acts of recognition

LEE PATTERSON

acts of recognition

essays on medieval culture

University of Notre Dame Press   Notre Dame, Indiana

Published by the University of Notre Dame Press
Notre Dame, Indiana 46556
www.undpress.nd.edu

Manufactured in the United States of America

Library of Congress Cataloging-in-Publication Data

Patterson, Lee.
    Acts of recognition : essays on medieval culture / Lee Patterson.
        p.   cm.
    Includes bibliographical references and index.
    ISBN-13: 978-0-268-03837-3 (pbk. : alk. paper)
    ISBN-10: 0-268-03837-6 (pbk. : alk. paper)
    1. English literature—Middle English, 1100–1500—History and criticism—
Theory, etc. 2. Literature and society—England—History—To 1500.
3. England—Civilization—1066–1485. 4. Historical criticism (Literature)
I. Title.
    PR255.P33 2010
    820'.9'001—dc22

                          2009038115

15152312

contents

preface

In preparing this collection of essays, two quotations have frequently been in my mind. One is Faulkner's well-known line from *Requiem for a Nun*: "The past is never dead. It's not even past." The other, more recent and less well known, is from a newspaper interview with Harold Pinter: "It's as if it never happened. It's all in the past and who cares? But let me put it this way—the dead are still looking at us, waiting for us to acknowledge our part in their murder."[1] The first passage is about the grip of the past on the present, the second about the responsibility of the present to the past. Faulkner refers to the way an individual's past distorts the sense of social responsibility (in this case Temple Drake's legal obligations); Pinter refers to the way the erasure of a social past (in this case the bloodshed caused by the invasion of Iraq) enables an evasion of individual responsibility (who cares?). Two dialectics are at work: between the past and the present, and between the individual and the social. These are dialectics familiar to every medievalist. What Faulkner and Pinter provide is the recognition that they bear a significance that must be defined as moral.

Whatever moral meaning the essays in this collection bear is, I hope, implicit—although not to the point of invisibility. I cannot pretend that even the most resolutely specific of them does not carry some sense that central human values are always involved, however local, even technical, the work. The dead *are* always looking at us, and our complicity in their murder is to forget them. The past *is* still present, no matter how rapid the rate of innovation. There is a deep continuity in human history. Were there not—if the past really were a foreign country where they do things differently—then we could not understand it at all.[2] But clearly we do, and we do because the past is, in a sense that we should not allow ourselves to ignore, us. Our responsibility to the past is a responsibility to the present; and only in understanding the dead as fully and accurately as we can are we able to understand ourselves. The most remarkable and yet often dismaying quality of the literature of the past is that it reads us while we read it. The one persistent recognition that emerged from writing these otherwise quite disparate essays is that whatever the text (*Beowulf, The Siege of Thebes, The Series*) and whoever the people (Henry V, John Clanvowe, Capt. Lawrence Oates), the values at issue remain central to contemporary life. I am not blind to the fact that this is a claim all historians—whether of literature or of the past *tout court*—almost always make. But that doesn't mean that it should not continue to be made, if only to remind those of us who seek to understand the past that we are simultaneously trying to understand the present—and, even more pertinently, our own lives, both professional and personal.

The first two chapters of this book are methodological. Chapter 1 has previously been published as the opening chapter of *Negotiating the Past: The Historical Understanding of Medieval Literature*, a book that appeared in 1987. Because that book is out of print, because the essay continues to be cited, and because its main points are still applicable to contemporary criticism, I have reprinted it here with a few revisions to indicate its continued relevance. The second chapter deals with pedagogy, and—with the help of the great sociologist Max Weber—the always vexed issue of how to manage in the classroom the inseparability of fact and value. The next three chapters deal with three of the less read English authors of the late Middle Ages, Sir John Clanvowe, Thomas Hoccleve, and John Lydgate. In all three cases the texts in question are used to illuminate a contemporary social phenomenon: the nature of court culture, the experience of the city, and the extraordinary act of self-making accomplished by King Henry V. Chapter 6—on what I have called "the heroic laconic style," a manner more familiarly known as the stiff upper lip—is most explicit in linking past to present, arguing that the bearing of the English aristocrat derives from a tradition that began in the early medieval world described in *Beowulf* and was quite deliberately reinvoked in response to the demands of nineteenth-century British imperialism. Chapters 7 and 8 deal with two Chaucerian texts, the little read *Complaint of Mars* and the widely read *Troilus and Criseyde*. Chapter 9 traces the topos of the gaze, and its companion the ecphrasis, from Virgil to Milton, with pauses along the way for discussions of Chrétien de Troyes and Dante. These three chapters are the most purely literary in the book. Oddly enough, the essay on the gaze is the oldest of the essays here reprinted, while the essay on the *Troilus* was just written. The final chapter is on the man whom I consider to be not merely one of the most influential of our medieval ancestors but one of the most important—Francis of Assisi. Here the issues of historical contextualization and psychological complexity, a complexity that is too often taken to be quintessentially modern, meet in a single figure. For this reason I have let this chapter stand as the book's final word.

The essays have been lightly revised throughout, largely to correct errors of fact and grammar and to rewrite passages that were poorly composed the first time. Whatever errors and uglinesses still remain are ill-favored things but, alas, mine own.

To thank those who have contributed to the making of this book would require me to list virtually everyone whom I have known and worked with over the past forty years. I shall therefore confine myself to a general expression of gratitude to professional colleagues who have been remarkably generous and to the students, both graduate and undergraduate, whom it has been my privilege and great good fortune to teach. I remember more of you than you think (even if I am an appalling correspondent) and always—well, almost always—with affection. In the spring of 2008, at Kalamazoo, a group of former graduate students, now colleagues, honored me with several special sessions. At the end I read to them lines from Yeats's "The Municipal Gallery Revisited" that I continue to believe characterize my experience as a member of the profession I entered many years ago:

You that would judge me, do not judge alone
This book or that, come to this hallowed place
Where my friends' portraits hang and look thereon;
Ireland's history in their lineaments trace;
Think where man's glory most begins and ends,
And say my glory was I had such friends.

acknowledgments

Chapter 1, "Historical Criticism and the Development of Chaucer Stud-ies," originally appeared in *Negotiating the Past: The Historical Understanding of Medieval Literature* (Madison: University of Wisconsin Press, 1987), pp. 3–39; chapter 2, "The Disenchanted Classroom," originally appeared in *Exemplaria* 8 (1996): 513–545; chapter 3, "Court Politics and the Invention of Literature: The Case of Sir John Clanvowe," originally appeared in David Aers, ed., *Culture and History, 1350–1600* (Detroit: Wayne State University Press, 1992), pp. 7–41; chapter 4, "'What Is Me?': Hoccleve and the Trials of the Urban Self," originally appeared in *Studies in the Age of Chaucer* 23 (2001): 435–68; the appendix to chapter 4, "Beinecke MS 493 and the Survival of Hoccleve's *Series*," originally appeared in *Old Books, New Learning: Essays on Medieval and Renaissance Books at Yale*, The Yale University Library Gazette, Occasional Supplement 4 (January 2001): 92–103; chapter 5, "Making Identities in Fifteenth-Century England: Henry V and John Lydgate," originally appeared in Jeffrey N. Cox and Larry J. Reynolds, eds., *New Historical Literary Study: Essays on Reproducing Texts, Representing History* (Princeton: Princeton University Press, 1993), pp. 69–107; chapter 6, "The Heroic Laconic Style: Reticence and Meaning from *Beowulf* to the Edwardians," originally appeared in David Aers, ed., *Medieval Literature and Historical Inquiry: Essays in Honour of*

Derek Pearsall (Cambridge: D. S. Brewer, 2000), pp. 133–57; chapter 7, "Writing Amorous Wrongs: Chaucer and the Order of Complaint," originally appeared in James M. Dean and Christian K. Zacher, eds., *The Idea of Medieval Literature: New Essays on Chaucer and Medieval Culture in Honor of Donald R. Howard* (Newark: University of Delaware Press, 1992), pp. 55–71; chapter 9, *"Rapt with Pleasaunce*: The Gaze from Virgil to Milton," originally appeared under a slightly different title in *ELH* 48 (1981): 455–75; chapter 10, "Brother Fire and St. Francis's Drawers: Human Nature and the Natural World," originally appeared in *Medieval Perspectives* 16 (2001): 1–19.

chapter one

Historical Criticism and
the Development of Chaucer Studies

By the early 1980s, the word *historicism*—indeed, the very word *history*—
had become highly charged both in the local field of medieval studies and
in literary criticism generally. And yet the charge was in each instance of
a different valence: for the medievalist the phrase "historical criticism"
was a code word for a densely annotated and narrowly argued reading of
an often aggressively moralistic cast; while for critics concerned with other
periods, criticism that advertised itself as historical raised expectations of
politically engaged readings of a progressive kind. The answer to the question why this should have been so—why should the historicism of the
medievalist have differed so sharply from that of critics working in later
periods?—is itself historical, and is inscribed with particular clarity in the
history of Chaucer criticism. Hence the focus of my attention here is upon
the two great critical formations, Exegetics and New Criticism, that served
Chaucer studies for almost twenty-five years as the most effective vehicles

I

for critical work. Moreover, the opposition they figured remains in force, although with a strange reversal in values. The apriorism and explicitly ideological commitments characteristic of Exegetics are now more likely to be found in work that defines itself as "theoretical," while the purportedly ideologically free empiricism claimed by New Criticism has attached itself to the kind of historicism now most commonly practiced. These are, to be sure, large generalizations that must accommodate many exceptions, but they do point to the persistence of an opposition that first emerged in the 1950s.[1] Despite this shift in values, these two attitudes—one aggressively historical, the other by and large indifferent to questions of historical understanding—are bound by their shared participation in the development of English studies. Their struggle has been essentially sibling in nature, and all the more violent for that. Here as often, the history of scholarship presents the features of a family romance, and its postures and polemics articulate no simple pattern of thesis and antithesis but a complex interweaving of piety with rebellion, covert borrowings entwined with ostentatious declarations of independence.[2] This dynamic was especially evident in Chaucer studies, where New Criticism and Exegetics were never on speaking terms, although each critical camp remained oddly and even obsessively aware of the other's presence.

When in the 1950s and early 1960s the work of D. W. Robertson first established Exegetics as a major force in the study of medieval literature, most medievalists hastened to position themselves vis-à-vis this new critical formation.[3] Some issued anathemas (Donaldson, Utley), some offered less global but still severe strictures (Bloomfield, Howard), some rather gingerly signed up as co-workers in the Exegetical vineyard (Kaske).[4] Without exception, however, these responses remained true to the empirical temper of American criticism by engaging Exegetics at the level of practice, attacking it for historical misrepresentation and interpretive inadequacy or, conversely, seeing in it new possibilities for critical work. Indeed, as Talbot Donaldson candidly acknowledged, such an approach was forced on the opposition by its inability to frame a theoretical objection.[5] The result of this pragmatism was that, despite and even because of the force of its practical objections, New Criticism was unable to confront Exegetics at the level of theory. Moreover, the silent but powerful New Critical reliance upon the educated sensibility as the final arbiter of interpretive common sense—a silence all the more impenetrable because of the necessary implicitness of sensibility itself—ensured that those opposed to Exegetics would decline to articulate a program of medieval literary studies to challenge Exegetics's easily replicated paradigm.

The result has been that Exegetics remained for all too many years, apparently against all odds, the great unfinished business of medieval studies. The point is not simply that the Exegetical method continued to be practiced but that it continued to arouse passions. Unable to absorb Exegetics and move on, Chaucer studies instead circled back almost compulsively to an apparently irrepressible scandal. Despite attaining a healthy maturity, Exegetics remained as combative and polemical as ever, while its opponents declined the passé title of New Critics but continued to denigrate a critical approach that was presumably beneath their notice.[6] And while in the twenty-first century this impasse might now seem to be of merely historical interest, as I have already suggested the confrontation between a systematic hermeneutic like Exegetics, with its commitment to an explicit interpretive method and a set of clear moral and political values, and a more eclectic, formalist, and only implicitly ethical approach like New Criticism, continues to be replayed in a variety of complicated formulations. Too often these formulations are reduced to a simplistic opposition between "theory" and "historicism." The real issue, however, is the difference between approaches that are systematic—in that they rely upon some *system* of thought, regardless of its content—and those that are explicitly empirical and therefore usually concerned with some form of historical context.[7] In short, the Exegetical *mode*, however reconfigured, remains with us, and remains a provocation to interpretive procedures that are heir—albeit in complex and often barely recognizable ways—to New Criticism.

The initial failure that allowed this opposition to continue in force was the inability of criticism to define a strategy of interpretation that would preserve both the indisputable scholarly findings of Exegetics and the humanist values that, as I mean to show, Exegetics sought to annul. Faced with the Exegetical meaning of the Miller's bagpipes, for example, or the Wife of Bath's deafness, or the Pardoner's eunuchry, critics opposed to Exegetics were largely silent, turning away from these iconographical details in favor of other, less apparently unilateral textual elements.[8] This evasion was especially marked in relation to the medieval tradition of exegetical reading itself, a tradition that Professor Robertson almost single-handedly brought to the attention of literary scholars but which criticism unwisely ignored.

The task of a fully informed Chaucerian criticism is not, however, to fend off Exegetical findings but rather to place them within a more inclusive understanding. Exegetical reading is, as everyone would agree, an authentically medieval mode of understanding; and it is one that is inscribed within Chaucerian poetry. Chaucer's poems both invite and, I believe, finally resist exegetical processing; and his characteristic poetic strategies are designed not only to evade but to explore the hegemonic power of institutionalized modes of medieval interpretation. Exegesis, in short, is itself one of Chaucer's subjects, and so vulnerable to his characteristic irony; and a fully responsive criticism must accommodate both this interest and the skepticism with which it is regarded. The failure of criticism to accomplish this task was perhaps most vividly shown by the continued production of readings motivated by a wholly unmediated Exegetics. Books and articles continued to appear throughout the 1980s that not only explicated the details of Chaucer's poetry in the terms established by Exegetics, but placed these explications in the service of total interpretations determined by Exegetical norms.[9] In sum, in 1985 John Fleming was able to say that Chaucer "is now widely though not universally regarded as *a conservative* Catholic Christian of his time"—the epithet (which I have emphasized) meaning to imply that Chaucer's religious beliefs are not simply part of his cultural situation, like his status as a royal servant or his residence in London, but the central concern of his writing.[10]

However much this assumption might foreclose fresh initiatives in Chaucer criticism, it remained in force as long as Exegetics was allowed to stand as the only fully articulated model of specifically *historical* criticism current in Chaucer studies. This is to say, again, not that there were not many different kinds of work (most of them implicitly ahistorical) being practiced in Chaucer studies, but rather that not only was there no widely known and generally acknowledged paradigm of historical criticism to be set against that defined by Exegetics, but that the issue of historical understanding per se had received virtually no general discussion within the context of medieval studies.[11] This was not, to be sure, a failure unique to medievalists. The inhospitality of Anglo-American literary culture as a whole to a philosophically informed historicism had largely condemned historical criticism to the benighted positivism of the nineteenth century, a darkness that only gradually yielded before the arrival of phenomenological hermeneutics, Marxism, and other European imports. Hence it was within the context of the development of historical criticism per se that Exegetics played a progressive role, not merely by its uncompromising insistence on the historicity of medieval poetry but by its careful articulation of the way in which such a program might be accomplished. And if the program is, as I hope to show, undermined by systemic weaknesses, it nonetheless remained for almost forty years the only game in town. Indeed, the opponents of the Exegetical project were for the most part united only by their opposition to Exegetics.

My purpose here, despite this polemical introduction, is less to argue a position than to offer an analysis of precisely this opposition.[12] Why did Exegetics remain unfinished business, an unassimilated challenge to the mainstream of Chaucer studies? There are, I think, a number of interrelated reasons, but all of them have their nexus in the question of what it means to be a medievalist. This is itself a historical and—above all—political question, and I therefore offer this chapter, like the book as a whole, as an exercise in what Professor Robertson would have called historical criticism.

I

The story begins with the medieval revival of the later eighteenth and nineteenth centuries and its relation to the scholarly effort to recover the vernacular literature of the Middle Ages. Popular medievalism in England divided into two major schools or attitudes, the most powerful representing the Middle Ages as universalist, institutional, and deeply conservative. Bishops Hurd and Percy, Sir Walter Scott, Coleridge and Wordsworth, Southey, Carlyle, Kenelm Henry Digby, Disraeli and the Young Englanders—these enthusiasts of things medieval celebrated the Middle Ages as a time when a harmonious society was held together by bonds of common faith and an unquestioned social order.[13] As the leading Young Englander, Sir John Manners, put it in his poem *England's Trust* (1841),

> Each knew his place—king, peasant, peer, or priest—
> The greatest owned connexion with the least;
> From rank to rank the generous feeling ran,
> And linked society as man to man.[14]

Manners articulated the program of the Young Englanders in, as he said, "a word": "let society take a more feudal appearance than it presents now."[15] These medievalists wanted a return to the past not merely in terms of vague ideals or romanticized trappings but institutionally, in the form of a strengthened national church and an authoritarian, hierarchically ordered society.[16]

In opposition to this conservative model the nineteenth century also saw the development of a conception of the Middle Ages as pluralist, primitivist, and above all else, individualist. This was the view made popular by Ruskin and Morris and, to a lesser extent, by the Pre-Raphaelites. Ruskin's enormously influential "The Nature of Gothic" argued that the medieval cathedral represented not a corporate Christian consciousness but the "out-speaking of the strong spirit" of the men of the north, and that its value resided less in its embodiment of religious values than in the rough imperfection that testified to the unconstrained labor of its individual makers.[17] Similarly, William Morris saw the great virtue of the Middle Ages in a heroic individuality that resisted "the degradation of . . . sordid utilitarianism." In line with a traditional liberal praise of Anglo-Saxon freedom and the native social forms through which it was expressed, Morris celebrated a voluntary "Fellowship of Men" that characterized medieval life at its best, and that found its finest (and last) expression in the gathering of the commons for the failed revolution of 1381.[18] For Ruskin and Morris, and for others like them, the Middle Ages were valuable not because of their powerful institutions of control and order but despite them. Spared both the classical importations that falsified Renaissance England and the dehumanizing industrialism that was currently disfiguring the nation, the medieval spirit was able to fulfill itself in forms hospitable to its original native vigor. In returning to the primitive origins of the nation these writers sought to recuperate an undergirding identity of spirit that could serve as an ideal of social coherence and unity to set against a contemporary society stratified by class divisions and riven by economic warfare. Rejecting the eighteenth-century idea of culture as the discriminating mark of social superiority, Romantic medievalists instead defined culture as an elemental and universal value that is the birthright of every member of the nation, and one from which too many had been alienated by a postmedieval history that should now be set aside.[19]

Although this conception of the Middle Ages was a minority view in nineteenth-century England, it was particularly congenial to the pioneers of early English studies. There are several reasons for this. One was the relative lack of state and institutional support for medieval scholarship in England, which meant that it was less easily appropriated by a conservative political apparatus. Nineteenth-century medieval scholarship in England tended to be an entrepreneurial activity, and the self-reliant individuals who engaged in it were naturally admiring of rugged individuality.[20] Another, more profound, reason was the congruence between the methods of German scientific historicism and liberal values. German scholars were themselves largely committed to a liberal political program that opposed both the absolutism of the right and the egalitarianism and revolutionary rationalism of the left. Their central political value was the protection of individual liberties, which they saw threatened by both church and monarchy and protected only by a powerful secular state.[21]

At a methodological level, they insisted that history is the sphere of the unique, of an irreducible individuality that must be grasped in all its specificity. And they privileged individuality not only as the object of study but also as the subject who studies, the scientific investigator who is able to arrive by painstaking labor at the original truth of things, whether it be the life of Frederick the Great or the *Nibelungenlied* in its authentic form. In sum, there was a profound affinity between German historical scholarship and liberal progressivism and individualism.[22]

This affinity can be seen in an explicit form in England in politically liberal scholars like J. M. Kemble and F. J. Furnivall. Both of these men became embroiled in controversies that pitted the new methods of German philology against an elitist antiquarianism, Kemble in the so-called Anglo-Saxon controversy of the 1830s, Furnivall in his sulfurous debate with Swinburne about the editing of Shakespeare some forty years later— two technical controversies that were in fact galvanized by political antipathy.[23] Furnivall was profoundly committed to the quintessentially liberal and Arnoldian idea that the study of the literature of the English past could serve to recover the organic unity that the class-divided society of the nineteenth century had lost, and at the opening session of the Working Men's College in Red Lion Square, where he taught for many subsequent years, he distributed copies of Ruskin's "The Nature of Gothic" that he had had printed at his own expense.[24] These instances of explicit political commitment, however, are less important than the fact that the vast majority of nineteenth-century medieval scholars of all political hues shared certain crucial interpretive assumptions. For one thing, despite their commitment to the idea of historical conditioning, these scholars in fact made little effort to correlate medieval literature to the institutions, whether social, political, or religious, of its period. On the contrary, medieval literature was in large part understood as the expression of a human nature valuably different from our own precisely because it was unconstrained by narrow and dehumanizing institutions. Old English literature was most often understood in the context of a pervasive Germanic primitivism that opposed native Anglo-Saxon values to "the blighting touch of Christianity."[25] So too with Chaucer, whose poetry was read in terms of an uncritical realism. Chaucer offered, it was thought, a representation of fourteenth-century life unmediated by preconceptions and undistorted by personal commitments; like his latter-day scholarly counterparts, he was above all else an independent individual who saw the truth of things and recorded it accurately. This is the Chaucer of Whig historiography, a disinterested but sympathetic observer, alert to the failings of his time but deeply understanding of the individual lives of his fellow citizens.[26] Far from being engaged in any local polemic, his poetry spoke to concerns that were part of the permanent fabric of human life.

But Chaucer's ability to trace what Blake had called "the Physiognomies or Lineaments of Universal Human Life"[27] required him, paradoxically, to rise above the very historical circumstances that scholars were, from another perspective, attempting to describe in all their specificity. In other words, there was within historicism a largely hidden debate between a conditioning historical context and a transhistorical humanism — a debate that continues in force in current criticism. In the nineteenth century this debate was virtually always silently resolved in favor of an idealist humanism, but in the work of the second generation of Chaucer scholars — Root, Kittredge, Manly, Lowes, Hammond, Tatlock, Patch, Dempster, Spurgeon and Malone — the paradox at the heart of the historicist project began to become visible.[28] These scholars dominated the field from the death of Furnivall in 1910 until the midpoint of the century. Their work falls into two sharply defined categories, which correspond not to differences among them — almost every scholar is represented in both categories — but to the internal division within historicism itself. On the one hand is an enormous and enormously valuable mass of sheer information, almost always presented in impressively learned articles and now enshrined in the notes to Benson's edition.[29] This work was accomplished through a laborious attention to detail, polyglot inclusiveness, and mastery of accurate techniques of recovery and restoration—through, that is, those procedures and values that successfully transformed the study of medieval literature from uncritical amateurism into a profession.

But the terms of this success prescribed inevitable and ultimately irremediable limitations upon the whole historicist project as originally conceived, limitations that are in certain ways still in force. Believing that natural science was successful because its methodology partook of the certainty and universality of the natural laws it sought to uncover, historicism in its positivist phrase assumed for itself a similar methodological purity. Since the results of its investigations were thought to be untouched by human hands, historicism ascribed to them an unqualified objectivity and an explanatory power that no merely thematic interpretation could possibly attain. In thus privileging extratextual data, historical criticism came to depend upon an unreflective factualism that foreclosed interpretive possibilities. Analogous, and equally prejudicial to the intersubjectivity upon which the humanist recovery of the past depended, was historicism's uncritical indulgence of its inevitable predilection for genetic explanation. After all, much of nineteenth-century historicism had been motivated by a desire to use the past, and specifically the medieval past, to prescribe a future, whether it was the restoration of the *ancien régime* in France, the reunification of Germany, or the dismantling of industrial techniques of labor management in England. Polemical explanation was virtually the raison d'être of historicism: knowing whence we came, so ran the argument, we would know what we should become. The mission of historicism was quite simply to historicize, to show that the present entities that had previously been understood in terms of universal principles or natural laws were instead the effect of prior causes. And this historicizing applied as much to literary texts as it did to political institutions.

The effect of these cognate aspects of historicism was to decompose the past in the very process of trying to recover it. By so definitively allowing the lines of explanatory force to run vertically, as it were, from the text back into the past that was to account for it, this brand of historicism devalued the possibility of lateral explanation in terms of function within the text itself. The first question it invariably asked of a puzzling element in the text was genetic, while the prevailing factualism disposed the answer to be a newly discovered item whose significance was taken to be self-evident. This procedure was most explicitly at work in the ubiquitous source study that characterized this phase of scholarship, but it was also visible in Manly's attempt to understand the pilgrims in terms of Chaucerian contemporaries, for instance, or in the persistent (and continuing) attempts to tie the poems to specific occasions.[30] In all of these cases Chaucer's poems were seen as effects to be explained by reference to their extratextual causes, explanations that were all the more powerful just because the causes *were* extratextual and therefore thought to be peculiarly objective in comparison to internal or subjective interpretations.

But if historicism was in danger of mummifying the very past it sought to revive, it remained nonetheless an essentially humanistic venture. The entire historicist project, we should not forget, was underwritten by the assumption of a transhistorical humanness that at once motivated and legitimized historical study. In the first volume of his *Grundriss der romanischen Philologie,* Gustav Gröber, the high priest of mechanistic positivism, echoed the idealistic Wilhelm von Humboldt in defining the object of philology as "the human spirit in language," and it was that *Geist,* ever varying in its manifestations but identical in its essence, that stood as the goal of historical study.[31] And while the idea of periodization, and the specialization of knowledge that it entailed, challenged the continuity between past and present that was at the center of humanist historicism, it never managed to destroy it.[32] Hence the other kind of work that the positivist literary historian produced in this period was the explicitly appreciative survey of Chaucer's poetry written by virtually every major scholar. The list begins with Root's *The Poetry of Chaucer* in 1906, includes Kittredge's famous 1915 lectures, Lowes's only slightly less celebrated ones of 1934, and Dempster's *Dramatic Irony in Chaucer* (1932), and concludes at midcentury with the career-capping books by Patch (1949), Tatlock (posthumously, in 1950), Lawrence (1950), and Malone (1951).[33] Two things stand out about these books. All of them present essentially the same Whig Chaucer as nineteenth-century criticism, and indeed except for greater accuracy could all have been written then. And with only the barest of exceptions none of them makes any real use of the massive historical detail that scholarship had succeeded in accumulating about Chaucer's poetry. In fact, there is in these books by eminent and powerful scholars a marked tendency to devalue scholarship itself.

This paradox is especially striking in perhaps the best of these books, John Livingstone Lowes's *Geoffrey Chaucer and the Development of His*

Genius (1934). Lowes begins by assuring his audience that they will be spared "the awe-inspiring *chevaux de frise* of technical Chaucerian scholarship" and uses an agricultural metaphor to let us know what he thinks of it: "technical erudition . . . may safely be left by the lover of poetry until its results have fertilized the common soil."[34] But having dismissed the very scholarship to which he had himself made such remarkable contributions, Lowes then offers in his first lecture a masterful summary of what he calls "the determining concepts of Chaucer's world," by which he means the kind of medieval astronomical, medical, and geographical knowledge that C. S. Lewis was later to anatomize in *The Discarded Image*.[35] Furthermore, in the second lecture he offers a biography of the poet and in the third an account of his reading, with an emphasis on Machaut, Froissart, and Deschamps. Having now prepared his audience with a substantial amount of scholarly information, Lowes then reverses field again and provides three scintillatingly appreciative lectures on the poetry that make virtually no reference to the preceding material at all. In short, historical scholarship and literary understanding have here little to do with each other. For Lowes, as for his colleagues, there were in effect two Chaucers: one is the fourteenth-century writer whose every word requires elaborate annotation, while the other is the purveyor of God's plenty who, as Root predictably said in 1906, "was in the world, but not of it," and who speaks with an immediacy that obviates the need for interpretation.[36] Either an antiquarian curiosity or an occasion for appreciative paraphrase, Chaucer's poetry fell prey to the ironic law of positivist historicism that decrees that the more that is known about a text the less it can be said to mean.

II

It is in the context of the perceived failure of this perhaps uniquely American brand of historicism that the rise of both New Criticism and Exegetics should be understood. As a general movement New Criticism was of course explicit in its opposition to historicism, both as a methodology and as a literary ideology entrenched within the university. Profoundly libertarian in its orientation, New Criticism sought to free poetry from the historicity in which scholarship had mired it so that it might become once again an agency for cultural reconstruction. For all its celebration of the work of art as a value in and for itself, New Criticism never abandoned the

Romantic and Arnoldian claim that literature offers the alienated reader a saving knowledge. Hence it was also opposed to a merely descriptive or appreciative criticism that devalued the capacity of literature to bear significant meaning. Moreover, New Criticism had very specific notions about the kind of meaning that poems could yield. Despite its insistence upon the objectivity of its interpretive procedures, New Critical practice was in fact underwritten by a familiar set of liberal and humanist values. It privileged pragmatic empiricism over a priori theorizing, an ethics of attitude over a code of rules, secular pluralism over doctrinal conformity, and above all the independence and self-reliance of the individual, who was understood not as conditioned by social practices and institutions but as an autonomous being who creates the historical world through self-directed efforts. In effect, New Criticism read all poetry as enacting a continual dramatization of this liberal humanist ideology. For the New Critical "poetics of tension," poetry was a battleground where the abstract certainties of the angelic imagination were subjected to the healthful testing of experience. The formal struggle within the poem between logic and texture (Ransom), or reason and emotion (Winters), or extension and intension (Tate), or the universal and the concrete (Wimsatt) was thematized into what R. S. Crane rightly identified as a set of "reduction terms": order and disorder, reality and appearance, nature and art, emotion and reason, and so on.[37] These are the topoi that the poem was then seen as figuring in a perpetual and irresolvable dialogue, the final meaning being the value of complexity itself. And even beneath this finality was the far stronger claim that meaning itself is a function of a deliberate act of choice. For New Criticism the poetic act is quintessentially the imposition of significance upon that which is otherwise without meaning, a gesture of creation that asserts the autonomy of the individual, just as the act of reading is best undertaken without social or institutional constraints.

While the early 1950s saw the appearance of a number of New Critical readings, it was Talbot Donaldson's edition and commentary of 1958, significantly entitled *Chaucer's Poetry: An Anthology for the Modern Reader*, that marked the full arrival of the New Critical Chaucer.[38] Suppressing all signs of the editorial and philological learning upon which it was based, and eschewing scholarly annotations and bibliographies, Donaldson's text proclaimed Chaucer's liberation from the erudite antiquarianism to which historicism had consigned him. And in his persuasively discreet commentary, Donaldson began to show the subtlety and depth of meaning that Chaucer's poetry could be made to yield when subjected to the interpretive procedures of New Criticism. Not surprisingly, the tenor of this meaning was consistent with the liberal humanism that underwrote the New Critical enterprise itself. Donaldson's Chaucer was a poet who persistently engaged his readers in a debate between the imperatives of cultural and religious authority, on the one hand, and, on the other, the irreducible complexity of lived experience.

But Donaldson went beyond thematics to argue that this is a debate implicit in Chaucerian form itself. Subscribing to the New Critical conception of poetry as dramatic rather than rhetorical, he both sharpened Kittredge's notion of the *Canterbury Tales* as a collection of monologues and applied the dramatic principle to texts, such as the General Prologue and *Troilus and Criseyde,* which had previously been ascribed to an authorial voice.[39] The effect of this strategy was twofold. First, in opening a gap between author and persona Donaldson allowed entrance to the New Critically sanctified principle of irony. No longer could Chaucerian statement, no matter how orthodox or conventional, be read as unqualified assertion, for it was now subject to the continual negotiations required by context. But secondly, he showed how these negotiations could be brought to a close. For the dramatizing of Chaucerian poetry meant that the referent of every statement was not an extrinsic system of value, whether or not historical, but the fictionalized personality who spoke it. At the center of Chaucer's poetry was character, and every statement should be read in the first instance as a characterizing device. What motivated Chaucerian poetry, then, was an aesthetic impulse toward mimetic fidelity regardless of the requirements of the absolutist morality of the Christian Middle Ages.

In effect, the New Critical revanche served to rewrite the traditional conception of the Whig Chaucer in terms that would resist the unwitting depredations of positivist historicism while allowing for the articulation of a more complex and powerful poetic meaning than descriptive criticism could elicit. Indeed, the New Critical preservation of the traditional image of the Chaucerian author, far from being just a pious gesture toward Chaucer scholars of yore, was itself a necessary part of the liberal humanism that New Criticism was anxious to protect. For just as Chaucer's poetry is an affirmation of the individual self, so must it be itself the effect of a commensurate individuality, of an author who is suitably distanced from his creation but remains the unmoved mover to whom responsibility can ultimately be referred. Even the distance itself is significant: masked by a series of ironic figurations, the poet is everywhere present but nowhere visible, a displacement that is the authorial equivalent of a poetry whose ultimate meaning is always implied but never stated (and hence requires the interpretive ministrations of the reader in order to be made explicit). Similarly, the aesthetic assumptions of New Criticism contained a powerful specific against historicism. As we have seen, the aetiological impulse of historicism sought continually to refer the elements of a text back to some prior cause, while its prevailing methodological factualism allowed these referrals to stand as sufficient explanation. But by insisting that the Chaucerian texts found their immediate origin in the fictive self of a pilgrim or narrative persona, New Criticism perforce invested their details with human value. No longer was it possible, for instance, to explain the mysterious Lollius as simply the mistranslation of a Horatian line that served to answer Chaucer's need for a Latin *auctor*. On the contrary, since the speaking voice was itself now a character, it too was endowed with a story, and Lollius, whatever his origins, necessarily played a part in it. Once identified, Lollius could no longer drop from critical sight but became a function in the narrative of the poem's telling, part of the speaker's ethical universe. So too, then, for historical scholarship in general. It could be seen as a kind of semantics, providing a glossary for Chaucer's topical lexicon but unable to read his poetic syntax, the organizing pattern by which meaning is made. And this was the task that could now be performed by a suitably informed criticism.

In its medievalist phase, then, and despite the polemical chasteness of Donaldson's textbook, New Criticism sought less to extract the poem from its historical context than to find strategies by which to reaffirm the humanist values that had motivated the historicist recovery in the first place. Rejecting the positivist factualism and academic mechanization that had brought about the mutual alienation of scholarship and criticism, this new generation of scholars reinstated the values of liberal humanism at the center of their procedures, using them as the interpretive principles by which they could make sense of the historical materials gathered by their predecessors. Donaldson's situating of character at the origin of Chaucerian discourse was one of the most powerful ways in which the materials of historical scholarship could be interpreted according to the values of liberal humanism. Similarly powerful, and theoretically more explicit, was the historical stylistics promoted by Charles Muscatine in *Chaucer and the French Tradition* (1957), a book that represents the most substantial and influential achievement of this phase of Chaucerian scholarship.[40]

The critical tradition against which Muscatine reacted was, as we have seen, one that privileged realistic immediacy while devaluing a highly figured and rhetoricized poetic, and it read the course of Chaucer's poetic career, and the history of virtually all later medieval poetry, as a progress from an empty courtly artificiality toward a vigorous and demo-cratic realism—a progress, of course, that matched the analogous devel-opment of society as a whole. But as the New Critics realized, while such a reading of literary history might make good sense politically, it contained an unwitting and devastating attack upon literature itself. For it assumed that the best kind of art is that which is most like life and therefore least like art. Committed as they were to defining and defending the literari-ness of literature as an essential quality that both protected literature from being misjudged by inappropriate standards and established it as an inde-pendent *Fach* worthy of professional study, New Critics found any scheme that devalued the artfulness of literary art unacceptable. Hence the an-nounced goal of Muscatine's project was to show that realistic writing, far from representing an unmediated access to the world, was itself a product of verbal art and therefore as conventional as the high style of courtly poetry—which meant by the same token that courtly poetry was wor-thy of being taken seriously. And as the subtitle of his book suggested (*A Study in Style and Meaning*), he argued that both the high and low styles of medieval literature were best understood as agencies of significance, deliberately chosen means by which values could be articulated.

This does not mean, of course, that Muscatine and his New Critical colleagues wished to attack the Whig account of literary history, with its optimistic story of the emancipation of the poetic imagination from the tyranny of imposed forms. On the contrary, Muscatine's account of medi-eval literature is underwritten by and supportive of precisely this liberal historiography, although his version is both less explicit and more sophis-ticated than its nineteenth-century precursors. Attacking in the first in-stance the fossilizing pressure of positivism, Muscatine insists that both the courtly and bourgeois styles themselves and the values they articulate are unconditioned by any specific historical formation. Each style is "an almost independent literary tool, tied less to a specific social class or specific genres than to a characteristic set of attitudes" (p. 59). "A conventional style," whether it be courtly or bourgeois, highly figured or conversational, is "independent of historical association" (p. 2), precisely because it articulates values that are transhistorical. These values are then themselves defined as expressive of different "levels of human apprehension of experience" (p. 3), apprehensions that are either idealistic or phenomenalistic, committed either to spiritual transcendence or to a practical and materialistic engagement with the world. And while Muscatine located this opposition at the heart of medieval culture in general and saw it as articulated in the disjunctions and juxtapositions of Gothic form, the very generality with which he described these values made it clear that they were in some sense common to all cultural life and that, indeed, their confrontation represented the energy at the heart of cultural history.

It was, in short, by positing a Hegelian conflict of idealist thesis and realist antithesis that Muscatine's humanistic literary history reinstated a realm of value above the world of otherwise inert scholarly facts. As well, the movement from thesis to antithesis told a story, and one that issued in the triumph of those values that are themselves central to liberal humanism. One of these values was the commitment to the growing emancipation of the individual, expressed here as the developing capacity of medieval writing to represent the self in all its depth and independence. So that while Muscatine agreed that the great weakness of courtly style is its "liability to lose that ultimate, delicate contact with human concerns that gives it meaning," he recuperated a master like Guillaume de Lorris by ascribing to his narrative "a kind of characterization" that is "created less through vagrant excursions into realism than through a richness and complication of the symbolic texture itself" (p. 40). No matter at what distance Guillaume's personification allegory stood from the historical world nor how homogenous its values, it remained validated by "a particular interest in psychology" (p. 40). Given the fact, then, that courtly style was justified by its capacity to represent character, it was inevitably the case that insofar as the bourgeois style articulated that psychology with greater density and detail it would surpass its courtly predecessor. Hence Jean de Meun's representation of La Vieille "shows the poet . . . catching into the web of the discourse elements dictated less by traditional satire than by a sense of the round, complex existence of the speaker herself" (p. 85), while on the contrary Faus-Semblant's disjunctive alternations between hypocrisy and honesty reveal an "abandonment of the literary approach," a failure that is stigmatized as "incomplete dramatization" (p. 92). In sum, Jean's invention of the dramatic monologue was presented by Muscatine as a grounding of traditional discourses in a self that encompasses and ironizes them but that is itself autonomously validated. On this account, the project of Jean's writing, and beyond him of the Chaucer who completes his initiative, is not to judge but to represent a self that stands as an ultimate and irreducible category of understanding, exempt from further analysis.[41]

In thus privileging, like Donaldson, the critical category of character, Muscatine witnessed to a similar loyalty to what a more recent criticism has called the ideology of the subject. This is, in the largest sense, a conception of the self as a self-identical entity defined through its difference from an externalized reality designated as society, or history, or the world; in a literary context, it is a positing of the author as the efficient cause of the text who is also the origin, and the proprietor, of its significance. As the central tenet of liberal humanism, this conception of the largely autonomous individual self is the foundation of Muscatine's literary historiography, where it functioned as both object and subject of the poetic process. For when Muscatine defined the goal of the medieval literary project as the representation of individual psychology, he necessarily posited as its source a poet who is motivated by a disinterested quest for mimetic accuracy and is therefore largely uncircumscribed either by programmatic commitments or by more profound social determinants. Chaucer's psychologized representation of the self presumes a corresponding autonomy on his own part: it is because he is free of polemical purpose or conditioning social ideology that he is able to give a sympathetic but carefully distanced representation of his world. Since objectivity is possible only to a dehistoricized and socially unconditioned subject, Chaucerian mimesis stands as the poetic equivalent of the liberal assertion of the freedom of the individual from a determining historical context.

This claim of disinterested sympathy was articulated by Muscatine in terms of the New Critical values of complexity and maturity. Subscribing to the New Critical principle "that the perennial significance of great poems depends on the multiplicity of meanings they interrelate" (p. 9), Muscatine saw Chaucer as the supreme instance of the poet who reconciles opposing values within a supervening order:

He sees the courtly and bourgeois modes, idealism and practicality, in ironic juxtaposition. He holds them in balance, sympathetically and critically, exploring each for its own essence and for the light it casts on the other. . . . He makes, more than any of his European contemporaries, a capacious, comprehensible order out of his legacy of style and meaning from the French tradition. (p. 120)

But where does Chaucer himself stand as he performs this act of stylistic counterpointing? Far from evading this question, Muscatine gave a forthright and powerful answer: securely within his own time. In defining that time, however, Muscatine turned not to the social conditions of the fourteenth century but to an idealist definition of the Gothic promoted by the Hegelian *Geistesgeschichte* of Wilhelm Worringer and, above all, Max Dvořàk, one that sees Gothic style as an aesthetic characterized by a juxtaposition of disparate forms and a distrust of the singular or monolithic attitude.[42] The effect of this representation of the Chaucerian context is to dehistoricize history, both by defining it at a level of idealistic abstraction and, more tellingly, by reading it as the external reflection of a determining Chaucerian selfhood. Muscatine tells us, in other words, not how Chaucer is a fourteenth-century poet, but rather how the fourteenth century is Chaucerian. By thus invoking an idealist definition of the Gothic, Muscatine was able to define a period style that was simultaneously conditioning and liberating, capable of standing outside itself and yet preeminently of its time. He defined, in sum, a mode of historical being that was by definition transhistorical, a paradox that corresponded with brilliant felicity both to a poet who is in but not of his time and to the needs of a critical tradition that was mired in its own hyperhistoricized consciousness and yet aspired to a vision of permanent truths.

III

Readers of Professor Robertson's work know that Exegetics represented a root-and-branch, no-holds-barred, take-no-prisoners attack upon the liberal humanist ideology that has dominated Anglo-American literary studies since their inception in the nineteenth century. It is precisely the absoluteness and ferocity of that attack that made Exegetics valuable, although at the cost of ensuring that it would never itself become the dominant critical mode. Moreover, the ambiguous *fortuna* of Exegetics derives at least in part from unwitting compromises to both its historicism and its antihumanism, gestures of accommodation that allowed the opposition to evade its challenge by attacking it for violations of humanist values to which it never really subscribed in the first place. In large part, I think, these compromises derived from a general resistance to self-understanding that characterized Exegetical criticism, and especially to an understanding of its own place in the history of medieval studies. This is the most complicated part of our story, for in seeking to counter the prevailing native values Exegetics went outside the Anglo-American tradition of medievalism to more congenial European formations. Specifically, Exegetics' most profound intellectual affiliations were with the European tradition of cultural history or, more properly, *Geistesgeschichte,* and at a more local level, with one of the few scholarly projects that harkened back to the conservative medievalism of the nineteenth century, iconography.

Despite occasional statements to the contrary, Exegetics was not originally undertaken to reinstate the historicism of the previous generation that New Criticism sought to displace. On the contrary, Exegetics shared with New Criticism a distaste for a descriptive historicism that explained the details of a text in terms of either naive realism or uninterpretive source study. Perhaps even more than New Criticism, Exegetics was motivated by a passion for meaningfulness, for discovering within the text a powerfully consistent set of values. But beyond this, Exegetics wanted to see meaningfulness as pervading the historical world itself, and as motivating those very facts that a positivist historicism regarded as wholly objective and therefore exempt from interpretation. Because of its fervor for making sense out of materials that less imaginative scholars saw as merely natural objects, Exegetics turned away from the narrow historicism of the Anglo-American tradition and toward the far more capacious and interpretively ambitious historicism of *Geistesgeschichte*—but with a difference.

While *Geistesgeschichte* was a multifarious enterprise, we can usefully enumerate its major premises so as to mark the points at which Exegetics diverged. In its original form, *Geistesgeschichte* embodied the commitment to unity or wholeness that characterized historicism in its original, Romantic form. In a reaction against the Enlightenment appeal to timeless laws and analytic reason, historicism insisted that all human phenomena had to be judged in terms appropriate to the supervening totality of which they were but parts. In political formulations this totality was the nation, specifically the German state that was struggling toward reunification in the early nineteenth century and whose unity was justified by appeals to the binding force of customary habits of long duration and, above all, to the underlying identity visible in a pure form in the Middle Ages. In terms of historical studies as a whole, this wholeness or *Ganzheit* was possessed by the various cultural periods, however defined. Each historical entity, and especially cultural artifacts, could be understood only in terms of all the other phenomena that together made up the period. What *Geistesgeschichte* finally aimed to understand was the spiritual radix of the historical period, the *diapason* (to use Karl Lamprecht's term) of which each individual entity was but a partial and symbolic expression.[43]

In its traditional formulation, cultural history insisted that this supreme object of historical knowledge must necessarily remain indeterminate; it was, in Huizinga's words, that "which is always before one's eyes and is never to be grasped."[44] This is because the crucial values of a culture are always immanent and dispersed, bespoken but never explicitly stated. The *Weltanschauung* which the individual cultural products of a period serve to express is necessarily inarticulate, a hidden but all the more potent spiritual condition that is perforce unknown to the members of the historical period. No more than a fish can understand the water in which it swims could a medieval man understand his medievalness. Culture is not learned behavior, inculcated by pedagogy and training, but an unspoken pattern that conditions the very possibility of life. Karl Mannheim cites a key statement by Dilthey—"*Weltanschauungen* are not produced by thinking"—and then comments:

> It needed the anti-rationalist movement within the cultural studies themselves, a movement which Dilthey first made a force in Germany, to make people realize that theoretical philosophy [i.e., explicit statements of value and meaning] is neither the creator nor the principal vehicle of the *Weltanschauung* of an epoch; in reality, it is merely only one of the channels through which a global factor—to be conceived as transcending the various cultural fields, its emanations—manifests itself. . . . As long as *Weltanschauung* is considered as something theoretical, entire vast provinces of cultural life will be inaccessible to historical synthesis.[45]

An artist's announced intention and even his explicit *ars poetica* are important not as circumscribing statements of meaning but as signs that must be themselves interpreted. "We must go beyond this 'immanent' interpretation and treat the theoretical confession as documentary evidence of something extra-psychic, . . . just as a doctor will take the self-diagnosis of one of his patients as a symptom rather than as a correct identification of the latter's illness."[46]

Given this definition of its task, *Geistesgeschichte* necessarily found the positivist scheme of cause and effect an inadequate methodology. Since its goal was to explain not the origin or evolution of cultural phenomena but their symbolic value, its method was consequently not explanatory but interpretive. Interrogating a wide range of materials in order to uncover their profound interconnectedness, the cultural historian applied what Gombrich called "the exegetic method."[47] And as Dilthey and others insisted, this method could not pretend to the objectivity that presumably characterizes the methodology of the natural sciences. Since the object of knowledge was a product of the human spirit, it required of the knower a corresponding spirituality. The very fact that we can know distant cultural objects at all is a function of the shared humanity that undergirds all of history, and to attempt to deny that humanity in the service of an unattainable objectivity is both to try to exempt ourselves from a historicity that conditions all experience and to discredit the very agency of understanding. Hence for Dilthey historical knowledge is the meeting of subjectivities, marked by contemplation (*Anschauung*) and intuition (*Ahnung*). Moreover, this process is necessarily and appropriately circular— the famous hermeneutic circle.[48] Cultural understanding obeys what Edgar Wind neatly designated "the dialectic of the historical document: that the information which one tries to gain with the help of the document ought to be presupposed for its adequate understanding."[49] Humanistic knowledge proceeds by a dialectical movement from parts to whole and back again, not by a linear accumulation of detail piled upon detail. In his account of the attitude which supports the enterprise of philology (in the largest sense), Leo Spitzer well described the values upon which *Geistesgeschichte* is based, and rightly stressed their essentially religious character:

> The philologician must believe in the existence of some light from on high, of some *post nubila Phoebus*. If he did not know that at the end of his journey there would be awaiting him a life-giving draught from

some *dive bouteille*, he would not have commenced it: "Tu ne me cher-
cherais pas si tu ne m'avais pas déjà trouvé," says Pascal's God. . . .
It is not by chance that the "philological circle" was discovered by a
theologian, who was wont to harmonize the discordant, to retrace the
beauty of God in this world. This attitude is reflected in the word
coined by Schleiermacher: *Weltanschauung*: "die Welt anschauen":
"to see, to cognize the universe *in its sensuous detail.*"[50]

At heart, as Spitzer suggested, the humanist piety that *Geistesgeschichte* displays toward the past is a barely displaced version of religious devotion.

Religious devotion, although in a fully explicit form, is also behind
the other, narrower enterprise that Exegetics draws upon, iconography.
The conservative medievalism of the nineteenth century gave rise to a
wave of architectural Gothicism, with the result that the great bastions of
institutional power—government, the church, universities, the courts,
and of course prisons—were housed in buildings that bespoke a profound
attachment to the feudal past.[51] So, too, in England and especially in
France, the restoration of ancient monuments became part of a larger
program of political restoration.[52] It was under these auspices that much
scholarly work was accomplished in deciphering Gothic symbolism. In
England the ecclesiologists of the Cambridge Camden Society not only
passed on church restoration and construction, but actually published an
edition of Durandus's *Rationale divinorum officiorum*.[53] But it was in France
that the most important work was done through the efforts of Napoleon
Didron (himself inspired by Châteaubriand's *Génie du christianisme*) and
other devout medievalists like the Abbé Cahier, work that culminated in
the enormously influential books of Emile Mâle. And it is Mâle and his
conception of iconography that stand in the most direct line of descent
behind Exegetics. "In medieval art every form clothes a thought," said
Mâle, and these thoughts derive from the works of "the theologian, the
encyclopaedist, the interpreter of the Bible."[54] The medieval universe is
profoundly symbolic—"In the Middle Ages the idea of a thing [is] always
more real than the actual thing itself" (p. 158)—and wholly unified: "All
the arts united in giving the people the same religious lesson. . . . *Liturgy,
drama and art teach the same lesson, make manifest the same thought. They reveal the perfect unity of the Middle Ages*" (p. 170; italics added).

One useful although admittedly incomplete way of understanding
Exegetics is as the return of the culturally repressed. The conservative

and institutional view of the Middle Ages that Anglo-American liberalism and pragmatic empiricism had not allowed into literary studies was reintroduced through the Trojan horse of French iconography and German *Geistesgeschichte*. For Exegetics articulated the perfect unity of Mâle's Middle Ages through the agency of a totalizing *Weltanschauung*. All elements of medieval culture, according to this view, bespeak the workings of a single radix or *diapason*. For Robertson this radix was the medieval "tendency to think in terms of symmetrical patterns, characteristically arranged with reference to an abstract hierarchy."[55] Much of the explanatory power of Exegetics derives from both the simplicity of this central conception and the comprehensiveness of its application. Most familiar to readers of Exegetical criticism is the ethical hierarchy established by the Augustinian law of charity, a powerful normative tool that unerringly locates all forms of human behavior upon a scale of spiritual value. But equally important are other hierarchies. Medieval ontology, for instance, privileges an abstract realm of absolute value over a historical or experiential world that can claim a merely contingent reality. Correspondingly, medieval aesthetics promotes meaning over mimesis, the nucleus of *sententia* over a deceptively beautiful cortex. And perhaps most important of all, the Middle Ages manifests throughout a clear cultural hierarchy, with the church at the top. As Robertson says, perhaps somewhat disingenuously, "the dominance of the church in the Middle Ages considerably simplifies the task of the historical critic."[56]

What simplifies it even more is that clerical culture is itself hierarchical, with the ubiquitous Augustine as not merely the leading but virtually the only *auctoritas*. Although Exegetical critics habitually cited an intimidatingly wide range of clerical writings, all are variations on the same Augustinian themes, a fact that far from impeaching the Exegetical method is entirely consistent with it. As Robertson explicitly argues, writers as divergent in space and time as Boethius, Rhabanus Maurus, Hugh of St. Victor, and Peter Lombard are engaged in providing "transcripts" or "elaborations" of Augustinian doctrines.[57] The inevitable next step in this exposition is then to assert the hegemonic authority of this clerical culture over medieval culture as a whole, an understanding that preempts the modernist opposition between religious or philosophical writing on the one hand, and poetry or literature on the other, in favor of a supervening hierarchy in which *all* medieval writing is "directed towards the establishment and the maintenance of those traditional hierarchies which were dear to the medieval mind" (*Preface*, p. 265). Unlike the babel of modern systems of description, medieval discourse was single and univocal, "able to discuss the goal of personal effort, of social effort, and of religious effort in a single terminology, and to come to an agreement about the general meaning of that terminology." It is ultimately this shared belief in the objectivity of a single set of values that makes possible the coherence, and the success, of medieval culture, and that accounts for the relentlessly normative and didactic nature of all medieval writing.

This catalogue of totalizings is then extended to include, for instance, the relationship between pictorial and literary art, or the capacity of medieval culture to absorb apparently indigestible items such as pagan writings or obscenity, or—most important—the analogous totalizing accomplished by the Exegetical hermeneutic at the level of individual texts. Indeed, the whole point of Robertson's Augustinian exegesis, as of Augustine's, is to harmonize the individual text with a supervening ideology. The central principle of Augustine's hermeneutic is that the text "should be subjected to diligent scrutiny until an interpretation contributing to the reign of charity is produced," and Exegetical readings consist in precisely such a scrutiny.[58] Moreover, the text produced by such an exegesis perfectly replicates the form of medieval culture as a whole, for it subordinates a wide range of disparate and potentially conflicting elements to the authority of an abstract *sententia*. And nothing, of course, could be more totalizing than the fact that that *sententia* is always and everywhere the same; what Robertson says about the final, heaven-directed stanzas of the *Troilus* could equally well be applied to all other poems and poets throughout the medieval centuries: "This, in effect, is what Chaucer has to tell us about love, not only here but in *The Canterbury Tales* and in the major allegories as well. It is his 'o sentence'" (*Preface*, p. 501). According to Robertson, the key principle of medieval aesthetics is the Augustinian definition of beauty as *convenientia*, which means the harmony that obtains when individual elements are organized according to symmetry and hierarchy in order to form a whole (*Preface*, p. 120). *Convenientia* is beautiful not so much in and of itself but because it replicates the divine order. The most massive medieval expression of *convenientia* is in one sense the Gothic cathedral, which articulates a divine plan through its scrupulous organization. And yet in a deeper sense the most extensive embodiment of *convenientia* is the Middle Ages itself. Imbued with what Robertson calls the "great civilizing concept" of charity, and rigorously organized according to the "convenient" principles of hierarchy and symmetry, medieval culture itself bespeaks a divine supervision.

But Exegetics went well beyond simply recuperating for literary studies a conservative, universalist, and institutional view of the Middle Ages. For the central force of its challenge was its antihumanism, that is, its questioning not merely the place of the individual in history but his or her very existence. For humanism, the individual is the privileged category that must be defended against all challenges. The task of the humanist historian is to define the canon of great writers that constitutes our literary past and to represent them as simultaneously articulating the values of their time and yet rising above them. The humanist's critical purchase upon past historical periods is grounded in an unchanging human nature, a transcendental subjectivity to which our own subjectivity responds and by means of which we understand. But Exegetics wholly rejected this scheme. There is no "unchanging human nature," but rather a humanness that is constituted anew by each cultural period. In contrast to modern assumptions, in the Middle Ages character was conceived not in terms of subjectivity, as a consciousness set over against that which it experiences, but rather in terms of ideology, as a structure of value. Since "psychological theories" are "features of the universe of discourse, and not of the realm of things, [they] do not exist before they are formulated" (*Essays*, p. 3); since the discursive formation of medieval culture did not articulate the idea of a value-free inner self, not merely was such an idea literally unthinkable but the experience itself was impossible. Culture not merely conditions individual consciousness but absorbs it entirely; just as each detail of a medieval cathedral witnesses to an underlying *ordo*, so each inhabitant of the medieval centuries is endowed with a single ideology. This is an effacement of the self that invests medieval discursive practices with absolute authority. Medieval culture is fully possessed of its own meaning, endowed with an unqualified self-understanding: able to know nothing other than itself, it knows itself completely. Hence the task of the historian is not to interpret but merely to describe; the past is not a hidden or discarded version of the self but wholly other, an object of knowledge and not a subject. If it is true, as Claude Lévi-Strauss has claimed, that "the ultimate goal of the human sciences [is] not to constitute, but to dissolve man," then Exegetics achieved that goal.[59]

There are many criticisms that could be made of this project, but most of those made to date have served primarily to distract attention from the full power of the Exegetical challenge. One of these criticisms is to object to the ruthless totalizing that Exegetics accomplished—an objection that has an obvious legitimacy. Another is to dismiss Exegetics as being merely what Ruskin called a "Gothic opinion," a medievalism constructed to provide arguments in a modern debate. It is unfortunately true that in its least interesting, most vulnerable form Exegetics could be read as simply the nostalgic projection into the past of the values that the modern world has wrongly abandoned. Nor was Exegetics much helped by its habit of characterizing the form of modernism it disliked (which, typically, it totalized into modernism per se) in abusive and reductive terms as sentimental, expressionistic, hedonistic, aesthetic and, above all, solipsistic. As the heat of its polemic revealed, Exegetics was itself deeply engaged in a contemporary debate, representing an anti-Romantic modernism that was a contemporary analogue to that which it admired in the past. And surely it was no accident that Exegetics emerged in the 1950s and that its polemics became most strident in the tumultuous 1960s, the decade that still functions as a kind of political litmus test.

But perhaps there is a third line of approach that can both respect Exegetical ambitions and yet get us closer to understanding both its practical successes and its subsequent exclusion from the mainstream of literary studies. Let us focus for a moment on its own intellectual heritage, both the native historicism that it rejected and the European procedures from which it fashioned an alternative. In his not dissimilar attack upon what he calls a humanistic anthropology, Michel Foucault issued a famous dictum: "It is comforting . . . and a source of profound relief to think that man is only a recent invention, a figure not yet two centuries old, a new wrinkle in our knowledge, and that he will disappear again as soon as that knowledge has discovered a new form."[60] In working toward its own new form of knowledge, Exegetics sharply revised the procedures of the *Geistesgeschichte* from which it derived its initial inspiration. A key principle of *Geistesgeschichte*, it should be remembered, is that the goal is for a knowledge that is by definition unavailable to the members of the culture being investigated. *Weltanschauungen* are forms of understanding that condition individual consciousness but are necessarily unknown to it, revealed (to quote Charles Peirce) not in the beliefs men parade but in the ones they betray.[61] Now as Foucault has pointed out, this notion of the unknown—the *Unbewusste*, the implicit, the inactual, the sedimented, the unthought—is itself a function of the modern creation of the subject; it is "the shadow cast by man as he emerged in the field of knowledge, . . . the blind stain by which it is possible to know him."[62] Entirely appropriately, therefore, Exegetics rejected the humanist hermeneutic of depth.

But what was to take its place? To judge from Exegetical procedures, the answer was, ironically enough, the very positivist historicism against which Exegetics reacted in the first place. Exegetical interpretations typically display the same reductive search for proximate causes and inert factualism as dominated the earlier, self-defeating historicism it sought to replace. Not only is a Chaucerian image to be explained in large part by reference to its source, with little or no regard to its function in the poem, but that source is itself exempt from interpretation. Hence by allowing the lines of explanatory force to run only from context to text rather than laterally as well, within the text itself, Exegetics avoided the narrative or literal understanding of an image—much to the dismay of more circumspect critics.[63] More tellingly, in dispensing with the humanist hermeneutics of depth Exegetics was unable to attend to the explanatory context itself, which remained wholly exempt from interpretation. For Exegetics, for example, what clerical writers said about love is not only an authoritative guide to what Chaucer must have meant but is itself transparent, neither requiring nor yielding to an interpretation that might reveal it as being itself determined by unacknowledged imperatives. Similarly, not only are hierarchy and symmetry the guiding principles of medieval culture, but they are everywhere stated to be so, statements that are expressions of that which is thought to be simply true rather than elements of a larger cultural conversation that requires interpretive effort if it is to be heard at all. Put bluntly, the *Weltanschauung* of medieval culture is neatly if illegibly printed in the marching columns of Migne's *Patrologia*.[64]

This revision of *Geistesgeschichte* in the direction of a positivist historicism is also visible in the Exegetical assumption of what can only be called a naive objectivism. Despite a considerable show of methodological sophistication, Exegetics characteristically defined itself in terms of a simplistic opposition between objective historicism and subjective criticism. For Exegetics, the problem of historical understanding was not epistemological but moral: on the one side are scholars who diligently seek to understand the past in its own terms, however much those terms might run counter to modern sensibilities, while on the other are aesthetes who, wallowing in what Robertson graphically described as "that rancid solipsistic pit into which the major tendencies of post-romantic thought have thrust us" (*Essays*, p. 82), prefer their own meanings to those of the documents they purport to study. In Robertson's most extended methodological discussion, the ideal scholar is defined as the Stylistic Historian who dispassionately describes the characteristics of other cultures while remaining himself uncircumscribed by any, a suprahistorical consciousness somehow exempt from the historicity that conditions all other forms of life.[65] This resolute refusal to confront the contingency of *all* historical understanding, or even to understand historicism itself as an intellectual formation profoundly shaped by its origins in the Romantic movement, made it inevitable that Exegetics would revert to the positivist methods of the past from which it sought escape.

Just this reversion, however, made possible the professional success of Exegetics, despite the widespread skepticism which its specific interpretations aroused. For its accommodation of *Geistesgeschichte* to the antitheoretical empiricism of Anglo-American literary scholarship allowed Exegetics to become a productive paradigm for literary work. Just as New Criticism offered its adherents a hermeneutic kit that included both interpretive techniques and the prescribed result—i.e., a reading contributing to the reign of humanism—so did Exegetics on its side. Endowed with industry and a library card, any competent scholar could produce the prescribed Exegetical reading for any medieval poem. In part, of course, it was just this predictability that kept Exegetics from becoming a truly dominant mode: the paradigm was too easily followed and the range of acceptability too narrowly defined to attract creative minds for long. Yet this kind of stricture really only repeats a familiar liberal lament ("It is all very dreary") while ignoring the abundance of Exegetical readings.[66] And the professional success of Exegetics, however circumscribed, is important not because it somehow proved the Exegetical representation of the Middle Ages to be correct but because it illustrated the process of professionalization itself.

As we might expect from its roots in the conservative, institutional medievalism of the nineteenth century, Exegetics had deep affiliations with the modern institution of medieval studies. Whether a physical institute, center, or program, or simply a normative idea of the way work on medieval materials ought to be undertaken, it is by means of the institution of medieval studies that the liberal modern university accommodated what was often presented as a conservative, institutionalist, and universalist conception of culture. That this is the ideology that underwrites the "interdisciplinary" programs of medieval studies common throughout North America has been made abundantly clear by the rash of self-explanations proffered by institutionalized medievalism. To cite just one statement among many: in speaking in 1979 at the fiftieth anniversary of the Pontifical Institute of Mediaeval Studies in Toronto, Gerhart Ladner noted the profound affiliation between "the universalist approach to medieval studies" and "the universalism of the Middle Ages" itself, and he eloquently described the "supra-individual and supra-political sense of community" of the Middle Ages that was, he felt, proving so attractive to contemporary students and that was itself embodied in the very institute whose anniversary was being celebrated.[67] Given its commitment to this idea of the Middle Ages, its privileging of Latin over the vernacular, its absolutist sense of historical periodization, and its conception of professional training, Exegetics was in theory if not in fact the method of choice for the literary side of medieval studies.[68] This means not that the Exegetical method was universally taught in programs of medieval studies, which is obviously not the case, but that Exegetics was powerfully in league with the very idea of medieval studies—with, that is, a professional superego brandishing paleographical handbooks, dictionaries of arcane tongues, German *wissenschaftliche* tomes, and all the rest of the paraphernalia that simultaneously torments and legitimizes the medievalist.

Yet for all its trumpeting of popularity and relevance, institutionalized medieval studies has appeared to many contemporary medievalists as more of a ghetto than an enclave, more prison than prelapsarian garden.[69] To nonmedievalists, it must be admitted, the isolation of medievalists from the mainstream of Anglo-American literary studies is a self-evident fact. The point is not the resistance of individual medievalists to the winds of change—indeed, literary medievalists seem all too anxious to be thought *au courant*—than the marginalizing of medieval literature as a force within literary studies as a whole. Its irrelevance is especially striking because it was, after all, in the name of the Middle Ages that the stranglehold of classical studies over nineteenth-century education was first broken, allowing vernacular literature to become an academic subject. As the work of Auerbach, Spitzer, and Curtius testifies, medieval literature was once at the center of the old humanist program. Now that that program has pretty well disappeared, one thing is clear: medieval literary study will not disappear into an enclave of bureaucratized positivism, protected only by an increasingly desiccated erudition. But will it ever regain its centrality?

Although the debate between Exegetics and New Criticism has followed an essentially nineteenth-century agenda, the issues continue to be relevant to contemporary life both within and outside the academy. The contribution of Exegetics to the study of medieval literature was that it promised to lay bare the political nature of this debate. With its virulent antimodernism and its polemical attack on the humanistic pieties of New Criticism, Exegetics articulated a conservative position with a force that not even a blandly pluralistic liberalism could evade. And yet in the last analysis Exegetics itself blunted its own attack. Refusing to take the problematics of historical understanding seriously, Exegetics reinstituted a naive objectivism that exempted it from the need to acknowledge its own place in history and led it to adopt the methods and values of an uncritical positivism. The result is that the debate over values that was at the heart of the confrontation with New Criticism was remystified, and then simply displaced into a simplistic argument between up-to-date critical sophistication ("theory") and old-fashioned erudition ("historicism"). Rehearsing this critical history allows us to see, then, that this current situation is, for all its sense of novelty to the participants, essentially a sterile repetition of the past. So as Lenin once said, "What is to be done?" Not a revolution, I think, but just what we should expect: the careful deployment of theoretical procedures responsive to the demands of history and the development of a theoretically informed historicism.

chapter two

The Disenchanted Classroom

If a life fulfilled its vocation directly, it would miss it.
—Adorno[1]

Discussions of pedagogy are subject to many different interests, not all of them compatible and some even disagreeable. The genre asks for descriptive pragmatism, a dispassionate account of the materials and strategies of teaching a certain body of texts. But as soon as one begins to reflect on why one does what one does in the classroom, self-justifying and polemical interests inevitably emerge. This essay will not pretend to have avoided such unattractive qualities, even as it argues against self-justification and polemic in the classroom. But whether acknowledged or not, pedagogical practice always rests on theoretical presuppositions, and in the second part of this essay I shall draw upon the work of Max Weber in order to define my own presuppositions. Then in the third part I shall argue that there is a connection between "responsible" pedagogy (in Weberian terms) and the kind of historicist criticism I try to use to explicate Chaucer's poetry in the classroom. However, I claim neither that what I shall describe as my practice *is* my actual practice—it is instead a model from which the imperfect reality of day-to-day work doubtless diverges—nor that this practice is appropriate for anyone else. While this essay offers a rationale for teaching literature that means to be valid in general rather than merely personal terms, it also argues that values are by definition incapable of proof, an incapacity that must also apply to mine. Finally, as a last demurral, I shall not appeal to student response as proof of anything. Teaching and learning are different activities, and to measure what students learn from a course in literature would require a serious investigation that cannot be accomplished by the sketchy course evaluations that typically serve as the sole evidence of classroom effectiveness.[2]

I

If the question of "what" cannot be divorced from "why," neither can it be divorced from "how." And "how" is conditioned above all by institutional requirements. At present the question of method is understood largely in the terms most influentially expressed by Paolo Freire in *The Pedagogy of the Oppressed*. As we all know, perhaps without quite knowing precisely how we know, a distinction has been established between a "banking model" of education, in which students are regarded as empty receptacles into which the all-knowing teacher "deposits" knowledge (bad), and "problem-posing education," in which the teacher, as a "culture worker," creates a dialogue with students in order, in Freire's words, to "develop their power to perceive critically *the way they exist* in the world *with which* and *in which* they find themselves; they come to see the world not as a static reality, but as a reality in process, in transformation" (good).[3] In this model—designed by Freire to confront the social needs of his native Brazil—the goal of teaching is to free students from the false consciousness that allows them to accept as inevitable life conditions that can be changed. At every stage the teacher seeks to subvert rather than encourage passivity, a process that requires not monologue but dialogue.

Current discussions of pedagogy ring with Freire-inspired manifestos. As the editors of an influential book of essays on teaching declare, "Pedagogy is about the linkage of teaching to social empowerment, leading to a politics of social strength, but in the context of shared social conceptions of justice and rights—that is to say, the radical pedagogy of the engaged intellectual is connected to the politics of everyday life."[4] Well, maybe. Given the heterogeneity of the students who attend the various kinds of post-secondary institutions available in the United States (not to speak of all the potential students to whom post-secondary education is closed), it would be wrong to declare that this is simply an inappropriate goal for American literary educators. But the Freire model does carry with it four assumptions that actually work against its premise of the dialogic equality of teacher and student. 1) It assumes that the student is actually *in* a condition of false consciousness concerning contemporary social conditions, which is—at least in my experience as both teacher and parent—a large assumption; 2) it assumes, perhaps even more egregiously, that the teacher is somehow uncontaminated by this false consciousness and perceives the truth of things; 3) it assumes that the goal of the teaching process is to transform the student's consciousness into that of the teacher, which hardly implies equality; and 4) it assumes that classroom education is capable of playing this kind of role in students' lives—lives about which most college and university teachers, quite properly, know little.[5] Even putting aside the very real pragmatic questions, then, one can legitimately ask whether the Freire model of pedagogy is capable of enacting, at least within an American context, the politics it promotes.

Obviously no teacher can be in favor of passivity or want to restrict engagement. But there are institutional realities that most discussions of pedagogical method ignore. The teacher is rarely in a position to decide unilaterally what size class he or she will be assigned; for a variety of reasons, most of them curricular and institutional, I have taught for some forty years in both public and private institutions without ever teaching an undergraduate Chaucer course as a seminar.[6] As a result, many of the discussions that stress either the value of "dialogue" in the classroom or the engagement of students' life experiences in the pedagogical experience become largely irrelevant.[7] The brutal fact is that as soon as class size moves beyond twenty-five or thirty, as soon as the room configuration is that of the lecture hall, with a podium or desk at the front and rows of seats facing it, and as soon as the course is formally designated as a lecture rather than a seminar, then there is no point in pretending to stage a dialogue. No lecture need be an uninterrupted monologue, just as not every seminar achieves the give-and-take of dialogue. But like it or not, in a lecture course the voice that is going to be heard most of the time is the teacher's.

One must therefore take seriously the limitations of the lecture form as a pedagogical method, limitations that have been depicted in especially mordant terms by David Punter. "Lecturing is a passive-aggressive mode of relating," says Punter, in which

> all fantasy power is invested in the lecturer, while the member of the audience is allowed to experience total irresponsibility [in order] to habituate the junior participant to powerlessness, and render him or her grateful for the condescension that may occasionally palliate the operations of absolute power.[8]

Despite its extravagance, and its assumption that teachers are stooges of the capitalist system who blindly reproduce its values in their duped victims/students, this description still contains enough truth to strike home. Which of us has not had the curious experience of being regarded simultaneously as both an omnipotent oracle dispensing truth before dutiful scribes and an infommercial host irritating viewers who are denied access to the remote control that would change the channel? Nevertheless, the inherent disadvantages of the lecture system can be ameliorated. Perhaps the most important way is through the section system used by many large universities, which allows undergraduates an opportunity to meet in a small group with a graduate teaching assistant. While the lecturer will visit these sections on occasion, my own policy is merely to observe so as to offer the graduate assistant whatever pedagogical advice might be helpful. A largely hands-off role is important to ensure the intellectual independence of the graduate assistants, who function best when they bring to the material viewpoints slighted by or opposed to those of the lecturer and so model intellectual independence for the students.

There are other, structural means by which the imbalances of the lecture system can be ameliorated. One is to use either in-class quizzes or daily exercises (e.g., journals) to ensure that the students do the reading before the lecture. For all the coerciveness (and infantilization) implicit in this procedure, it does preempt one of the most unpleasant of pedagogical experiences. This is when the teacher strongly suspects that the students have not done the reading but pretends that they have; the students *know* they have not done the reading but feign attentiveness to a largely incomprehensible lecture; and the teacher then treats this attentiveness with a jaded tolerance that silently admires the students' dramatic abilities while being irritated at the bad faith everyone is displaying—all the while trying to deliver an interesting lecture to the members of the audience who *are* prepared. In any case, the unpleasantness of the quiz method can itself be ameliorated. One way is to make the quizzes very easy, so that a student who has done the reading will get a high grade; a second is to substitute the quizzes for a mid-term and/or final exam, so that students get a genuine compensation at the busiest times of the term for working conscientiously at other times; and a third is to offer an optional final exam, with short, quiz-like questions, for those who have done so badly on the quizzes—or have declined to attend the lectures—that they need a last-minute reprieve.[9]

Another way to soften the impersonality and imbalance of the lecture system is to develop a lecture style informal enough to allow for—and to invite—discussion from the floor. Whether this is possible depends not just on the lecturer's personality but also on the size of the class, the nature of the room, and—perhaps most important—the character of the institution. Whatever the reason, such informal exchanges between lecturer and student are in my experience much easier at some institutions than others. This has nothing to do with how "good" the students are but rather with expectations, specific to each institution, about teacher-student relations and the responsibility of each party for the effectiveness of lecture courses. In some institutions this responsibility is felt to be shared, while in others it is thought to rest exclusively with the lecturer. *Why* this should be so is to me a mystery, but that it *is* so is unmistakable.

Finally, the lecture format can be softened by inviting students to participate in the performance. In most of my courses, and in all lecture courses, I offer the students a variety of options for doing the written work of the course. Students can, for example, write anywhere from one long to three short critical essays; or they can substitute for one or more essays a different sort of writing, such as a short story based on one of the texts—the most memorable instance was a retelling of *Troilus and Criseyde* in the context of World War II Germany—or even an original Canterbury tale, sometimes in Middle English verse, sometimes not. It is a prejudice of

academic culture to assume that the only form of work that engages mean-
ingfully with literature is the critical essay—a form that the vast majority
of students will never again be called upon to produce after graduation.
It is a similar prejudice to assume that the only form of work that counts
is written. In fact, when students are offered the opportunity to engage
in some kind of performance relevant to the materials of the course the
results are often stunning. These have ranged from an accomplished performance of the Miller's Tale to a one-act opera based on the Prioress's
Tale. But whatever the students have produced, it has defined the cultural
space of the class as open to all members.

II

Even if we grant that the lecture format need not be as alienating as is
sometimes assumed, it still remains true that the intellectual purpose the
course hopes to achieve is largely dependent on the instructor's decisions.
To discuss the goals of education these days is to enter a controversy in
which academics' appetite for the pleasures of self-righteousness finds free
rein, where the satisfaction of pointing out others' limitations not only
guarantees but authorizes one's blindness to one's own. Nonetheless, it is
finally impossible to discuss teaching anything, including Chaucer, without candidly acknowledging that the practical choices one makes derive
from value commitments. In what follows I shall define my own classroom
decisions by contrasting them not to the pedagogical practices—of which
I know nothing—but to the critical arguments of other Chaucerians. I do
not assume that these arguments are in fact transferred in whole or even in
part into the classroom: I am simply extrapolating from critical writings
the pedagogical consequences they entail. If I am wrong in these extrapo-
lations, it is an error of misunderstanding rather than malice, an error for
which I apologize in advance.

The debate about course content entails two components, one relevant to humanities teaching in general, the other specific to medievalists.
First, if for the purposes of analysis we think of our teaching in terms of
knowledge and values, where should our emphasis fall? Second, should
we teach medieval literature primarily in terms of its relevance to or difference from contemporary life? These questions are interrelated: an ex-

plicit emphasis on values in the classroom sits more comfortably with a present-minded approach, while past-mindedness leads to a focus on historical knowledge. These alternatives are far from exclusive: no one can teach Chaucer without also teaching how to read and pronounce Middle English accurately, and no literature course can avoid a persistent involvement in the fundamental skills of literary interpretation. Indeed, this second topic—too easily dismissed as mere "close reading" and sometimes thought to be both politically inert and culturally passé—remains a central and necessary preoccupation of *every* literature course, regardless of its level or subject matter. Nor should this be a matter for lament, as English professors sometimes seem to think. The penetrating analysis of texts is a difficult but crucial competence for young men and women entering an economy whose rewards are increasingly reserved for a professional and managerial class skilled in verbal analysis. Whether or not we like the way the global economy is developing, part of our job as teachers must be not merely to credential our students but to prepare them to compete successfully in a harsh economic world from which many of us (myself included) are institutionally shielded. This may make us complicit with the injustices of that world, but we can hardly confirm our virtue as challengers of the system by declining to provide our students with the tools they need to prosper in a labor market from which we have withdrawn. I shall return to this question of the responsibility of the intellectual at the end of this essay, but for the moment my point is simply that every literature course, including a Chaucer course, not only must but should focus on the skills required for accurate reading and effective writing.[10]

One way to enter the controversy over how to balance a present-minded emphasis upon values with a past-minded emphasis upon knowledge—again, all the while acknowledging that these alternatives never present themselves in a pure form—is to turn to an earlier moment in academic history when these issues presented themselves in a different but still recognizable form. In 1917 Max Weber delivered a lecture to an audience of German university students on the topic of "Wissenschaft als Beruf"—a title typically translated as "Science as a Vocation" but perhaps better understood as "Scholarship [or even Knowledge] as a Vocation."[11] Weber's essay, and his scholarly position as a whole, is often misrepresented as promoting a naive claim to objectivity, a disengaged intellectual neutrality, and a pedantic retreat into specialization as a goal in and of itself.[12] These misunderstandings are caused by not locating the lecture either in relation to Weber's thought as a whole or to the intellectual traditions within which he worked. Indeed, much of the recent concern in Anglo-American literary studies over questions of critical method ignores the historicist and hermeneutical theory developed by German thinkers from Dilthey to Gadamer and Habermas. This may be because Anglo-American cultural studies escaped from a naive empiricism and objectivism only much later than the German tradition and under the poststructuralist tutelage of French interpreters of that tradition: Heidegger as reread by Derrida, Nietzsche as reread by Foucault, Freud as reread by Lacan. The result has been to declare the problem of the methodology of the cultural sciences a pseudo-problem by consigning difficult concepts like objectivity and validity to the dustheap of an outworn metaphysics. In addition, the intense particularism of recent American life, and of American academia especially, has meant that questions that smack of universalism—such as those of methodology—have been seen as simply disguises for bids for power by one identity group (typically white males) at the expense of others. If, in Carroll Smith-Rosenberg's words, women's history can only be legitimately written from a feminist standpoint because of "women's absolute Otherness," then the common ground on which methodological questions can be discussed diminishes to zero.[13]

Unlike many contemporary theorists, Max Weber was interested not in transforming society, nor in imagining utopianist alternatives, but in understanding the role that scholarship and pedagogy could legitimately play within the world as he took it to be. To many Weber's realism is a not unadmirable "heroic cynicism"; to others it is a quietist acceptance of, even a spiteful apologetics for, bourgeois capitalism.[14] Certainly in this lecture, Weber is as always intensely aware of the socio-cultural context. Locally this meant the growth of nationalist pan-Germanism spurred by the military and political crises of 1917: much of Weber's methodological pronouncements were delivered in response to the growing pressure of the right-wing nationalism that would, after his death in 1920, develop into Nazism. More broadly, the context to which he addressed himself was a world that was, in the one Weberian term that remains current, "disenchanted." The progressive domination of the world by practical reason means, wrote Weber, that "there are no mysterious incalculable forces that come into play, but rather that one can, in principle, master all things by calculation."[15] And calculation can teach us how the world works but not what it means. As Weber says, with typical acerbity, "I may leave aside altogether the naive optimism in which science—that is, the technique of mastering life which rests upon science—has been celebrated as the way to happiness. Who believes in this?—aside from a few big children in university chairs or editorial offices." And he goes on to cite Tolstoy: "Science is meaningless because it gives no answer to our question, the only question important for us: 'What shall we do and how shall we live?'" (p. 143).

In methodological terms, Weber insists that values remain incapable of scientific—that is, empirical—demonstration. In an earlier essay, he had also explained that

> only positive religions—or more precisely expressed: dogmatically bound *sects*—are able to confer on the content of *cultural values* the status of unconditionally valid *ethical* imperatives. . . . The fate of an epoch which has eaten of the tree of knowledge is that it must know that we cannot learn the *meaning* of the world from the results of its analysis, be it ever so perfect; it must rather be in a position to create this meaning itself. It must recognize that general views of life and the universe can never be the products of increasing empirical knowledge, and that the highest ideals, which move us most forcefully, are always formed only in the struggle with other ideals which are just as sacred to others as ours are to us.[16]

Knowing as much about the world as we do, Weber urges us to admit, with a realism that recommends tolerance, that the values by which we live cannot be defended by appealing to canons of validity.

How, then, can people make sense of their lives? Weber's answer is the notion of *Beruf*, translated as "calling" or "vocation." In *The Protestant Ethic and the Spirit of Capitalism* (1904–5), he argues that the sixteenth-century collapse of Catholicism generated "a feeling of unprecedented inner loneliness of the single individual" through the withdrawal of a providential deity and its replacement with the distant Protestant, and specifically Calvinist, God.[17] This "disillusioned and pessimistically inclined individualism" (p. 105) found its salvation neither in ritualized religion nor in monastic withdrawal but instead in a "this-worldly asceticism":

The only way of living acceptably to God was not to surpass worldly morality in monastic asceticism, but solely through the fulfillment of the obligations imposed upon the individual by his position in the world. That was his calling. (p. 80)

This notion of vocation, a definition of "labour as an end in itself," was essential to the development of the morality required by capitalism: "The ability of mental concentration, as well as the absolutely essential feeling of obligation to one's job, are here most often combined with a strict economy which calculates the possibility of high earnings, and a cool self-control and frugality which enormously increase productivity" (p. 63). The notion of vocation in the Calvinist scheme of salvation provided the model from which other notions of vocation developed, not least those that now hold sway in the professions of law, medicine, science, and in the academy. In sum, we live not only in a disenchanted world, in which the connection between fact and value, between *is* and *ought*, is definitively broken, but in a capitalist world that provides existence with meaning in terms of a life of labor defined by the ideology of vocation.[18] As Carlyle said, "Blessed is he who has found his work; let him ask for no other blessedness."[19]

These, according to Weber, are the conditions of modern, disenchanted life, and there are only two possible responses: a futile, even self-deluding rejection, or a clear-eyed, pragmatic acceptance. Rejection can be accomplished by what he calls "an ethic of commitment" (Weber's word is *Gesinnungsethik,* which can also be translated as "an ethic of ultimate ends" or "an ethic of conviction"); acceptance entails what he calls "an ethic of responsibility." These are terms whose relevance to the vocation of teaching I wish to explore at some length.

The ethic of commitment is a response to what Weber calls "the ethical irrationality of the world," the fact that the conflict of values cannot be resolved by empirical means. Unwilling to accept disenchantment, some inspire themselves with "the flame of pure intentions";[20] they seek to "break out of the disenchanted world . . . [through] self-clarification and self-determination in opposition to, and no longer within, the iron constraints of society."[21] In the context of pedagogy, the ethic of commitment tempts the teacher to become a preacher or prophet, an "impresario" (p. 137) of the lectern. But "the prophet and the demagogue do not belong

on the academic platform" (p. 146), in part because of the power relations that structure the educational situation,[22] in larger part because the
teacher should not promote values that are by definition beyond empirical demonstration. On the contrary, "The task of the teacher is to serve
the students with his knowledge and scientific [i.e., scholarly] experience
and not to imprint upon them his personal political views" (p. 146). Indeed, Weber went further, opposing the prevailing view that the role of
the university was that "of forming the minds of men and of propagating
political, ethical, aesthetic, cultural or other views."[23] In this he rejected
the idea, central to German intellectual life, that the purpose of education
was the formation (*Bildung*) of the student's personality by imbuing it
with the deepest, most permanent ideals of German *Kultur*.[24] And with
this idea he rejected as well the deep complicity of the German universities with the state that financed them. Indeed, Weber was resolute in insisting that academic freedom meant independence from government intervention, an idea first promoted by Wilhelm von Hulmboldt at the very
beginning of the German university tradition and, although under increasing pressure, still central to American post-secondary education.[25]

The "ethic of responsibility" that Weber opposes to the ethic of commitment must be understood in relation to one of his most important—
and most misunderstood—ideas, that of *Wertfreiheit* or value-freedom.
This has both a methodological and a pedagogical dimension. Pedagogi-
cally, value-freedom means that the teacher must distinguish, as best he or
she can, between the meaning of the cultural objects under scrutiny and
their value. "Consider the historical and cultural sciences," says Weber.

> They teach us how to understand and interpret political, artistic, lit-
> erary, and social phenomena in terms of their origins. But they give
> us no answer to the question, whether the existence of these cultural
> phenomena have been and are *worth while*. And they do not answer
> the further question, whether it is worth the effort required to know
> them. (p. 145, emphasis in original)[26]

Weber here raises two interrelated points. One is that teaching the "cultural sciences" requires a reticence about questions of value because they
seek not to measure the past by the standards of the present but to explain cultural phenomena "in terms of their origins." As Weber argues

throughout, the purpose of education is to provide knowledge not about what ought to be but about what is, to explain the *functioning* of cultural practices and particulars, in the sense of their historical causes and meanings (what he also calls "the internal structure of cultural values" [p. 146]), rather than their *significance,* in the sense of their value to us.[27]

Weber's second point is about specialization, which he promotes for four reasons. The first is that the initial goal of education must be to teach the student to think "independently" (p. 134), an independence that is impossible unless the student is endowed with both the historical information and the conceptual and methodological tools to offer solutions to cultural problems. Second, the segmentation and rationalization of modern life means that productive work is possible only through specialization, a narrowing of focus that is a prerequisite for the attainment of vocational satisfaction: "A really definitive and good accomplishment is today always a specialized accomplishment. And whoever lacks the capacity to put on blinders, so to speak, and to come up to the idea that the fate of his soul depends upon whether or not he makes the correct conjecture at this passage of this manuscript may as well stay away from science [i.e., scholarship]" (p. 135). Third, specialist training disabuses the student of the notion that empirical knowledge can solve the central problems of life: "One does *not* wish to see the deepest and most intimately personal decisions in life, the ones in which a man must rely on his own resources, jumbled up with specialist training, and that one wishes to see them solved by the student in the light of his own conscience, not on the basis of any suggestions from his teachers."[28] And finally, Weber argues that only specialist training provides the student with the conceptual ability to recognize facts ("especially those which he finds personally inconvenient"[29]) and to draw from them the appropriate conclusions. This ability has not merely a technical value. On the contrary, being taught how to follow out the relation of means to ends, of actions to consequences, can bring the student to understand the way in which "such and such a practical stand can be derived with inner consistency, and hence integrity, from this or that ultimate *weltanschauliche* position" (p. 151). Put simply, given the values you espouse, then certain life choices are consistent and others are not. "Thus, if we are competent in our pursuit," argues Weber, "we can force the individual, or at least we can help him, to give himself an *account of the ultimate meaning of his own conduct*" (p. 152; emphasis in original). Clearly this is an ethical lesson, but one that can be learnt only if the teacher seeks not to impose upon the student his or her own values.

The self-denying severity of Weber's thinking on pedagogy depends throughout on the fact-value distinction that he expresses in the controversial notion of *Wertfreiheit*. Since post-structuralist thought would seem to have demolished any such notion, it may be well to explain briefly what Weber meant by it. As we would expect of a thinker who emerges from the tradition of Nietzsche and Dilthey, Weber is intensely aware that any such distinction is, in practical terms, difficult to draw, and—following Dilthey—he rejected the simplistic empiricism that would apply the methodology of the natural sciences to the study of cultural practices and products. As he says, with some exasperation,

> I would rather not discuss any further whether it is "difficult" to distinguish between statements of empirical fact and practical value-judgments. It is. . . . [Indeed], it is possible, precisely when one appears to be eliminating all practical value-judgments, to suggest them very strongly, following the well-known formula, "Let the facts speak for themselves."[30]

As this formulation suggests, Weber is quite aware that all knowledge is developed within a value-laden socio-historical context that determines not merely the object of inquiry but the methodology and, to an important degree, the results. Weber called the historical situatedness of scholarly inquiry *Wertbeziehung*, which can be awkwardly translated as "value-relatedness." But if value-relatedness is unavoidable, it has as its counterpart *Wertfreiheit*: scholarship may be interdependent with its cultural moment, but it can also achieve at least some measure of independence. This partial independence is possible by means of what Talcott Parsons, the most important American sociologist influenced by Weber, calls "the familiar norms of objectivity both in verification of statements of empirical facts, and in logical inference and analysis." As Parsons says,

> a particular subvalue system must be paramount for the investigator, that in which conceptual clarity, consistency and generality on the one hand, empirical accuracy and verifiability on the other are the valued outputs of the process of investigation.

Value-freedom thus means "freedom to pursue the values of science within the relevant limits, without their being overridden by values either contradictory to or irrelevant to those of scientific investigation."[31] In short, "value-freedom" refers to the rigorous application of empirical methods within the context of a project that is necessarily defined by the investigator's values.

This idea was important to Weber not because it guaranteed "objectivity." On the contrary, he was perfectly aware that "the most certain proposition of our theoretical sciences—e.g., the exact natural sciences or mathematics, is, like the cultivation and refinement of the conscience, a product of culture," and he insisted that "all knowledge of cultural reality . . . is always knowledge from *particular points of view*."[32] But he nonetheless thought it possible to protect scholarly investigation from what he called "party-political" opinions, those political programs that are consciously adopted and explicitly pursued within the context of one's life as a citizen.[33] More important, he thought it possible, through a process of rigorous self-examination, to become aware of the relation of party-political opinions to one's larger value structure; in saying that students could learn to understand the relation of their value system to various courses of action, he assumed that their teachers were capable of the same process. Hence he maintained that, for all its difficulty, it was not merely possible but necessary for

> the academic teacher [to] impose on himself the unconditional obligation of rigorously making clear to his audience, and above all to himself, in each individual case (even at the risk of making his lectures boring), which of his statements on that occasion is an assertion of fact, either logically demonstrable or empirically observable, and which a practical value-judgment. To do this certainly seems to me to be a straightforward requirement of intellectual integrity, once the distinction between the two domains is conceded: in this case it is the absolute minimum that is required.[34]

In part this rigorous program was necessary if teachers were to avoid gratifying both students and themselves by playing the prophet in a disenchanted world: "academic prophecy will create only fanatical sects but never a genuine community" (p. 155). In a larger sense, however,

Weber's program is motivated by a limited but genuine idealism. If in a disenchanted world all activities are subordinated to pragmatic ends, then scholarship offers a space of resistance: because of its *wertfrei* character it can escape from the iron cage of pragmatic rationality and pursue the goal of a knowledge that is valuable in and of itself.

III

Weber's pedagogic imperatives constitute only one program among many and can make no claim to correctness.[35] But his analysis of the cultural context of modernity within which we live and work, and the kind of lives and work that are therefore both possible and valuable within that world, claims our attention for a number of reasons. For one thing, to accept Weber's central principle that the triumph of rationality precludes any means of ascertaining the validity of any one set of values over others is to become deeply skeptical of the notion—currently prevalent on both the right and left—that universities are appropriate places in which to teach civic virtue. And even if such a goal were thought both desirable and possible for the university, one must be even more skeptical of the idea that literature provides an appropriate means. To be sure, one cannot disagree that *in the last analysis* "everything is political." But the number of steps that a careful textual reading must take before this "last analysis" is reached undermines the force of whatever moral lesson might be taught. As Paul de Man has unpopularly but persuasively argued, "attention to the philological or rhetorical devices of language . . . transform[s] critical discourse in a manner that would appear deeply subversive to those who think of the teaching of literature as a substitute for the teaching of theology, ethics, psychology, or intellectual history"—or politics.[36] On the contrary, the best a careful rhetorical analysis can finally provide is the "negative knowledge" that "it is not . . . certain that literature is a reliable source of information about anything."[37]

The values that the teaching of literature *can* plausibly promote are not party-political opinions but the more general habits of mind that Weber designates as "intellectual integrity" and "independence of mind." By intellectual integrity he meant nothing more (nor less) than that the basic rules of empiricism be observed: as much of the evidence as possible must be incorporated, especially facts that are "inconvenient" both to the hypothesis being pursued and to one's own commitments; conclusions must be consistent with the evidence; and, above all, every effort must be made to observe the perplexing but still feasible distinction between "facts" and "values." By "independence of mind" he meant the capacity to pursue an intellectual project to its conclusion, regardless of its implications, and the ability to recognize that just as life choices are distinct from (although hardly irrelevant to) intellectual endeavors, so too specialized knowledge can provide little guidance in making them. For Weber, this independence could be accomplished only through a focused effort—through specialization—that made possible the skill and knowledge required for cogent results.

How are these educational goals—the essence of Weber's ethics of responsibility—to be pursued? The way I have chosen is to attend above all to the historicity of texts. This is not to say that historicist scholarship does not itself entail party-political opinions, nor that a course designed from a historicist standpoint cannot be pursued according to an ethic of commitment.[38] But in the classroom, historicism need make few or no claims about the present.[39] Its central ambition is to discover original meaning—that is, the meaning of a text to its author, to its original audience, and in the largest sense, to history itself.[40] That this ambition is philosophically controversial and intellectually difficult should be no cause for criticism, since the same strictures apply to all critical enterprises of any scope. As Adorno has said, "Every thought which is not idle . . . bears branded on it the impossibility of its full legitimation."[41] Historicism wants to understand nothing less than what Chaucer meant when he wrote his poems, what the poems meant to the society within which they circulated, and—at a higher level of abstraction—how the poems connect not just to the self-aware intentions of the poet and the explicit expectations of his audience but to larger patterns of social practice and ideology. Despite the profusion of discussions of historicist theory and practice, there is nothing particularly esoteric or complicated about this. Historicism concerns itself with the literary traditions upon which Chaucer drew, with the political, economic, social, and cultural environment within which he lived, and with the ways in which his poetry—in both form and content—is related to the local context of late fourteenth-century life and to the larger structures of the historical process, specifically the transition from the Middle Ages to modernity. That this is a strenuous program is true, but the goal is perfectly clear: to understand Chaucer's poetry as above all a phenomenon of late fourteenth-century England.

There can be no sense here of an "absolute" or "totalized alterity," of trying to recover the past in a pure or unadulterated form.[42] The distinction between past and present is not only not absolute but methodologically nonexistent: we know the past only in the terms that the present makes available to us. Every investigation of whatever sort begins by eliciting various significances from a text, a process necessarily and appropriately governed by modern interests. But the question is what happens then. Does one try to understand how these significances were or were not figured by other medieval cultural objects and practices? Or does one locate these significances in relation to modern culture? It is only at this relatively late point in the process of understanding that distinctions among different ways of being interested in the past can be made. Marshall Leicester is right to insist that his readings of Chaucer's poems, for all their disregard for historical context, are not ahistorical but are instead "a preliminary contribution to a . . . properly historical account of the Middle Ages."[43] That Leicester himself does not move beyond this preliminary stage neither supports nor challenges his interpretations. For he is interested not in a historical argument but in describing the way Chaucer's poetry can be read in terms of certain modern, largely psychoanalytic preoccupations—preoccupations whose connection to medieval writers other than Chaucer remains to be demonstrated. A "properly historical account," on the other hand, is concerned to provide such a demonstration, which in no way limits its access to theoretical formulations such as psychoanalysis. But it is required both to accommodate its interpretive schemes to the empirical canons that govern historical investigation per se and, as well, to discover how its textual interpretations relate to the cultural practices of Chaucer's England. At its best, then, historicism is both a restrictive *and* an expansive practice: it imposes methodological limits at the same time as it widens the field of inquiry.

The double process of restriction and expansion required by historicism is appropriate to a pedagogical program governed by Weber's ethic of responsibility. However politically charged our interpretive schemes, however vivid the analogies we draw between past and present, the final and definitive resort of historicist inquiry must always be to fourteenth-century England. The last question it asks of a text is not "What does this mean to us?" but "What might it have meant to them?" The effect of this imperative is to interpose, at least for a moment, a protective pause before the closure of understanding, a moment of deferral that can encourage the reader to listen to voices distant in time and different in purport. And by insisting that texts must be related to contexts, historicism can present literature as providing not values upon which to pass judgment, nor examples to be pressed into the service of current preoccupations, but problems that require solutions. By no means the only way to maintain the disinterestedness needed to avoid an ethic of commitment, and hardly providing a guarantee, historicism nonetheless erects systemic barriers that can help to protect us from our own enthusiasms.

Because most students know next to nothing about late fourteenth-century England, teaching Chaucer historically does require some special materials. But the teacher isn't starting from scratch. Many students enter a Chaucer course with an interest in things medieval gleaned from a variety of unofficial sources—an inspiring high-school course, a trip to Europe, the movies, an early obsession with Dungeons and Dragons or their video counterparts, or medievalized fantasy books by authors like Tolkien or Piers Anthony. However fragmentary and idiosyncratic, this knowledge provides a core of experience that can be developed toward a deeper interest in a more formal historical knowledge. This further development can be accomplished in a number of ways. For myself, I provide the students with a Course Pack of nine or ten essays drawn largely from the work of historians: in an appendix I have listed the repertoire from which I currently draw these essays, a list that is subject to continual revision.[44] These essays are read within the first four or five weeks of term, and the students fill in a worksheet on each essay that focuses on central points. Students are given as well a list of some twenty books relevant to the period and of the standard bibliographies. The goal is to provide fundamental information about the period that can then serve as a point of reference throughout the term and show students how to follow up on more specific interests.

But in practice, what does teaching Chaucer historically entail? A good example is provided by the *Book of the Duchess*, not least because it has a conspicuous if enigmatic historical pertinence that current criticism has largely disregarded. Recent critical discussions of the poem focus on topics that have an obvious modern interest: the inability of language to represent reality, the colloquy between dreamer and black knight as a psychoanalytic "talking cure" for a neurotic mourner, the narcissistic subjectivity of the bereft male, the poem as an originary moment of a national literary culture, and—perhaps above all—the way in which the poem stages a dialogue between men that programmatically excludes the woman to the point of actually requiring her death.[45] In this last kind of reading, Blanche's death is not the subject of the poem but the occasion that makes possible male homosociality, just as the interpretations of the poem accomplished by male critics accomplish a "heroic" bonding between critic and poet. These critics are by and large uninterested in medieval literary and social contexts; indeed, for Louise Fradenburg, Elaine Tuttle Hansen, and Gayle Margherita the place of the feminist critic within the contemporary world of Chaucer studies is of greater interest than the place of Chaucer within the late fourteenth century. These three critics explicitly found their readings upon an ethic of commitment.

That the issues this criticism finds in the poem are really there can hardly be doubted: they have been, in one form or another, the common currency of criticism of the poem for half a century. The question, rather, is the relation of these issues to the historical context in which the poem was written and read.[46] This context is constituted in part by the general crisis of the aristocracy that became increasingly acute as the century progressed (see the essays by Bolton, Dyer, Faith, Hilton, Macfarlane, and Myers), in part by the conditions of the aristocratic court culture within which Chaucer wrote all his poetry (with the possible exception of the *House of Fame*) prior to the *Canterbury Tales*. To understand this latter context is to deal with the difference between *maker* and *poete*, to assess the ambiguous status of the *maker* within the court, and in general to explore the way in which aristocratic culture used a series of literary and quasi-literary practices as a form of symbolic capital—all under the growing pressures being felt by the English governing classes (see the essays by Starkey, Olson, Green, and Benson).

In dealing with the *Book of the Duchess*, then, the question of narcissism is treated not psychoanalytically but socially. In the *Fonteinne amoureuse*, Machaut had provided a penetrating critique of the aristocratic habit of privatizing political problems and recasting them into the language of *fine amor*: for Machaut the *fonteinne amoureuse* is the fountain of Narcissus, established by Venus and carved by Pygmalion.[47] In drawing on this poem for his account of Ceys, Alcyone, and Morpheus, Chaucer reveals the dangers inherent in the "douce ymagination" that absorbs the lover and that the poet feeds.[48] So too, the analogy that the poem establishes between the aristocratic activities of hunting and versifying has a social valence: one demonstrates power over the land and its inhabitants (both human and animal), the other power over language. In this light Chaucer's decision to write in English is seen less as a matter of asserting nationalist pride than of defending class prestige: the poem demonstrates that English is as elegant, as fashionable, and as articulate as French, thus making it clear that the maternal tongue is not only not the exclusive property of the commoner but finds its highest mission when it expresses aristocratic interests.[49] And the poem's interest in the inability of language to represent reality, and specifically a relationship of trusting mutuality— so that we get an elaborate discussion of courtship but almost none of achieved love—clearly has a social meaning. For the world of courtly ambition in which the poem is located stresses both the verbal facility of the courtier (with its playful masquerades) and the "trouthe" of the man of honor (with its demand of full commitment), capacities that are not just different but dangerously contradictory. Linguistic misrepresentation is in this world less a philosophical than a political problem, especially given the growth of retaining as the primary mode of social bonding among the knightly class. In this connection, it is relevant to observe that Gaunt granted Chaucer his annuity of £10 on June 13, 1374, just five days after he was appointed Controller of Customs and left the royal household.[50]

The central historical problem the poem poses is about its relevance to John of Gaunt: why would it be in his interest to be represented as the black knight? This is a good question for the classroom because it is at once conspicuous and difficult to answer.[51] The answer is unlikely to be found in speculations on the personal relationship between Blanche and her husband. For one thing, sexual fidelity seems to have been no more one of Gaunt's virtues than of the other men of his time and class. Everyone knows of his involvement with Katherine Swynford before and during his marriage to Constance of Castile, but less well known is the fact that in 1358 or 1359, very close to the time of his marriage to Blanche on May 20, 1359, he had a daughter by a woman named Marie de Saint-Hilaire, one of the Queen's ladies-in-waiting—a daughter named, with to us amazing gracelessness (or bad luck), Blanche.[52] More important, by invoking at the end of the poem "A long castel with walles white" (1318), Chaucer makes all too clear that the true value of Blanche of Lancaster to Gaunt was the property and title that survived the person whose death his poetic alter ego had just been so plangently lamenting. Indeed, that Chaucer could include so obvious a reminder of the economic and political rationale for the marriage within an elegy suggests that medieval men (and perhaps women as well) were less disturbed by the *Realpolitik* of aristocratic marriage—or perhaps less sentimental about marriage per se—than modern critics sometimes think they should have been. But quite apart from either Gaunt's sexual history or his personal feelings for Blanche, about which we know nothing, the representation of courtship in the *Book of the Duchess* is so stylized and derivative as to render moot the question of emotional appropriateness. The interesting (and potentially answerable) question is not, "Did Gaunt feel this way about his dead wife?" but rather, "Why did Chaucer represent Gaunt in this particular way?"

An answer to this question must begin then with the representation of the black knight. His eloquence and emotional intensity are a given: like any aristocrat, he can talk the talk and walk the walk of love. But he is also youthful: he is only twenty-four and "Upon hys berd but lytel her" (455–56), while Gaunt was twenty-nine when Blanche died and so somewhat older when the poem was composed. He is not merely a loyal but a submissive, even timorous lover: he provides a vivid account of his terror at having to speak to the lady and his despair at her initial rebuff (1182–1257). And above all, he is nothing but a lover. As he says, in one of the poem's few enigmatic passages, as a youth he could have followed "other art or letre" (788) but "I ches love to my firste craft," adding, with unexpected bitterness, "Therfore hit ys with me laft" (791–92). The reason for his bad decision was that he didn't know the consequences: because he was governed by Idleness,

> Al my werkes were flyttynge
> That tyme, and al my thoght varyinge.
> Al were to me ylyche good
> That I knew thoo.
>
> (801–4)

Lacking judgment, he chose unwisely and now, apparently, has no recourse.[53]

The picture one gets of Gaunt from the historical record is of an immensely ambitious and energetic man who could never quite find the proper stage for his talents. He may have been, thanks to his marriage and to the early death of Blanche's co-heir (her older sister, Maud), one of the richest and most powerful men in England. But he was still only the king's third surviving son, and after the births of the Black Prince's two sons, Edward in 1365 and Richard in 1367, he must have known, despite the death of his older brother Lionel in 1368, that he was never likely to become king of England. He consequently focused his attention on foreign ventures: from 1369 until 1376, when the Black Prince died, he never spent a consecutive twelve months in England. The most serious of these ventures was the marriage to Constance in September 1371 and the assumption of the title of King of Castile and León the following January, events which may well predate the composition of the *Book of the Duchess*.[54] And what historians have called Gaunt's "princely hauteur," his "blazing temper," and his "powerful and exigent personality" must have been well in evidence by the time he was in his late twenties or early thirties, when the poem was written, while it seems to have been only later in life that he developed what capacity he had for "politic flexibility."[55]

Given this account, the problem of the appropriateness of the portrait of the black knight solicits a number of hypotheses. One can argue, for example, that the very inappositeness of the portrait makes it politically useful: a powerful and overbearing young man intensely concerned with making a public career for himself is here presented as a wholly private figure, subordinate both to his lady and to his own feelings. One can also see in the poem the powerful strain of noble pathos so prominent in chivalric literature, especially in the Arthurian romances that most noble households seem to have possessed. This is a theme that stresses the burden of eminence and the unwarranted misfortune that afflicts the ambitious honorman, and by staging and endorsing the powerlessness felt by the powerful it provides a defense of privilege. The theme is central to both *Troilus and Criseyde* and the Knight's Tale, although presented in those poems in a progressively more critical light. Yet the *Book of the Duchess* is also something of a mirror for this prince, suggesting in its oddly skeptical account of its young lover's career choice the dangers of youthful impulsiveness—and yet by representing this as a fault of youth exempting the now older Gaunt from its critique. Finally, whether these hypotheses be found persuasive is, in the classroom, less important than what they make visible—the kind of knowledge and imagination historical understanding encourages and enables.

IV

At a time when academics feel the need to engage their political convictions in action, the kind of teaching I have described may seem a timid retreat from the vividness of the present into the pallid world of historical specialization. Yet Weber is surely right in arguing that specialization is the best way for the scholar-teacher to adhere to an ethic of responsibility while avoiding the powerful appeal of an ethic of commitment.[56] Moreover, as Weber's own life demonstrated, no scholar needs to or should take a vow of celibacy in regard to the civic responsibilities of the citizen outside the academy. But civic duty is a different part of life; and while all of us want to understand our lives as wholes, the way we achieve that understanding is a personal matter that is strictly irrelevant to our professional practice.

That these two areas of life can be pursued with success while respecting the difference between them is well illustrated by the example of Noam Chomsky. Chomsky insists that his specialist work as a linguist and his civic work as a critic of American foreign policy are distinct enterprises: "What special knowledge I have concerning language has no immediate bearing on social and political issues. Everything I have written on these topics could have been written by someone else."[57] Indeed, Chomsky goes further by arguing that intellectuals should not think that their expertise grants them a special capacity to understand the truth of anything other than their specialty. The realities of public life are not "inaccessible to simple people," as intellectuals sometimes like to think. "In the analysis of social and political issues," Chomsky continues,

> it is sufficient to face the facts and to be willing to follow a rational line of argument. Only Cartesian common sense, which is quite evenly distributed, is needed . . . if by that you understand the willingness to look at the facts with an open mind, to put simple assumptions to the test, and to pursue an argument to its conclusion. (p. 5, ellipsis in the original)

Chomsky's "Cartesian common sense" is equivalent to Weber's "intellectual integrity" and "independence of mind." To help students to develop this capacity cannot be the most immediate purpose of a Chaucer course, but it can be one of its underlying assumptions. Indeed, one could hardly ask more of any course than that it promote open-mindedness, encourage the testing of simple assumptions, and teach the pursuit of an argument to its conclusion.

Appendix

Judith M. Bennett, "Public Power and Authority in the Medieval English Countryside," in Mary Erler and Maryanne Kowaleski, eds., *Women and Power in the Middle Ages* (Athens: University of Georgia Press, 1988), pp. 18–36.

Larry D. Benson, "Courtly Love and Chivalry in the Later Middle Ages," in Robert F. Yeager, ed., *Fifteenth-Century Studies: Recent Essays* (Hamden: Archon Books, 1984), pp. 237–57.

J. L. Bolton, "Crisis and Change in the Agrarian Economy," chapter 7 of *The Medieval English Economy 1150–1500* (London: Dent, 1980), pp. 207–45, 354.

Christopher Dyer, "Late Medieval Society," chapter 1 of *Standards of Living in the Later Middle Ages: Social Change in England c. 1200–1520* (Cambridge: Cambridge University Press, 1989), pp. 10–26.

Rosamond Faith, "The Class Struggle in Fourteenth-Century England," in Raphael Samuel, ed., *The People's History and Socialist Theory* (London: New Left Books, 1981), pp. 50–60.

Chris Given-Wilson, introduction to *The English Nobility in the Late Middle Ages* (London: Routledge and Kegan Paul, 1987), pp. 1–25, 181–83.

Richard Firth Green, "The Court of Cupid," chapter 4 of *Poets and Princepleasers: Literature and the English Court in the Late Middle Ages* (Toronto: University of Toronto Press, 1980), pp. 101–34.

Rodney Hilton, "Social Concepts in the English Rising of 1381," chapter 17 of *Class Conflict and the Crisis of Feudalism: Essays in Medieval Social History* (London: The Hambledon Press, 1985), pp. 216–26, 330–31.

Maurice Keen, "The Clerical Estate," chapter 10 in *English Society in the Later Middle Ages 1348–1500* (Hambledon: Penguin Books, 1990), pp. 240–70, 312–13.

Kay E. Lacey, "Women and Work in Fourteenth and Fifteenth Century London," in Lindsey Charles and Lorna Duffin, eds., *Women and Work in Pre-Industrial England* (London: Croom Helm, 1985), pp. 24–82.

Alan Macfarlane, "English Economy and Society in the Thirteenth to Fifteenth Centuries," chapter 6 of *The Origins of English Individualism: The Family, Property and Social Transition* (New York: Cambridge University Press, 1979), pp. 131–64.

A. R. Myers, "The Tragic Dilemma," chapter 1 of *England in the Late Middle Ages, 1307–1536*, 2d ed. (Harmondsworth: Penguin, 1963), pp. 1–22.

Glending Olson, "Making and Poetry in the Age of Chaucer," *Comparative Literature* 31 (1979): 272–90.

M. M. Postan, "Markets, Towns and Gilds," chapter 12 of *The Medieval Economy and Society: An Economic History of Britain in the Middle Ages* (Harmondsworth: Penguin Books, 1972), pp. 233–52.

Michael J. Sheehan, "Choice of a Marriage Partner in the Middle Ages: Development and Mode of Application of a Theory of Marriage," *Studies in Medieval and Renaissance History*, n.s. 1 (1978): 1–33.

David Starkey, "The Age of the Household: Politics, Society and the Arts c. 1350–1550," in Stephen Medcalf, ed., *The Later Middle Ages* (New York: Holmes and Meier, 1981), pp. 225–90.

Sylvia Thrupp, "A General View of the Middle Strata of the Nation," chapter 7 of *The Merchant Class of Medieval London, 1300–1500* (Ann Arbor: University of Michigan Press, 1948), pp. 288–319.

chapter three

Court Poetry and the Invention of Literature

The Example of Sir John Clanvowe

"The language of poetry naturally falls in with the language of power. . . . The principle of poetry is a very anti-leveling principle. . . . Poetry is right royal. It puts the individual before the species, the one above the infinite many, might before right."[1] Hazlitt's disillusioned comments on the politics of poetry—comments prompted by what he feared were the antidemocratic attitudes of his beloved Shakespeare—express a common embarrassment. So many poets are so politically incorrect that to admit one's interest virtually amounts to self-conviction as a reactionary—unless, of course, one chooses to convict the poet instead. For medievalists the situation is if anything worse. Having chosen to immure ourselves in the distant past, does not our willful irrelevance make us automatically guilty? Indeed, the resurfacing of political concerns in medieval studies since the 1980s seems to represent an attempt at political rehabilitation in two senses: not only do we wish to show that the issues that animate other members of the professorate concern us as well, but in finding even medieval literature political we show that we must be *hyper*-political ourselves.[2]

The irony in all this is that the Middle Ages has been, ever since its invention as an object of scholarly study in the seventeenth century, one of the most highly politicized sites of historical knowledge. This was especially the case during the formative period of medieval studies in the nineteenth century: since the Middle Ages was understood to be the time when European civilization most became itself, medievalists were responsible for discovering the true political and cultural character of their various national states. Hence their work was invested with a weighty political value. A vivid example is Fustel de Coulanges's claim that the Prussians defeated the French in 1871 because they understood the Middle Ages better.[3] Not, of course, that there was *a* Middle Ages. Always at issue was what Gaston Paris called the "double manner of understanding the Middle Ages." Was it the golden age of the monarchy, the nobility, and the Church (as the Ultramontane Léon Gautier asserted), or the source of "modern freedoms, municipal independence, and the control of government by the people" (as the liberal Paris himself preferred to think)?[4] And in literary terms, the argument was whether the essence of the national literature was martial and pious (i.e., aristocratic) or realistic and satiric (i.e., bourgeois). Were its origins to be found among the nobility or lower down the social scale?

The political temperature of English studies has generally been lower than across the channel, but these debates have nonetheless left their mark on our scholarly enterprise. If we look at the first stage of the repoliticization of medieval studies, in the 1980s, we can find two Chaucers that roughly correspond to Gaston Paris's two Middle Ages. In a book published in 1986, Paul Olson presented Chaucer as a courtier-poet serving "a royal government in quest of social order," and the *Canterbury Tales* as a "poetic commentary on the state of the commonwealth" that expresses the views of that government.[5] Not surprisingly, Olson's Chaucer is a didactic allegorist whose poems speak a message of moral and social governance. On the other hand, Paul Strohm's *Social Chaucer*, published in 1989, presents a poet socially "at large within the turbulent and ill-defined middle ranks of society," the "middle strata" that bespeak the new social possibilities available in late fourteenth-century England. And this location enables what Strohm calls the "tonal variation" of Chaucer's poetry, his "mixture of styles and tones of voice," his ability to "entertain different perspectives and tolerate a high degree of contradiction between them," and his exploitation of "mixed perspectives and open forms," "abrupt shifts in direction and tone," and "an urbanely impartial attitude."[6]

My purpose in this essay is not to adjudicate between these two accounts but instead to challenge their shared, unspoken assumption. For Olson Chaucer's ideological commitment to the court entails a poetry of didactic straightforwardness; for Strohm, since Chaucer's poetry is complex and subtle he must be located within the "middle strata" instead of within an ideologically narrow court. For Olson, Chaucer's location in the court entails ideological commitment; for Strohm, Chaucer's ideologically uncommitted writing entails a location outside the court. For both critics, in other words, the court cannot be the site of the kind of formally intricate and thematically negotiable writing that we now take literature to be. I want to suggest, however, that while Strohm is right in thinking that Chaucer's poetry is complex, subtle, and eschews explicit ideological commitment, Olson is also right in thinking of him as a court poet— at least until the time when most of the *Canterbury Tales* was composed. In other words, I want to propose that the court is indeed a site where literature is produced, that it is even the most important of such sites in the crucial period of the late fourteenth century, when a vernacular literary tradition was in the process of self-conscious formation. Hazlitt was right when he said that "the language of poetry naturally falls in with the language of power." But it is also a language whose final allegiances can never be predicted.

The focus of my argument, however, is not upon Chaucer himself. Although Chaucer's way of writing was formed from within the court and largely reflected its interests, he also regarded it as a historical origin to be transcended. In the *House of Fame* he presents a trenchant commentary on both the vagaries of service in the prince's court and its effect on literary ambition; and the *Legend of Good Women*, both in its Prologue and in the individual Legends, groans under the harsh demands of an insensitive monarch and the burden of both political and cultural authority. Under the influence of the Italian humanists, and especially Dante, Chaucer aspired to a view of the poet as speaking not to local but universal values: this is the meaning, for example, of the passage at the end of *Troilus and Criseyde*, derived from the *Thebaid* and *Inferno* 4, where he instructs his poem to kiss the footsteps of Homer, Virgil, Ovid, Horace, and Statius. As A. C. Spearing has said, Chaucer was "the father of English poetry in the sense that before him there was no such thing as an *idea* of English poetry," an idea derived in large part from *trecento* Italy.[7] In sum, he shares with the humanist tradition—the tradition in which Strohm writes—the belief that historical contingencies such as the court must be transcended for literature to be produced.

Such ambitions are not visible, however, in the writing of the fully-fledged courtier-poet Sir John Clanvowe. Clanvowe was a chamber knight in the household of Richard II, one of the so-called "Lollard knights," and a member of what has come to be called Chaucer's circle.[8] Almost exactly the same age as Chaucer (both were born in the early 1340s), he was both a friend and literary colleague.[9] Two works have been ascribed to him: a religious treatise called *The Two Ways* and a poem, until the end of the nineteenth century thought to have been written by Chaucer and known as *The Cuckoo and the Nightingale*, but now accurately entitled *The Boke of Cupide* and correctly, I believe, ascribed to Clanvowe. This poem must have been written in the late 1380s or early 1390s: it alludes to the Knight's Tale and the Prologue to the *Legend of Good Women*, both written in the late 1380s, and Clanvowe died in 1391. The poem is a debate between a cuckoo and a nightingale set within a dream, the topic being the nature of love. The nightingale promotes unswerving amorous devotion, the cuckoo a blunt skepticism, and although the cuckoo seems to win the debate— at least he leaves the nightingale speechless—it ends inconclusively: the cuckoo is driven off, but when the nightingale asks the other birds for reparation they refuse to act, deciding instead to hold a parliament the following St. Valentine's Day to consider the case. The poem itself then ends with the nightingale singing a lyric—we are given only the first line, "Terme of lyve, love hath withholde me"—that awakens the narrator.[10]

The poem used to be much admired—Milton imitated it and Words-worth translated it—although now that it has fallen out of the Chaucer canon it is apparently little read, or at least little written about.[11] Gervase Mathew called it "clearly a court poem"—a poem specifically "of the court" rather than a "courtly" poem expressing aristocratic values in general.[12] It is an elegant and witty instance of court *makyng,* a text that represents amorous conversation in order to generate amorous conversation within the court. Hence recent critics have called the poem "a courtier's frippery," a poem composed to provide "intellectual and social diversion and amorous dalliance among a minuscule élite group," in the words of Rossell Hope Robbins, and therefore bearing "little relation to reality."[13] But the court is as real as anything else, and in the late fourteenth century it had itself become, as we shall see, a major political issue. Moreover, the self-designation of court poetry as mere entertainment, far from precluding relevance, may well enable it: triviality can be used to represent reality as well as to escape from it.

The lyric line that concludes the poem provides an instance: "Terme of lyve, love hath withholde me" (289). Read as a courtly dictum, this line means simply that the nightingale has wholly committed herself to love. But it also bears a topical political sense. In Middle English to "withhold" someone means to retain them: it is the term used in the indentures of retaining that began to be written in English just after this time.[14] Hence the line should be translated, "I have been retained for life by love." Now it can hardly be a coincidence that it was at just this time—beginning, that is, in 1389—that Richard began to indulge, systematically and extensively, in life retaining.[15] The nightingale's service to the God of Love is thus not merely metaphoric but defined by a specific form of indenture, and the poem is asking questions about lordship and service that have a topical relevance.

In fact, the poem can be read as a kind of political allegory. It opens by citing Chaucer's Knight's Tale, where Theseus comments on Cupid's power—"The god of love, a! benedicite, / How myghty and how grete a lorde is he!" (1–2)—power that Clanvowe represents as utterly unrestricted: "al that euere he wol he may, / Ayenst him ther dar no wight say nay" (16–17).[16] Moreover, the nightingale is not only "loves seruaunt" (148, 159) in a conventional sense but a creature whose very being derives from Cupid. He provides the terms in which her identity is defined, the conditions of her existence, the structure of value by which she understands the world: "in that beleve I wol bothe lyve and dye" (162). Service to this God requires not merely one's loyalty but one's selfhood: "He that truly loues seruaunt ys, / Were lother to be schamed than to dye" (159–60). And to be the servant of this lord precludes any alternative: "For who that wol the god of love not serve, / I dar wel say he is worthy for to sterve" (133–34).

But this conception of love's power, defined by the narrator and promoted by the nightingale, is challenged and finally subverted in the course of the poem. For one thing, the opening citation from the Knight's Tale contains a hidden critique, since Theseus's words were in their original context ironic: he was mocking the ferocity with which the young lovers Arcite and Palamon fight over a lady who is unaware of their very existence much less their love.[17] Second, and more important, throughout the debate the cuckoo attacks the legitimacy of Cupid's authority. For him Cupid is nothing but a tyrant—"love hath no reson but his wille" (197)— and his court is correspondingly capricious: "In this court ful selde trouthe avayleth, / So dyuerse and so wilful ys he" (204–5). This critique invokes the standard medieval definition—prominent throughout the Middle Ages—of the tyrant as a figure of angry self-indulgence, a ruler who abrogates the rule of law in favor of the "illegal power of his will," to cite one of the article's of Richard's deposition.[18] And when the nightingale defends Love as a lord who rewards the man "whom him likes" (195), for the cuckoo, as for medieval political thought in general, this is not only no defense at all but a profound indictment. This is also an indictment that speaks to the conditions of Ricardian kingship, and in a language familiar in contemporary poetry. For if, as is generally accepted, Alceste's cautionary injunctions to the God of Love in the Prologue to the *Legend of Good Women* comment on Richard's tendency to what Chaucer calls "wilfulhed and tyrannye" (G, 355); and if John Gower's revision of the *Confessio amantis* bespeaks his awareness that Richard is less the benevolent Cupid who presides over his parliament of lovers in Book 8 of the *Confessio* than the tyrant whom he was to excoriate in the *Chronica tripertita*; then surely Clanvowe's willful Cupid is another commentary on Ricardian kingship.

Oddly enough, however, the poem presents its dictatorial Cupid as oddly ineffective, as an impotent tyrant. In part Clanvowe again makes his point by means of Chaucerian allusion. It is on "the thirde nyght of May" (55) that his narrator goes forth to perform his love service, the same date on which Palamon escaped from prison (1463) and met Arcite in the grove where he too was performing love service. And again there is a battle: after the nightingale is reduced to tears, she begs the God of Love to come to her aid and is rescued by the narrator himself, who drives the cuckoo off by throwing stones at him, thus reducing the heroic combat of the Knight's Tale to comic contretemps. Not only does Cupid decline to help his loyal servant, but when the nightingale asks the other birds to "do me ryght / Of that foule, fals, vnkynde bridde" (270), they also demur by insisting upon holding a parliament at which the cuckoo can defend himself, and to which must be summoned the eagle "our lorde" and the "other perys that ben of recorde" (276–77). Only at this parliament, to be held on St. Valentine's Day at Woodstock before the Queen's chamber window "shal be yeven the iugement, / Or elles we shul make summe acorde" (279–80). In effect, then, Cupid disappears from the poem as a figure of authority, replaced by a parliament constituted by carefully prescribed procedures and uncertain in its outcome, and held, moreover, before the Queen but with neither her authority nor participation— a gesture that not only excludes the King but limits the role of royalty per se in parliamentary deliberations. Clanvowe's Cupid, then, is less the all-seeing sun god before whom Chaucer quakes in the Prologue to the *Legend of Good Women* than a *deus absconditus* whose servants must rely upon a stone-throwing buffoon for defense and turn to an independent and uncertain parliament for justice. This ineffectiveness gives special point to the nightingale's concluding song: "Terme of lyve, love hath withholde me" (289). A life retainer, she has learned in the course of the poem a bitter lesson about the unreliability of her lord. Clanvowe is thus saying two, not entirely consistent things: on the one hand, the God of Love's tyranny is rightly castigated by skeptics and wisely restrained by parliament; but on the other, he is unable to protect those upon whom his authority rests and who most nearly feel the pressure of his ambition. His power is both excessive and inadequate, his aspirations at once illegitimate and ineffective.

It is tempting to explain this paradox in terms of Clanvowe's biography. Clanvowe first entered royal service in 1373 as a knight of the household of Edward III, and he was inherited by Richard upon his accession to the throne in 1377. Later Richard included him among the "new group of chamber knights, clearly men of the king's own choice," who were installed in 1381.[19] Throughout his career in the royal household he participated in military campaigns, including Richard's Scottish expedition in 1385, and he performed the usual diplomatic and administrative services typical of his rank. But probably because he was a generation older than the king he never became one of his favorites, and in 1388, although he was dismissed from the household by the Lords Appellant, he avoided more severe punishment.[20] The following year he returned to the household upon Richard's reassumption of power, but in 1390 he and his friend

William Neville seem to have obtained permission to join the Duke of Bourbon's crusade against Tunis. The following year they both died in Constantinople, probably while on pilgrimage. Walsingham included Clanvowe as one of the so-called Lollard knights in the royal household, and it seems clear that he and the men with whom he associated shared the purist, biblicist piety that was widespread in the late fourteenth century and that the Lollards developed into a full-blown, theologically sophisticated heresy.[21] This was not, however, a religious style much favored by the king, who was drawn to more established forms of piety: even the anti-royalist Walsingham praised Richard for his defense of the faith, and the king's religious preferences are perhaps best shown by his patronage of Carthusian monasticism.[22]

Given this history, it is not unreasonable to see Clanvowe as being in a complex relation to the court, at once central and detached. He had witnessed both Richard's incipient tyranny in the period 1382–86 and its chastening by the Lords Appellant working through Parliament in 1386 and 1388. And while he did not himself suffer greatly in 1388, many of his colleagues did. His enlistment in the crusade of 1390, and then in the pilgrimage of 1391, perhaps bespeak a desire to distance himself from a court in which he had lost confidence. If we are to read the *Boke of Cupide* at the level of conscious intention and topical relevance, then, perhaps we do best to see it as at once a critique of Richard's tyranny and a lament for Clanvowe's stalled career, as at once satire and complaint.

II

But topical decoding can hardly encompass the full range of the political meaning of Clanvowe's poem. Court poetry, after all, is not merely a kind of writing but a social practice, and one laden with ideological value. Literary historians have rightly insisted on the instrumental, pragmatic nature of court poetry, its role as part of the "courtly conversation" so essential to courtly recreation.[23] But if this writing entertained court servants, it also trained them: it provided what *la belle dame sans merci* called a "school" of "fayr langage," teaching its students, in Christine de Pizan's wonderful phrase, to "parler mignot."[24] From the time of its medieval beginnings in the eleventh century, courtliness had always made verbal facility a central value: *facetus* is virtually a synonym for *curialis,* and it means both "elegant" and "clever," both "refined" and "witty."[25] According to another medieval definition, a man who is *facetus* is one who can get what he wants out of words, whether a subtle meaning or a desired effect.[26] And if to be courtly is to be adroit with words, the riddles, acrostics, *jeux partis,* and *demandes d'amour* that are preserved, either intact or in allusion, are evidence of the assiduity with which this talent was practiced and displayed.[27] According to Thomas Usk, a sergeant-of-arms in Richard's court, Love teaches her servants "to endyten letters of rethorike in queynt understondinges."[28]

As Usk's phrasing implies, a correlative courtly talent is the capacity to interpret, to read with understanding the elegantly metaphoric and topically allusive language of the court poem. In the *Prison amoureuse,* for example, Froissart explains that a courtly poem is "a gloss of something which cannot or must not be openly stated."[29] So too, in the *Livre messire Ode,* written by Oton de Grandson while at the Ricardian court in the 1370s and 80s, the narrator overhears a lover grieving for the loss of his sparrow-hawk but fails to understand that he is speaking "par poetrie" and really means his lady.[30] And in the *Book of the Duchess* Chaucer had already used the same device but had lain bare the social meaning it contains: his narrator's inability to understand the Black Knight's metaphor of the chess game is a function of his lower social status. It is this interpretive alertness, even suspicion, that led Puttenham in the sixteenth century to call the trope of allegory—"which is when we speake one thing and thinke another"—"the Courtly figure," one known not only to "euery common Courtier, but also [to] the grauest Counsellour."[31]

As literary historians have shown, court writing was in no sense the preserve of a special group of professional poets.[32] The demise of the minstrel in the late fourteenth century represents not merely a shift from one kind of taste to another but the *deprofessionalization* of writing per se. No longer was literary activity confined to a particular group of specially trained men but became instead the preserve of the court as a whole. Hence the fact that not only do none of the large number of documents that record Chaucer's career refer to him as a writer, but that his career was probably not advanced by his literary activity.[33] To have acknowledged that Chaucer could do something special that other members of the court could not would have been to undermine the socially legitimizing function of courtly *makyng*. According to Deschamps's *Art de dictier*, there are two kinds of music: a "musique artificiele" played on instruments by "le plus rude homme du mond," and a "musique naturele," the harmony of verse ("une musique de bouche en proferant paroules metrifiées") inspired by the "amorous desire to praise ladies" that inhabits gentle hearts.[34] A great many courtiers did in fact write poetry: we have the names and some of the poems of over a dozen noble *makers* from late medieval England, as well as the rather bizarre fact that Richard II wanted his epitaph to compare him to Homer.[35] Indeed, one of the tasks of the professional poet (if the title be admitted at all) was to collaborate with the patron in the production of the courtly text. Froissart's *Prison amoureuse*, for instance, records the way in which the poet instructed his patron, Wenceslas of Brabant, in the art of making, and both this text and the later *Méliador* contain poems by both authors.[36] The same is true of Machaut's *Fonteinne amoureuse*, which describes the departure of Jean, duc de Berri, into exile and incorporates several of the Duc's laments. Indeed, it is not impossible that in Chaucer's *Book of the Duchess* the rather inept lyrics ascribed to the grieving Black Knight were really written by John of Gaunt, to whom the poem was dedicated.

This expansion of literariness to include the court as a whole also helps to account for a pronounced generic shift in the literary system of fourteenth-century England. Romances and histories, almost entirely in prose, continued to be copied and read, as library lists and manuscript survivals demonstrate. But the literature of fashion produced within the court—excluding works of instruction—was almost exclusively lyric. This category includes not only lyrics per se—the many "compleyntis, baladis, roundelis, virelais" that Lydgate ascribed to Chaucer and that must have been written by other courtly versifiers in the hundreds—but also the new genre of the *dits amoureux* produced by Machaut and Froissart.[37] For all their apparently narrative form, these works are in fact sets of lyric performances enclosed within a narrative frame: they provide lyrics with a context that is, in their usual, freestanding state, only implied. The *Book of the Duchess*, largely derived from the *dits amoureux*, is the first poem to transfer this form into English; and while there are no Chaucerian poems that fully replicate the French paradigm, we can recognize in the roundel of the *Parliament of Fowls*, in the complaint of *Anelida and Arcite*, in the ballade of the Prologue to the *Legend of Good Women*, and above all in the many lyric moments, both celebratory and lamenting, of *Troilus and Criseyde*, the presence of the lyric impulse.[38] We also recognize it in the *Boke of Cupide*, in the nightingale's lyric outburst in defense of love (149–62), a song appreciated even by the cuckoo: "thou spekest wonder faire" (166), he admits.

This privileging of lyricism not only encourages the production of the small scale, intricately wrought verse that best displays the verbal talents courtliness admires, but also reminds us that court poetry is part of the aestheticization of life to which late medieval court culture as a whole was dedicated. Just as cuisine transforms food into art, just as *haute couture* transforms the body into a visual display, so court poetry transforms language and feeling into the elegant artifice of lyric. The court poet must balance, in the words of Daniel Poirion, "le désordre de la passion et l'ordre de la parole."[39] On the one hand he languishes in sorrow, fearful of madness ("ʒe haue broken þe balance / Of my resoun," says one poet) and brought by "cruell peyne" to the point of death: "I dee! I dee! so thrillith me that thorne!" Yet he is also the artist who crafts these feelings into a beautiful artifact. These lines are spoken by a female narrator in a poem that is in fact written by a man, and written in order "to Obey [the] hie commaundement" of an unnamed princess: in the epilogue the poem is revealed to be a precious offering.[40] French literary historians especially have insisted that court poetry is a "jeu des formes," aspiring to pure aestheticism and seeking to create a cultural *hortus conclusus* where the aristocratic "culte égocentrique" can find a fulfillment impossible in the difficult historical world of the late Middle Ages.[41]

But it is also more than this. For we must never forget that court poetry is not just an escape from history but also part of it: it is a social practice designed to create courtiers. The court is what Brian Stock has called a "textual community," a "microsociety organized around the common understanding of a script."[42] The court lyric provides a paradigm not merely for behavior but for an internalized ethic: it allows specific structures of feeling to be experienced as rational and appropriate. Certainly lyricism is privileged because it is the literary form that best allows for the theatricalization of the courtly self. But perhaps more important, it also provides a way to discipline the aspiring courtier. It creates "rhetorical man" from the inside as well as from without.[43]

The notion of the courtier as a self-made man, constructed by social practices specific to the court, has particular force in Ricardian England.

Already in the latter years of Edward III, the business of government had become increasingly concentrated in the king's household, and especially in the *camera regis* into which the aging monarch withdrew.[44] The court also became less itinerant, confining its movement to a small area around London. In 1376 Parliament responded by banishing from court not only the hated Alice Perrers but those courtiers who, in the words of Peter de la Mare, the Speaker of the Commons, "scoff and mock, and work for their own profit," an appropriate description of men well practiced in courtly *facetiae*.[45] Many of these men, moreover, came from very humble backgrounds, and included a group of merchants whom the peers would certainly not have considered to be of gentle status.[46] But this house-cleaning could not solve the problem in the long term. When the young Richard assumed authority in the early 1380s, he also surrounded himself with *familiarissimi* and allowed the household to function not as "the focus of the aristocratic community" as a whole but as his *privata familia*.[47] Moreover, Richard's development of the court as an exclusive society wholly dedicated to the fulfillment of the wishes of the king was not simply a matter of personal style. It was also part of a political program aimed at dispossessing the traditional ruling class of England and replacing it with a courtier nobility created by Richard and located largely in the household.[48]

Not surprisingly, then, throughout the 1380s attacks continued to be made upon the court. These attacks can be documented in 1380, in 1381 (when Parliament complained about both evil counsellors and the "outrageouses nombre des Familiers esteantz en l'hostiel"), in 1386–87, and finally, and with bloody consequences, in 1388.[49] To be sure, questions of policy were at issue, and especially the war with France, which Richard sought to resolve but which most of the nobility were eager to continue. But ultimately of more importance was the king's attitude toward both the nobility, the peerage that he excluded from his councils, and toward the very idea of nobility itself. It was bad enough that Richard banished from his councils those who thought it their right to be there, replacing them with men—and mostly very young men—whom he found personally congenial: John Beauchamp, Simon Burley, Michael de la Pole, and, above all, Robert de Vere (as the nightingale says of the God of Love, he rewards "whom him likes" [195]). But what was worse was his degradation of the very idea of nobility. For Richard persistently violated the link between land and status upon which noble identity had traditionally rested. When Thomas of Woodstock was created duke of Gloucester in 1385 he was given not the land needed to support his dignity but simply an annuity; and when John Beauchamp was created Baron Kidderminster, the title was conferred as a personal honor, that is, without a barony—an event unprecedented in English history. Richard's creation of a courtier nobility thus offended a central principle of aristocratic identity: he defined it according to the ideology of courtliness rather than the economic and political realities of power. When in 1385 he created de la Pole earl of Suffolk, he said in the patent of creation that "we believe that the more we bestow honors on wise and honorable men, the more our crown is adorned with gems and precious stones." As Anthony Tuck comments,

> The aristocracy, in Richard's view, existed to shed lustre on the crown, and the practical implication of this view is that the titled nobility do not need any independent territorial standing or any great wealth or military reputation to justify their ennoblement: title depended upon royal favour, and upon the particular noble's relationship with the crown.[50]

For Richard the nobility was not an independent body with its own political rights but simply an embodiment of the king's magnificence, its titles dependent on his will.

By concentrating the power of government in the court, Richard was able to give free play to his absolutist impulses. Much has been written about Richard's sense of his own supremacy: he not only entitled himself "entier emperour de son roiaulme" but also sought to become Holy Roman Emperor, an enterprise in which the Wilton Diptych, with its startling analogy between the court of Heaven and Richard's earthly court, perhaps played a role.[51] The elaborate public ceremonies and devices of which he was fond seem to have had a counterpart in a highly developed court ritual.[52] Richard had a keen sense of the honor due the king, and the magnificence of the court—both its physical environment, on which Richard lavished huge sums of money, and its elaborate ceremonial—played a major role in promoting his sovereignty.[53] This fact was not lost on contemporaries. In 1395 Roger Dymmok's attack on the Lollards, dedicated to Richard, included a detailed defense of the *magnificentia* of the royal court against its critics: he addressed the king as Royal Magnificence and argued that sumptuous display was an appropriate demonstration of power.[54] As Patricia Eberle has said, Richard was "the first English king to cultivate magnificence in the style of his court, self-consciously and on principle, as a means of enforcing his autocratic rule."[55] Not just his famous and much-hated white hart livery, but court fashion per se, indeed *fashionableness* per se, became an expression of Richard's political program.

Richard's definition of the court as an expression of the royal will was a way of not merely promoting himself to others but reaffirming to himself his sense of his unbridled authority. In the royal household, as in noble households generally, the authority of the *paterfamilias* was unquestioned.[56] For Richard, the absolute dominion he exerted over the court was a model for the kind of governance he wished to impose upon the nation as a whole. We have, in fact, a striking account of Richard's manner of holding court. On feast days

> he leet ordeyne and make in his chambir a trone, wherynne he was wont to sitte fro aftir mete vnto euensong tyme, spekynge to no man, but ouerlokyng alle menn; and yf he loked on eny mann, what astat or degre that evir he were of, he moste knele.[57]

The chronicle source of this passage dates this behavior in 1398, at the very end of Richard's reign; but in the F-Prologue to the *Legend of Good Women*, written a decade earlier, Chaucer's account of the angry gaze of the sun-like God of Love implies a characteristic Ricardian style: "his face shoon so bryghte / That wel unnethes myght I hym beholde," says the poet, while Love himself "sternely on me . . . gan beholde, / So that his loking dooth myn herte colde" (232–33, 239–40). Richard's anger and imperious bearing were much commented upon by contemporaries, and historians have seen them as psychological analogues, if not causes, of his political program.[58]

For the nobility, the aristocratic lifestyle was above all martial and chivalric, a conservative self-understanding that had been reinforced by the years of war with France.[59] Now the king wanted to end that war, and was simultaneously promoting a lifestyle that celebrated elegance of dress, subtlety of speech, and sophisticated and perhaps indelicate forms of recreation, innovations that challenged more traditional conceptions of chivalric virtue. This was a lifestyle, moreover, that was above all dedicated to the idea of *fashion*, which privileged a self-chosen élite of new men who were more concerned with surfaces and manners—the "newe gyse"—than with a substance they themselves lacked.[60] If, as Norbert Elias has argued, the civilizing process is marked by the transformation of a warrior into a courtier nobility, then late fourteenth-century England provided a particularly intense moment in that long process.[61]

Not surprisingly, then, the Ricardian court aroused strong reactions among contemporaries: as Eberle has rightly argued, the late fourteenth century saw a politics of courtly style. As we would expect, Richard's courtiers were attacked for their elaborate clothing, but these complaints were only a metonymy for larger concerns. There was also continual criticism of the courtly style of speech as, for example, in Walsingham's famous attack on Richard's courtiers as "knights of Venus rather than knights of Bellona, more valiant in the bedchamber than on the field, *armed with words rather than weapons, prompt in speaking but slow in performing the acts of war*."[62] There were recurring complaints that Richard surrounded himself with young men who misled him with what one chronicler called their *laciuiis verbis*.[63] Gower inveighed against "the bland words of the cunning" men who were misleading Richard, clever courtiers who were so young as not to realize how culpable were their *facetiae:* "To boys, it is not wrongdoing but joking, not dishonor but glorious sport."[64] According to another poet, court games were in fact conspiratorial plots: "Whan falshed lawheþ, he forgeþ gyle; / Half in malice is his play."[65] And in the blunt words of yet another poet, "Falshede is called a *sotilte* / And such a nome hit haþ hent": the word *sotilte* refers here to court games and theatricals.[66]

The problem of truth-telling at court is a habitual topic of discussion in court texts. The court is a dangerous place: in the words of one poem, "Thow wenyst he be thy frend; he is thy foo certeyne," so "Whate euer thow sey, / A-vyse the well."[67] Even the lover's song must be carefully guarded: "whan thou . . . criest like a nightingale," advises another poem, "Be ware to whom thou tellest thy tale."[68] Given these anxieties, courteous speech is on occasion defined not as periphrastic and ornamental but as blunt and direct: let your language be "curteis et brief," advises one Anglo-Norman poem, two terms that are usually antithetical.[69] There is much advice in court literature on sage speaking, with attacks on obscure or ambiguous speech, on mocking and joking, on the *facetiae* that in other contexts are the courtier's stock in trade: here the ideal seems to be the discourse of Chaucer's Clerk, "short and quyk and ful of hy sentence" (I.306).[70] And there is also praise for the man who will risk the wrath of the prince to tell the truth directly.[71] For truth-telling at court is a dangerous activity—"who say soth he shal be shent" becomes a proverbial phrase in the late fourteenth century. "I kan & kan nauȝt of court speke moore," says Langland nervously.[72]

Moreover, the truth-teller cannot get a hearing in such a world, for his frank words will not even be understood. For the author of *Mum and the Soothsegger*, the crafty Mum is "right worldly wise of wordes," while the Soothsegger "can not speke in termes ne in tyme nother, / But bablith fourth bustusely ass barn vn-y-lerid."[73] Unable to speak the discourse of the court, the Soothsegger can find no audience for his "trewe tales."[74] And his exclusion is graphically illustrated in the alliterative style of the poem itself, with its distinctly unmetropolitan, non-royal provenance. The same attitude is present in another alliterative poem, *Sir Gawain and the Green Knight*, which is structured by the relationship between royal and provincial courts. It may even be that the representation of the "childgered" Arthur, "bisied [by] his ȝonge blod and his brayn wylde," and presiding over an elegantly gamesome court, is meant to reflect Richard. But whether the poem has this topical relevance or not, it is clear that its central social opposition is between monarch and nobleman, metropolis and hinterland.[75] Also clear is the direction of the critique: far from being in need of instruction in courtesy, Bertilak's court reveals an effortless command of the intricacies of court behavior, especially the "luf-talkyng" of which Gawain, "þat fyne fader of nurture," is supposed to be the master. Indeed, not only does the lady battle Gawain to a standstill in their "dalyaunce of . . . derne wordez" (1012), but she becomes the agent who reveals the superficiality of Gawain's understanding of the meaning of games, and specifically of the "Crystemas gomen" (283) with the Green Knight to which he has committed himself. From this perspective, the poem's message is that not only is the provincial court as well versed in fashionable behavior as that of King Arthur, and not only does it maintain a warrior ethos (witness Bertilak's hunting) that the Arthurian court has evidently lost, but it actually understands the meaning of court practices more profoundly than the royal court that thinks itself to be the center of fashion. The poem reveals both the connection between games and "trawþe" and the full meaning of "cortaysye," a term that is here, as in *Pearl* and *Cleanness*, expanded to incorporate large ethical and spiritual meanings.[76] Finally, this kind of poem fits well with its origins in the Cheshire-Shropshire region of northwest England. For this was an area that had very close relations with the crown—Cheshire was a palatinate county with which Richard had a special relation at least as early as 1385—and yet that remained fiercely independent and enthusiastically in support of a war that Richard sought to end, an enthusiasm that actually generated several armed uprisings in the 1390s.[77]

The point is that *Mum and the Soothsegger* and *Sir Gawain and the Green Knight*, poems that are at once well informed and yet critical of court values, focus much of their attention on the verbal practices current in the court. Because the soothsegger cannot speak in "termes" his advice is not heeded; and while Gawain knows "the teccheles termes of talkyng noble" (917), not only is his proficiency less absolute than he assumes but he does not really know the terms' full meaning. Both poems present the court as a place where people have a special way with words, perhaps even speak a special dialect (one courtesy book calls it "cointise"). But while this facility may confirm their sense of social superiority, it alienates them both from the nation as a whole and from deeper, more permanent values.[78]

III

The relevance of this context to the *Boke of Cupide* is twofold. First, the poem explores with particular acuity the practice of courtly self-fabrication, the way in which courtier identity is socially constructed rather than, as aristocratic ideology requires, naturally given. This topic is staged in the role assigned to Clanvowe's narrator. He is on the one hand a typical instance of the long-suffering lover, catching a lovesickness in May—"Bothe hote and colde, an accesse every day" (39)—and assiduously performing his love service. Yet he is also "olde and vnlusty," a dissonance that should be read neither biographically nor comically but socially, as a statement about the stresses of self-fashioning. For his devotions are performed in a way that is unmistakably mechanical. He says he cannot sleep because of the "feueres white" that assail him, yet adds that "hit is vnlyke to me /

That eny herte shulde slepy be, / In whom that love his firy dart wol smyte" (41–45): he is awake because he knows it would be inappropriate for a true lover to sleep.[79] So too, his love service is to go into the woods to hear the nightingale before the cuckoo: he does this because he has heard the "comvn tale" (48) that this signals good fortune. His behavior, in other words, is not instinctive but that which is required of one who would be known as a lover.

A sense of the theatricality of his performance, its quality as learned rather than natural behavior, is also implied by two Chaucerian echoes. The initial action of the poem is organized according to the pattern established by Chaucer's narrator in the F-Prologue to the *Legend of Good Women*. As in the F-Prologue, the narrator of the *Boke of Cupide* starts by entering a green meadow "poudred with daysye": "Al grene and whit, was no thing elles sene."[80] And he too hears a harmonious birdsong, a "foules ermonye" sung by birds that have chosen mates "vponn seynt Valentynes day" (83, 80): in the F-Prologue the birds sing "alle of oon acord" in honor of "Seynt Valentyne" (130–70).[81] But in the F-Prologue the narrator's love service—his passionate worship of the daisy—is both "constreyned" by "gledy desir" (105), a "fir" he continues to feel even while writing the poem (106), and is set in opposition not only to the books he abandons every May but to a court that ritualizes such passion into the cult of flower and leaf. In the course of the poem the intensity of the narrator's feelings is subdued to the demands of court poetry, demands that are made explicit in the subsequent dream and that the poem as a whole, with its repeated legends of subordination and constraint, enacts. But in the *Boke of Cupide* this dialectic is reversed: it is the waking love service that confirms the authority of cultic forms of behavior, while the dream, much to the narrator's consternation, puts this authority into question. What we have, then, is not the disciplining of a potentially rebellious court servant, as in the F-Prologue, but the reluctant recognition by a court servant that he has laboriously rendered service to a lord much less powerful than he had first thought.[82]

The other Chaucerian allusion that can help us understand Clanvowe's narrator has a similar effect. It is when he has fallen into "a slombre and a swowe, / Not al on slepe, ne fully wakynge" (87–88), that Clanvowe's narrator hears, to his dismay, not the nightingale but "that sory bridde, the lewede cukkowe" (90). This narrative configuration derives

from Book 2 of *Troilus and Criseyde*: "on Mayes day the thrydde" (56)—
the same day on which Clanvowe's poem is set—Pandarus suffers from
"a teene / In love" (61–62) and takes to his bed; and the next morning,
"half in a slomberynge," he hears the song of the swallow Procne, who
"with a sorowful lay / . . . gan make hire waymentyng" (64–65). And just
as a disparaging precursor precedes the appearance of the nightingale in
Clanvowe's poem, so too here: at nightfall on this same day Criseyde hears
a nightingale outside her window singing "a lay / Of love" (921–22). There
are doubtless several reasons why Clanvowe has rewritten a tragic Chaucerian pattern into comedy, but the most obvious effect is to associate his
narrator with Pandarus. We might think that the relation is one of likeness, an affinity between Pandarus the ineffective lover and Clanvowe's
"old and vnlusty" (37) narrator. But such a reading depends upon mis-
conceiving Pandarus as simply a comic character; on the contrary, as Gervase Mathew has said, "he is an experienced English courtier of the late
fourteenth century, . . . a man of cultivated sensibility, facilely expressed
emotions and quick stratagems—all qualities then prized."[83] Pandarus
has mastered not only the "chere of court"—when he visits Criseyde and
her ladies, "of this and that they pleide" with "many wordes glade, / And
frendly tales" (2.148–50)—but also the sophisticated innuendo that constitutes court dialect, what he (and others) called "wordes white" (3.901,
1567).[84] In a poem in which the relation of words to meaning is always at
issue, Janus-like Pandarus is the presiding spirit.

Clanvowe's narrator, on the other hand, is a flat-footed, wooden version of the labile courtier: he mechanically acts out a ritual of love service and defends his lord by throwing stones at a bird. In fact, the cuckoo's
parting shot—"Farewel, farewel, papyngay!"—provides a shrewd critique.
A parrot is a quintessential courtly bird, as the context in which it typically appears in medieval poetry attests: Gawain has parrots embroidered
on his helmet covering (611), in the *Romaunt of the Rose* the God of Love's
garment is similarly embroidered "with popynjay, with nyghtyngale" (913),
Langland's Imaginatyf uses them as an emblem of the "riht ryche men þat
reygne here on erthe" (C, 14, 172), and in *Susannah* the elegant garden
is inhabited with parrots and nightingales (75).[85] There is even a French
romance devoted to the *Chevalier du Papegau*.[86] In fact, in *Mum and the
Soothsegger* the word is used to designate a courtier to whom the commons,
represented as magpies, fruitlessly complained: "piez with a papegeay par-

lid of oones, / And were y-plumed and y-pullid and put into a caige."[87] But the parrot also has characteristics that allow it to function as an emblem not just for the courtier but for the courtly overachiever: its gaudy plumage, its status as the plaything of the rich, and its ability to rehearse, with mindless enthusiasm, the phrases it has been laboriously taught— these rendered it an apt symbol of the fawning, too-perfect courtier.[88] In other words, the cuckoo's mockery is directed not simply at the narrator's alliance with the nightingale but at a certain excess, a zealousness to follow courtly prescription—whether it be in the performance of his own love service or in throwing stones to protect Love's servant, the nightingale— that witnesses to effort, application, toil. What the narrator lacks is the quintessential courtly value that Castiglione was to call *sprezzatura*, a virtue that court texts had promoted since the eleventh century. It is the effortlessness that implies natural superiority, the "calculated underplaying of talents" that bespeaks an excess of talent, the grace possessed by the true aristocrat that assumes "the natural or given status of one's social identity and [denies] any earned character, any labor or arrival from a social elsewhere."[89] But the fabricated nature of courtier identity is all too visible in Clanvowe's narrator, a truth to which the "unkind" cuckoo draws attention with his parting epithet.

The other way in which the *Boke of Cupide* interrogates the social practices of the court is in its focus on the question of verbal decorum. For the nightingale the cuckoo's song is "elynge" (115) or tedious. But the cuckoo retorts that "my songe is bothe trewe and pleyn" (118) so that "*euery wight* may vnderstonde me" (121); and he criticizes the nightingale for not only "breke[ing]" the song "in [her] throte" (119–20)—which evidently refers to a fashionable mode of singing—but for singing in French: "I haue herd the seye 'ocy! ocy!'" says the cuckoo, "Who myght wene what that shulde be?" (124–25)[90] This is a complaint that reflects contemporary discussion about the politics of language. On the one hand is the élitist dialect of the nightingale, a discourse that requires an armature of special knowledge and specific ideological commitments to be understood: "ocy" is not only the traditional literary representation of the nightingale's song, and is not only in French, but encapsulates in a single word the absolutist ideology that is at the center of courtliness. As the nightingale says, "who that wol the god of love not serve, / I dar wel say he is worthy for to sterve" (133–34).[91] The alternative to this coded discourse is the cuckoo's truth-telling, which is not only understood by "euery wight" (121, cf. 150) but possesses a self-evident validity: "What nedith hit ayens trweth to strive?" (145).

By giving the cuckoo the discourse of truth, the poem validates his position: he is the courageous soothsegger so rarely found at court. And the fact that he is here driven off by a narrator eager to prove his loyalty to a tyrant would seem simply to confirm his virtue, and to ratify the oppositional valence of Clanvowe's poem. For all his "cherles herte" (147), the cuckoo's political independence allows him to see truths that are closed to the ideologically bound nightingale. He is kin to other marginal figures who destabilize the official views of medieval culture: Marcolf, the cynical peasant who mocks Solomon's sublime wisdom; the many unauthorized voices that impede the progress of *Piers Plowman*, beginning with the importunate "lunatik" who interrupts the establishment of the king's governance with a riddling blessing (B, Prologue, 123–27); the "foules smale" in the *Parliament of Fowls*, who demand that the cultic rituals of the gentle birds not be allowed to thwart their mating habits; and the Miller of the *Canterbury Tales*, who refuses to accept Harry Bailly's deferential management of the tale-telling game.[92]

But as these analogies also suggest, to assume that the poem simply ratifies opposition is in the final analysis impossible. In fact the *Boke of Cupide* asks a deeper, more troubling question: does the intrusion of marginal values represent a genuine challenge to authority? Even assuming that the cuckoo possesses the "trweth," do the complexities of court discourse automatically foreclose its declaration? Is it possible to be at once inside and outside the court, to challenge its assumptions in a language it can understand? For what is striking about the fate of the cuckoo's voice in the poem is less its final, inevitable exclusion than the way in which it is gradually absorbed into court discourse. In the course of the poem the cuckoo is transformed from the independent truth-teller into the stock figure of court satire, able to rehearse only his own narrow, overdetermined message. And he expresses it, strikingly enough, in the same periphrastic, allusive style that we associate with court discourse.

At the beginning of the poem the cuckoo's challenge was, as we have seen, abrasively explicit: far from being a lord worthy of service, the God of Love is a willful tyrant who at once abuses and neglects his servants. But in the next stage of the debate he returns to his traditional role as the harbinger of adultery: "Yf thou be fer or longe fro thi make, / Thou shalt be as other that be forsake, / And then shalt thou hoten as do I" (183–85). The effect of this shift is to reduce the cuckoo from political truth-teller to agent and presiding spirit of cuckoldry: he becomes simply the conventional "cukkow ever unkynde" (358) of the *Parliament of Fowls*, the "fol kokkow" who speaks "of myn owene autorite" (505–6) and cares only for his own interests (603–9). Second, this attack is itself phrased in a language of periphrasis and metaphor that demands careful interpretation. This is partly true of the lines just cited, but even more so of those that precede them:

> What! louyng is an office of dispaire,
> And oon thing is ther in that ys not faire;
> For who that geteth of love a lytil blysse,
> But if he be alway ther by ywysse,
> He may ful sone of age haue his eire.
>
> (176–80)

Skeat provides a persuasive gloss for these difficult lines, but the point is less their specific meaning than the difficulty itself: this is hardly the speech "bothe trewe and pleyn" (118) of which the cuckoo has earlier boasted.[93] Far from speaking in opposition to court dialect, the cuckoo has now been absorbed within it: he has become the other by which the court defines and ratifies its own practices. Just as Chaucer's cuckoo joins in the fashionable roundel with which the *Parliament of Fowls* concludes (it is sung to a tune composed in France), so by the end of Clanvowe's poem the cuckoo no longer poses a threat to courtly social practices. Hence the poem projects as its own sequel a highly traditional and fully courtly parliament-of-birds poem.

To explain this dynamic of cancellation as simply an effect of Clanvowe's personal history is inevitably reductive. But the little we know of his situation, and of his response to it, does provide a biographical context that is worth our attention. I have already suggested that Clanvowe's relation to the inner circle of the royal household was complicated, that he may have found the Ricardian court a not entirely congenial environment. Yet what was his alternative? To turn to the Appellant opposition would not only have been an act of betrayal but would have required him to assume an attitude toward the war, and toward chivalric heroism generally, that would have been antipathetic. For despite his military career, he seems to have been detached from the more conventional chivalric attitudes associated with the anti-court party. There are two pieces of evidence to support this claim. One is a well-known passage in *The Two Ways,* in which Clanvowe attacks those who are "greete werryours and fiȝteres and þat distroyen and wynnen manye loondis, . . . and of swyche folke men maken bookes and soonges and reeden and syngen of hem"; and he contrasts them to those "þat wolden lyuen meekeliche in þis world and ben out offe swich forseid riot, noise, and stryf, and lyuen symplely. . . . Swiche folke þe world scoorneth and hooldeþ hem lolleris and loselis, foolis and schameful wrecches."[94]

The other evidence is Clanvowe's truculent testimony in the famous dispute between Sir Richard Scrope and Sir Robert Grosvenor over a coat of arms. Like the other witnesses, Clanvowe was asked what he knew of the arms in dispute, and replied that he knew them to belong to Scrope. When asked to expatiate, however, he declined to offer a survey of the campaigns on which he had served with Scrope, surveys that were provided by the other witnesses. On the contrary, he brusquely refused to discuss the matter at all:

> He said that if a man asked him all the questions in the world he would always answer in the same way, that all the times he had fought in the king's campaigns he had never seen any other man carry these arms nor use them except the Scropes, and before this dispute he had never heard of Grosvenor nor of his family.[95]

The irritated comment of Sir Nicholas Harris Nicolas, the document's nineteenth-century editor, nicely captures the tone of this testimony: "the deposition is chiefly remarkable for the petulance which [Clanvowe] displayed at being interrogated" (2.438). Alone among the 250 witnesses, Clanvowe declined to discuss his military career.

What is also striking about this testimony for our purposes is the mode of this refusal: rather than debate, Clanvowe retreats into silence. We see much the same strategy at work throughout *The Two Ways.* Searchers after Clanvowe's heterodox religious opinions have been disappointed in the treatise: for Anne Hudson, it is "an insipidity" and "an anthology of puri-

tan pious sentiment," and even K. B. McFarlane found it "a farrago of pul‑
pit commonplaces."[96] But McFarlane also understood where its hetero‑
doxy was to be found:

> The only trace of Lollardy is in the silences. Clanvow [sic] says noth‑
> ing in favour of confession, pilgrimage, the veneration of the saints,
> the effectiveness of the sacraments, nothing at all about the priest‑
> hood. He ignores the Church as an institution altogether. He was a lay
> preacher and has assumed to himself at least as much of the clergy's
> functions. That was what aroused the Church's resentment against the
> lay party.[97]

It is by not speaking that Clanvowe expresses his resistance to estab‑
lished religion, just as a similar silence serves to criticize the honor code
that drove Scrope and Grosvenor to a six-year struggle over a coat of arms.
This is also the silence into which the cuckoo is banished. The *Boke of
Cupide* demonstrates that the court cannot be spoken to in any language
but its own, a language able to accommodate and neutralize all criticism.
To speak "trewe and pleyne" is finally impossible: within the court all dis‑
course becomes nuanced, multivalent, facile. The *Boke of Cupide* cannot
help but be a courtier's frippery. But silence has its own force, the elo‑
quence of taciturnity. "Lerne to say wele, say litel, or say noȝt," advises
one court text, a progressive diminishment of voice that matches the
cuckoo's gradual exclusion.[98] It is perhaps in a similar silence that Clan‑
vowe's deepest thoughts on the politics of poetry at the Ricardian court
are to be found.

IV

Let us now return to our original question. Is court poetry by definition
so narrow in its interests, so local in its focus, so bound in its ideology,
that it stands in opposition to the form of writing we have come to call
literature—a writing that aspires to a more fully inclusive vision of human
experience? Or is it not the case that the "double voicing" characteristic
of court poetry, and the very inevitability of its return to its historical con‑
text, is itself productive of literary discourse?

The coding of the political in terms of the amorous that we have observed in the *Boke of Cupide* is in no sense unusual. The plaintive tone of so much court poetry, its staging, over and over again, of the single scene of (in Derek Pearsall's words) "the lover and his mistress for ever frozen into ritual gestures of beseeching and disdain" articulates what was called, as early as the twelfth century, the *miseriae curialium*.[99] The description by Peter of Blois of the anguish of courtiers awaiting advancement replicates the lexicon in which lovers will lament throughout succeeding centuries: "They delight in ardors; what is heavy grows light, what is bitter turns sweet, and our martyrs, though they are weak, do not feel their toil."[100] Whether the service be compelled by lady or by lord it is service nonetheless, and in either case the courtier is a helpless suppliant for the grace of an omnipotent figure far beyond him, a passive petitioner who can do little to affect his own future.[101] In this sense the quintessential courtly form is the complaint: it is at once wholly disinterested, an act undertaken on the assumption of the uselessness of lament—"What shall I say, to whom shall I complayn? / I wot not who wyll on my sorus rewe"—and yet profoundly pragmatic: only a lover so devoted as to pursue a hopeless suit is deserving of grace.[102] However, occasionally the real purpose of this erotic poetry becomes visible: the troubadour Elias Careil confesses that "I'm not singing to gain sexual pleasure / but for honor and profit."[103] To be sure, we hear this admission only rarely, since part of what makes a courtier worthy of reward is his ability to represent inconvenient truths with the discretion of subtlety.

But court poetry is in no sense restricted to a single, pragmatic function. In fact, much of it is much less a naked bid for advancement than a meditation on the conditions of court life considered in their widest relevance. Many court poems reflect upon the painful self-discipline that aspiration requires: "throughe gouernance growethe grace," as one poet ambiguously says.[104] They also stage a specifically courtly ambivalence: on the one hand the courtier's desire to escape from a highly competitive and untrustworthy environment, on the other his yearning to perform, to dazzle. These are intensely private poems designed to be overheard: "Vnto myselffe a-lone / Thus do I make my mowne," says the lover—lines that begin an elaborately turned virelai.[105] They stage moments of aloneness—"My selfe and I, me thought we wer Inow," says the lover in *La belle dame sans merci* (86)—but then people them with either personified abstractions or representative examples of the courtly population. And these poems speak as well to the disappointments of the noble life per se. Oton de Grandson's *Livre messire Ode* is an almost unrelieved litany of lament that bears a close relationship to the exiled and disinherited Oton's miserable personal history; Charles d'Orleans's poems return over and over to the issue of *troth*, not surprising for a man trapped by sharply conflicting loyalties; and the lyrics ascribed to William de la Pole, duke of Suffolk, express a pattern of constraint and aspiration that takes on a particularly telling valence when correlated with his unhappy life.[106] And we should also remember that these are poems that in many instances mean exactly what they say: they are written by men living in the overwhelmingly male (and masculine) world of the court and, given the medieval requirement of hypergamy, competing for a very few women, all of them above their station.[107] In the court lyric, a lady is sometimes just a lady.

But above all these are poems about complexity, specifically the complexity of personality and manner entailed by court life. Their energy derives from the opposition between an absolutist idealism—the monolithic claims of love, the unalloyed intensity of desire, the singularity of erotic selfhood, the unconditional joy capable of satisfying all needs—and the complex world of contingency that frustrates its realization. On the one hand is the lover burdened with a self-possessing, self-possessed desire; on the other are the impediments to love—the impassive lady, the faithless man, the mockers who scorn love's law, the very conditions of a social life that precludes absolutes—against which the poet can only pose the impossible voicing of a desire he can never fully express. Every courtly poem is in effect a debate, whether between a nightingale and a cuckoo or, as is more commonly the case, between feeling and form, love and the language of love. Over and over again court poets lament the insufficiency of speech. "Of þis swete nek if I more say, / Me þink my body breke yn tway, / for sorow I may no lenger speke": the palpability of the female body both generates and stands as an analogue to an overwhelming and inarticulate male desire.[108] In another poem the lover decides to "vn-bynde" his care by writing a letter which "A-boute my hede I woll . . . wynde, / Tyll sche her-selfe hit wyll vnbynde": the lover becomes an icon of love, the bearer of a message that can be expressed only by silent witnessing.[109] Or the lover seeks "to tell you Myn entent," but is foiled by both his incapacity ("y haue nothere gamyn ne gle") and the circumstances ("We may not speke but we be schent"), a failure of expression that his thwarted and so all the more powerfully eloquent poem at once intensifies and ameliorates.[110] In a variant of the same dynamic, and one with special relevance to the *Boke of Cupide*, a lover tells his lady that his words will "be bothe true & playn," a promise that the smoothly artful poem in which it is embedded belies.[111] And so on. Writing is at once the means of communication and the barrier that impedes it, a gesture toward the intensity and singularity of feeling that generates it but which it can never finally encompass. In the words again of Christine de Pizan, the lover may desire to speak "a voix simplette" but he always ends up talking "mignot."[112]

In the most general terms, then, the court poem explores the vicissitudes of simplicity in a world of complexity. Driven by a desire for the absolute but caught within the world of the contingent, the nightingale song of the courtier is constantly accompanied by the raucous tones of the cuckoo. This is a counterpoint that captures a doubleness at the very heart of courtliness. On the one hand, the court is ostensibly composed of "euery wight that gentil ys of kynde," in the words of Clanvowe's nightingale (150), men and women whose easy elegance bespeaks breeding. These courtiers exist not only to serve the prince but, in the elegance of their dress and speech, as in the artful shaping of their personalities, to embody his magnificence. Yet the subtlety and nuance this symbolism entails subverts the absolutism to which it is in service, just as the courtier's fabrication requires a discipline that ill sorts with the claim of instinctive superiority. So too, to know and bow to the will of the prince requires a psychological penetration, and an alertness to the complexity of human intention, that is hardly consistent with the ideal of instinctive love and service courtly idealism promotes. Lydgate describes how the prince's "frowne" causes the courtiers to whisper among themselves—they "priuely wol rowne / Whan a prynce doth vp-on hem frowne"—but with each arriving at his own meaning: "Everych conclude[s] lich his fantasye."[113] Far from creating a court unified by the unquestioning desire to reflect his own image, the monarch instead generates an interpretive insecurity that alienates his courtiers from himself and each other. Instead of the uniformity of will and the simplicity of desire to which it aspires, and which its literature means to celebrate, the court is in fact heterogeneous and self-conflicted, a complexity its writing inevitably if uneasily acknowledges.[114]

As we have seen, then, this dialectic of court writing, mediating between absolutism and contingency, uniformity and heterogeneity, self-identity and dispersion, has both a topical meaning for the politics of the Ricardian court and relevance to the ideological formation of courtliness in general. But it also performs cultural work of another sort: it generates a mode of writing that comes to constitute, for much of English literary history, literature itself. Court poetry incorporates a set of irresolvable antinomies: interest and disinterest, work and play, the desire to transcend the social context and yet an unavoidable need to recuperate and refigure it. It posits a twofold audience—one engaged in mere dalliance, another capable of reading ironically—just as it generates an author who does and does not mean what he says. It thus entails a mobile, disunified self capable of assuming a variety of incommensurate subject positions. And it deploys a language not only laden with rhetorical tropes and topoi but capable of understanding its own rhetoricity—a language located, in Paul de Man's phrase, "in the void of . . . difference."[115]

These are the characteristics that in succeeding centuries certified a certain kind of writing as aesthetic, distinguishing it from other, non-literary writing. This distinction is not ontological but historical: we now realize that literature is less a specific kind of writing than a writing that is taken, for a variety of reasons, to be literature. But the historical effect of the distinction is beyond dispute. The court provided, in other words, a site not just for the production of specific literary works but for the development of literary discourse per se. To be sure, it was hardly the only site in which this discourse was produced in late medieval England;[116] and a *sine qua non* for the emergence of the *idea* of literature was the Italian humanist ideology of a transhistorical writing. But it was in the court that the language of power became the language of poetry. And because of the shape of subsequent literary history—the overwhelming dominance of Chaucer's court poetry in the fifteenth century, and the location of Skelton, Wyatt, and Surrey in the Tudor court—this event proved to be decisive. We should not be surprised, then, that the first court poet in English was also the father of English poetry, nor that the courtier John Clanvowe produced a poem that Milton and Wordsworth found worthy of imitation. Whether he knew it or not, he was making literature.

chapter four

"What Is Me?"

Hoccleve and the Trials of the Urban Self

To redeem the past and to transform every "It was" into "Thus
would I have it!"—that only do I call redemption!
                    —Nietzsche, *Thus Spoke Zarathustra*

More than one self per organism is not a good recipe for survival.
            —Antonio Damasio, *The Feeling of What Happens*

As the *Male Regle* nears its end, Hoccleve asks, with the willful naiveté
that makes his poetry at once enigmatic and endearing, "Ey, what is me
þat to myself thus longe / Clappid haue I?"[1] Hoccleve is the most strenu-
ously autobiographical poet of early English literature: not until at least
Donne, or perhaps even Wordsworth and the high Romantics, do we find
his equal in self-observation.[2] To the first critics of Hoccleve's poetry, as to
more recent commentators, these self-representations are understood as

conventional poses required for thematic reasons. This understanding locates his account of his misbehavior in the *Male Regle* within a penitential context, establishing a pattern of sin followed by contrition, while it
reads his dialogue with the almsman in the *Regiment of Princes* as both providing a cautionary example of misgovernance to Prince Henry and as
motivating the poem's petition for relief from poverty.[3] And Hoccleve's remarkable account of his madness and the social isolation it forced upon
him in his late *Complaint* has also been interpreted as a penitential exercise, a story of sin and contrition, with the other items that comprise the
so-called *Series* being located within the same moralizing context.[4]

Other critics, more alert to the literary and psychological complexities inherent in all acts of self-representation, have avoided claiming that
Hoccleve's autobiographical protagonist is simply an everyman adopted to
prove a moral point. But they have continued to read his various accounts
of himself as essentially strategic, poses adopted depending on the needs
of the communicative situation. Here the argument is primarily that Hoccleve wears the mask required of the subordinate who wants his superior
audience to listen to his importunities and advice. As John Burrow puts
it, "Hoccleve makes a fool of himself to amuse the great man," a reading
that is at one point endorsed by Hoccleve himself, when he admits—in
a poem written for Edward, duke of York—that the poem serves as "an
owtere of my nycetee / For my good lordes lust and game and play."[5] And
in the *Male Regle* he admits that "who so him shapeth mercy for to craue, /
His lesson moot recorde in sundry wyse" (397–98): strategy is evidently
never far from Hoccleve's mind. As James Simpson has said, "Hoccleve
the poet is extraordinarily sensitive to the conditions of discursive exchange," conditions in which he is presumed by modern critics to be always at a disadvantage.[6] In sum, the general consensus can be summarized
in Paul Strohm's dictum: "the medieval (and pre-modern) self is more
likely to deploy the self, not as the ultimate center of interest, but as an
imaginative exemplification of broader issues."[7]

But there are problems with allowing this familiar assumption to
dominate our interpretations of Hoccleve's writing. For one thing, it tends
to ignore the urgent specificity, the dogged relentlessness, and the sheer
ubiquity of Hoccleve's self-descriptions; and for another, it presumes that
a culture that privileged the universal, that sought to understand particularity by reference to absolutist patterns, made attention to individuality
for its own sake impossible.[8] Hoccleve's exasperated and exasperating

question, "what is me?"—an inescapably blunt formulation that stands symbolically for the persistent self-reflexivity of his writing as a whole[9]— is, this essay will argue, the fundamental topic of all of his writing. What we would call his individuality, both his particularity as this specific person and, more important, his own *sense* of his particularity, both his self-consciousness and consciousness of self—is at once Hoccleve's treasure and his pain, at once that which he most insistently displays and that from which he most persistently seeks escape. Hoccleve's obsessive concern with representing his own inner life is less a strategy directed to some larger literary goal than the goal itself.[10]

In what follows I shall begin with an account—drawn partly from the *Regiment of Princes* but primarily from the so-called *Series*—of Hoccleve's individuality. In providing a summary reading of the *Series*, I mean also to show that Hoccleve seeks, albeit in vain, for the Nietzschean redemption described in this essay's epigraph. His poetry as a whole, I argue, tries always to fit the self into a coherent and unifying narrative that will provide Hoccleve with a sense of self-controlled direction. And yet the very nature of the self he simultaneously possesses and is possessed by makes this redemptive closure unattainable. But is this failure of accommodation simply an effect of Hoccleve's unique, even accidental eccentricity, a peculiarity of the personality that allows of no further explanation? The final two sections of the essay will propose two reasons for Hoccleve's dilemma. One is political, deriving from the conditions of cultural life under the Lancastrians, and will be explicated by means of a survey of the major poems of Hoccleve's career. The other is social, deriving from the conditions of material life prescribed by the bureaucratic context of Westminster and, above all, the urban context of London. Before we reach these explanations, however, we must first define as clearly as possible the nature of the selfhood that Hoccleve finds so puzzling: "What is me?"

I

The dialogue with the almsman in the *Regiment* prefigures with startling if serendipitous accuracy Wordsworth's meeting with the leech gatherer.[11] Throughout this extended conversation Hoccleve fends off his inter-

locuter's offers of the consolations of philosophy and theology with a continual return to the specifics of his condition as a Privy Office clerk dependent on an unreliable Exchequer. Yet it is this very specificity that renders
the dialogue with the almsman unproductive: unable to submerge himself
into the universalized humanity that is the proper object of philosophy
and theology, he remains immune to consolation. As the almsman himself acknowledges, moralizing clichés are of little interest to Hoccleve: "I
see wel smal effect / Or elles noon my wordes in thee take" (1814–15).[12]
Nor can Hoccleve's condition be understood simply as moral failure, an
inability to accept the quietist endurance the almsman advises. When
he says, rather oddly, that the "cause and ground" of his despondency
is "the lak of olde mennes cherisshynge" (793–94), he is pleading not
for patronage—especially since the poem is addressed to the distinctly
young Prince Henry, who was about twenty-five at the time of the poem's
composition—but for affection and support from this particular old man.
Yet we are also awkwardly aware that the conversation with the old man
is cast in the formal mode of a literary topos, the dialogue between wisdom
and folly, age and youth, experience and innocence.[13] These dialogues are
everywhere in medieval literature, but Hoccleve's most immediate model
is almost certainly Chaucer's Pardoner's Tale, where rioters whose behavior is only a slightly more extravagant version of Hoccleve's carry on
a conversation with an old man whose topic is also, although they do not
know it, despair and repentance.[14] If, then, the dialogue of the Regiment is
an obvious literary fiction, the recognition of the topos fights with the
autobiographical impulse that it partly enables, partly defeats. The poem
then becomes nothing more (nor less) than an instance of a man talking to himself, what Hoccleve himself calls one of those "troubly dremes
drempt al in wakynge" (109): the attempt to break out of psychic self-
enclosure by writing a poem is less an act of healing than a further symptom of the disease. According to the almsman, whose own biography bears
a suspicious resemblance to Hoccleve's, "Whil thow art soul [solitary],
thoght his wastyng seed / Sowith in thee" (201).

This condition of simultaneous self-enclosure and self-fragmentation—the setting up of parts of the self as if they were other than the self,
only to have them either collapse back into the self or, worse, fly apart—
is characteristic of Hoccleve. In the Regiment he describes himself as vic-
timized by reified aspects of his own personality—figures such as "Thoght"

and "Wach"—so that his restless anxiety is inflicted *upon* him rather than willed *by* him.[15] His alienation is both psychological and social: he is as much a stranger to himself as he is to others. Hence he explains the disorder of the *Regiment*—he admits that "this pamflet / Noon ordre holde[s]" (2060–61)—in terms of the dispersal of elements of his own personality: "Anothir day, whan wit and I be met, / . . . and han us freendly kist, / Deskevere I wole that now is nat wist (2063–65). How strangely specific is this image! Hoccleve's wit is so much not a part of himself that he can imagine kissing it as one might a friend returned from abroad.

The most detailed and powerful account of Hoccleve's psychic condition is both described and represented by the compilation of five texts that in the manuscripts remain without a title but to which Eleanor Hammond ascribed an uncertain unity by naming the *Series*.[16] First comes the *Complaint*, a soliloquy in which Hoccleve describes his anguished effort to understand both the mental illness that afflicted him five years previously and the social ostracism that has been its continuing effect; then the *Dialogue* with a Friend, who seems unwilling to accept Hoccleve's own account of his recovery and suggests to him that instead of undertaking, as he himself proposes, the translation of a work on the art of dying that he fulfill a promised commission for Humphrey of Gloucester; the third item is then the poem for Humphrey, the *Tale of Jereslaus's Wife*, a work drawn from the same narrative tradition of "accused queens" as Chaucer's Man of Law's Tale, to which it makes clear reference; then—without any transition— the previously mentioned work, translated from Heinrich Suso and called by Hoccleve *Lerne to Dye*; and finally, at the Friend's instigation, and apparently superfluously, an unpleasantly misogynist narrative about a deceitful prostitute and her foolish victim called the *Tale of Jonathas*.[17]

Most discussions of this compilation seek for overriding themes that can provide coherence to a very odd collection of texts—themes such as the notion that illness is an effect of sin and can only be cured by confession, or that all life is best seen as but a preparation for death (with the *Lerne to Dye* as both the textual and spiritual center of the work), or that the work is an effort at both psychological and social rehabilitation.[18] These attempts are persuasive to the extent that they describe not the text Hoccleve wrote but the one he tried to write. The *Series* is both difficult and interesting because the sense it makes is not conceptual but experiential: we can understand it only by tracing the twists and turns by which it approaches but finally evades coherence. It records the workings of a consciousness for which self-knowledge and social acceptance are at once goals to be achieved and conclusions to be avoided.

In the *Complaint* Hoccleve describes madness as self-fragmentation. He says that "[my] wylde infirmitee . . . me out of myself caste and threew" (40–42); "the substance of my memorie / Wente to pleye as for a certeine space" (50–51). Even his physical behavior, as reported to him by others, reveals a decentering and dispersal: "heere and ther forth stirte I as a ro" (128), "My feet were ay wauynge to and fro," "myn yen soghten euery halke" (131–33). Analogously, the return to sanity is described as a re-collection of the scattered parts of the self: his memory "retourne[d] into the place / Whens it cam" (54–55), and "my wit were hoom come ageyne" (64); ever since, he assures us and himself, "My wit and I han been of swich accord / As we were" (59–60); "Right so, thoghe þat my wit were a pilgrym / And wente fer fro hoom, he cam agayn" (232–33; see also 247–49). Yet by personifying memory and wit as distinct from the self, Hoccleve's spasmodic psychomachia posits a division within the very self that he wants to present as unified and self-identical.

More significantly, the *Complaint* sets up strategies for confirming the healthful unity of the self that actually reveal the opposite. In the work's best known passage, Hoccleve poses before a mirror in order to fabricate a bearing that will persuade his friends that he is as mentally sound as he knows himself to be (155–68). Seeking to construct an outer appearance that will correspond to the inner reality, Hoccleve implicitly confirms a split between what one is and what one is seen to be, between inner self and social role. Hoccleve discovers that he can never *pretend* to be himself: since he must "peynte contenance, cheere and look" (149), he cannot possess the instinctive and unproblematic identity to which he aspires. So too, by depending upon others to confirm his psychic integrity is to acknowledge that identity is not a given unity fully within one's own possession but a product of social interaction. And with this recognition that there is no means to prove either to himself or to others that he is fully *self*-possessed, Hoccleve arrives at an impasse that ironically replicates the very emotions and behavior he claims to have put behind him:

> O lord, so my spirit was restelees,
> I soghte reste and I nat it fond,
> But ay was trouble redy at myn hond.
>
> (194–96)

Since his friends avoid him he is denied the "communynge" (217) that would demonstrate his sanity: just as the self is revealed to be a collection of disconnected fragments, so Hoccleve stands as an isolated individual "among the prees" (191).

At this point in the poem occurs a moment that will reward close attention, for it exemplifies the movement of the *Complaint*, and indeed of the *Series*, as a whole. Bidding farewell to happiness—"Adieu my good auenture and good chance!" (273)—Hoccleve then undergoes an emotional about-face in the very act of writing the poem.

> And as swythe aftir thus bethoghte I me:
> "If þat I in this wyse me despeire
> It is purchas of more aduersitee;
> What needith it my feeble wit appeire
> Syn God hath maad myn helthe home repeire?
> Blessid be he, and what men deeme or speke,
> Suffre it, thynke I, and me nat on me wreke."
>
> (274–80)

Until this point the poem has been written in the present tense: the *Complaint* asks to be read not as the reported narrative of a previous experience but as a present tense event, taking place in the act of writing. Yet suddenly, with the first line of this stanza, we shift for a moment into the past tense—"And as swythe aftir thus bethoghte I me"—before returning to the present. For a moment the poem ceases to be a record of immediate, ad hoc musings and becomes instead an account of what was once thought. The effect is to create an instability in the very form of the *Complaint*—an effect very like that created later, in the *Dialogue*, in the inclusion of an apparently irrelevant passage about coin-clipping and counterfeiting (99–196). Whose voice do we hear? Is it that of man speaking *ex tempore*, describing a condition that exists in the moment of its utterance? Or one speaking from the perspective of the present looking back upon a confused moment in the past that has now been understood? When at the end of the stanza Hoccleve promises not to avenge himself on himself—"Suffre it, thynke I, and me nat on me wreke" (280)—he engages in the same act of self-doubling that the stanza enacts temporally.

It is shortly after this awkward convolution that Hoccleve turns to "a boke" (310), a dialogue between Reason and "a wofull man" found

originally in Isidore of Seville's *Synonyma*.[19] Overwhelmed by the problem of self-understanding, Hoccleve now transforms his subjectivity into
an object by conforming it to an orthodox pattern. The protagonist of
Isidore's book, as Hoccleve presents him, is a man who has sinned (320),
who is now despairing (328–36), and is comforted by Reason's message
that "Swiche souffrance is of mannes gilt clensynge" (349), that God cas-
tigates those whom he loves (356–57), that rather than complaining the
sufferer should repent and ask God's mercy (365–71). Having fallen into
a psychological depth he is unable to fathom, in other words, Hoccleve
seeks escape in a comfortingly familiar paradigm. But in a pattern that will
be repeated throughout the *Series,* as soon as resolution is offered it is withdrawn, a withdrawal here marked in the literal action of the poem. Before
he can finish translating the book its owner asks for it back, a rupture that
is then repeated in the next section of the text when the Friend's importunate knocking on the door interrupts Hoccleve as he is finishing the very
Complaint we are in the process of reading.

 The movement of the *Series* as a whole follows just this pattern of
resolution undone by rupture, producing a text that for all its agitated ani-
mation is unable to advance toward its goals of integrating the self with
itself and the individual within society. In the *Dialogue* Hoccleve seeks
to enforce the religious understanding of his illness at which he arrived
in the *Complaint* by projecting a pious text, the *Lerne to Dye,* as the final
work of a man who now locates himself at the end of his life: "the nyght
approchithe, it is fer past none, . . . Ripnesse of deeth faste vpon me haast-
ith" (245–47). But the Friend interrupts this familiar act of medieval self-
termination by redefining Hoccleve's illness not as spiritual but merely
physical: God may have cured him, but "Of studie was engendred thy
seeknesse" (379). In pursuing this argument the Friend provides a powerful account of Hoccleve's capacity to lose himself in books:

> ioie hastow for to muse
> Vpon thy book and there in stare and poure
> Til þat it thy wit consume and deuoure.
>
> (404–6)

These lines describe exactly the process by which Hoccleve, in the *Complaint,* allowed his own, unsatisfactory selfhood to be absorbed by the protagonist of Isidore's tract. Moreover, not only does the Friend redefine

Hoccleve's program for health as being actually part of the disease, he also persuades him to set aside the translation of Suso and instead to reenter the social world by producing a poem once promised to Duke Humphrey, a poem that will serve as a palinode for Hoccleve's earliest work, the *Letter of Cupid*. Once again, then, progress toward both literary and personal closure is derailed, as Hoccleve turns back to his attempt of twenty years earlier to gain entrance into the now-vanished courtly world within which Chaucer once so gracefully moved.

Personal integration is now dependent on social integration. By gratifying Duke Humphrey's request Hoccleve will establish for himself a stable and familiar social identity as a court poet. To do so, however, he must prove that his first effort at court poetry, the *Letter of Cupid* (1402), is not in fact misogynist, as the Friend claims (a charge to which we shall return). Hoccleve offers two defenses, both derived from Chaucer. The first invokes the self-defense offered in the General Prologue:

> therof was I noon auctour;
> I nas in þat cas but a reportour
> Of folkes tales; as they seide, I wroot:
> I nat affermed it on hem, God woot.
> Whoso þat shal reherce a mannes sawe,
> As þat he seith moot he seyn & nat varie;
> For, and he do he dooth ageyn the lawe
> Of trouthe. He may tho wordes nat contrarie!
> (760–67)

The second defense, derived from the Prologue to the *Legend of Good Women*, is that the poem is really *not* an attack on women but a defense: "I to hem thoughte no repreef ne shame. / What world is this? How vndirstande am I?" (773–74).[20] Nonetheless, the misunderstood Hoccleve agrees to produce a palinode, both to regain the good graces of women and to please Humphrey, duke of Gloucester, whose "lust and desir," says the Friend, is "with ladyes to have daliance" (703–6). To a contemporary aristocratic audience, this phrase would have been more than a conventional courtly compliment. For at just this time Humphrey was involved in prenuptial negotiations with Jacqueline of Hainaut, the mistreated wife of the Duke of Brabant.[21] It is clear that the ever-politic Henry approved of this match—Jacqueline stood as godmother to Henry's son during this time[22]—and in an era when aristocratic marriage was a political matter there can be no question of scandal.[23] But there still remain awkward disjunctions between Hoccleve's account of Humphrey as an elegant courtier devoted to the service of ladies, his concurrent actions as a hard-headed politician using marriage to advance his own and national interests, and the tale that Hoccleve now produces for Humphrey's delectation—a story about how a woman is abused by men for both material and sexual purposes.

Derived from the *Gesta romanorum*, the *Tale of Jereslaus's Wife* describes the violent assaults on the virtue of the loyal wife of the Emperor of Rome when her husband leaves her in the care of his unscrupulous brother. As an offering to Duke Humphrey, who was at this very time functioning as *custos* or Lieutenant of England while his brother the king pursued his French ambitions, and who was currently engaged in marriage negotiations, the tale is thus a distinctly tactless choice. If this historical context reveals Hoccleve's inability to serve as a dependable source of aristocratic flattery, the tale's *literary* context shows that he was equally ineffective at understanding—or perhaps accepting—the poetic identity required by the cultural world of the Lancastrians. The *Tale of Jereslaus's Wife* has a pattern of structural repetition, and a heroine notable for her patient constancy, that inevitably recall Chaucer's Man of Law's Tale. Now the Man of Law's Tale served Chaucer as a way to disown his *own* palinode for *Troilus and Criseyde*, the *Legend of Good Women*.[24] So that both by his insult to Gloucester and by his pattern of Chaucerian allusions, Hoccleve tries to claim for himself the same kind of political non-alignment, and the same assertion that literature—when properly understood—can rise above mere party allegiance, that Chaucer maintained in the Prologue. He is nostalgically invoking, at a time when Lancastrian control was at its most successful, a Ricardian world in which his desired kind of writing—socially and politically disinterested—might have found a place.

We should thus not be surprised that when the Friend reappears to read the tale he remonstrates at the lack of a moralization, which he then himself provides the poet, apparently from another manuscript of the *Gesta*.[25] For the moralization removes the tale from the awkwardly apt context of Humphrey's political and marital ambitions and locates it within the indeterminate universality of moral truth. Nor is it odd that the moralization is followed, with no transition, by the translation from Suso that it was meant to replace, the *Lerne to Dye*—a tacit withdrawal by Hoccleve from the attempt to reassume the identity of court poet. Yet here even traditional wisdom is cast into a narrative form that represents yet again Hoccleve's sense of a fragmented and besieged yet oddly truculent selfhood. The work gestures toward but finally fails to achieve the closure that Hoccleve has been seeking. "Blessid is he that can see the endynge" (899), it counsels, and its central theme is that life must be lived in constant awareness of death. Yet while Hoccleve declines to translate the whole of his source, a replay of his inability to translate all of Isidore's *Synonyma*, he does provide what at least *looks* like a definitive closure by translating, as a coda, the account of the bliss of Heaven given in one of the lessons for All Hallows Day. Because this is the very day (November 1) which the *Complaint* gives as its date of composition, as well as the date, five years previously, when Hoccleve's sanity returned to him (50–56), we are encouraged to think that the end has finally come round to the beginning, that the fragments of both personal history and literary composition have been re-collected into a whole.

But of course not so—for the *Series* does not end here but has, as an ostentatious and wholly indigestible supplement, the *Tale of Jonathas*, a story of the repeated betrayal of a naive young man by a prostitute and his horrifying act of revenge. Again we see the return of the old Hocclevian themes—the betrayal of trust, the impossibility of learning from experience, sin manifested as sickness, confession as the only cure—but now given a darkly vengeful turn. Now there is no cure for sin, confession is useless, wanton youth is wasted without compensation, and the only legitimized action is brutal retribution. That the tale is viciously misogynist is certainly true, but it is also typically self-defeating. A tale that broods with increasing bitterness upon the wiles of women is at the end dedicated—amazingly—to "my lady westmerland." This was Joan Beaufort, a very formidable woman indeed: daughter of John of Gaunt and Katherine Swynford, she was not only the king's aunt but the second wife of the immensely powerful Ralph Neville, first earl of Westmorland. More to the point, Lady Westmorland had persuaded the earl to strip his eldest son of his inheritance for the ultimate benefit of the eldest of *her* sons, Richard Neville, earl of Salisbury—and, incidentally, the husband of Chaucer's granddaughter.[26] How could Hoccleve possibly have thought it appropriate to dedicate this particular tale, which describes a woman persuading a young man to part with his inheritance and then being savagely punished, to this particular woman? The *Tale of Jonathas* bespeaks a mind at odds with itself, filled with a mixture of ambition and resentment, desperately trying to make moral sense of experience but pushed finally into a vengeful negativity that could only rebound upon itself.

The *Series* is thus a set of dismal if fascinating *Notes from the Underground*. As we all know, Jacob Burckhardt notoriously said that in the Middle Ages "man was conscious of himself only as a member of a race, people, party, family, or corporation—only through some general category."[27] Contemporary medievalists, myself included, have used this statement as a stalking horse in our efforts to rehabilitate medieval individualism. But Burckhardt's dictum can usefully remind us that while individuality may have been possible for medieval men and women, it was not always a happy condition.

II

Hoccleve's earliest poem of any ambition is the *Letter of Cupid*, and the circumstances of its composition and reception provide an index to the difficulties faced by a young poet under the new Lancastrian regime. The poem is a translation and revision of *L'Epistre de Cupide*, a poem written by Christine de Pizan in May 1399.[28] Christine's poem takes as its premise that ladies of the court—of the *familia Cupidinis*—have sent a petition to the God of Love asking for relief from the misbehavior of men, and the poem is Cupid's sympathetic reply.[29] But Christine's poem dismisses the sophisticated *doubles entendres* and elegant ambiguities of court poetry by centering itself on a straightforward and deeply felt insistence that women are worthy both in themselves and as men's natural companions (713–44). There is no honor to be won by attacking women, says Christine: they are men's mothers, sisters, and friends, and a companionable mutuality ought to obtain between men and women.[30] In her autobiographical *Lavision Christine*, Christine explains the occasion for the writing of the poem. She says that she sent her son to England in 1399 to join the household of John Montague, the earl of Salisbury. After Richard's deposition, and after Montague's execution for his part in the plot against Henry in January 1400, she was then asked to send Henry her poems and to join her son in England by becoming Henry's court poet. But she refused, and was able to extricate her son from England sometime between the end of 1401 and the first six months of 1402.[31]

Hoccleve's version of Christine's poem, dated May 1402, can thus plausibly be seen as his attempt to persuade Henry that an English man could serve as a court poet at least as well as a French woman. Hoccleve's *Letter of Cupid* therefore turns the poem away from the uncomfortable moralism of Christine's original and toward an elegantly undecidable *jeu d'esprit*, largely by omitting her account of the basic equality of the sexes. Yet this course has its own dangers. In endowing the poem with a cryptic ambiguity—is it a defense of women or an attack upon them?—Hoccleve does succeed in rendering it an appropriate *objet d'art* for a court world in which, as Richard Green has said, "the distinctions between art and life, illusion and reality, game and earnest, have become strangely blurred."[32] But within the context of the Lancastrian household, dominated by Henry's understandable anxiety about disloyalty and betrayal, would ambiguity have been highly prized? Late medieval love fantasies, for all their apparent frivolity, are in fact virtually incapable of avoiding allusion, whether or not intended, to harsh political realities. Examples that come immediately to mind are Chaucer's Prologue to his *Legend of Good Women* and his friend John Clanvowe's *Boke of Cupid*.[33] And in his own poem Hoccleve follows Christine in describing how men "by sleighte and sotiltee" have brought down kingdoms:

> Betrayen men nat Remes grete and Kynges?
> What wight is þat can shape a remedie
> Ageynes false and hid purposid thynges?
> Who can the craft tho castes to espye
> But man, whos wil ay reedy is t'applie
> To thyng þat souneth in to hy falshede?
>   (85–90)

These lines could hardly have amused the king. For here was one of his own men rewriting, in a witty parody of the official style that he used in his work as a clerk in the Privy Seal (the king's most intimate government office), a poem that dwelt on deceit and disloyalty, and that was associated, albeit tangentially, with the disloyal John Montague, himself a courtly poet of considerable reputation. The point is not that Hoccleve did his job badly but that he did it too well. By rejecting the absolutist categories of Christine's Cupid—men are all bad, women all good—and by removing from her poem its firm moral basis in the equality of the sexes, Hoccleve created a text that was open to a variety of interpretations.

But there was little room for such ambiguity in a political world committed to the regulation of discourse by lay and clerical authority working hand-in-hand.[34] In 1401 the anti-Lollard statute *De haeretico comburendo* prescribed not just the burning of heretics but that "all books of suspect orthodoxy . . . be surrendered to the nearest bishop at forty days notice," a clause that was interpreted with distressing latitude.[35] It was also in 1401, according to Adam of Usk, that

> one William Clerk, a writer of Canterbury, but born in the county of Chester, was condemned by the judgement of the court military, and was first reft of his tongue, for that he had uttered against the king wicked words, laying them to the charge of others, and then of his right hand wherewith he had written them, and lastly by penalty of talion, because he had not made good his charges, was beheaded at the Tower.[36]

Hence in *Mum and the Soothsegger*, the sophisticated Mum is "right worldly wise of wordes," while the Soothsegger, unable to master the subtle language of the court (he "can not speke in termes ne in tyme nother, / But bablith fourth bustusely ass barn vn-y-lerid") can find no audience for his "trewe tales."[37] In November 1407 Arundel introduced to the Convocation at Oxford thirteen constitutions to control Lollardy (they were formally issued in 1409) which represented, in the words of Peter McNiven, "a serious attempt to introduce a firm system of censorship. . . . The general theme of the 'Constitutions' was that it was necessary to forgo critical consideration of the rôle and rites of the Church, academic freedom, intellectual independence, theological inquiry, and the advancement of knowledge and understanding in the interests of preserving and strengthening the authorised safeguards against spiritual instability."[38] In a climate in which theological heterodoxy was not merely thought to entail political sedition but, in the case of Sir John Oldcastle, actually did, Hoccleve's persistent refusal to be explicit, and his awkward allusions to sensitive political issues, could hardly have been expected to win him inclusion within the circles of power.

Hoccleve's most significant poem after the *Letter of Cupid* is the *Male Regle*. Written sometime between late September 1405 and late March 1406, the poem appears to be nothing more than a humorously autobiographical account of Hoccleve's rather trivial transgressions against the God of Health combined with a begging poem asking that his annuity be paid. But when placed in its political context, it reveals itself to be even more available to disquieting interpretation than the *Letter of Cupid*.[39] For it is a poem about misgovernance, financial irresponsibility, and ill health. Throughout his reign, and especially in the first half, Henry IV was in grave financial difficulties. Despite his promise upon assuming the throne that he would "live of his own," by 1404 there was general agreement that the Lancastrian regime was at least as bad as the Ricardian in its continual demands for money.[40] In the face of Parliamentary pressure, the Council agreed, in August 1404, to suspend the payment of all annuities — an act that directly affected Hoccleve. Although, as Peter McNiven has shown, "exemptions were made for various categories of annuitant, [they were] mainly already well-endowed persons headed by the king's own relatives,"[41] an unfairness that must have been particularly galling to a man like Hoccleve left without other resources.

Then when Parliament met in October and November 1404, the Commons renewed its old demand that Henry disendow the Church to obtain the funds he required. Archbishop Arundel, Henry's most indispensable supporter, argued in response that the expropriation of the Church would provide a precedent for the abolition of all property rights. The Commons finally agreed instead to a large subsidy, but appointed two so-called War Treasurers to oversee the expenditure of funds. Henry sought to get around this condition by appointing as one of these treasurers Thomas Neville, Lord Furnivall, who was, with his brother Ralph Neville, the earl of Westmorland, a loyal supporter. It is to Furnivall, who can aptly be described as one of Henry's cronies, that Hoccleve addresses his poem.

To these financial insecurities should be added the growing issue of Henry's own poor health. In early June 1405 Henry either ordered or acquiesced in the execution of Archbishop Scrope, and according to popu-

lar rumor it was at this time that he contracted the wasting disease—
thought at the time to be leprosy—that rendered him from time to time
unable to rule and from which he was eventually to die.[42] Hoccleve's poem
is written in the persona of a sick man addressing a personified Health,
has an extended discussion of the dangers of flattery and the need for the
ruler to have men about him who will tell him when he is hated, relies
heavily on political metaphors, meditates on the problem of counsel and
"rakil wit," deals—albeit comically—with the problem of martial valor
and questions of honor, and petitions for the payment of legitimate debts.
Is it, then, a poem about Thomas Hoccleve or about Henry IV? Raising
most of the current questions about the fitness of Lancastrian rule, it is, in
more senses of the phrase than either Lord Furnivall or the king would
have appreciated, a poem about ill rule. And that it provides an acute
commentary on current conditions in the disguise of a confession of personal weakness is perhaps the most severe reproach it raises: not only can
the truth not be told, but the failure of the governors is exacted on the
bodies and in the lives of the governed. It is, in sum, an apparently personal poem that can barely hide its political subtext, a poem in which private conditions reciprocally cause and are caused by public effects.

In 1410–12 Hoccleve wrote his most popular poem, the *Regiment of
Princes,* a book of governance addressed to the young Prince Henry.[43] Perhaps because Hoccleve saw in the prince the possibility of a less tightly
controlled cultural environment,[44] the poem allows itself a surprisingly
wide latitude in its critique of the Lancastrian style of governance.[45] Take,
for example, the opening exemplum of the *Regiment,* which illustrates the
sorrow that a crown brings to the wearer. This is a truth that at the time
of writing was vividly displayed in the political misery and physical illness that were weighing down the dying king. But it is also a truth that the
ambitious prince—all too eager for his own chance at kingship—was
showing himself as temperamentally unable to appreciate. Again, Hoccleve warns the prince against "Brekynge bondes þat stablisshed were /
Mankynde to profite" (2232–33), and he blandly hopes that no one in
this land could be accused of breaking an oath (2241–47). How could
Henry have missed the relevance of this cliché to the Lancastrians? After
all, the Northern rebellions that dominated the first half decade of their
reign were fueled by the memory (or rumor) that Bolingbroke had sworn
on his return to England in 1399 not to seek the crown, and by his now-
disregarded oath when becoming king that he would live on his own

resources. And speaking of royal finances, Hoccleve's blistering attack on royal prodigality (carefully prefaced with an assertion of loyalty: "In al my book yee shul nat see ne fynde / That I youre deedes lakke or hem de-spreise" [4397–98]) is surely relevant to the notoriously precarious and wasteful royal household—a problem exacerbated by the prince's expen-sive campaigns in Wales and not likely to be improved by the current forays of an English army into France.[46] Indeed, given this military adven-turism, the call for peace with which Hoccleve ends the *Regiment,* and his argument that a king who loved "trouthe and justice" would seek peace "by matrymoyne" rather than war (5392–94) has a rather tactless pertinence.[47]

Nor is this all. Take the gloomy meditations with which Hoccleve opens the poem as a whole:

Me fil to mynde how that nat long agoo
Fortunes strook doun thrast estat rial
Into mescheef, and I took heede also
Of many anothir lord that hadde a fall.
(22–25)

In the marginal gloss with which Furnivall guided the reader in his EETS edition, as well as in a footnote, he assures us that this passage refers to Richard II, but would a contemporary audience have been so sure?[48] What about the incapacitating and soon-to-be-fatal illness that was at this very moment afflicting Henry IV? And if the poem was written—or even published—after November 1411, what about the dismissal of Prince Henry and his council by a newly invigorated king?[49] The vagueness of the reference certainly allows for Furnivall's interpretation of the allusion, but when located in its specific time and place it takes on a more ominous significance.

On March 1, 1410, Arundel and the king condemned an obscure and almost pathetically vulnerable Lollard named John Badby to be burnt, at least in part so as to make clear to Prince Henry and his supporters that the old order had not yet passed.[50] Hoccleve reports this terrible event as a way of celebrating the prince's mercy and yet his ultimate commitment to orthodoxy. But Badby's execution also appears in the poem in the context of Hoccleve's account of his own mental anguish and social alienation: the almsman has just warned him that his unhappiness—the "thoght lurk-ynge thee withynne" that leads "streight way to desconfort" (274, 268)—

makes him vulnerable to "the feendes sly conclusioun" that leads men to despair, just as others are led into heresy at "the feendes instigacioun" (278, 283). This placing makes clear the extent to which, with internal dissensions and external dangers having created a climate of suspicion, any expression of discontent could be read as a challenge to political and/or religious authority. Moreover, in his account of Badby's execution Hoccleve takes the occasion to report in some detail the victim's heretical views: that the eucharistic wafer remained "brede material" (291) after the consecration and that a priest's power to "make God" is no greater than "a raker's or swiche anothir wight" (293).[51] After describing, apparently quite accurately, the prince's efforts to save Badby and the heretic's obduracy, Hoccleve adds that Badby's outward appearance made it impossible for any but God to know "if he inward hadde any repentance" (321)—an emphasis on the inward and spiritual at the expense of the outward and formal that was at the very heart of Lollardy. Finally, Hoccleve declines to speculate on the ultimate fate of Badby's soul, but assigns to "dyvynes" the responsibility to "speke and muse / Where his soule is bycome or whidir goon" (323–24)—an oddly agnostic response to the very issue that was claimed to legitimize the burning of heretics alive. It is hardly surprising that some medieval reader should have crossed through these stanzas in one of the manuscripts—an all the more significant gesture since this particular manuscript was almost certainly designed as a presentation copy for a noble patron, probably one of the prince's brothers.[52]

A brief glance at a later poem that appears to be nothing more than a vituperative rejection of Lollardy in favor of official orthodoxy also reveals a more complicated scenario.[53] In the *Remonstance Against Oldcastle* Hoccleve begins not, as we would expect, by attacking Lollardy per se.[54] The poem falls into two distinct parts: the first thirty-four stanzas (272 lines) are addressed to Oldcastle, the second thirty stanzas (240 lines) to the heretics who have led him astray. In the holograph manuscript, Huntington MS 111, there is a large initial at line 273, encouraging the reader to notice a redirection in the theme of the poem at that point.[55] The first thirty-four stanzas urge Oldcastle not to betray his knightly identity by meddling in matters that belong to clerics. In part this advice is almost pedestrian in its practicality: Oldcastle should avoid reading the Bible and stick to Lancelot of the Lake, Vegetius, the Seige of Troy or of Thebes— "thing þat may to th'ordre of knyght longe" (198). Or if he must read the Bible, then Judges, Kings, Joshua, Judith, Paralipomenon, and Maccabees would be appropriate, because they are both "autentik" and "pertinent to chiualrie" (207–8). But the central element of Hoccleve's argument is more profound. Just as Oldcastle's very identity depends upon an unquestioned transmission of ancestral titles and lands, so too orthodoxy has been passed down to us by "our faders." To turn to heresy is thus to break a doctrinal line of transmission as crucial to one's selfhood as inheritance itself. Therefore, Hoccleve urges Oldcastle, apply yourself

> To thyng þat may to th'ordre of knyght longe.
> To thy correccioun now haste and hie,
> For thou haast ben out of ioynt al to longe.
>
> (198–200)

Only after concluding this part of the poem with a prayer for Oldcastle's salvation does Hoccleve turn to a rather predictable attack on Lollard doctrines. And not until the final three stanzas (480–524) does Oldcastle reappear, when he is urged to "retourne knyghtly" (496) to orthodoxy and, just as important, to join Henry and his men in France: "How can a knyght be / Out of th'onur of this rial viage?" (503–4). Only, concludes Hoccleve, if "the cursid fiend [has] changid [his] gyse!" (508)—transformed him from his true self into something false, inauthentic, counterfeit. In sum, then, Hoccleve understands heresy less in terms of religious error than as a deviation from the selfhood prescribed by society—an understanding almost inevitable for a man who feels himself to be chronically "out of joint."

In addition to the sensitive questions of Lollardy and its violent suppression, the general picture that Hoccleve provides of Lancastrian England in the *Regiment* is anything but affirmative. In discussing the fate of old soldiers who fought in France, for instance, Hoccleve describes the nation as a harsh and friendless place: "I see routhe and pitee exylid / Out of this land. Allas, compassioun! / Whan shul yee thre to us be reconsylid?" (862–64). Similarly, the almsman's oddly extravagant attack upon extravagant dress reveals a world not merely of excess but of social fraudulence (you cannot tell the man from the lord—or perhaps the true king from the false), indiscipline (sons no longer obey fathers), and violence (men cannot defend their lords from attack in the streets with their long sleeves)—a world in which, in other words, governance has failed. Much later in the poem Hoccleve explicitly laments, "The riot that hath been withyn this land / Among ourself many a wyntres space" (5216–17), a lament that echoes the complaints of the Parliament of January 1410, which referred to the need for "bone et substanciall gouvernance."[56]

Perhaps the most thoughtful and most pointed commentary that the poem offers the prince, however, is in its extensive treatment of the theme of father and son.[57] Hoccleve exemplifies justice with the story of the Roman consul who wished to punish his son's adultery with blinding, but his son's popularity with the people persuaded him not to. In response, however, he poked out one of his son's eyes and one of his own so that the letter of the law would be observed. "Now if tomorwe fil ther swich a chance," asks Hoccleve, "Sholde men fynde so just governance?" (2769–70). Would a contemporary father, holding to a rigid standard of justice, refuse to countenance or forgive his son's transgression, even if he must partake of the punishment himself? Lamenting a lost standard of integrity, the story is relevant to both king and prince—the prince, in seeking to displace the king as ruler of England, has transgressed, but the king—himself a usurper—is unwilling to apply the law to his son. Hoccleve's example thus speaks with awkward pertinence to what must have seemed to many the Lancastrians' unseemly squabbling over the spoils of kingship and the lack of integrity to which it witnessed.

Similarly, throughout the poem Hoccleve establishes a symbolic connection between himself and Prince Henry. Both are fatherless: Hoccleve is the negligent son who now mourns his absent father Chaucer and must make do with the tiresome and often irrelevant almsman; Henry is equally in need of paternal wisdom but must make do with Hoccleve, who seems to provide little more than a translated and abbreviated anthology of counsel (what Pearsall calls "unexceptionable moral principles that should guide a prince's behavior"), wisdom Hoccleve assures Henry that he already knows.[58] In the past it was different: Alexander had Aristotle, the Roman republic had Cicero, Augustus had Virgil, and Richard II had Chaucer. But the continuity between past and present—like the continuity between father and son—has been broken; and the agents of this rupture are the Lancastrians. It seems unlikely that the political meaning of these meditations on the relationship between the generations would be lost on a prince who took care, almost immediately upon assuming the throne, to reinter the body of his neglected predecessor, Richard II.[59]

If Hoccleve were really trying to produce, as the almsman advised, something "fressh and gay" for the prince to "desporten him by nyght"

(1906, 1903) he can hardly have thought he succeeded. This is doubtless why he draws attention throughout the poem to the need for a king to listen to the truth-teller rather than to "Favel" the flatterer (e.g., 2934–47, 3039–101, 4439–73) and to forgive the poet who speaks with wit (e.g., 3389–3409).[60] The point is not that Hoccleve was either a particularly shrewd or a particularly courageous political observer: all of the unpalatable things his poem says about the Lancastrian regime were, to judge from Parliamentary petitions and chronicler's reports, common knowledge, and doubtless part of the daily conversation of those who lived and worked in the ambit of Westminster. The point, rather, is that Hoccleve was temperamentally incapable of fashioning himself to fit the system, of adopting the untroubled public identity of a deferential servant to the crown. He was neither as shrewd and detached as Chaucer, nor as self-protective as Lydgate.[61] On the contrary, he was an individual who performed even the most familiar and practiced of roles, the adviser to the prince, in a way that called attention to the way both he and prince failed to meet conventional expectations. He was, in short, a man for whom the social identities available in Lancastrian England failed to explain to himself the "me" that he evidently found so troubling.

Indeed, even Hoccleve's role as a royal servant—a clerk in the office of the Privy Seal—is presented as suppressing, and therefore making all the more intense, his sense of individuality. In the Privy Seal he was little more than a scribe, composing letters according to strict formulas, the nature of which he himself exemplified in his *Formulary,* with some 1,100 differently worded but equally dehumanizing bureaucratic prototypes.[62] His description in the *Regiment* of his work at the Privy Seal shows the way in which psychic and bodily unity is bought at the price of social isolation and physical pain. The mind of the writer is both coordinated with eye and hand—"Mynde, ye, and hand—noon may from othir flitte, / But in hem moot be joynt continuance" (997–98)—and the mind itself is made "al hoole, withouten variance" (999). But the result of this unity is social isolation: typical urban workers "make game and play, / And foorth hir labour passith with gladnesse; / But we laboure in travaillous stilnesse" (1011–13). Hoccleve is describing not only the difference between one kind of labor and others, but the way in which a fully developed bureaucracy like the Privy Seal establishes a specialized division of labor that requires both social isolation and a denaturing segmentation of the individual. While working Hoccleve has, for once, "al his wittes hoole" (1004). But this psychic unity is possible only because unproductive aspects of the self that allow one to be both oneself and to enter into a larger social whole have been obliterated.[63] One might also suggest that at Westminster, as often in the working world of the late Middle Ages, Hoccleve was caught up in what Jacques Le Goff has called "the chronological net" of mechanical time, the temporality of "urban monads" that supplanted the natural time of the countryside.[64] In 1365–67 clocks were installed in the tower at Westminster Palace, and mechanical time-keeping would have contributed to the rule-bound and segmented world of those who labored in the government bureaucracy.[65]

Hoccleve's insistence upon his individual particularity must be in part understood, then, as an effect of the society in which he lived and wrote. In the words of Peter McNiven, the Lancastrians "deliberately followed a course of action designed to offer total certainty in both religious and secular affairs at the price of conformity to a rigorously orthodox and traditional authority."[66] A society that insists upon conformity makes particularity not merely visible but unavoidable. This is especially the case when uniformity is brought about, as in the reign of Henry V, by a carefully fostered cult of personality. For this kind of conformity is paradoxically created by celebrating an individual, a form of nation-building that is almost guaranteed to generate the resistance of other individualities.[67] By detailing the highly specific conditions of his social and financial life,[68] Hoccleve draws attention to *his* individuality, to a selfhood that can be accommodated neither to the bland clichés of advisory rhetoric nor to the homogeneity of deferential loyalty. This is why he insists, in the one well-known moment of this little-read poem, that Chaucer be not merely remembered but that his bodily image be presented to the reader: the "fressh lyflynesse" (4993) of Chaucer that Hoccleve carries in his memory must be reproduced in the "likness" (4995) of a picture drawn on the page. Chaucer is important to Hoccleve less for the virtues and values he represents, and less for the paternal sustenance he may have provided, either in life or death—admirable as they may be—than as an instance of a particular person whose bodily selfhood, with its inimitable appearance and manner, carries a power that surpasses the conventional formulas of praise.[69] Hoccleve, we remember, is someone for whom mental images are particularly compelling. If this is the characteristic that separates him from others, that individualizes him by isolating him within his mind, it is also the characteristic that makes him a poet, that associates him most tangibly with his great original.

III

I turn now to a second explanation for Hoccleve's uncomfortable sense of selfhood. If the conditions of life under the Lancastrians, especially for those enmeshed within its bureaucratic net, explains in part his awareness of his individuality and even peculiarity, one must also take into account his identity as a resident of London.[70] Hoccleve was almost certainly, like so many others, a migrant to the city: his surname suggests he came from the village of Hockliffe in Bedfordshire, located just within the area defined by a forty-mile radius to the north and east from which London drew most of its migrants.[71] Estimates of the population of the city to which he came range from a low of 35,000 to a high of 80,000.[72] But whatever figure turns out to be most likely, the disparity between city and country must have been at least as great in a diminished post-plague London as it was when, around 1300, the city had a pre-plague population of some 100,000. The city to which Hoccleve came was probably less densely crowded than in the past, but it must nevertheless have felt congested to a rural migrant. Certainly the governors of the city were alert to the ease with which disorderly crowds could gather in the narrow streets and squares of the city, and civic ordinances repeatedly and nervously prohibit unauthorized gatherings.[73]

The sense of a densely packed and potentially unruly crowd is present in many of the London writers of the later Middle Ages. When Chaucer, for example, describes the gathering of the audience for Theseus's tournament at Athens in the Knight's Tale, he stresses both the size of the crowd and its density: "Unto the seetes *preesseth* al the *route*" (2580). Whether this description actually reflects his own experience at the 1390 Smithfield tournament outside London is less important than the sense of urban crowding it expresses.[74] A similar sense of concentrated and disorderly humanity is present in the final scenes of the *House of Fame*: among the busy "congregacioun" (2034) of the House of Tydyngs rumors that are "encresing ever moo" pass among it just as a fire spreads "Til al a citee brent up ys"

(2077–80); and when the people rush together to observe the mysterious "man of gret auctoritee" they form a chaotic jumble of humanity—"alle on an hepe" (2149). So too, in the *Tripartite Chronicle* Gower refers to the inhabitants of London as "a multitude of people like the sands of the sea."[75] And in describing a journey to Westminster and London in search of justice, the early fifteenth-century poem "London Lickpenny" describes the "prese" and "gret rout" at the courts, and then the chaos of buying and selling that fills the London streets and that finally drives the narrator back to the country.[76]

Not only would London have been experienced as crowded and noisy, it would also have seemed to a rural immigrant to contain a radically heterogeneous population. As well as migrants like Hoccleve, many of whom must have maintained their old country customs and even dress, there were also large alien communities of Germans, Flemings, and Italians. And London street life would have displayed a far more heterogeneous and more closely contiguous population of rich and poor, exalted and lowly, privileged and disempowered, than would have been found in any single place in the country. David Wallace has described London as embodying not a single value but rather "a discourse of fragments, discontinuities, and contradictions"—a heterogeneity that was an effect not simply of different economic and political interests but of different social and national identities.[77] Finally, of course, London (like Westminster) was the locale par excellence of the money economy. Both "London Lickpenny" and *Piers Plowman* represent the city as a place of endless "chaffering," where all values are rendered equivalent by their reduction to a cash value. In the confession scenes of Passus V of the B-text (V.297–340) Gluttony describes not just a tavern but a London tavern: his companions include Clarice of Cockslane (one of the locales for London prostitutes), "a Rakierre of Chepe" (i.e., a scavenger of Cheapside), and Godfrey of Garlekhithe, another London neighborhood. The interesting thing about this scene is that it focuses on the bartering between Clement the Cobbler and Hikke the Hackneyman over a cloak and a hood. For Langland, and for many others, the central activity of the city is a "chaffering" that reduces all things to a single standard of worth—a standard that is not only arbitrary but also, within the religious context of the Church that Glutton has foregone, worthless. There is perhaps even a sense that the tavern, as the place where this kind of bargaining goes on, is the quintessential locale of the city. In the *Canterbury Tales* the Tabard Inn is where a standard is sought that will render all the tales—and the people who tell them—equivalent.

Density of population, heterogeneity of type, and the dominance of a money economy: these are three of the central elements that constituted life in late medieval London. One of the inevitable effects of such a way of life, as we now know full well, is the erosion of a sense of community and with it a social identity securely grounded in a set of shared values. That this effect was experienced in medieval London is suggested by the way in which external, formal codes—such as gild regulations, city laws like curfews and restrictions on places and kinds of residence, sumptuary laws, and the civic displays that asserted the unity and hierarchy of the urban community—were used to identify and control the independent integers that comprised the city population. Another response was the development of deliberately created communities to provide the intimacy and social support that city life precluded: parish gilds and fraternities are the most visible form of these communities (London had no fewer than 108 parishes), but we should also include such ad hoc arrangements as the so-called, and probably fictional, "Court of Good Company" to which Hoccleve alludes in his balades to Henry Somer.[78] Hoccleve shows himself eager to be submerged within larger, intimate relationships—what in the *Series* he calls "communyng"—yet even here he simultaneously insists on his own conspicuous difference from others.

It may also be that Hoccleve's own specific location in the urban world contributed to his sense of painful isolation and/or proud independence. He worked not in London but in Westminster; he was a member of a bureaucracy not a gild; he was almost certainly not a freeman or citizen of the city (an exclusion that applied to about three-quarters of London's residents); and before his marriage he lived at the Inn of the bishop of Chester, which was located not within the city proper but outside the city walls in the western suburbs. In the 1370s another poet—Langland—had described the individualism of the city dweller in his account of the London waferer Haukyn. For Langland, Haukyn's spiritual failure derived not simply from the fact that he was constantly distracted by city life into activities that precluded a concern for his soul. More important was his assertive individualism: he was "so singuler by hymself" as to constitute what Langland calls "an order by hymselue, / Religion sauȝ rule and resonable obedience."[79] Haukyn wanted to be conspicuous—"to haue a bold name" (289)—and so was a braggart and tale-teller "In towne and in Tauernes" (303). He was, in sum, not unlike the self-description Hoccleve gives in the *Male Regle*: a man filled with self-doubt and a sense of isolation who compensated by a brittle tavern gaiety.

It has been said that Hoccleve is England's first city poet, the comparison being made to Charles Lamb.[80] In John Burrow's words, Hoccleve

> is a poet of *urban* companionship, evoking already something of that distinctive, almost cosy, sense of familiarity which unites those living in the busy 'press' of a great town who actually happen to know each other, either socially or at the office.[81]

But Hoccleve is far more urban than urbane, more alert to the solitude of the man who lives amidst the crowd than to the possibilities for intimacy. If we are looking for his successor in the English literary tradition, we are more likely to find it among the great modernists than the minor Romantics. As a failed effort at personal and social reintegration, the work to which the *Series* demands comparison is not one of Elia's genial essays but the abrasive encounters, formal fragmentation, and unconvincing religiosity of *The Waste Land*. It cannot be coincidental that T. S. Eliot was also a migrant to the city, also a clerk in a large bureaucracy, also spiritually lost in the anonymity of the metropolis. Perhaps the most urban of poets are those to whom the city is most strange.

Appendix to Chapter 4

Beinecke MS 493 and the Survival of Hoccleve's *Series*

Beinecke MS 493 is a modestly sized manuscript (288 x 208 mm) of 134 folios, written on paper except for vellum leaves that encase most of the
ten gatherings. It is written in an ungainly and cramped secretary book
hand of the fifteenth century, dated by Malcolm Parkes to 1450–75.[1] The
manuscript contains three English poems of the fifteenth century, the
period eloquently if now notoriously characterized by Eleanor Hammond
as "an age lacking in enthusiasms and convictions, an age of dull sense-
perceptions and low creative power, that [tended] to the expression of
those didactic and melancholic feelings which the torpid or the conven-
tionalized mind considers 'decorous.'"[2] The first item in the manuscript is
a five-part work by Thomas Hoccleve which Hammond entitled *Series*.
Second is the *Danse of Machabre* by John Lydgate.[3] And the last item is
Hoccleve's other major work, the *Regiment of Princes*. Until very recently
the best that could be said about Hoccleve was that he was, in the words
of the author of the only book about him, "a poet very much a product of

his age."[4] As for Lydgate, he has only recently, and only partially, recovered from the assessment offered by Derek Pearsall in 1970: "the torpor of his mind is stirred [only] when some favourite moral commonplace is threatened."[5]

The manuscript lacks any illumination. It is lightly but intelligently rubricated for the first half, but then rubrication disappears almost entirely except for truncated Latin glosses. From here on the only guidance available to the reader are initials with illuminated champ sprays placed at what are evidently thought to be significant divisions in the text, but many of which are in fact quite random. On the other hand, clear divisions that are marked in other copies of the text are here ignored. With these contents, then, and given its unexciting format, MS 493 is one of the more modest treasures in Yale's Beinecke Rare Book and Manuscript Library. But sometimes even unpromising materials provide an opening into a past whose existence would otherwise remain unsuspected. What follows is an inquiry both preliminary and speculative, despite the fact that paleography rightly privileges the conclusive and mistrusts speculation. This essay will be neither deeply erudite nor prudently cautious, but perhaps these infractions of scholarly decorum will find compensation in its attempt to rescue Beinecke 493 from the category of the mediocre.

The obvious question to ask of the manuscript is one of arrangement: what is a small poem by Lydgate—the *Danse of Machabre* is only 672 lines long, a mere bagatelle for the usually otiose Lydgate—doing between Hoccleve's only two major works?[6] The five parts of the *Series* total over 3700 lines, plus two substantial stretches of prose, while the *Regiment of Princes* is over 5400 lines long. Moreover, it is by no means clear that the two Hoccleve poems would naturally have been grouped together, since one was extremely popular and the other something of an embarrassment. The *Regiment of Princes*, written in 1411–12 for Henry V while he was still Prince of Wales, was one of the most popular works of the fifteenth century, with forty-three extant manuscripts.[7] This figure compares very favorably with the *Canterbury Tales* (57 mss), the three versions of *Piers Plowman* (50 mss), Gower's *Confessio Amantis* (40), Lydgate's *Fall of Princes* (30), and Chaucer's *Troilus and Criseyde* (a mere 16). There were good reasons for the success of Hoccleve's poem: it is written in a plain and unpretentious style, proffers the bromides of the age, and—perhaps as significant—includes encomia to the two heroes of what people living in the increasingly chaotic years of the later fifteenth century remembered as England's golden age. One is Henry V himself, about whom there co-alesced a powerful cult of political nostalgia as the disastrous reign of his son collapsed into civil war. Even the lightly rubricated Beinecke MS is careful to indicate in the margin that it is "Kyng henry þe fyfte" whom the poet is celebrating.[8] The other hero is Chaucer, whom Hoccleve des-ignates as his literary father, and whom the Lancastrians assiduously pro-moted as England's first national poet.[9] Indeed, Hoccleve supervised the patronal manuscripts of the *Regiment,* and made sure that an illumination of Chaucer was included in them. This illumination survives in only three of the manuscripts, with six others mutilated in a way that suggests— rather woundingly—that their owners valued Chaucer's picture more highly than Hoccleve's verse.[10]

But if the *Regiment* was a popular poem, for its associations as much as for its content, the *Series* evidently was not. It survives complete in only five manuscripts and in a fragmentary form in two others. One of the complete versions is in Hoccleve's own hand (Durham Cosin V.iii.9) [D], which contains only the *Series* and is dedicated to Joan Neville, the countess of Westmorland.[11] There also survives another holograph of the fourth of the five parts of the *Series,* the *Lerne to Dye,* in Huntington Li-brary MS 744, fols. 53–68v [H].[12] Apart from these authorial manuscripts, the *Series* survives—as in Beinecke 493—only in conjunction with the *Regiment* and Lydgate's *Danse of Machabre,* as follows: Bodley Arch. Selden supra 53 [S] (*Regiment, Series, Danse of Machabre*), Bodley 221 [B] (*Series, Danse of Machabre, Regiment*), Laud misc. 735 [L] (*Series, Danse of Ma-chabre, Regiment*), Yale Beinecke 493 [Y] (*Series, Danse of Machabre, Regi-ment*), and, missing the *Tale of Jonathas* and the *Tale of Jereslaus's Wife,* and in conjunction with a number of other texts, including several by Chau-cer, in Coventry City Record Office MS Accession 325/1 [C] (*Regiment, Series, Danse of Machabre*).

Even an incomplete collation of the five non-authorial manuscripts shows that the texts of the *Series* in four of these five manuscripts, like the texts of the *Regiment,* are very closely related (C is the partial—but only partial—exception).[13] Selden holds a place of special authority among all five. For one thing, it is by far the earliest of the five, having been written in the 1420s, soon after the composition of the *Series* in 1421–22.[14] Hoc-cleve died in 1426 and Lydgate's *Danse of Machabre* was composed in the same year. This dating places Selden very close to the point of origination of the five manuscripts of which it is the likely progenitor. Furthermore, several of the variants unique to SBLYC point toward the kind of minor tinkering that, as John Bowers has shown, is typical of scribes but is also present in the two versions of *Lerne to Dye* transcribed by Hoccleve himself and might therefore be authorial. Here are several examples from a passage in the *Complaint*:

D	But as soone as it is bicomen drye (272)
SBLYC	But as soone as *that* it bicome is [*or* becommys] drye
D	Rial might and eerthely magestee (274)
SBLYC	Rial might and *all* eerthely magestee
D	The wyse men wel knowen this is sooth (279)
SBLYC	The wyse men wel knowen *that* this is sooth
D	Londe rente cattel gold honour richesse (281)
SBLYC	Londe rente cattell gold honour *and* richesse
D	Þat for a tyme lent been to been ouris (282)
SBLYC	Þat for a tyme *ben lent us* to been ouris

More suggestive of authorial revision are the following instances from *Lerne to Dye*:

DH	More to thee profyte shal be my lore (78)
S	Gretter profite shal be to þe be my loore
BLY	Gretter profite shal to þe be my lore
C	Gretter profite shal be to þe my lore
DH	And now myn ende comth hens mot y go (106)
SBLYC	And now neiȝeth myn ende hens moot y go

These variants, and others like them, show that, at least for the *Series*, SBLYC form a distinct group. As other variants show, and is suggested as well by their identical format, BLY form a subgroup, with C divergent.[15] Furthermore, the many unique variants in the carelessly copied C, and its lack of agreement with D or DH where S diverges, argue that it too descends from S, although either directly or by a different route from BLY. In sum, then, collation argues that S is the likely source of the text of the *Series* in the other four non-authorial manuscripts.

By leading us to this small family of manuscripts, then, Beinecke 493 helps us to see that the circulation of Hoccleve's *Series* was not only limited but crucially dependent on the availability for copying of either S

or—an always possible if, given the dating, unlikely case—a lost progenitor. This lack of popularity is hardly surprising, not because the *Series*
is an uninteresting or unaccomplished text—far from it—but because it
is so very peculiar according to the norms of fifteenth-century taste. The
work consists of five parts. First comes a *Complaint,* an autobiographical
soliloquy in which Hoccleve describes his anguished effort to understand
both the mental illness that afflicted him five years previously and the
social ostracism that has been its continuing effect; then a *Dialogue* with a
Friend about what Hoccleve, as a writer, should now do after his recovery,
either translate a treatise on the art of dying (which is Hoccleve's choice)
or, the Friend's proposal, produce a poem already promised to Humphrey,
duke of Gloucester, the king's youngest brother. Hoccleve resolves the debate by doing both, first producing a poem for Humphrey called the *Tale of
Jereslaus's Wife,* which tells of the sufferings of a noble lady at the hands
of her husband's brother; then translating and versifying part of a treatise originally written by Heinrich Suso and called by Hoccleve *Lerne to
Dye*; and finally, at the Friend's instigation, and apparently superfluously,
adding an unpleasantly misogynist narrative about a deceitful prostitute
and her foolish victim called the *Tale of Jonathas* and dedicated—in the
holograph—to the countess of Westmorland.

This is not the place for a full explication of this remarkable work,
but three examples of its way of proceeding can provide some idea of just
how peculiar the *Series* is. First, in the *Complaint* Hoccleve produces a kind
of autobiography that is not merely rare in medieval literature but merits
the title unique.[16] For instance, he describes how he poses before a mirror in order to fabricate a bearing that will persuade his friends that he
is mentally sound. But all he succeeds in doing is confirming that there is
an unbridgeable gap between what one is and what one is seen to be, between inner self and social role. Put simply, Hoccleve discovers that one
can never *pretend* to be oneself; and both here and throughout the poem
Hoccleve's poignant laments for his social isolation, and for his inability
to make visible the inner self, make of the *Complaint* something very like
a fifteenth-century *Notes from the Underground.*

The two other examples help to explain Hoccleve's predicament as
what he called himself in the *Regiment*: "nobody's man." The *Tale of Jereslaus's Wife,* written for Humphrey, records, among other things, the political and sexual misbehavior of the emperor's brother while "steward"

of the empire in his brother's absence. Since Duke Humphrey was at this very time serving as the king's lieutenant in England while Henry was in France, Hoccleve's narrative has an obvious and stunningly tactless political relevance. Finally, after translating an unexceptionably moralistic section of Suso's work as *Lerne to Dye*, Hoccleve unwisely accepts his friend's advice and adds, as a wholly indigestible supplement, the *Tale of Jonathas*. The tale records the way in which a deceitful woman persuades a naive young man to part with his inheritance, only to get her comeuppance in a particularly barbarous way. The autobiographical themes of the *Complaint*—the betrayal of trust, the impossibility of learning from experience, sin manifested as sickness, confession as the only cure— return in this tale only to be deflected from Hoccleve himself and given a darkly vengeful turn. Moreover, a tale that broods with increasing bitterness upon the wiles of women is then dedicated—amazingly—to "my lady westmerland." This was Joan Neville, the second wife of the powerful Ralph Neville, first earl of Westmorland. Most important, Lady Westmorland had persuaded the earl to strip his eldest son of his inheritance for the benefit of the eldest of *her* sons.[17] How could Hoccleve have thought it appropriate to dedicate this tale, which describes a woman persuading a man to part with his inheritance and then being savagely punished, to this particular woman? Having an even more obvious topical relevance to its dedicatee than even the *Tale of Jereslaus's Wife*, the *Tale of Jonathas* is so offensive that it betrays a mind filled with a mixture of ambition and resentment and pushed finally into a vengeful negativity that could only rebound upon itself.

In sum, the only part of the *Series* that comfortably accords with conventional fifteenth-century taste is the *Lerne to Dye*. If we now return to our original question about the arrangement of the manuscripts in which the *Series* survives—the small family of five that derive from the Selden manuscript, a family that contains our own Beinecke 493—this fact will be crucial. For it is in Selden that we first find Lydgate's *Danse of Machabre* placed directly after the unpalatable *Series*, a position it retains in all five of the other manuscripts.

What do we know of the *Danse of Machabre*? Fortunately, quite a lot. In the Prologue to the poem Lydgate tells us that he translated it from a French original whose text was actually painted, in 1424–25, on the walls of the Cemetery of the Holy Innocents in Paris.[18] In 1426 Lydgate was in

Paris as a member of the retinue of Richard Beauchamp, earl of Warwick, so there is every reason to think that the translation was made then.[19] This brief poem consists of a series of dialogues between Death and members of the various estates, ranging from Pope, Emperor, Cardinal, and King to Friar, Child, Clerk, and Hermit. Far from exhibiting a morbid fascination with death, which from Huizinga onward has been taken as characteristic of the autumnal Middle Ages, this poem—the earliest surviving instance of the genre—focuses instead upon the social and satiric elements of the form.[20] Here Death is the great leveler who mocks worldly pretensions; and the poem aims at undermining one of the most cherished beliefs of medieval Christians, that you can in fact take it with you, that you can use your earthly wealth to procure heavenly benefit, that you can—in Joel Rosenthal's phrase—"purchase paradise."[21]

We also know that in 1430 an important citizen of London, John Carpenter, Clerk of the City from 1417 until 1438, had Lydgate's translation, suitably revised, painted on the walls of the cemetery at St. Paul's Cathedral known as the Pardon Yard, where it remained until the wall was demolished in the sixteenth century. And it appears as though Carpenter's interest generated manuscripts of both versions of Lydgate's poem. Of the fifteen manuscripts of the poem that survive, nine represent Lydgate's initial translation, and six others the revision that became known, according to John Stow, as "the dance of Poules."[22] Of the nine manuscripts of the first version, five are especially closely related: these are the same five manuscripts that contain the two Hoccleve works.

If we now ask why Lydgate's *Danse of Machabre* was added to a collection of Hoccleviana, we can arrive at a plausible answer. Lydgate was the most popular poet of the century, and to judge by extant manuscripts eventually surpassed even Chaucer in readership.[23] But Hoccleve's important work was over by the middle of the 1410s, and by 1426 he was dead, while Lydgate was a semi-official court poet of the Lancastrian regime, already author of a number of large-scale works commissioned by the most powerful men of the realm. On the other hand, to judge by rubrics, Hoccleve's name was not one that carried much weight, and it is likely that most readers did not even know that he was the author of the *Regiment*. For example, although the scribe of Beinecke 493 knew that Hoccleve wrote the poem, at the end of the *Regiment*—which in 493 is also the end of the manuscript as a whole—the scribe identifies the work as the

De regimine principium by Egidius, by whom he means Giles of Rome, the author of one of Hoccleve's sources. In this the scribe follows the usual practice: of the forty-three manuscripts of the *Regiment*, only nine identify Hoccleve as the author.[24] In short, while Lydgate was the major author of the fifteenth century, Hoccleve was obscure and even offensive. By ending the manuscript with Lydgate's *Danse of Machabre*, then, the organizer of the Selden manuscript provided Hoccleve's *Series* with a thoroughly reputable epilogue, and with an authorial name freighted with cultural capital.

Moreover, the Selden manuscript provided its readers with another way in which Hoccleve's most peculiar work could be accommodated to the conventional tastes that Lydgate was so much better at gratifying. At the beginning of the *Lerne to Dye* in Selden there is an accomplished tinted drawing of a skeleton threatening a dying man lying in bed.[25] This is the only illumination in the manuscript, and it serves not only to draw attention to the most conventional part of the *Series* but to link it to the unexceptional Lydgatean text at the end. If one wanted Hoccleve's *Series* to survive, what better way of accomplishing this than to stress the moral probity of the manuscript? The small tail of Lydgate's *Danse of Machabre* can thus help ensure the survival of the large, rather ill-behaved dog of Hoccleve's *Series*.

Who might be interested in performing this charitable act of cultural rescue? My candidate for the savior of Hoccleve's *Series* is that same John Carpenter who was responsible for painting "the dance of Poules" on the cemetery wall in 1430. Carpenter's literary interests were extensive. In 1419, as Clerk of London he had compiled the famous *Liber Albus*, a massive work that included the regulations that governed the administration of the city and an index to the precedents contained in the city's archives. His dealings with Lydgate included not only the revision of the *Danse of Machabre* into the Dance of Paul's but also the provision to the poet of a detailed description, in Latin, of the pageant that welcomed the newly crowned Henry VI to London in 1432, a description from which Lydgate fashioned most of his English poem commemorating the event.[26] Carpenter has also been proposed as the patron of a work called *The Libelle of Englyshe Polycye*, written between 1436 and 1438, which presented in aggressive terms the attitude of the London merchant community toward the government's foreign policy.[27] More to the purpose of our investigation, Carpenter was one of the executors of the will of Mayor Richard Whittington—he of the mythical cat—who died in the spring of 1423. One of the beneficial uses to which Carpenter put Whittington's substantial wealth was to build a library at the Guildhall, a project not specified in Whittington's will but consistent with his wish that his money be used for works of charity.[28] The idea of the library was almost certainly Carpenter's, and when he died himself in 1442 he left a number of books to the same library.[29] As he said in his will,

> if any good or rare books shall be found amongst . . . my goods which . . . may seem necessary to the common library at Guildhall, for the profit of the students there, and those discoursing to the common people, then I will and bequeath that those books be placed by my executors and chained in that library, under such form that the visitors and students thereof may be the sooner admonished to pray for my soul.[30]

By this clause Carpenter sought both to enrich his community's intellectual resources and to benefit his own soul.[31] Did he also, by including among those "good or rare books" a work such as the Selden manuscript—or perhaps even the Selden manuscript itself—perform another act of charity by preserving from oblivion the lifework of a literary friend?

That this question is more than merely a pleasant fantasy is suggested by two facts. One is that Hoccleve and Carpenter were indeed friends. Among Hoccleve's poems is a charming "Balade" addressed to Carpenter. In it Hoccleve laments his debts but refrains from asking Carpenter to pay them off. On the contrary, he rather oddly asks Carpenter to protect him from his creditors—"To be betwixt hem and me swich a mene / As þat I mighte kept be fro duresse" (23–24).[32] In asking that Carpenter protect the impecunious poet from the enforcers employed by fifteenth-century loan sharks, Hoccleve was actually referring to an important moment in London political life. In July 1422 Richard Whittington—no longer mayor but still influential—played a trump card in his long and bitter dispute with the Brewers Guild. At his insistence, the City Council not only fined the Brewers the substantial sum of twenty pounds for overpricing their ale but ordered several of their officers to be imprisoned until the fine was either guaranteed or paid, an unusually harsh action. Yet when the Brewers asked John Carpenter, the Clerk of the City, what they should do, he told them to go home and forget the whole matter, saying that the action against them "was not done at þat tyme bot for to plese Richard Whityngton."[33] In other words, Carpenter stood between the Brewers and the vindictive Whittington as Hoccleve asked him to stand between himself and his creditors. In Carpenter's pragmatic sense of proportion and generosity, and in Hoccleve's willingness to joke with him about a political contretemps that was far from trivial, we can perhaps sense the contours of a friendship that could solace even the lonely Hoccleve. Is it merely sentimental speculation to suggest that Carpenter was the kind of man who would not just protect an impecunious poet from exigent creditors but preserve his idiosyncratic work from the ravages of time?[34]

The second piece of evidence that points toward Carpenter as a donor who might have given a copy of a Hoccleve-Lydgate manuscript to the Guildhall is small but tantalizingly, even exquisitely, suggestive. You will remember that Carpenter's will said that "if any good or rare books shall be found amongst . . . my goods which . . . may seem necessary to the common library at Guildhall" that it should be "placed by my executors and chained in that library." Arch. Selden supra 53 is preserved in a binding of the late fifteenth or early sixteenth century. The binding is undistinguished, but for one thing: it bears upon it the impression of the staple to which a library chain was once attached.[35] I myself cannot resist the pleasant thought that this impression is the sign of a far deeper if less permanent impression, one compounded of literary appreciation and human affection.[36]

Making Identities in Fifteenth-Century England

Henry V and John Lydgate

Courting the Significant Other

The courtship to which the title of this section alludes was recently entered, not for the first time, as a metaphor for academic collaboration by Brian Stock, who rather lamented its pertinence. "There are," he said, "fewer areas of agreement than there might be between empirical historians and students of literature. [We have achieved] neither marriage nor divorce but rather, after the fashion of medieval romance, endless extensions of an increasingly frustrating courtship."[1] Over a hundred years ago Gaston Paris, one of the founders of medieval literary criticism, confidently announced that "we regard the poetic works of the Middle Ages as above all documents of history."[2] Yet after all this time we have apparently made little progress in brokering a permanent and emotionally satisfying relationship, or even a working partnership, between literature and history. Moreover, this extended courtship has recently been made more difficult by the arrival of a mysterious suitor, also from France, who has whispered a seductive message to literary critics quite different from that of Gaston Paris, a suitor who has promised an erotic isolation filled only with words, eliminating the need for contractual relations with the world outside. Historians, for their part, while observing this development with polite curiosity, have continued to believe that Isidore of Seville's definition of history as *narratio rei gestae* is more helpful than Derrida's dictum that "il n'y a pas de hors-texte."[3] While acknowledging that history is constructed rather than found, they have largely set aside metaphysical doubt in favor of practical tasks. Contemporary historiography, and especially that of the Middle Ages, operates for the most part within what Dominick LaCapra has called "a 'documentary' or 'objectivist' model of knowledge": it relies upon an archive of "informational documents" whose value is taken to be primarily factual or referential, it practices an objectivist method that sees subjectivity not as the necessary condition of understanding but as a dangerous contaminant, and it operates within a system of periodization that seems often to predetermine what a text can and cannot mean.[4] Since the texts of interest to literary critics are typically constructed within an intricate rhetorical system that makes them unproductive of hard data, and since their interpretation manifestly precludes verifiability, they rarely figure in historical accounts of the period. Indeed, historians of late medieval England seem rarely even to read the work of literary critics.[5]

On their side, literary critics have done little to persuade their historian colleagues that their analyses can provide fresh access to the realities of the medieval past. Not that there are not many literary critics who are concerned with historical contextualization.[6] But for the most part this kind of work proceeds with little attention to recent poststructuralist thought, as if the linguistic turn taken by cultural studies had obviously led up a blind alley. On the other hand, critics who do apply contemporary theory to medieval texts tend to operate under the sign of Ezra Pound's modernist dictum to "make it new." Concerned to claim for medieval literary studies a currency usually denied it, they deploy the often esoteric — and often counterintuitive — discourse of the literary criticism *du jour*. Moreover, and more important, the programs that drive these studies tend to preclude specifically historical insights. For the very medievalness of the text under scrutiny — in effect, its historicity — is the embarrassment these theoretically *au courant* readings seek to redeem. And since this historicity is a function of the social realities of the medieval world, they tend to disappear as well.[7]

Hence what we almost entirely lack is work that can show that historical understanding can actually be enabled rather than avoided by poststructuralist thought, that the enterprise of poststructuralism, and particularly the deconstruction that is its fundamental element, can be more than a local fashion, more than a seductive exaggeration of the procedural caveats and natural skepticism we have always already employed. In sum, I will argue that this exotic French import can reveal for us not just what makes the medieval past like the modern present but what makes it different as well; that it can elucidate social practice as well as literary form; and that it can be an agency not to divide but to bring together historians and literary critics.

To claim for deconstruction a capacity for *historical* analysis will seem quixotic to many. It has become customary to describe deconstruction as, in Terry Eagleton's words, "a hedonist withdrawal from history, a cult of ambiguity or irresponsible anarchism."[8] Since the deconstructionist is thought to wallow in a timeless aporia of pure textuality, any access to either history or historiography must be foreclosed.[9] Yet in fact deconstruction, at least in conception if perhaps too rarely in enactment, is nothing if not a historicism. Its central insight is that Western philosophic thought, and the social practices it credentials, bases itself upon an order of meaning conceived as primary, transcendental, and beyond history—an origin from which all other, merely historical instances are derived. As Derrida says, logocentrism is the belief in an origin or priority that is seen as "simple, intact, normal, pure, standard, self-identical, in order *then* to conceive of derivation, complication, deterioration, accident, etc."[10] But the process actually works the other way around: the logos is not given but derived, "a determination and effect within a system that is no longer that of presence but of differance."[11] However the deconstructive program may be enacted in individual instances, its fundamental insight is a challenge to idealism, essentialism, and transcendentalism—to all those metaphysical gestures by which Western thought has sought to avoid the historical, the material, and the social.

In this sense, then, in its relentless unmasking of transcendental value as historically contingent and historically constructed, deconstruction should be considered as part of the Enlightenment project of modernity rather than as either an offshoot of Nietzschean irrationalism or as a cynical, *fin-de-siècle* postmodernism.[12] And many of the critical practices to which it has given rise have in fact proven to be genuinely liberatory. In demystifying the theology of the origin, deconstruction has shown that identity is relational rather than essential: just as for Saussure language is a system of differences without positive terms, so for deconstruction metaphysical thinking and social practice are not founded upon an essential being but organized according to a set of binary oppositions — thought and language, God and history, essence and existence, the individual and society, ego and id, male and female, white and black, straight and gay, and so on. What deconstruction seeks to unmask are the suppressions and elisions — the ideological constraints — that make possible these polarities. Its characteristic strategy is to show that each element, far from being either coherent in itself or independent of its designated other, harbors within itself an unacknowledged affinity with its opposite. Identity includes difference, difference masks identity: just as nothing is ever fully identical with itself, neither is it wholly different from the binary opposite in relation to which its identity is established.

Thus deconstruction, far from either denying the reality of history or its availability to knowledge, is a critical practice that seeks to understand how "reality" is put into place. When Derrida notoriously says that "there is nothing outside the text," he is restating in a deliberately provocative way the position actually held by many sociocultural historians, that reality is culturally or discursively produced, that — in Jonathan Culler's words — "the realities with which politics is concerned, and the forms in which they are manipulated, are inseparable from discursive structures and systems of signification."[13] While such a program *could* lead to the neglect of the social, economic, and political institutions by which power is enforced, it need not; and while it *could* lead us to submerge agency into structure, nothing requires that it do so. Indeed, if we locate deconstruction within historiographical practice rather than in opposition to it, then it can be seen as a style of analysis that can help us to understand the production of cultural meanings.

The particular object of analysis in this essay is the making of identities in late medieval England, specifically the monarchial identity of Henry V and the poetic identity of John Lydgate. The oddly equivocal term "identity" refers in the first instance to social identity, those distinctive characteristics that allowed Henry V and Lydgate to meet the definition of monarch and poet, a process that involved as well larger contemporary identities, especially the English national identity so much in the process of formation at this time. A second object of attention is the way in which disparate elements, personal as well as political, were consolidated to form a unity or identity of character and of interest. In this sense identity is the result of a process of making identical—by imposing direction and overcoming division, correcting waywardness and suppressing dissent. Finally, this essay proceeds on the assumption that this kind of analysis, far from being anachronistic, accords with (although it can hardly replicate) medieval habits of thought. Or, more precisely, and less modestly, I mean to suggest that bringing deconstruction so explicitly into the arena of medieval studies can benefit both parties. Deconstruction and the poststructuralist formations that have followed from it may become more conscious of their own historical origins, and medieval studies, as a working practice, more alert to its affiliations with other contemporary ways of thinking. If medieval culture did not invent the binarism of identity and difference, it reinvented it in spades, so much so that the Middle Ages is often defined by nonmedievalists in terms that imply identity and deny difference. Conformity, fixity, and obedience are assumed to be everywhere; diversity, mobility, and skepticism are less easily found. Indeed, part of my argument is that in early fifteenth-century England the language of identity and difference provided both Henry V and John Lydgate with sanctioned symbolic meanings that could be used in the service of political and literary stabilization. Yet I wish also to suggest that the intensity with which this language was deployed was a symptom of anxiety rather than certainty, both a reflexive dependence on old modes of persuasion and a doubt about their effectiveness. I wish to suggest, in other words, that the awareness that binarism is constructed rather than simply given is not unique to modern much less postmodern thought, that even a so-called premodern or traditional culture like the Middle Ages could recognize—albeit hesitantly and reluctantly—its own self-constructions for what they were.

I have chosen to discuss these two men in order to bring within the same interpretive practice a historical figure whose career epitomizes everything history has privileged—*res gestae* not only done in the public arena but done with consummate success—and a writer who all his life

remained an observer. But the two men nonetheless had extensive dealings with each other: Henry seems to have known Lydgate throughout
most of his adult life, and Lydgate produced a number of important poems
at the king's request, especially the massive *Troy Book*, begun in 1412 but
not completed until 1420. The object of my attention here is the *Siege
of Thebes*, an ambitious poem written in 1421–22, and although not the
product of an actual commission nonetheless attentive to the king's success in France. Finally, Henry and Lydgate have always been considered
typically, even reassuringly medieval. Certainly Henry was acutely conscious of traditional values and practices, and modern historians have
seen him as a man who made the medieval monarchy work.[14] Indeed,
the subtitle of the first twentieth-century biography of Henry—Charles
Lethbridge Kingsford's *Henry V: The Typical Mediaeval Hero* (1901)—
accurately sums up, in its admiration as in its assertion of representative-
ness, the modern consensus.[15] So too, some rather irresolute efforts to define Lydgate as an early humanist and as therefore proto-modern have been
subsequently, and persuasively, rejected, especially by Derek Pearsall, whose
Lydgate is a thoroughly conventional poet who "medievalizes" every potentially progressive bit of material that comes his way, and especially the
poetry of his great predecessor, Chaucer.[16] These opinions are, I believe,
essentially correct. But what might be questioned is their unspoken assumption that both Henry and Lydgate were somehow *unproblematically*
medieval, that they lived their medievalness naturally and without self-
consciousness. For if identity is never given but instead made through a
double process of inclusion and exclusion, then we should be alert to the
discursive materials and political and poetic strategies by which Henry V
and Lydgate constructed themselves. And in this investigation we can
perhaps also understand the larger cultural imperatives that encouraged
these two men to adopt identities that were not simply traditional but
traditionalistic, identities that were conspicuously and even deliberately
"typically medieval."[17]

Siege of Thebes: Identifying the Monk of Bury

Born about 1370, Lydgate began writing poetry in the first decade of the
fifteenth century, and for fifteen years or so his career followed a double
path. On the one hand, he produced an extensive body of court poetry

whose primary effect was to affirm the supremacy and stability of the noble class, poetry such as "The Complaint of the Black Knight" (1402–3?) and "The Temple of Glass" (1404?). A poetry of private amorousness set in an ideal landscape protected from the winds of history, the elegant figuration and extravagant emotions of this writing endorse the social superiority of its protagonists. And the *maker* responsible for its production presents himself as simply a transparent vehicle for the articulation of these values, a loyal subordinate whose craftsmanship allows him to deploy the cultic language of courtliness without taking part in its practices— an exclusion all the more pronounced when the poet is, as here, a monk.

On the other hand, and at the same time, Lydgate was commissioned by Henry to produce the massive *Troy Book* (1412–20) and, in all likelihood, the similarly monumental *Life of Our Lady* (1409–11?). Here he functions not as courtly *maker* but as a writer of weighty texts whose very existence witness to the monarch's historical legitimacy and spiritual seriousness. Moreover, in writing the *Troy Book* Lydgate provides Henry not just with a history—the genre most fully associated with monastic literary production—but with an authoritative version of the Trojan history that had, at least since the time of Henry II, served to support the monarchial legitimacy of insecure English kings.[18] For in representing Henry as the patron of what was taken to be the founding moment of English history, Lydgate was both affirming Henry's proprietorship over the national culture and, in invoking the concept of *translatio imperii*, asserting the principle of genealogical transmission that underwrote medieval political legitimation. In these texts, then, Lydgate functioned not as the dutiful purveyor of the discourse of a class from which he was by definition excluded but as a monk providing his sovereign with the monastically generated materials needed to sustain royal authority—a function also performed by other Benedictines such as Thomas Elmham and Thomas Walsingham.[19]

In the uncommissioned *Siege of Thebes*, a poem begun in the spring of 1421 and completed before Henry's death on August 31, 1422, Lydgate took it upon himself both to exemplify and to promote his role as the monastic supporter of Lancastrian rule, as worthy of becoming, as he did, "poet-propagandist to the Lancastrian dynasty."[20] The *Siege* promotes this poetic vocation in a number of ways. For one thing, as commentators have long noted, the text serves as a rudimentary *mirour de prince*: not only is each of the male characters carefully located on a scale of chivalric and regal virtue, but Lydgate provides explicit and straightforward directions on virtuous governance.[21] His twofold message is that peace is preferable to war and, a topic relentlessly repeated, *trouthe* is preferable to duplicity or *doublenesse*. In part this topic is political: the sorry history of Polynices and Ethiocles teaches us to treasure unity and avoid the "Cokkyl of envye and debat" sown by "the olde Serpent" (4663, 4668–69).[22] And in part it is ethical: the cause of the war is the "doublenesse of Ethiocles" (1778), who—having "lefte trouthe" (1783) and become "false and double of entent" (2068)—refused to honor the agreement with Polynices that they should rule Thebes in alternate years. Consequently a ruler should be "pleyn and hool as a Centre stable" (1724) and should avoid "eny doublenesse, / Variaunce or vnsicrenesse, / Chaunge of word or mutabilite" (1747–49). These oft-repeated injunctions are then drawn together at the end, and given contemporary point, through a citation from the Treaty of Troyes (4698–4703), the accord signed in May 1420 by Henry and Charles VI that designated Henry as Charles's heir and "reunited" the crowns of France and England. While Lydgate's point at its simplest is that war can be avoided only if solemn agreements are honored, it draws on the larger metaphysical assumption that the opposition of "trouthe and resoun" to "falshed and tresoun" (2639–40) is built into the structure of reality. On the one hand, argues the poem, are integrity, simplicity, consistency, and self-identity; on the other duplicity, complexity, variability, and self-contradiction.

The *Siege of Thebes* presents itself, moreover, not just as articulating but as itself exemplifying this absolutist opposition. Claiming that its promotion of *trouthe* over *doublenesse* is its "sentence hool, withoute variance" (54), the poem presents itself as an instance of perfect self-identity. As Lois Ebin has shown, throughout his career Lydgate promoted a remarkably crude semiotics.[23] For him the poet is a verbal craftsman whose "rethorik" "adournes" or "enlumynes" or "enbelissches" or "aureates" received truths in order to illuminate in turn the mind of the reader. According to this model, the form-content dilemma that rhetoric had always posed is no dilemma at all, and neither is the transmission of truth over time. The poet reads the truth out of one text, incorporates it into another, and passes it on to an audience that receives it clearly and completely—the "sentence hool, withoute variance." Although drawn from the unexamined clichés of medieval literary theorizing, this simplistically didactic poetics ignored all those complexities of interpretation and figuration that me-dieval hermeneutics and rhetorical theory had in fact treated with great sophistication.

In the *Siege* Lydgate provides two demonstrations of this kind of "el-loquence." One is in the narrative itself, where he presents examples of the poet as civic authority, first in his account of the founding of the city by the harpist Amphion, then in the representation of the prophet Am-phiaraus (or Amphiorax, as Lydgate calls him).[24] Lydgate mentions only to set aside the darker version of the Theban founding by Cadmus and his dragon warriors—a founding myth that his sources use to establish the pattern of fratricidal violence and fatal recursion that will come to con-trol Theban history—in favor of a model of Ciceronian eloquence. Am-phion's raising of the walls by his music and his subsequent exile of Cad-mus become for Lydgate a figure for the power of Mercury over Mars, and demonstrates the importance of eloquence in the provision of good gover-nance.[25] Similarly, the prophet and priest Amphiorax functions in his nar-rative as the voice of prudent restraint, and we are clearly meant to see the disaster as caused at least in part by the Argives' refusal to attend: "for al his elloquence / He had in soth but lytyl audience" (3811–12).

Lydgate's other demonstration of his poetics, of far greater complexity, resides in his appropriation of Chaucer's *Canterbury Tales.* By presenting the *Siege* as a tale told by Lydgate the pilgrim as the first tale on the *return* journey from Canterbury, Lydgate the poet deals with the anxiety of influ-ence by literally joining the Chaucerian project. But in fact, while repre-senting himself as a Chaucerian, Lydgate misrepresents Chaucer's poem. By positing a return trip Lydgate ignores Chaucer's final understanding of his pilgrimage as unidirectional and, at the end, presided over by the Parson. Instead he reinstates the Host's discredited festive model of a cir-cular movement centered upon the Tabard Inn. Not only is the displace-ment of the Host by the Parson that Chaucer had engineered in the Par-son's Prologue here undone, but this Host is a petty tyrant—"ful of wynde and bost" (80)—interested only in mirth. "Thow shalt be mery who so þat sey nay," he threatens Lydgate and demands that he

> leyn a-side thy professioun.
> Thow shalt not chese nor þi-self withdrawe,
> ȝif eny myrth be founden in thy mawe,

Lyk the custom of this Compenye;
For non so proude that dar me denye,
Knyght nor knaue, Chanon, prest, ne nonne,
To telle a tale pleynly as thei konne,
Whan I assigne and se tyme opportune.

(132–39)

Unlike Chaucer's Host, whose treatment of the pilgrims varied from jocular familiarity to gallantry and even obsequiousness, Lydgate's Host is simply overbearing; and whereas Chaucer's Host admired sententiousness as well as jollity, and bowed at the end to the Parson's authority, Lydgate's version demands a universal mirth: "Telle vs some thyng that draweþ to effecte / Only of Ioye!" (170–71).[26]

This reduction of an original complexity to uniformity is perhaps what we should expect when Lydgate "medievalizes" a pre-text. But this transformation is not a reflexive conservatism but part of a strategy of self-representation and identity formation. For Lydgate simplifies the *Canterbury Tales* in order to provide a context in which his own monastic integrity—his seriousness as the noble rhetor poet—will be most visible. Chaucer's multivalent *Tales* are reduced to a uniform frivolity in order to provide a foil for Lydgate's seriousness: it is his difference from Chaucer that establishes Lydgate's identity. By misrepresenting the *Canterbury Tales* as a mere *divertissement,* Lydgate legitimizes his own weighty history. This process of self-definition through difference is implicit as well in the tale he now tells. For whereas Chaucer began his outward journey with the Knight's Tale, a thematically complex and skeptical rewriting of the Theban legend, Lydgate begins the return journey with a historiographically traditional and thematically unambiguous version of the same material: "the sentence hool, withoute variance." He will, moreover, tell this story of origins from its beginning, providing a prequel to the Knight's Tale.[27] Chaucer's Knight had merely gestured toward the full Theban story, while Chaucer himself—in *Anelida and Arcite* and the "Complaint of Mars"—provocatively entangled Theban history with erotic supplements. Now Lydgate, fulfilling his monastic responsibility by carefully following "myn Autour" (3972) throughout, will restore the history to both narrative wholeness and thematic clarity.[28]

An analysis of the *Siege of Thebes* in terms of identity and difference thus reveals a clear pattern. For one thing, Lydgate here constructs his own identity as pious monk and advisor to the sovereign, in part through his self-representation within the *Siege* itself, in part by claiming a traditional monastic integrity in historiographical matters, in part by asserting his literary difference from Chaucer.[29] For another, he relies upon what can aptly be termed a poetics of identity: we are assured that his representation of the literal and moral truth of Theban history coincides at every level with its "real" or original meaning, a meaning whose self-evidence his carefully crafted language enforces rather than complicates. Meanwhile, the lesson Theban history teaches is itself about identity versus difference, about integrity and unity (*trouthe*) versus duplicity and division (*doublenesse*). And finally, as the citation of the Treaty of Troyes implies, the poem affirms an identity of interest between poet and sovereign: working together, they can achieve the "Pees and quyet, concord and vnyte" (4703) that is the goal of good government. This is, at any rate, the straightforward program that the poem proposes, although, as we shall see at the end of this essay, its enactment reveals a complexity of motive, and a resistance to power, that is interestingly un-Lydgatean.

The Making of a Monarch

When Henry V became king of England on March 21, 1413, Lancastrian sovereignty faced fundamental problems. For one thing, the constitutionality of Henry's position was far from certain. Not only was he the son of a usurper, but for about eighteen months, during 1410–12, he had himself been in implicit and at times virtually open rebellion against his father. There was also grave concern about the capacity of the Lancastrian regime to govern, for it seemed to have done little to solve the problems that had brought Richard's monarchy into disrepute. Law and order were inadequately enforced, the king's household was hardly less bloated and overbearing than under Richard, and Henry IV himself had been preoccupied with physical illness and spiritual apprehension.[30] Not surprisingly, then, Henry V was threatened within less than a year of his accession with the serious rebellion led by his old companion in arms, Sir John Oldcastle, and then, on the eve of what would become the Agincourt campaign, with the Southampton plot hatched from within his own court. Clearly the legitimacy of his authority was far from universally or even widely acknowledged, and when his ambassadors laid claim to the crown of France, the predictable French reply was that he had no right even to the crown of England.

In seven years Henry succeeded brilliantly in overcoming these and other disabilities, establishing himself not just as the legitimate king of both England and France but as the embodiment of the English nation as a whole. The narrative of this triumph is well known, and historians have explicated in important detail its administrative, political, diplomatic, and military aspects. But what has not been described is Henry's own self-construction as a monarch within the discursive field of early fifteenth-century England. Both in image and in practice Henry's kingship defined itself in terms of the contemporary language of public virtue, the same language that Lydgate deployed so skillfully in the *Siege of Thebes*.

The major theme of contemporary writings concerned with the public or communal interest—and few texts do not express such an interest—is the advocacy of unity or concord against the fear of division or disunity. The poet of MS Digby 102—so well informed about public opinion that he may even have been a member of Parliament—welcomed Henry's accession in 1413 by praying that "Among oure-self, god send vs pes" since "ȝif ȝiþt be raysed, / Þan stroye we oure awen nest."[31] For him the royal crown symbolized national unity: "What doþ a kynges crownes signyfye, / Whan stones & floures on sercles is bent? / Lordis, comouns, & clergye / To ben all at on assent" (lines 9–12). And when in 1414 he urged Henry to make "pes wiþ-ynne," to bring together "All ȝoure reme in vnyte," he was actually echoing the speech given by the Chancellor, Bishop Henry Beaufort, at the opening of the Leicester Parliament.[32] Similarly, a macaronic sermon delivered after the death of Oldcastle in 1417 stresses above all the need to reunify the kingdom: "Nostrum regnum quod est unum corpus" is the preacher's theme, and he celebrates the reign of Edward III when "clerus and þe laife huius terre wer knet to gedur in uno fagot and brenden super istum ignem"—with, that is, the fire of perfect charity.[33] In his poem commemorating Henry's reinterment of the body of Richard II in Westminster Abbey in 1413—itself a significant affirmation of continuity and hereditary legitimacy—Hoccleve recalled that "this land wont was for to be / Of sad byleeue & constant vnion" and begged Henry to return it to its former integrity.[34]

Not surprisingly, the king's enemies were seen as both agents of division and as themselves self-divided. Lord Scrope, a member of the Southampton conspiracy, was described by the loyal monk John Capgrave as a typical double-dealer: "Sobir was the man in word and chere; and undir that ypocrisie had he a ful venemous hert."[35] And for the *Brut* all the Southampton plotters were motivated by duplicity, by "fals couetyse and treson."[36] Oldcastle and the Lollards were the most obvious targets for invective since, as Hoccleve (among many others) put it, they were attacking "the vnitee / Of Holy Chirch."[37] God is "feith right, trouthe, & al bountee" (184), he says, a source of integrity who, as he put it in another poem, will both keep Henry "in feithful vnitee" and smite the Lollards, who have introduced difference where there should be identity: "Dampnable fro feith were variance!"[38] In the *Brut* the word "false" rings like a chime throughout the description of Oldcastle and Lollardy: they are "fals heritikis" who pursue "fals treson, to haue slayn þe King," a "fals purpos," a "fals ordinaunce & worchyng," a "fals purpos & ordinaunce."[39] Contemporaries understood the Lollards as false or duplicitous because they were incomprehensible as people who were sincere, who truly believed different articles of faith: since doctrinal difference was a denial of the God who is, in Hoccleve's words in the *Regiment of Princes* (written for Henry in 1412–14), both "þe auctour of trouthe" and "trouthe itself" (2393, 2411), it was a perversity possible only to the self-divided or self-deluded. Hence the contemporary chronicler John Strecche described Oldcastle as a "fictus hereticus," since a "true heretic" was a contradiction in terms; and a brief alliterative poem of 1415 presents the Lollards—despite a ferocious sincerity all too evident in their texts—as "gylers" who "Momelyn with here mouthes moche and malys in hert, / And of a mys menyng maketh a faire tale, / Vnder flateryng and fair speche falsehede foloweth."[40] Indeed Lydgate himself, in a poem written in 1413–14 and addressed to Henry, warned that the religiously heterodox are also politically unreliable: "He may dissymule with a feynyd hewe, / But take good heede."[41]

We can see from these examples how the complexities of contemporary politics were cast into the moral and metaphysical language of unity and division, identity and difference. What is perhaps surprising, however, is that this same language was applied to the central event of Henry's reign—the war with France—and applied across an extraordinary range of detail. The war was typically described not as the conquest of a foreign nation but as the recovery of the king's inheritance, not as a confrontation with the other but as reunion with part of oneself. When Henry invaded Normandy in 1415, according to a contemporary panegyric, the

Gesta Henrici Quinti, he was simply seeking to recover that "which belongs to him entirely by right dating from the time of William the first, the Conqueror, even though now, as for a long time past, it is thus withheld, against God and all justice, by the violence of the French (*violentia Gallorum*)."[42] And when he conquered Normandy, he emphasized the legitimacy of his sovereignty both by presenting himself as William's rightful successor as Duke of Normandy—he wore the ducal robes in Rouen in 1419—and by returning the duchy "aux Usages et Coustumes qui estoyent en nostre dit Paiis au temps de noz Predecesseurs," usages and customs that predated the French seizure.[43] Nor was Henry's sense of recovering that which was already his restricted to Normandy: the major theme of royal propaganda—which includes not just the *Gesta* but parliamentary and other pronouncements—was that justice required Henry to reclaim the dynastic rights that had belonged to the English royal line (with which Henry was thus firmly associating himself) since at least the reign of Edward I.[44] And Henry took care to compile and to circulate dossiers of historical documents that supported his case, an example of what one historian has called his "romantic legalism."[45]

Since Henry already possessed France *de jure* if not *de facto,* the war was to be understood not as a struggle between two separate nations but as the rebellion of a disloyal people against its rightful sovereign. It was, in effect, a civil war: the *Gesta* called it an internal battle (*prelium intestinum*) in which fraternal blood (*fraternus sanguis*) was being shed. The goal of Henry's invasion was to be understood as the restoration of England and France to an original unity: "Would that the French nation might soon attain to peace and unity [*ad pacem et unitatem*] with the English," disingenuously lamented the *Gesta.*[46] Nor was it simply official texts like the *Gesta* that purveyed this view: according to the chronicler John Hardyng, the purpose of Henry's wars was to "make an vnyon / Betwyx Englonde and Fraunce" (744), while in the *Troy Book* Lydgate said that the war was undertaken so that "Yngeland and Fraunce / May be al oon, withoute variaunce."[47] Indeed, as early as 1411, in the *Regiment of Princes,* Hoccleve had claimed that since God deplores "þe hateful discorde" (5315) between France and England, Henry should "Purcheseth pees by wey of mariage" (5403): "By matrimoigne pees and vnite / Ben had" (5394–95).[48]

Contemporaries well knew that what made France vulnerable to English schemes was its own internal division, strife lamented by French writers from Christine de Pizan to Alain Chartier.[49] Far from gloating over the fratricidal self-destruction of the enemy, however, an English poet like Hoccleve saw it as an unnatural condition—an "vnkyndly disseueraunce" (5310)—that bespoke a suicidal lack of integrity: "Thi self manaseth þi self for to dye," he says to the French nation, "Thi self destroye, and feble is þi victorye! / Thow hast in þi self stryven oft" (5292–94). Consequently, the Treaty of Troyes was seen as an act of unification. Undertaken "for the peaceful reintegration of the kingdoms of France and England" (*pro Franciae & Angliae Regnorum reintegranda pace*), it made the crowns of France and England—if not the nations themselves—one. According to the English version of the treaty,

> both the Crounes, that is to sey of France and of England, [shall] perpetuelly be togedyr, and be in Oone and in the same Persone, . . . and . . . both Roialme[s] shull be Governed from that tyme, that We [i.e., Charles VI] or ony of oure Heires [i.e., Henry V and his descendents] come to the same, not severally, under divers Kynges in oone tyme, but undir oone and the same Persone, the whiche for the tyme shall be Kyng of either Roialme and Soverayn Lord.[50]

As a definitive sign that this unity was not forced but natural, not a novelty but a reclamation, the language of the treaty referred to the principals in familial terms: Henry was for Charles "nostre cher fils" and he and Queen Isabelle loved him "comme pere & mere" (896). As for Charles's legitimate son, the dauphin, who had murdered John of Burgundy at Montereau the previous fall, he was mentioned in the treaty only to be excluded from the family unit as a treacherous and deceitful interloper.[51] With the replacement of the dauphin by Henry, then, the French royal family, and by implication the French nation, had been restored to moral integrity and domestic unity.

If we are to grasp how thoroughly the discourse of difference and identity structured contemporary thinking, we must also attend to the language by which national identities were being constructed in the latter half of the Hundred Years War.[52] Beginning in earnest with Henry's 1415 invasion, the governing classes of both England and France, concerned to transform a dynastic quarrel into a national campaign, took pains to generate a sense of national feeling by appealing to a fear and dislike of the opponent.[53] On the English side, French difference—the difference, that is, that set the French apart from both the English and from themselves—was understood as duplicity and double-dealing. The overriding theme of English war propaganda was what the *Gesta* called *Gallicana duplicitas,* what another text called *duplicitas Francorum* and *fraude Francorum.*[54] As early as the 1340s the English had contrasted "their own reasonableness, innocence, and even naiveté [to] the 'foxy cunning' and 'treachery' of the French," who pretended one thing only to do another *(unum agens et aliud simulans).*[55] For the vernacular chroniclers of Henry's reign the French were "dobil," full of "fraude and sotilte," practiced in "ymaginacionys, congettis and sleythis."[56] English writers often complained about the deceit even of their allies, the Burgundians: the "fals flemynges . . . loved vs neuer 3it, by the roode, / ffor alle here fals flateryng fare," complains one poet bitterly, and another blamed John of Burgundy's murder on his own foolish manipulations as much as on the treachery of the dauphin.[57] So when Philip of Burgundy abandoned the English at the Congress of Arras in 1435, Lydgate berated him in a language of French duplicity versus English integrity that was by now highly traditional: the English ambassadors had sought "of hool affeccioun . . . to haue concluded a parfyt vnyoun" but were thwarted by (of course) Philip's "doblynesse."[58]

This distinction between the frank, wholehearted English and the devious, guileful French—a distinction still to be found in English national self-identification[59]—extends even to contemporary characterizations of the two languages. This linguistic issue is especially telling, for it shows how profoundly politicized the discourse of identity became, and provides an analogue at the level of national policy for Lydgate's reductive poetics. In his *Treatise on the Astrolabe,* written "in my lihte Englissh" about 1392, Chaucer had said that "the King [is] lord . . . of this langage," although Richard II may in fact have preferred French. But it was the Lancastrians, and especially Henry V, who adopted a "policy," in John Fisher's words, "of encouraging the development of English as a national language." Beginning perhaps as early as 1415 but certainly by the time of his second invasion of France in 1417, Henry worked to make English "an official language of central administration"—and with such personal direction that the bureaucratic vernacular promoted by his Chancery was actually modeled on the king's personal style (the King's English indeed!).[60]

Lydgate was naturally hypersensitive to this royal policy, and in dedicating the *Troy Book* to Henry he says it was written "For to obeie with-oute variaunce / My lordes byddyng" (73–74), including Henry's command that it be written "in englysche" (106):

> By-cause he wolde that to hyȝe and lowe
> The noble story openly wer knowe
> In oure tonge, aboute in euery age,
> And y-writen as wel in oure langage
> As in latyn and in frensche it is;
> That of the story þe trouthe we nat mys
> No more than doth eche other nacioun.
>
> (111–17)

The *Troy Book* is thus conceived as a work of national history (a "noble story") whose "trouthe" would submerge class differences ("hyȝe and lowe") within an overarching sense of a national identity equivalent to those of "eche other nacioun."

What accompanied this state-generated linguistic nationalism was a distinction between the French and English languages on the same moral and metaphysical grounds that were used to distinguish the nations as a whole. When the Brewers decided to keep their guild records in English, they explained (in Latin) that they had done so because

> our mother-tongue, to wit the English tongue, hath in modern days begun to be honourably enlarged and adorned, for that our most excellent lord, King Henry V, hath in his letters missive and divers touching his own person [*personam suam propriam*], more willingly chosen to declare the secrets of his will [*secreta sue voluntatis*], and for the better understanding of his people, hath with a diligent mind procured the common idiom (setting aside others) to be commended by the exercise of writing.[61]

The *materna lingua* is evidently the natural medium for speaking about oneself and revealing the secrets of the will—for expressing, that is, one's essential selfhood: it is as distinctively and reliably indicative of a man's identity as his mother. Correspondingly, French was thought to be both foreign and capricious, both different from English and meretricious in itself.[62] This distinction was at no time more urgent to the English than when they negotiated with their enemy—since, as one of Henry's captains said, "Certes all the ambassadors that we deal with be incongrue, that is to say in old manner of speech in English, 'they be double and false.' "[63] A striking example are the negotiations of John of Gaunt and Richard, duke of York, with Philip of Burgundy and Jean, duc de Berri, in 1394. According to Froissart, the Englishmen had a difficult time of it, "car en parlure françoise a mots soubtils et couvers et sur double entendement" while they "ne le veulent entendre que plainement"; in Lord Berners's early sixteenth-century translation, "the Frenchemen . . . were full of subtyle wordes, and cloked perswacions and double of understandynge," a verbal subtlety "which Englysshemen use nat in their langage, for their speche and entent is playne."[64] In order to protect themselves from the devious French these plainspoken Englishmen submitted "aucune parlure obscure et dure ou pesant" to the scrutiny of their learned clerks, who would make sure that it was "examinée et visitée et mise au cler." Froissart goes on to say that the English excused this suspiciousness by saying that since they had not learned French in childhood, they were not of the same "nature et condition" as the Frenchmen. What might they have meant by this elliptical phrase is suggested by Lord Berners's significantly expanded translation of these three words: "And the Englysshmen to excuse themselfe, wolde say, that Frenchemen lernynge suche subtlties in their youth, muste nedes be more subtyle than they"—a passage that shows Lord Berners preserving his self-image as a plain speaker by employing the verbal manipulations he is censuring in his Gallic opponents.

Linguistic self-images again became a matter of diplomatic policy in December 1418, when, with the help of the papal legate Cardinal Orsini, Henry V sought to establish the terms of negotiation with the French. Henry complained to Orsini that although the French wanted to conduct business in French, he preferred Latin, which is *indifferens omni Natione*.[65] When the French demurred, Henry continued to insist that all business be conducted "in a language which I can speak, understand, and write, that is, English or Latin"—certainly a disingenuous requirement from a man who for the first decade of his public life had conducted his correspondence and official business in French. The impasse was resolved by Orsini's proposal that all documents should be kept in French and Latin, and that in cases of disagreement the Latin version should be authoritative. But that more than diplomatic jockeying was at issue here is suggested both by Henry's insistence—which implies a real anxiety—and by Orsini's explanation that Latin is required as an interpretive standard "because of the equivocations and interchangeability of French words" (*propter Æquivicationes & Sinonima Verborum Gallicorum*). Apparently Italians also thought that French was a language of unreliable ambiguity.

If the terms in which English identity was established were integrity and truthfulness versus duplicity and guile, we should not be surprised that Henry's royal identity was constructed in essentially the same terms. To a degree unusual even for a medieval monarch, Henry was taken to represent, even to embody, the nation as a whole, and he became a figure of fascination and awe for his contemporaries. His glories were commemorated in no fewer than five fifteenth-century Latin biographies, and although only one English biography survives, there is evidence that at least three others were written.[66] Given the fact that most medieval kings received no biographical treatment at all, this abundance witnesses to the remarkable degree to which Henry was able to identify the nation with himself.[67] And he accomplished this not only by his military and political genius—which should never be underestimated—but also by a careful strategy of self-construction that accorded with the values he was determined should prevail.[68]

The most evident means by which Henry defined himself as embodying the integrity or *trouthe* of the nation as a whole was his lifelong self-representation as a *vas electionis*, an agent of the God who was "þe auctour of trouthe." As early as the Welsh wars of his youth, he asserted that "la victoire n'est pas en la multitude de poeple . . . mais en la puissance de Dieu," a theme that reached its height with Agincourt.[69] Although most contemporary chroniclers knew full well that the stunning English victory was due at least in part to the lack of discipline of the French, there was none who did not also see in it the hand of God.[70] The theme of providential guidance was expressed with particular insistence in the magnificent pageant that greeted Henry on his royal entry into London in November 1415. The *Gesta* described how Henry was met with a tower with a statue of St. George with a sword and a scroll reading *Soli deo honor et gloria*, and then passed by another tower where was "enthroned a figure of majesty in the form of a sun and emitting dazzling rays," and with the motto *Deo gracias*, "the tributes of praise to the honour and glory not of men but of God." The king, dressed in purple (the color of Christ's passion), walked in the midst of the procession with a small retinue: "Indeed, from his quiet demeanor, gentle pace, and sober progress," said the *Gesta*, "it might have been gathered that the king, silently pondering the matter in his heart, was rendering thanks and glory to God alone, not to man."[71]

Was this ostentatious humility? Or self-effacing arrogance? Only oxymorons can express something of the manipulated and manipulating complexity of Henry's self-presentation. In other respects Henry's promotion of the almost theocratic grandeur of Lancastrian royalty was more straightforward. Examples are the changes in the coronation ceremony that stressed providential presence, and the expansion of the law of treason to include *lèse majesté*, so that an attack upon the king, including verbal derogation, was an attack upon the nation itself.[72] Nor was it only on festive occasions that Henry stressed the divine aura that encompassed the royal person. He was famously alert to royal prerogative, demanding not just that ambassadors stand in his presence but that they not even look him in the face; and he would often sit under a canopy—as, for instance, when he received the surrendering citizens of Harfleur in 1415—that signified an authority derived from above.[73] And Henry's personal piety was famous: woe to the man who would interrupt his prayers while he communed with his Lord.

The *Gesta*'s description of Henry's "sober progress" in the victory procession in London—the *Brut* refers to him as "sad," i.e., solemn—is an early instance of a widespread attention to Henry's gravity, a seriousness of demeanor that bespeaks not merely resolution but a sense of higher purpose. John Page's poem on the *Siege of Rouen* describes Henry hearing mass "solemp with semeland so sad" and only then receiving the citizens of Rouen:

> Alle stylle he stode that whyle,
> Nothyr dyd he laughe nor smyle,
> But with a countenaunce fulle clere,
> And with a fulle lordely chere,
> Nor to mylde, nor to straunge,

But in a mene withowtyn change,
His countenans dyd he not a bate,
But stylle he stode and in astate,
Or hym lyste to geve an answere.[74]

This quiet uniformity of manner—what the version of Page's poem included in the *Brut* describes as being "ay in oon withoute chaunge"—
characterizes Henry throughout these writings.[75] Even his early misbehavior as Prince of Wales (in Frulovisi's oft-quoted phrase, he "exercised
equally the feats of Venus and Mars") was turned to this purpose by providing the occasion for his almost religious conversion into Henry V:
"And aftir his coronacion," says Capgrave, "he was everne turned onto
anothir man, and alle his mociones inclined to vertu."[76]

The foil most persistently used to set off Henry's mature sincerity was
not his own youthful excess but the frivolity of the French in general
and the dauphin in particular. The almost certainly apocryphal story of
the gift of the tennis balls was designed to set Henry's seriousness of purpose and laconic brevity against the dauphin's trifling.[77] On the eve of
Agincourt the French frolicked—they "made mony grete fires, and moche
revell with hontynge, and played our King and his lorde3 at þe dys" (378),
says the *Brut*—while Henry prayed; and his unassuming speech to his
troops bespeaks a depth of seriousness, and a piety, that more flamboyant
rhetoric would have betrayed: "'Thanne,' said our King, 'nowe is gode
tyme, for alle Engelond prayeth for vs; and þerfore be of gode chere, &
lette vs go to our iorney.'"[78] Pious, dutiful, letting his actions speak louder
than words, and bearing a very stiff upper lip indeed, Henry was presented
by the contemporary sources as a striking instance of a now-familiar British national stereotype—the leader who eschews flamboyant gestures and
bombastic words, whose depth of feeling is expressed by a terse matter-
of-factness, who does his duty under difficult circumstances while modestly ascribing his triumphs to a force greater than himself.[79] And that this
gravity was consistent with conquest rather than disaster—that it was
equanimity in triumph rather than, as the heroic ethic had traditionally
prescribed, resolution in defeat—made his economy of gesture all the
more persuasive.

The construction of Henry's identity as an ideal type of the national
character was not, however, simply image-making. For Henry's energeti-

cally pursued royal policy sought to place himself at the center of the nation's life, to provide his compatriots with not just a cynosure but the executive will that would bring them to coherence and direction. One of his first tasks was to reunite the governing classes of the country by imposing royal authority upon an increasingly lawless gentry. This he accomplished by deftly manipulating a system of royal rewards and punishment and, above all, by directing noble belligerence away from civil disorder and toward foreign conquest. Crucial to this disciplinary process was both the king's ability to behave with resolute and principled consistency— one of his epithets was *Justicia*—and the skillful deployment of his own prestige.[80] When he sought to reinvigorate a negligent judicial system, he relied on the Court of King's Bench, a court so "closely identified with the person and interests of the king [that] its proceedings were invested with peculiar authority."[81] And again, he was less interested in punishment than in reconciliation, a process accomplished largely by offering malefactors the opportunity to regain their monarch's grace by participating in the war in France: as Edward Powell says, "We may suspect that the courtrooms of 1414 had an aura of the recruiting-office about them."[82] Once these men entered into Henry's host they were again subject to a discipline rare in medieval warfare: Henry not only punished his soldiers for unauthorized depredations upon the populace but instituted military practices such as muster and review.[83]

There was, indeed, hardly an area of public life where Henry did not place himself at the center. Even while in France he insisted on maintaining close supervision over English affairs, and he took a personal interest in the details of administration throughout his ever-expanding French possessions, especially Normandy.[84] McFarlane characterized him as "the king who kept personal control of every branch of government," a control directed not just toward structuring and disciplining national practices but also toward placing the king always at the center of the national life.[85] His monastic foundations, for example, the most ambitious of any English monarch, were designed to produce, in Jeremy Catto's phrase, "a 'gigantic power-house of prayer' for the Lancastrian dynasty."[86] He also instituted liturgical changes that solicited spiritual support from his subjects, sponsored William Lyndwood's *Provinciale*, a codification of English practice in church government, and in the spring of 1421 initiated a thoroughgoing reform of the Benedictine order—an event that had, as I shall shortly propose, an effect on the writing of the *Siege of Thebes* by the Benedictine Lydgate. His opposition to Lollard deviancy was unremitting—the Lollards called him "the prince of prestis and our uttir enmy"—and during his reign the Sarum Rite, refined at his monastery of Syon by Clement Maydeston, was promoted as the single authorized liturgy for the church in England.[87] In sum, in a striking prefiguration of the Tudor Reformation, Henry firmly and decisively brought religious life under state control. Nor was it only religious practice that Henry sought to supervise: in 1419 he had his brother Thomas, duke of Clarence, codify and register coats of arms, beginning the process by which the previously unregulated diffusion of armorial bearings was centralized, with the monarchy as the fount of honor.[88] Finally, even his choice of royal servants witnessed to what has been called the "personal dominance" of the king, a centralization that brought the business of governing "to new levels of professionalism and skill."[89]

In summation, then, Henry practiced what we can appropriately call the politics of identity, in the several senses in which that term has been used. His own monarchical identity stressed not just ethical integrity but psychological coherence, an unconflicted, forthright, and even artless selfhood confident in its values and resolute in pursuing its interests, a selfhood in which difference was subordinated to identity, *doublenesse* (as both ethical duplicity and psychological complexity) to *trouthe*. Furthermore, Henry was assiduous both in identifying the nation's interests with his own and in seeking to bring the various elements of fifteenth-century English society into identity with each other and with himself. This public policy was underwritten by an absolutism that was perhaps instinctive, perhaps deliberately fostered. But it succeeded not only because of Henry's extraordinary energy and skill, but also because it could draw upon a discursive field that named coherence and identity as proper while stigmatizing fragmentation and difference—and that endowed this opposition with the nationalist values of a country at war. In many ways Henry was a conservative, even reactionary monarch, and we can see deep within his actions the great universalist dream of the Middle Ages. He was genuinely committed to overcoming the scandal of the Great Schism—"ffor to make vnyon in hooly chirche," as a contemporary put it—and he always maintained that the reunification of France and England was only a prelude to the larger reunification of Christendom that he would accomplish with a crusade to the Holy Land.[90] Yet he was also a preview of things to come, the age of absolutism that Europe was about to enter.[91]

Cracks in the Pedestal

While Henry's making of himself and his world was immensely successful, even at the moment of his greatest triumph—in May, 1420 he married Catherine and was designated heir to the throne of France—troubling complications were visible. The form these difficulties took is of interest to us because they show that the discursive field within which Henry operated so effectively also imposed restrictions that limited his largest ambitions. To be sure, Henry's problems were material as well as ideological. By 1419 the recruitment of soldiers and especially captains for service in France became difficult, so much so that the crown seems to have resorted to rather desperate means for finding "volunteers": in a letter of March 1420 one agent tells Henry that he will be recruiting at the sessions of the Court of King's Bench at York "opon the Deliverance of the Gaole there, and a Cession of the Pees also."[92] So too, Parliament was becoming increasingly reluctant to approve taxes for the war: in the Parliaments of December 1420 and May 1421 no money was granted, and in December 1421 only a small grant of one-fifteenth was approved.[93] Nor was it only men and money that were becoming more difficult to secure. "In 1418," we learn, "both archbishop Chichele and bishop Repingdon complained of the negligence, torpor and inaction with which their mandates to make patriotic prayers had been treated."[94] Apparently even spiritual support was becoming hard to come by.

There were no doubt many reasons for this waning of enthusiasm: the inevitable disillusionment when the brilliant victories of Harfleur, Agincourt, and Rouen gave way to the dispiriting prospect of a long, hard conquest, especially given the defeat and death of Clarence at Baugé in March 1421; the sense that since the king had now recovered his kingdom in France, its rebelliousness was a French, not an English, problem that should be paid for with French revenues; and a general lack of interest in foreign adventures when local concerns were so much more visibly pressing. But Henry's problems were ideological as well as practical. In the Parliament of December 1420 the Commons petitioned for the reenactment of a statute of 1351 that declared that the crown of England should never be subject to the crown of France.[95] Indeed, the Treaty of Troyes that had been signed six months earlier had already acknowledged English anxiety over its identity as an independent nation. After asserting, in a passage that has already been quoted, that the crowns of France and England shall "perpetuelly be togedyr . . . in Oone and in the same Persone" and that both realms shall also be governed "undir oone and the same Persone," the treaty then adds:

> Kepyng ne the les, in all maner other thynges, to ayther of the same Roialmes here Ryghtees, or Custumes, Usages, and Lawes; not makyng subget in ony manere of wise oone of the same Roialmes to th'oder, nor puttyng under, or submittyng the Ryghtes, Lawes, Custumes, or Usages of that oone of the sayd Roialmes, to the Ryghtes, Lawes, Custumes, or Usages of that other of the same.[96]

The crowns are one but the nations are separate; the governing authorities are the same but the systems of government are different. This is a condition that is perhaps constitutionally conceivable, perhaps even practically possible. But it is also one that sets up within the discourse of identity and difference an intolerable contradiction.

The Commons' petition expressed a concern for English separateness—for preserving the national identity that Henry himself had so assiduously developed.[97] And this concern allows us to see that the language of identity and difference had in fact been used in two, mutually exclusive ways. On the one hand, there was the insistence on English integrity versus French duplicity, presenting England as politically unified and ethically coherent while France was riven by internal divisions and corrupted by duplicity. Yet on the other hand, there was also the claim that the war was undertaken to heal the rift between the fraternal nations England and France, to bring back to unity—to oneness and integrity—two crowns that were in truth parts of a single whole. In a sense, Henry was simultaneously prosecuting two different wars: a national war that required his compatriots to conceive of themselves as citizens of a state threatened by a foreign power and a dynastic war that defined them as vassals loyal to their feudal lord and committed to regaining his rights. These conflicting identities then began to emerge as Henry moved closer to achieving the goal that perhaps not even he had fully believed within his grasp, and in the clauses of the Treaty of Troyes, as in the parliamentary statute six months later, it began to disturb his inexorable progress toward synthesis.

The best evidence of this disturbance can be found in the efforts that Henry's heirs made, beginning immediately upon his death and continuing for most of the next two decades, to generate support for what came increasingly to be felt as a *damnosa hereditas*.[98] Their impossible task was to demonstrate that the dual monarchy was not a constitutional and conceptual monstrosity but a desirable, even natural political arrangement. But given the privileging of singularity and unity, is it imaginable, as Lydgate put it, "to weer too crownys"?[99] A particularly interesting attempt to silence these questions was produced in the year after Henry's death, when the duke of Bedford commissioned a genealogical poem from Laurence Calot, a French clerk, and had it illustrated by an accompanying manuscript picture. The painting—a later copy of which survives—traces out with elaborate care the descent of the royal lines of England and France and their ultimate unification in the young Henry VI, only two years old at the time.[100] (See figures 1 and 2.) The picture is rigorously symmetrical: a central lozenge, which includes portraits of the Capetians from St. Louis on and is labelled the "Directe ligne de France," is framed by a band on the left, labeled the "ligne collateralle de France" and containing portraits of the Valois kings, and by an identical band on the right, which contains portraits of the "ligne d'Angleterre" from Edward I to Henry V. At the bottom of the page the bands curve together to join in a portrait of the infant Henry VI, over whose head hover two angels. These angels bear the crowns of France and England: here two become one.

Or do they? The purpose of the design is to present the random walk of the royal politics of England and France—a politics deformed by the accidents of reproduction, the hazards of the marriage market, the uncertainties of battle, and by insanity, incompetence, and betrayal—as a process of unbroken rectilinearity, a development so orderly as to be both inevitable and, in its visual representation, self-evident. Yet those hovering angels, holding two crowns over a single infant head, form an image whose instability denies ideological closure. The angels must hover forever while Henry must remain forever *infans*, incompetent, and heir to a split legacy whose contradictions he could hardly be expected to resolve. The picture's function is to make Henry's dual monarchy plain, to render it

Fig. 1. Manuscript illustration. British Library MS Royal 15. E.vi., fol. 3r. © British Library Board. All rights reserved.

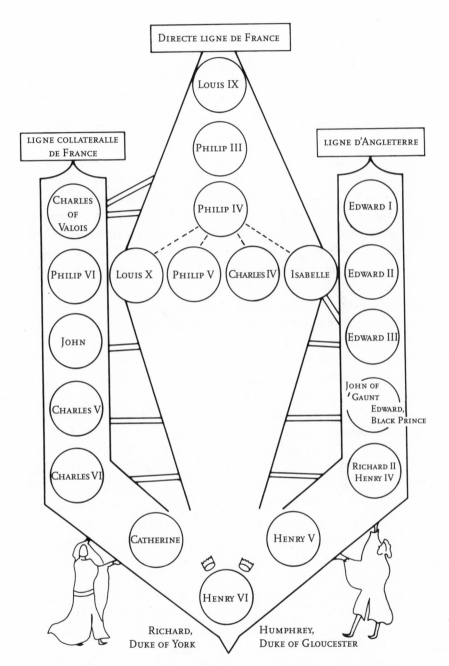

Fig. 2. Schematic representation of Figure 1. Prepared by Christopher L. Brest.

before the viewer in terms that are as direct and unmediated as the gene-alogical process—the "lignes" of descent—by which his royal authority had been passed on to him. Yet this very directness and self-evidence pre-scribe a picture that cannot be painted, and promote an authority that cannot be enforced. A king with two kingdoms and two crowns is by no means unfamiliar to the Middle Ages—indeed, the pope wore *three*—and Kantorowicz has taught us that because kings, like other ruling fig-ures, were both mortal persons and immortal offices they were subject to "innumerable germinations."[101] So it is not doubleness per se that causes the problem, but the practical reality of uniting France and England. In using this ungainly form of representation—which angel is going to get the crown on first, and then where will the second one go?—the picture is curiously at odds with itself: it makes visible the very difference it was meant to deny.

That there was a credibility gap among the French, for whom Calot's poem and its accompanying picture were initially intended, was only natural. But there was also a problem in England, and the propaganda campaign mounted there included a translation of Calot's poem by none other than John Lydgate. Commissioned by the earl of Warwick in 1426, in Lydgate's "The Title and Pedigree of Henry VI" the discourse of iden-tity and difference—called here "trouthe" and "variaunce"—is deployed with an insistence, even an obsessiveness, that pushes it to the break-ing point.[102] The premise of the poem is that Christ, "Prince and souerain Lord / Of vnyte, of peas, and of accorde" (75–76), "hath for vs so gra-ciously provided, / To make al oon that first was devided" (142–43), a "vnyte" (156) that the poem will make visible and self-evident: "we may *se* with euery circumstaunce / Direct the lyne of Englond & of Fraunce" (136–37). This political submergence of difference into identity has an analogue in the poem's own method. Its sequential structure lays out the genealogical line "in order ceriously" (40), a structure identical with the putative rectilinearity of Henry's descent "from þe stok riall / Of Seint Lowis" (225–26); and its own meaning, we are assured, "woll nat vary" from the "truth[e]" (107). Moreover, Lydgate insists that he is both a faithful translator of Calot's original—"In substaunce filowyng the sub-staunce / Of his writyng and compilacioun" (62–63)—and a loyal ser-vant of the earl of Warwick, whose "precept first and commaundement" (12) he here fully enacts. Finally, the poem is designed to bring about in its reader/viewer the uniformity and self-identity it everywhere displays, "To put awey all maner [of] variaunce, / Holy the doute and þe ambyguyte" (6–7). Asserting identity and rejecting difference in every dimension, "The Title and Pedigree of Henry VI" bespeaks by the very ardor of its commitment the tenacity of the doubts it means to remove.

Henry V's enterprise was projected and justified in terms of identity and reunion—two would become one—but it concluded in difference and division: one was encumbered with two. No symbolic discourse, whether painting or poetry, could resolve this dilemma, and in Lydgate's "Title and Pedigree"—as in his other poems supporting the dual monarchy—we witness a collision between language and fact, between rhetoric and reality, that Lydgate's poetics of identity refused to contemplate.[103] We witness universalism—both Henry's and Lydgate's—pushed to its discursive limits and beyond by the realities that rendered its ambitions unattainable. After his death, the absolutist politics of identity that had guided Henry in the construction of both himself and his world finally confronted differences that neither military nor linguistic *force majeure* could subdue: differences between French and English culture, between dynastic rights and national interests, between the imperial ambitions of the chivalric class and the local concerns of the nation at large, and between a heroic father and his saintly son.

As for Lydgate, it is not only in his translation of Calot that we can recognize anxiety and even the intuition of failure. If we now, at the end of this essay, turn back to 1421–22, and to the *Siege of Thebes*, there becomes retroactively visible Lydgate's own skepticism toward his identity as a spokesman for Lancastrian interests, and perhaps even an acknowledgment that poetry and power can never be brought to a perfect identity of purpose.

Identifying the Writer

Although I have described the general historical setting within which the *Siege of Thebes* was produced, there is as well a more specific context that needs to be described. In the spring of 1421 Henry undertook a campaign to reform Benedictine monasticism in England. In March he wrote to the abbot of St. Edmunds (Lydgate's monastery) asking him to summon a meeting of the order. The meeting, presided over by the abbot and attended by the foremost monks in England, convened in Westminster on May 7. It was opened by an address by the king directing the order to dispense with recent innovations and return to Benedict's original foundation, what Henry called the *pristina religio monachorum:* we recognize here both Henry's desire to exercise royal control over the nation's spiritual institutions and his politically motivated belief in the power and purity of historical origins.[104] Naturally the monastic community politely demurred, explaining its deviations from Benedict's rule by reference to the dispensing power of the abbot and the precedent of later canonistic authority. At any rate, by June the king had returned to France, never to return to England alive, and when the monastic commission set up to consider the king's suggestions reported in 1423, the question was good and truly moot.

While the records of the May meeting maintain a blandly official tone, we do have access to a more vivid monastic reaction. This is a contemporary sermon, probably preached by John Pauntley, monk of St. Peter's, Gloucester, and probably before the king, just before his return to France on June 10, 1421.[105] Written in a mixture of Latin and English, and witnessing to an equally mixed attitude toward the king, this sermon can serve as an analogue to the *Siege of Thebes,* which was being written by another Benedictine at exactly the same time. On its face the sermon is a paean to Henry's leadership: although the ship of the kingdom is sailing across what Pauntley calls (in bad Latin) a *duplici mari*—a double sea that symbolizes both "welth and prosperite" and "woo and adversite" (p. 88)— it is under the sure hand of this "wise mariner and most worþi werriour" (p. 91). Henry's success, however, is interpreted not as a tribute to his own virtues but as a reward for his protection and renovation of God's church: "Just as *he hath qwyt* God, so God has rewarded him; just as his love has advanced God and the church, so *his wele and honour* have been advanced" (p. 92). Having thus established the priority of religious values, Pauntley then launches into a gloomily monkish warning about the dangers of chivalric achievement, an admonition he illustrates with a somewhat tactless reference to the death of Henry's brother Clarence only three months earlier.

> There is neither faith nor stability in worldly glory; worldly honor is
> *a sliper þinge and elvich;* now it is, now it is not; today a man, tomorrow

not; today a lord, tomorrow *a lost man;* today *a dowti werrour,* tomorrow dead in the field . . . . So, *be þou never so worþi a werrioure, never so wise a governour,* even if you attain the highest point of honor, even if you sail over high seas *of welth and prosperite, be þou ones passid þi path schal wex fulle pleyn, þi worþi dedes* will be forgotten *and passe out of mynde.* (pp. 92–93)

Finally, turning to Henry's intervention in Benedictine affairs, he agrees that the religious life has declined from its original integrity:

> Neither regulars nor seculars live as they ought. Our conversation and way of life is not as it once was. Our coat is of another color. Our life is not like the lives of our old fathers. *Many brekkes* are in every part of our ship. . . . But we will be saved by *oure sovereyn lord.* (p. 95)

This passage would certainly seem to justify the editor's opinion that our author "betrays no uneasiness about the king's concurrent attempt to reform the Benedictines" (p. 87). And yet the examples he gives of the high standards from which current monks have fallen away are instances of neither spiritual fortitude nor meditative transcendence but of political resistance to presumptuous monarchs:

> Once the lords temporal and spiritual were touched and moved by the spirit of God. . . . Behold this spirit moved the holy doctor Saint Ambrose to excommunicate the mighty emperor Theodosius because his ministers recklessly killed many innocent people in a particular city. This spirit moved saint Thomas of Canterbury to resist king Henry II and to spill his own blood for the liberty of the Church. The life of these men was such that they did not fear to reprehend sin, they dared to speak the truth, they placed the fear of God before themselves. (p. 94)

Here, then, is a Benedictine performing his traditional role as advisor to the prince in a way that is, if not explicitly critical, at least highly complex. The monarch is saluted for his achievements, but reminded that they are an effect of his devotion to Holy Church; celebrated for his leadership, but warned that pride goeth before a fall; praised for restoring the monastic order to its former integrity, yet informed that this integrity is defined by the admonishment of abusive monarchs. Whatever Henry may have thought of this performance, it masterfully deploys traditional *topoi* to express both submission and independence, to identify its speaker with the royal program and yet to insist that the different interests of monk and king be respected. And it provides a telling analogue to Lydgate's similarly ambivalent text.

To be sure, we should hardly be surprised that the *Siege of Thebes* cannot live up to its disingenuous assertions of transparency and self-identity. As literary critics never tire of pointing out, literary texts are always complex and self-conflicted, and it takes no great interpretive subtlety to show how the *Siege* undoes itself through narrative digressions and thematic indecision. But rather than explain this irresolution globally, by reference to properties inherent in literature or even language, a procedure that itself universalizes and dehistoricizes, I prefer to invoke the specificities of Lydgate's situation. For one thing, Henry's proposed reformation of the Benedictine order helps to account for Lydgate's self-presentation in the literary context in which he places the *Siege*: he is a monk who is conscientious in performing his penitential and civic duties and yet alert to Harry Bailly's administrative challenges to his sense of monastic integrity. In effect, the Prologue to the *Siege* implies that the king's program to reform his order is both unwanted and unnecessary: just as the pilgrim Lydgate resists Harry's overbearing directives, so the monastic establishment as a whole needs no political direction in order to perform its traditional functions. Thus Lydgate asserts both compliance with and independence from unreasonable commands, a double response not unlike that of John Pauntley's uncompromisingly ambiguous sermon.

Rereading the poem in the light of this more complex relationship between patron and client, we can see that while at one level it is an admiring commentary on Henry's French war, telling the story of the recovery of a kingdom by its rightful ruler through the enforcement of "Couenauntys and conuencioun / Imad of olde" (3774–75), it also tells of fratricidal struggle that ends in bleak devastation. Indeed, its deepest message is that using war to right wrongs is a course of action whose performance is brutalizing and whose outcome is uncertain. Even the moral differences between Polynices and Ethiocles, and between the Argives and Thebans—differences, after all, upon which the efficacy of the entire narrative depends—are not consistently maintained. Both Polynices and his

Argive allies often behave in ways that impeach their moral superiority, and even the supremely virtuous Tydeus—who serves the poem as its premier mirror of princehood—ends his life gnawing in rage at the head of his enemy.[106] To be sure, none of the details that upset the clarity of the poem's moral structure is added by Lydgate to his source; and Statius's *Thebaid,* to which every medieval version of the Theban legend must finally be referred, is unremitting in its insistence that all that war can ever accomplish is the moral degradation of its participants. But in the spring of 1421, as the implications of Henry's triumph were beginning to come clear, it was this narrative that Lydgate chose to rewrite, a choice that entitles us to recognize that its darker meanings have contemporary relevance.

Nor is the poem's antiwar message the only or even the most telling way in which it challenges Henry's successes. For to invoke the Theban legend as a commentary on contemporary events was to summon up a dangerously subversive historiography. In medieval as in classical writing, Thebes was the site of endlessly repeated acts of hubric impiety and internecine slaughter. Most important, the grim history of Thebes was one of blind repetition: from its foundation by Cadmus's fratricidal dragon warriors through to its final extinction in the internecine combat of Ethiocles and Polynices, Thebes was a site where the inexpiable bloodletting of family violence was endlessly repeated. Even a bare list of Theban victims tells the story: Cadmus's wife, Harmonia (the daughter of Mars and Venus and recipient of the famous and fatal Theban necklace, made by Vulcan as a bitter wedding gift), Semele (whose son, Dionysius, became immortal at the price of his mother's death), Agave (mother and murderer of Pentheus), Niobe (wife of Amphion, and responsible for the deaths of her children), and even Amphiaraus, not a Theban at all but a victim of its curse: his wife, Euriphyle, betrayed him to his death on the Argive campaign against Thebes because she was bribed by Harmonia's necklace. The exemplary figure of Theban history, as the Middle Ages well knew, was Oedipus, whose parricide and incest trace the central pattern of violence and repetition, of family slaughter and of blind recursion to the source.[107]

Given this significance, the Theban story inevitably called into question both the commitment to purposive action and the rectilinear transmission of value from the past that underwrote the medieval monarchy. This underwriting was articulated in medieval historiography by another classical legend, that of Troy. Troy served the Western monarchies as their founding myth of origins because it maintained that fall is followed by rise, that heroic achievement can be reachieved, that empire can be translated both geographically and temporally, and—most important—that a historical origin can provide a secure foundation upon which the future can be built. But Theban history challenged all these assertions by revealing a profound corruption at the very source of historical action: in the *Siege of Thebes* Lydgate names it "ynfecciouin called Orygynal" (2565), a phrasing that correlates the biblical concept of original sin with the antique sense of a fatal impurity, an irredeemable pollution.

Both psychologically and historiographically, then, Theban history questions the myth of origins promoted by Trojan history. For this "tale of woes," as Statius called it (2, 267), there is in effect no history, no linearity, no transmission, just the futile reenactment of a fatal desire. This is why we can say that Theban history deconstructs medieval historiography, that it articulates an anxious skepticism that medieval culture sought always to hold at bay. But there had been an earlier occasion in the English historiographical tradition when the toxic Theban story was allowed to contaminate the Trojan foundation myth. This was Chaucer's *Troilus and Criseyde*, a Trojan poem that harbored an insistent and finally fatal Theban subtext.[108] In his own Trojan poem Lydgate assiduously avoided such dangerous material, a perfect example of his habitual simplification of Chaucerian complexity. But in the *Siege of Thebes*, begun immediately after the completion of the *Troy Book*, he allowed it voice. And if, in correlating this Theban material with Henry's triumph, he issued a monitory warning, he also offered a shrewdly ironic self-assessment. In the Prologue to the *Siege* he had in effect defined himself as an anti-Chaucer, as the serious historian who avoided Chaucerian frivolity and irresolution. Yet in the final analysis he wrote a poem that included its own opposite, the same strategy that Chaucer had so brilliantly used in *Troilus and Criseyde*. Despite himself, Lydgate discovered that he was Chaucerian after all.

chapter six

The Heroic Laconic Style

Reticence and Meaning from *Beowulf* to the Edwardians

Come, friend, you too must die. Why moan about it so?
Even Patroclus died, a far, far better man than you.
And look, you see how handsome and powerful I am?
The son of a great man, the mother who gave me life
a deathless goddess. But even for me, I tell you,
death and the strong force of fate are waiting.
                                    —*Iliad* 21.119–24[1]

The near oxymoron of my title can best be explained, at the outset, by one of its most famous instances. Capt. Lawrence Oates was a member of Robert Scott's doomed expedition to the South Pole in 1910–12. On the fatal return trip his frostbitten feet would no longer allow him to continue walking, and—knowing he was damaging the chances of survival of the others—he decided he must sacrifice himself to the greater good. In the midst of a blizzard he went to the door of the tent, saying "I am just going outside and may be some time"—and walked off to his death. "It was," Scott wrote in his diary, "the act of a brave man and an English gentleman. We all hope to meet the end with a similar spirit, and assuredly the end is not far." Nor was it. Less than two weeks later Scott wrote his famous Last Entry, a verbal gesture that was faithful to Oates's selflessness: "For God's sake look after our people."[2]

This essay will develop the ideas implicit in these heroic acts. The first is that the "national characteristic" of British verbal self-restraint—whether understood as the time-honored stiff upper lip or as a knowledgeable (or perhaps self-protective) refusal to indulge in unwarranted enthusiasm—is part of a continuous tradition that goes back a very long way: specifically to the Scandinavian and Germanic literatures of the Middle Ages. Second, this national characteristic is undeniably class specific: not just Oates's self-sacrifice but his self-deprecating understatement is central to Scott's definition of his comrade as a gentleman. And third, when looked at in the context of Victorian and Edwardian culture—that is, at the time when English imperialism was at its apogee, which is the larger context of Scott's expedition—the medieval *origins* of the laconic heroic style were rediscovered as an important aspect of the medieval revival which spoke directly to late nineteenth-century conditions. The question of whether it still speaks to ours is something for the reader to decide.

These three arguments will be developed by way of three seemingly disparate examples, in very different genres. The origins and original meaning of heroic understatement, as expressed in early medieval literature, will be reconsidered in the case of *Beowulf*, which itself can be seen as a meditation on, rather than merely an instance of, heroic laconicism. The second example might equally be seen as a retroactive comment, from the perspective of the turn into the twentieth century, on the late Victorian epic of colonialism: the extremely popular novel *The Four Feathers* by A. E. W. Mason, first published in 1902, just a decade before Scott's expedition, but set in the late 1880s. The third actually preceded the appearance of *The Four Feathers* and harks back in its topic to the first. Neither poem nor melodramatic novel, W. P. Ker's magisterial *Epic and Romance*, published in 1897, is obviously related both to *Beowulf* by its focus on the

medieval heroic poem and to *The Four Feathers* by its chronological situation, and, I shall argue, by its implied critique of its own era.

I

Given the significance that Ker's book will play in the closing section of
my argument, an appropriate place to begin to explore the meaning of the
laconic style is with his favorite literary genre, the Icelandic sagas. These
narratives display throughout a hard-bitten wryness and a persistent use
of negation and understatement.[3] Here are two examples from *Grettir's
Saga*. On one occasion Grettir attacks a ghost who lives in a barrow, kills
it after a ferocious fight, and then returns home, late for dinner. When he
is upbraided by his master for his bad manners in coming in late, he replies:
"Many a small thing happens late at night."[4] Or take this well-known
"death-jest," as it is called. Atli is being attacked by his enemies:

> Suddenly Thorbjorn came rushing up to the door, and with both
> hands he drove the spear into Atli's waist, forcing it right through
> his body. Atli said, as he received the thrust, "Broad spears are be-
> coming fashionable nowadays." With that he fell forward onto the
> threshold.[5]

In both cases the laconic style appears to be simply a way of expressing superiority: is the "small thing" that happened late at night to Grettir the
killing of the ghost or the rebuke from his master? When Atli comments
on the broad spear he both shows his unconcern for death and mocks his
killer for being merely fashionable. But, in fact, the laconic style is so com-
pressed, so terse and abrupt, that we cannot be entirely sure *what* is meant.
Perhaps Grettir does regard killing the ghost as a small thing; perhaps Atli
is in fact showing that he too is an aficionado of spears. The effect of the
telegraphic style is to intimate a whole spectrum of moral discriminations
without ever making them explicit. This then raises other questions: is this
moral system unstated because it is incoherent, or because it is so simplistic that it needs no exposition, or because—on the contrary—it is so
intricate that to express it is to betray it, that it must be lived rather than
articulated? There is no clear way of deciding among these possibilities: by

its very terseness the laconic style allows for an abundance of interpretive opportunities.

These comments can be expanded by reconsidering *Beowulf*. As readers have long noted, the poem's style is defined by understatement, displacement, indirection, allusion, obliquity, and reticence. Litotes, "the figure of speech in which much less is said than is meant," is, as with much heroic poetry, the characteristic mode of *Beowulf*.[6] Speaking of the reaction of the Danes to the death of Grendel, the poet says that "his death did not seem painful to any warrior" (841–42); when Beowulf uses the giants' sword to decapitate Grendel, "the edge was not useless to the warrior" (1575–76); when the messenger comes to the waiting Geats to tell them of Beowulf's demise, "little was he silent" (2897); and so forth.[7] According to Frederick Bracher, this kind of understatement occurs in *Beowulf* once every thirty-four lines, and Bracher demonstrates that it occurs far more frequently in heroic, non-religious poems than in those with an explicitly Christian subject, and, surprisingly, that it never occurs in prose.[8] But while negation may be the most obvious form of reticence in the poem, it is by no means the only one. Fred Robinson has described the poem's appositive style—its reliance upon paratactic juxtaposition—as being "especially rich in implicit meaning" and as therefore "logically reticent." In combination with its use of compounds and variation, and an open syntax that allows meaning to be construed in a variety of ways, the style of the poem is "more suggestive than assertive, more oblique than direct. . . . [It] creates the impression of restraint and reticence in the poet's voice, a voice which often seems to supply facts without an accompanying interpretation of them."[9] For Robinson the effect of this style is to make possible the complex mixture of "admiration and regret" with which the Christian poet regards his pagan past: it has "the ability to entertain two simultaneous points of view that are necessary for the resolution of poignant cultural tensions."[10] Guided by this suggestive account, I wish to explore some other ways in which the laconicism of *Beowulf* functions to articulate meanings that perhaps by their very nature resist verbal formulation.

In the essay that initiated the modern tradition of *Beowulf* criticism, J. R. R. Tolkien stressed both the elemental, inhuman quality of the poem's breathtaking monsters and their relation to "the evil side of the heroic life," which he characterized as malice, greed, and destruction.[11] Edward Irving extended this insight from the moral to the social sphere: as well as representing "the Other, the Darkness," Grendel "seems to be representative at times of an evil and arrogant individualism that is wholly destructive in its effects on society and has some connection thematically with the feuds smoldering below the surface of the poem or with a figure like Heremod, type of the self-willed and wicked king."[12] In 1974 Harry Berger and Marshall Leicester carried these suggestions still further by not only demonstrating the way the poem connects the monsters and the feuding spirit, but by arguing that the monsters function as "allegorical displacements of the evil" that is enacted in the violence of the feuds. Moreover, this displacement is a form of willed ignorance, in which insoluble social problems are reconfigured in simpler forms so that an act of cleansing or reparation, however ultimately ineffective, can take place. As Berger and Leicester explain,

> The story of Grendel [and the other monsters] is like those narrative myths which, in primitive and traditional societies, serve to block further explanations by giving definite answers that set the curious mind at rest—and serve often to distract it from the underlying insoluble sources of social stress.[13]

Lastly, Ian Duncan provided further, lexical evidence on the equivalence between Beowulf and the monsters he exterminates, and on the obstructive, obscuring dialectic between the monster-killing narratives and those of the various feuds.[14] Where Duncan differs from Berger and Leicester, however, is on the question of the relation of the protagonists of the poem, and especially Beowulf himself, to this dialectic. For Berger and Leicester, Beowulf and his fellows are alike in being incapable of understanding the fatality built into their social world: it is, for these critics, "a predictable structure dynamically at work beyond the consciousness of the men locked into it" and they "are asleep to the latent motives and consequences" of their actions (pp. 49, 46). This is a society, they believe, that creates history behind its own back, and is incapable of understanding the consequences of its own social practices. Duncan, on the other hand, while not directly discussing the question of the warriors' knowledge of their situation, sees the tension between secrecy and openness as a central theme in the poem. "Secrecy in itself generates malignity, breeds dragons," he proposes; but Beowulf's heroism consists in his ability to "join *wordas* and *worcas* in transparent, performative unity, by carrying out his boasts" (p. 123).

The poem's reticent, allusive style functions as a way to make vivid this tension between the open and the hidden. More important, if litotes is "the figure of speech in which much less is said than is meant," then the various modes of understatement—negation, laconicism, displacement, allusiveness, and silence—are ways of making meaning visible in the very act of hiding it. When the warriors, and especially Beowulf himself, deploy these kinds of understatement, we are required to consider whether they are aware (or intended by the poet who speaks through them to be so aware) of the full dimensions of their situation. By examining several of the extensive speeches delivered by Beowulf himself, we can see that Beowulf himself and perhaps only he (along with the poet) possesses that awareness. His language reveals a consciousness painfully mindful of that which it would rather avoid but which it finally chooses—heroically—to confront.

A salient instance is Beowulf's verbal contest with Unferth. This is at once a display of his credentials as a fighter of monsters, a demonstration of the linguistic dexterity that the true leader must possess, and a verbal warm-up for the more serious contest that lies ahead: the animosity stirred up by Unferth will be displaced into the fight with Grendel. The crux of Beowulf's defense against Unferth's mockery is that he, unlike his competitor Breca, killed sea-monsters during the rowing contest, and so protected other sea-farers from their depredations. Beowulf describes the slaughter of the sea-monsters with a laconic joke: "I served them with my excellent sword, as was fitting. Not at all of that feast did they have joy, those dealers in crime, that they should eat me, sit about a banquet on the sea-bottom" (562–64). And he concludes this part of his speech with the famously elliptical statement, "Fate often saves an undoomed man, when his courage is good" (572b–73). Although he says that "I do not much boast of it" (586b), Beowulf is clearly contrasting his heroism to the ineffectiveness of the Danes. The feasting of the sea-monsters that Beowulf prevents stands in contrast to the feasting that the monster Grendel engages in nightly: Grendel "takes his pleasure," says Beowulf, "kills and feasts, expects no fight from the Spear-Danes" (599b–601a).[15] The subtlety of Beowulf's statement here is less in its obliqueness—he concludes his comments with an explicit boast that he will accomplish that which the

Danes have failed to do (601b–605)—than in its mastery of metaphor and its clear grasp of the reality of the situation. He knows exactly what Unferth is about in his challenge, just as he knows of Unferth's unsavory past, and he meets it with a shrewd mixture of grim humor, heroic resolve, and cheerful self-promotion. Whatever may have been hidden in Unferth's challenge has now been brought into the open, and there can be no doubt about either Beowulf's intentions or—for all his politeness to Hrothgar— his assessment of Danish failure. Yet both anchoring and unsettling his speech is that strangely unresolved metaphysical musing: "Fate often saves an undoomed man, when his courage is good." For all of the social acuity that the verbal contest with Unferth articulates, this gnomic statement shows that Beowulf refuses to forget that his ultimate fate may or may not be subject to his own control. And it is precisely his ability to maintain a resolutely balanced cosmic perspective, neither self-destructively fatalistic nor naively self-reliant, that encourages us to grant Beowulf a full understanding of the world in which he enacts his heroism.

A second example of Beowulf's use of the laconic style is his response to Hrothgar's complaint that Grendel's dam has eaten Aeschere. When summoned to the king's side Beowulf is innocently cheerful, asking if Hrothgar had, "in view of this urgent summons" (1320), passed a pleasant night. "Don't ask about happiness," Hrothgar testily replies, and then implicitly blames Beowulf for having roused Grendel's dam to her act of vengeance. Beowulf tactfully not only ignores the ungratefulness of this charge, but overlooks the fact that until now neither Hrothgar nor any of the Danes has mentioned Grendel's dam at all, an omission that has placed Beowulf and his Geatish companions at risk. "Don't sorrow, wise king," he says instead. "It is better for every man to avenge his friend than much mourn" (1384–85). Ignoring Hrothgar's own responsibility for Aeschere's death, even to the point of applying to him the now wholly inappropriate epithet "wise" (*snotor*), Beowulf again invokes a gnomic saying that is blandly consoling, yet—for those who are alert to implication—critical of Hrothgar's inaction. As always, readers will have to decide for themselves how much irony to hear in Beowulf's statement. But for those who read his words as carefully crafted both to solace the old man while obliquely acknowledging his failure, they stand as further evidence of a consciousness that is more capacious than that of his fellows and specifically of the "wise" Hrothgar himself.

In both of these instances Beowulf makes visible, if not explicit, meanings that would otherwise remain at best implicit, more likely entirely hidden. Appropriately then, his actions literally bring to light that which is hidden, the monsters who lurk in dark and secret places. Despite the audience's privileged knowledge of the Grendelkin's descent from Cain and their biblical meaning, the poem still insists on their mysteriousness. We can only guess at Grendel's motives because the poet expresses them in a passage famous for its difficulty: the enigmatic statement that he cannot approach the throne to receive rings "because of the lord" (or the "Lord") invites us to consider the condition of being Grendel without giving us any real access to *his* consciousness.[16] He is a "terrible walker-alone" (*atol angengea* [165a, 449a]), a "goer in shadows" (*sceaugenge* [703a]), motivated by "unknown malice" (*uncuðne nið* [276b]), who attacks in the night (*deorcum nihtum* [275b]), an "alien spirit" (*ellorgæst* [807b, 1349a] like his mother (see 1617a, 1621b), whose home is a "hiding-place" (*heolster* [755b]) or "secret land" (*dygel lond* [1357b]), the dark and murky mere into which the hero must descend. In this mysteriousness Grendel and his mother—like the equally undefined dragon—embody not just the feuding principle but the "secret hostility" (*beadurune* [501a]), the "malice-caused sorrow" (*inwidsorge* [831a]), the "slaughter-anger" (*wælnið* [85a, 2065a, 3000a]) and "sword-hate" (*ecghete* [84a, 1738a]) that motivate—in ways that the poem declines fully to explain—the violence of tribal life. If Beowulf's task is to "keep watch against monsters" (668b), it is also to stand against the "malice-nets" (*inwitnet* [2167a]) that kinsmen weave for each other with "secret craft" (*dyrnum cræft* [2168a]). And he does this by making known that which is hidden.

This responsibility for revelation is fulfilled in heroic action by Beowulf's display of Grendel's arm, of his head, and finally of the dragon and his hoard: "the hoard is revealed" (3084b), announces the poet, albeit at the price of the hero's life. But more important than these displays of monstrosity are the two striking acts of explication by which, in a typically displaced and litotic way, Beowulf reveals the deepest significance of the heroic life. The first occurs after Beowulf's return from Heorot to Hygelac's court. Beowulf has come to know that Heorot is a place of open secrets, where reality is faced, if faced at all, only with difficulty. One of these realities, carefully preserved behind a facade of what must be merely formal respect, is that Hrothgar is a king incapable of providing his people with the protection they require. Another, as we have seen, is that there is not only one but two monsters who must be exterminated. A third, brought forward by Wealhtheow in a typically allusive and tortuous way, is the enmity between Hrothulf and Hrothgar, and the threat this poses to her sons, Hrethric and Hrothmund. Here the truth is so sensitive, and so dire, that Wealhtheow's carefully crafted speech of entreaty to Beowulf is preceded—and perhaps even elicited—by the cryptically presented story of the fight at Finnsburh, which tells how another Dane, Hengest, followed "the world's custom" in exacting revenge upon his enemies and how another Danish queen, Hildeburh, suffered the deaths of both her son and her husband.[17] The parallel between Hildeburh and Wealhtheow is obvious enough, but what is important for our purposes is that the scop's song of the tragedy of Finnsburh is sung during the *celebrations* for the death of Grendel and reminds us (as well as Wealhtheow and Beowulf) that Heorot cannot so easily be cleansed. Indeed, the events later that night, when Grendel's mother comes to take her revenge, makes that all too clear.

This is all the more true of the deepest, darkest open secret about Heorot: that regardless of Beowulf's heroics it is doomed to destruction. At the beginning of the poem, when the great hall is described as the summation of Hrothgar's glorious reign, we are suddenly told, almost as an afterthought, that the hall—"tall and wide-gabled"—was in fact waiting for "the hostile surge of hateful fire; nor was it yet at hand that the sword-hate of son-in-law and father-in-law after deadly enmity would arise" (82b–85). Later the poet makes an even more cryptic allusion to these events: during the battle with Grendel it seems as if the hall is about to fall apart, but, says the poet, it is so splendidly built that no one had the ability to destroy it "unless the embrace of fire would devour it with heat" (781b–82a). The modern reader, endowed with the elaborate apparatus that accompanies editions and translations of the poem, knows that this passage refers to the coming feud between Hrothgar and Ingeld which will entail the burning of Heorot. Whether a contemporary audience would be able to surmise the meaning of these cryptic lines is uncertain. The poet is careful to provide for his audience a full account of this episode elsewhere, but how could it know that this passing comment referred to that future event? The important point for our purposes is that the poet provides this information not in his own voice but in Beowulf's account to Hygelac of his visit to Heorot (2024–69a). In other words, the poet endows Beowulf with knowledge of the future tragedy that awaits Heorot, which must affect his sense of his apparently successful mission. He has cleansed the hall through his heroic battles, but he knows that this accomplishment—like everything else in his world—is merely temporary. Beowulf can thus be under no illusions about the historical, indeed the metaphysical, structure of his world.

When we look more closely at Beowulf's account to Hygelac of the inability of the Danes and the Heathobards to settle their feud we are able to appreciate the depth of his understanding of the social practices of his world. For Beowulf does not simply tell Hygelac (and the poem's audience) that the exchange of women does not always (or perhaps ever) work as a means of reparation. On the contrary, he provides a vividly imagined account of the way in which vengefulness reemerges through the very means designed to suppress it. It is the Danish attendant of Freawaru who wears the Heathobard armor that arouses the old spear-warrior to test the feelings—"the resolve of the heart" (*hreðra gehygd* [2045b])—of the young Heathobard. Throughout Beowulf's account the emphasis is on the way the "grim-minded old man" (2043b) infects his younger tribesman with his "painful words" (2058a) so as to bring about "the evil of war" (2046a). This is a story within a story in two senses: the whole episode is encapsulated within Beowulf's account of the killing of Grendel (2002–9, 2069b–2143), and the old man's speech is then itself contained within the imagined action of the collapse of the truce between the Danes and the Heathobards.[18] The effect is not only to enforce the link between the feuding principle and Grendel, but to provide us with a sense of Beowulf moving ever more inward in his quest for the source of the "slaughter-hate" (*wælnið*) that drives the violence of the heroic world. Moreover, the scene that Beowulf imagines puts at its center an act of story-telling very similar to that in which he is himself at the moment engaged. The old man uses not just the sight of his father's weapons being borne by a Dane to tempt the young Heathobard to violence but provides him with an interpretation in the form of a narrative: "Now here the son of I know not which of those murderers struts in the hall, boasts of the murder, and bears the precious objects that by right you should own" (2053–56). In effect, Beowulf provides not just an account but an *example* of the way in which narrative—the rehearsal of the grievances of the past—creates new occasions for violence. These are the conditions, he is saying, in which there

can be no friendship without deceit (2067–68). Just as the giving of Freawaru to Ingeld ultimately allows for the destruction of the peace it is intended to establish, so the retelling of the old stories of violence becomes
itself a source of violence. We remember that the story of Hengest's vindictive slaughter of his Jutish hosts at Finnsburh—so similar in its motivating occasion to the future Beowulf predicts for Freawaru's thane—was
rehearsed by the Danish scop as part of the celebration for Grendel's defeat.[19] Beowulf's reconfiguration of that story in the context of his own
narrative of Grendel's death could hardly be more pointed: a society that
obsessively, even lovingly remembers the past will inevitably repeat it.

In granting to Beowulf a knowledge of the significance of his words
I am taking seriously the poet's decision not merely to place them in his
mouth but to endow them with special relevance to both the social and
the psychological dynamics of tribal violence. The second act of narrative revelation, by which Beowulf lays bare the cultural meaning of his
heroic world, is even more startling in the depth of understanding it displays. This is his speech prior to the confrontation with the dragon in
which he recounts the tragic history of King Hrethel. Again, the context
is crucial. Beowulf is saying farewell to his thanes: "his mind was sad, restless and ready for death" (2419b–20). He takes his leave by what we can
now recognize as a typical strategy of narrative displacement. First he tells
the story of the death of Herebeald, killed accidentally by his brother
Hæthcyn, and of the terrible inaction forced upon their father Hrethel;
and he then expands upon this story with another vividly imagined scene,
this time of a father grieving for his outlaw son hung upon the gallows.
In part, as critics have pointed out, Beowulf is confronting his own dilemma: if he takes action against the dragon, he dooms his people to the
enmity of the Swedes in a feud whose details provide the envelope in
which he embeds this central story; if he refuses this challenge he dooms
himself to the anomie that undoes Hrethel.[20] But in a larger sense, as the
vivid account of the anguish of the father who must watch his son die
shamefully and without recompense, Beowulf is questioning the cultural
foundations of his world. As Linda Georgianna has skillfully argued, in
this speech Beowulf "calls into question the coherence and meaning of
the heroic world, which depends substantially on vengeance and fame to
lend meaning to death."[21] More, with his extended simile of the grieving
father, Beowulf confronts the ultimate futility of all forms of action, and

hence all forms of speech, in the heroic world. The father looks at his son's empty dwelling-place, the silent wine-hall, and he goes then to his bed, chanting grief-songs. "To him," Beowulf concludes, "it seemed too wide, the land and the dwelling" (2461b–62a). This sense of emptiness exceeds the social and legal problem of reparation, even for the shameful death of a son. The Beowulf who is speaking, we remember, is "sad, restless and ready for death." This story summarizes the sorrow and futility not just of Germanic heroism, but—although this is a thought we resist thinking—perhaps of all life. And by placing this speech in the mouth of his hero, the poet allows us to believe that Beowulf himself understands this terrible possibility, that at the moment of farewell he too experiences an unassuageable emptiness. Yet his expression of this harsh understanding is brief and displaced: not only does he himself not chant grief-songs, he does not even allow himself to repeat those of the bereft father. We have here, then, the laconic as narrative strategy, a story and a context that allow for depths of meaning that a fuller, more straightforward account would misrepresent.

In the Old English poem known to modern readers as "The Wanderer" the speaker acknowledges that his lament is not just useless but indecorous, perhaps even shameful. "I know indeed," he says,

> that it is a fine custom for a man to lock tight his heart's coffer, keep closed the hoard-case of his mind, whatever his thoughts may be. Words of a weary heart may not withstand fate, nor those of an angry spirit bring help. Therefore men eager for fame shut sorrowful thought up fast in their breast's coffer.[22]

The wanderer speaks now in part because he is alone—he "sat apart in private meditation"—and in part because he has confronted the ultimate reality of an irredeemable and unassuageable mortality against which he possesses no recourse other than speech. In a "middle-earth in which each day fails and falls," in which "wine-halls totter, the lord lies bereft of joy, all the company has fallen, bold men beside the wall," the last, final gesture is the lament that Beowulf denies himself—a gesture that the mourner himself recognizes to be unavailing against the bitter truth of the transience, and inconsequentiality, of human life. Perhaps, as the poet says in the poem's final lines, "it will be well with him who seeks favor, comfort from the Father in heaven, where for us all stability resides." But the wanderer himself is denied this comforting platitude, a poetic discretion that might give pause to even the most pious reader.

II

I turn now to the reemergence of reticence in the late nineteenth century, first in the definition of the English gentleman and then as a central value in the scholarly recovery of the Middle Ages. To be sure, between the medieval Germanic heroic age and the ideology of imperial heroism that flourished in Victorian England lies the entire code of chivalry, a development that defined the values of class difference in part as habits of verbal behavior. Derek Brewer has described Malory's language as "colloquial and ceremonious—the style of a fifteenth century gentleman," and he comments on "the dramatic terseness that also characterizes Malory's style, indicative of a certain practical, man-of-the-world's tone, of a desire to get on with the story, and an English gentleman's feeling that he does not need to underline the effects and significance of his words."[23] In the Victorian and Edwardian periods, as in the late medieval, English culture was again intent not merely on asserting gentlemanliness—as in Scott's comment about Capt. Oates—but on trying to define it, even to theorize it. The key figures here, at least for my purposes, are Newman, Pusey, and Ruskin. Newman developed the concept of "reserve," by which he initially meant the idea of withholding certain theological doctrines from audiences unsuited to receive them. But inevitably a religious strategy became a social practice: in the words of James Eli Adams, "Reserve might become . . . the social embodiment of some form of inward, spiritual elevation; . . . it could be the outward index of an inner depth that distinguishes the man possessed of a calling."[24] Pusey called this quality a "retiredness and absence of self," and we can recognize in it the paradox of a structure of personality that resists "the gaze of the multitude while nonetheless soliciting its attention, . . . a 'hiddenness' [that becomes] a sign of social and moral exclusivity."[25] Analogously, Ruskin defines the gentleman as someone who feels deeply, who participates sympathetically in the sufferings of others, but who makes manifest his emotions precisely by declining to display them. As Joseph Bizup nicely puts it, the reserve of the Ruskinian gentleman "is the theatrical display of the lack of display, and . . . signifies that the gentleman experiences a depth and intensity of feeling not available to the common man. . . . True reserve is the outward manifestation of that sympathy which moves the gentleman to alleviate the sufferings of others."[26]

The connection between this understanding of gentlemanliness and the laconic style can best be illustrated by prose fiction, specifically by one of the most popular and influential novels of Edwardian England. This is *The Four Feathers* by A. E. W. Mason, first published in 1902.[27] The popularity of the book is hard to overestimate. Forty years later, in 1942, over a million copies had been sold, and the book still remains in print.[28] It, and other books like it, provided for British society a model for heroism that had—and perhaps still has—an enormous appeal. And not only for the British: it was (in an irony that is almost too apt) the favorite book of the Norwegian explorer Roald Amundsen, who carried it with him on his successful race to the South Pole against the ill-fated Scott expedition on which Capt. Oates uttered his famous last words.[29] And it also, as we shall see, provided both a style of deportment and an imagery of personal worth that had a visible effect on a British society that endured the militarization required by both the First and Second World Wars.

The *Four Feathers* is set at the time of the campaigns in the Sudan. While the chronology of the novel is not made precise, it covers six years after the death of Gordon at Khartoum in 1885 and before the final conquest of Omdurman in 1896 by Kitchener—later known as Lord Kitchener of Khartoum or "K of K." While taking the rightness of the British cause for granted, *The Four Feathers* is not, in fact, an imperialist novel. It tells the story of Harry Feversham, heir to a glorious military heritage: his father fought in the Crimean and holds annual "Crimean nights" at which stories of heroism and cowardice are told. Unlike his hard, uncomprehending father, Harry is in fact a Ruskinian gentleman, reserved on the outside but full of imagination and empathy within. Throughout his childhood he is tormented with fears that he will dishonor the family, that he is a coward at heart. Although he joins the army, when he learns that his regiment is to sail for Egypt his self-doubt leads him to resign his commission on the pretext that his first responsibility is to his fiancée, Ethne Eustace. But he then receives, in Ethne's presence, a box containing the cards of three of his regimental comrades, each accompanied with a white feather. On learning the reason for this strange offering—that they are accusing him of cowardice—Ethne breaks off a feather from her fan, presents it to Harry, and dismisses him, apparently forever.[30]

The body of the novel has two themes. One is the story of Harry's closest friend, John Durrance, a natural soldier unacquainted with self-doubt, who is blinded by sunstroke in the Sudan and in his blindness comes slowly to understand the meaning of Harry's disgrace and disappearance. The other is the story of Harry's rehabilitation, accomplished by performing anonymous acts of heroism in the Sudan that persuade his regimental colleagues, and finally his fiancee, to receive back their white feathers. For our purposes there are two issues to be stressed. One is that heroism is defined here not by acts of derring-do but rather by quiet, anonymous, patient endurance—by a kind of penitential suffering in the service of others. The other is that the novel throughout privileges silence over speech, symbolic gesture over expressive articulation. It is almost Jamesian in its celebration of the hidden and the repressed. But it is explicit about one matter, its definition of what does and does not constitute a gentleman. Here is the account of Durrance—whose very name points to endurance as the greatest heroic virtue:

> He was a soldier of a type not so rare as the makers of war stories wish their readers to believe. Hector of Troy was his ancestor; he was neither hysterical in his language nor vindictive in his acts; he was not an elderly schoolboy with a taste for loud talk, but a quiet man who did his work without noise, who could be stern when occasion needed and of an unflinching severity, but whose nature was gentle and compassionate. (p. 247)

On the other hand, here is Mason's account of the other kind of soldier:

> Captain Willoughby was known at his club for a bore. He was a determined raconteur of pointless stories about people with whom not one of his audience was acquainted. And there was no deterring him, for he did not listen, he only talked. He took the most savage snub with a vacant and amiable face; and wrapped in his own dull thoughts, he continued his copious monologue. In the smoking-room

or the supper-room he crushed conversation flat as a steam-roller
crushes a road. He was quite irresistible. Trite anecdotes were sand-
wiched between aphorisms of the copybook; and whether anecdote
or aphorism, all was delivered with the air of a man surprised by his
own profundity. If you waited long enough, you no longer had the
will power to run away, you sat caught in a web of sheer dullness.
Only those, however, who did not know him waited long enough;
the rest of his fellow-members at his appearance straightaway rose
and fled. (p. 250)

Ungentlemanliness is here defined, if you look closely, as neither vulgarity
nor braggadocio but as insensitivity, as a lack of imagination, a failure
of sympathy. Willoughby is not just a bore but a man who speaks too
much because he lacks the inner selfhood that is the precondition for self-
possession and reserve.

The Four Feathers had a long Nachleben that shows both its influence
and how easily its subtle understanding of heroism could be debased.
The novel was almost certainly the source for one of the most infamous
practices of the First World War, the White Feather Brigade initiated by
Admiral Charles Fitzgerald in August 1914, the first month of the war.
This was comprised of ladies who would hand out white feathers to men
in civilian clothes; Geoffrey Parker, the distinguished war historian, tells
how his grandfather, himself an invalid, saw a woman try to give a white
feather to a man with an amputated arm, at the end of which was a hook.
The woman did not notice the disability, and the man swung at her with
the hook, knocking her and her feather to the ground.[31] The cruelty of the
entire enterprise, with its massive lack of sensitivity, is the exact opposite of all that Mason's novel tried to promote.[32] The other significant aspect of the book's legacy was its cinematic afterlife. No fewer than six
film versions have been made, the first in 1915 (the date testifying to its
importance in providing a model for British soldiers condemned to trench
warfare), the most recent in 2002. The best known is Alexander Korda's
version made in—again, note the date—1939. This is one of what is
called Korda's imperialist trilogy, the other two being Drum and Sanders
of the River.[33] Encouraged by the anti-appeasement bloc in the British government, Korda earned with these films the title of the Kipling of the
Kinema—"K of K," in other words, the cinematic Kitchener.[34] His Four

Feathers is indeed an imperialist film: it begins with the shameful abandonment of General Gordon at Khartoum and concludes with the glorious capture of Omdurman, with many "fuzzie wuzzies" exterminated in the process. But for all its vulgarity, Korda's film did keep to one of the central values of the novel, the laconic style, by adding a detail not present in the original. When Harry Feversham disguises himself as a Singali tribesman so that he can perform his acts of reparation, he pretends to have been forcibly rendered mute by having his tongue cut out: throughout much of the movie, consequently, Harry never says a word. As Ralph Richardson, playing the blinded Durrance, comments, "A man comes to understand these things," and the less said the better.

III

My last exhibit is another *fin de siècle* celebration of the laconic style, also chronologically related to Scott's fatal expedition. It also happens to be central to the development of medieval studies within the academy. In 1897 W. P. Ker published his first and most important book, *Epic and Romance*. Ker's topic was hardly original. Since at least the sixteenth-century the relative merits of epic and romance had been debated in terms of a constantly changing theory of genres. But Ker inherited this debate in the terms it had acquired from German romanticism. He accepted the premise that culture had moved from a condition of simplicity and authenticity to one of complexity and imitation, from—as Schiller put it—the naive "simple sensuous unity" of man's original condition to the sentimental "artificial age" of modernity.[35] For other thinkers, the contrast was between epic objectivity—Hegel called the epic "the memory of an essential mode of being once directly present"—and self-reflexive romanticism.[36] For Ker this cultural opposition had a generic counterpart in a stark contrast between epic and romance.

But if Ker's book remained within the terms of romantic thought it redefined the nature—indeed, the very chronology—of the Middle Ages. For him the true Middle Ages was represented not by the chivalric spectacle and romantic intensity of which so many of his contemporaries were enamored. On the contrary, he saw the essence of the Middle Ages as residing in the Germanic spirit of the north—a spirit that was gradually corrupted by the dominance of southern, and specifically French, influences. But far from sharing the democratic politics of Victorian Teutonists like the socialist William Morris and the liberal historian E. A. Freeman, Ker was a Tory radical whose most immediate predecessor was Carlyle. We may doubt that he admired Carlyle's address to the industrialists of his day as "Sons of the icy North" and his comparison of them to "Thor red-bearded, with his blue-sun eyes, with his cheery heart and strong thunder hammer."[37] Ker disliked what he called Carlyle's "groaning and agony," his "eloquent, metaphorical, imaginative prose"—which, as he said, "spoil[s] the market for sober people"—but he quoted with approval Carlyle's description of democratic Britain as composed of "twenty-seven millions, mostly fools."[38]

According to Ker, the true division between the Middle Ages and modernity was not the Renaissance but the twelfth century: his crucial date was 1100. He chose this date not only because of its proximity to what he called "the victory of the Norman knights over the English axe-men" at Hastings—however shopworn, the myth of the "Norman yoke" appealed to Tory radicals like Disraeli, Carlyle, and (we may presume) Ker himself[39]—but because the twelfth century was when genuine epic gave way to inauthentic romance. For Ker, "medieval romance" was virtually a contradiction in terms. It is, he said,

> almost as factitious and professional as modern Gothic architecture. . . . The term "medieval" ought not to obscure the fact that it is modern literature, . . . which has its beginning in the twelfth century.[40]

As for medieval epic, although the *Song of the Cid,* the *Song of Roland, Beowulf,* and the *Nibelungenlied* are representative if flawed instances, its pure, unadulterated form could be found only in the Icelandic sagas.[41] "The great imaginative triumph of the Teutonic heroic age was won in Iceland," Ker argued (p. 181); it is there that he found "the finest expression and record of the spirit and the ideas belonging properly to the Germanic race in its own right, and not derived from Rome or Christendom" (p. 57).

It was the social condition of Iceland that made this accomplishment possible. Medieval Iceland, he thought, represented a society that was at once intensely individualistic and uniformly aristocratic. As Ker explained in his lectures on the Danish ballads, delivered in 1900, "It is possible for a nation to be gentle all through—'the Quality' not a separate caste from the Quantity."[42] In *Epic and Romance* he argued that

> The ideas that took the Northern colonists to Iceland were the ideas of Germania—the love of an independent life, the ideal of *the old-fashioned Northern gentleman,* who was accustomed to consideration and respect from the freeman, his neighbours, who had *authority by his birth and fortune to look after the affairs of his countryside,* who would not make himself the tenant, vassal, or steward of any king. In the new country these ideas were intensified and defined. (p. 58, my italics)

These social conditions generated a literature that focused with particular intensity upon the individual. In an address to the Viking Club, delivered about 1900, Ker said that "the remarkable thing in the sagas, the real secret of the Icelandic mind, is that nothing is really valuable except the individual character. . . . Their story-telling . . . is founded on a sense of reality, an imaginative knowledge of character; on whatever it is that makes a difference between a true dramatist and the preacher" (CE 2.122). He meant by this that the Teutonic epic declined to articulate its values in an explicit code of heroic conduct, but embodied them in characters faced with ultimate choices. The sagas describe a limited number of what Ker called "tragic situations": the conflict of honor and kin, the necessity of a good man carrying out a course of action he knows to be wrong, the battle in a narrow place, loyalty to a hopeless cause, "the last resistance of a man driven into a corner" (p. 293). But these situations give rise to no ethical speculation, for all of the pressure is internalized and embodied in the characters themselves. As Ker said, in a passage central to his thinking,

> The Sagas, which in many things are ironical or reticent, do not conceal their standard of measurement or value, in relation to which characters and actions are to be appraised. They do not, on the other hand, allow this ideal to usurp upon the rights of individual characters. They are imaginative, dealing in actions and characters; they are not ethical or sentimental treatises, or mirrors of chivalry. (p. 206)

It was this reticence, this reserved, laconic formality, this "spirit of negative criticism and restraint" (p. 212), this "economy of phrasing" (p. 213)
and "moderation of language" (p. 265) that Ker most admired in the sagas.
And its disappearance was occasioned by romance: "as gentlefolk become
more ideal and ostentatious, and their vassals more sordid and dependent"
(p. 8), these unspoken values had to be replaced with an explicit, and
therefore superficial, code of conduct. Ker summed up the difference in
the following passage:

> An ideal, defined or described in set terms, is an ideal without any re-
> sponsibility and without any privilege. It may be picked up and traded
> on by any fool or hypocrite. *Undefined and undivulged*, it belongs only
> to those who have some original strength or imagination or will, and
> with them it cannot go wrong. (pp. 202–3, my italics)

Ker not only admired this reticence but also practiced it. His account
of the sagas is powerful in its commitment: one cannot read his book and
not want to read the sagas. But he refused to define, in any systematic or
even coherent way, the values they express. Modern books on the sagas
often include chapters like "Life Values and Ideals."[43] But Ker disavowed
all such efforts at abstract definition: if you don't understand why these
stories are valuable; if you don't appreciate what he called, in a grudging
concession to explicitness, "the ideas of loyalty, fellowship, fair-dealing,
and so on" (p. 304); then there is no point in trying to explain them to
you. Indeed, the isolation and peculiarity of Iceland—its complete lack
of relevance to the rest of Europe—is not a drawback but precisely what
makes it most valuable. He was convinced that "the Sagas are the great
victory of the Humanities in the North" (p. 210), but he also insisted that
"Iceland in the sagas [is] utterly different from all the rest of the world"
(CE 2.123). With heroic resignation, and perhaps (it must be admitted)
some complacency, he said that "it is part of the fate of Icelandic literature that it should not be influential in the great world, that it should fall
out of time, and be neglected, in the march of the great nations. It is in
this seclusion that its perfection is acquired, and there is nothing to complain of" (p. 269). And in his lecture to the Viking Club he made the
same point more pungently: "The Icelandic settlement was (and remains
in history) a protest against all the ordinary successful commonplaces of

the world" (*CE* 2.121). Partly acknowledging the paradox of *lecturing* on that which is perfected by neglect, he concluded his paper to the Viking Club with this passage:

> The question will not be asked here, "What is the use of it all?" It may be difficult to explain in what consists the value of Icelandic literature to the great world, which gets on so easily without it. . . . [Iceland] has its reward in being itself. (*CE* 2.128)

Indeed, the great world *has* gotten on without the sagas, as has the little world of literary criticism. If we were to ask which of Ker's two opposed genres have triumphed in the world of literary criticism, the answer would have to be romance. In medieval studies the most important response to Ker's book was Eugene Vinaver's 1957 article "From Epic to Romance," the germ of his influential book, *The Rise of Romance* (1971), in which he argued that romance represented both a literary and a cultural advance upon epic.[44] But in much larger ways the literary sensibility of the contemporary academy is still dominated by a romance aesthetic. New Criticism and Deconstruction both witness to its influence, and—primarily through the work of Northrop Frye—romance itself has become the quintessential genre of modernity. With its narrative intricacy, its obsessive self-consciousness, and its celebration of deferral as both narrative style and interpretive practice, romance is still the genre of our times.[45]

But it would be wrong to leave Ker's book with this melancholy assessment. It was written, as I have said, within the context of a centuries-long European debate, initiated by the cinquecento recovery of Aristotle's *Poetics* and the beginnings of vernacular genre theory. But it was also written in the 1890s, and it should be placed within that more local context. In a sense this is to read the book against its grain, since it avoids any allusion to its contemporary world: it is apparently as detached from *fin-de-siècle* England as heroic Iceland was from Europe. This refusal to acknowledge the form and pressure of the time is characteristic of Ker's work. In the essays he wrote during the Great War there are only two oblique references to that cataclysmic event. One is in 1916, when in an address to the English Association he applauded Henry James's decision to become a British subject; the other, in 1915, is his choice of Jacob Grimm as the topic for an address to the Philological Society—an address in which, with ostentatious (and admirable) independence, he praised Grimm for being able "to give colour and warmth to the history of the German race" (*CE* 2.232). Was this a way of saying that scholarship transcends politics? We may well think so, especially since the lesson that Ker drew from Grimm's life was an obliquely defiant *Fay ce que voudras*—do what you will.

Nonetheless, if *Epic and Romance* is read in its historical context much about it becomes more highly charged. The 1890s were the Yellow Decade, the time of Decadence, Imagism, and Symbolism. It was also the time of the Fabian Society, the founding of the London School of Economics and the British Labour Party, and the beginning of the Boer War. Where in this energetic world should we locate Ker's *Epic and Romance*? The answer, I think, is that Ker's book—implicitly and, at rare moments, even explicitly—is part of a self-consciously Counter-Decadent movement. Ker's Middle Ages were certainly not those of William Morris, Aubrey Beardsley, or Arthur Machen; and in a decade when—as Victor Plarr later said—"one had . . . to be preposterously French," Ker's view of the quintessentially French form of romance as a collection of "vanities, wonders, and splendours" (p. 34) was an anti-Gallic protest.[46] But there are deeper matters at issue than taste in literature. For one of the central values of Decadence was self-division—precisely that which Germanic epic, perhaps wisely, refused to contemplate. In *The Picture of Dorian Gray*, written in 1890, just four years after Stevenson's *Dr. Jekyll and Mr. Hyde* (1886), Oscar Wilde has his protagonist "wonder at the shallow psychology of those who conceive of the Ego in man as a thing simple, permanent, reliable, and of one essence."[47] According to Arthur Symons's manifesto, *The Symbolist Movement in Literature* (1899), "Every artist lives a double life," and in *Arms and the Man* (1894), Shaw's protagonist went even further in celebrating the fragmented personality: "Which of [my] six [selves] is the real man? That's the question that torments me. One of them is a hero, another a buffoon, another a humbug, another perhaps a bit of a blackguard. And one, at least, is a coward."[48] When only one of Shaw's protagonist's selves was a hero, in a play that interrogated, under its Virgilian title, the long cultural history of militarism, one can understand that Ker's celebration of the heroic age was more than simply a reactionary Teutonism. On the contrary, in early medieval literature he found represented a selfhood simplified by its confrontation with the unalterable reality of death. If this poetry presented a "drama of strong characters"

(p. 37), they were made strong by what he called "a knowledge not too elaborate or minute, but sound and clear" (p. 69)—the knowledge, that is, that life is temporary, death inevitable. For Ker this knowledge is epitomized in the hero's last words in the Old Norse *Hamðismál*: "if we die to-day, if we die to-morrow, there is little to choose. No man may speak when once the Fates have spoken" (p. 141). For Ker, psychological complexity is possible only for a person, and a society, that willfully ignores the inescapable fact of death. To speak of the unreality of modern life is to forget that all life is, from the perspective of death, unreal—and therefore, in a paradox that the Icelandic hero would have understood but never sought to express, the only reality. Either to lament or to celebrate artificiality is to miss the point.

Ker's admiration for reticence must also be understood in the context of what we may call the late nineteenth-century crisis of language. The central element of this complex phenomenon relevant here is the notion that compared to spoken language, "written language [was] . . . linguistically artificial and inauthentic."[49] This meant that linguistic usage was beyond the control of the cultural elite, and that the English language—and with it the English nation—was condemned to contamination and decay. And here Victorian cultural critics invoked the inevitable analogy to Rome: just as classical Latin had collapsed into the vulgar tongues by contamination with the Germanic barbarians, so too would English, by its very expansiveness and imperial dominance, become corrupted as a prelude to the collapse of the British Empire itself.

The response of the Decadents to this fear was not to condemn but to celebrate the polyglot, the artificial, and the factitious in language. In his notorious foreword to Baudelaire's *Fleurs du mal* (1867), Gautier defined decadence linguistically:

> This style of decadence is the last effort of the Word, called upon to express everything, and pushed to the utmost extremity. . . . Such is the inevitable and fatal idiom of peoples and civilizations where factitious life has replaced the natural life, and developed in man unknown wants.[50]

In England the celebrant of this fallen polyglossia was Walter Pater, whose own lapidary style and practice of treating English as a "dead language" were deeply antipathetic to Ker. For Ker valued above all else the simple and the spontaneous: where Pater would labor over the finely wrought pages of his essays, Ker—whose platform performances were legendary—preferred to construct his essays from scripts provided by a stenographer in attendance at his lectures.[51]

Ker's admiration for reticence, and his own refusal of grandiloquence, can therefore be seen as a protest against the linguistic exorbitance of his contemporaries. In his reserve, in his insistence that a value is most valuable when left unexpressed, Ker is part of the Counter-Decadence of the 1890s. Contemporaries with similar views would include the Tory journalists W. H. Henley and Charles Whibley (who was to edit Ker's essays after his death), and poets like Kipling, Hardy, Housman, and John Davidson, all of whom participated in the 1890s revival of the ballad—the literary form that, in its laconic brevity, Ker thought nearest to the heroic epic.[52] In one of his later essays Ker the nominalist complained that in literary criticism "the spirit of the age is a dangerous demon": poets should not be reduced to being mere reflexes of their historical moment (*CE* 1.129). Yet Ker the reluctant Hegelian also knew that the spirit of the age was a powerful force that few could resist. In *Epic and Romance* he both stands outside his time and reacts to it—very much like Beowulf, in fact. When he celebrates "the hardness of the Sagas" (p. 217) we can see that the alternative to this male strength is the sexual lability of Wilde or Beardsley; when he says that much of the art of romance writers like Chrétien de Troyes "is bestowed in making pedantry look attractive" (p. 333), or when he claims that Boccaccio's *Teseide* "might be taken as the first example in modern history of the pernicious effect of classical studies" (p. 364), his target is the classicist Pater. As Ker must have known, *Epic and Romance* was a polemical book: like the saga heroes he so much admired, the book meant far more than it said.

IV

Most readers will feel, no doubt legitimately, that the values that support the verbal phenomenon this essay explores are part of a past that is well left behind. Aristocratic violence legitimized by a self-protective hauteur, a masculinist community of values so intimately shared as to need no articulation (colloquially known, and experienced, as the old boys' club), imperialist exploitation masked by an ethic of self-sacrifice, and above all

a male silence that refuses to confront unpleasant emotions honestly—
it would not be unreasonable or even unfair to understand the laconic
style in these terms. But to stop here would be to accede too easily to the
pleasures of a self-righteousness in which an enlightened present often
likes to indulge when thinking about the benighted past. It would also,
I think, misunderstand the effect of these examples. One of the most active fields of sociolinguistic research has been the description and evalu-
ation of male and female speech.[53] Two of the salient points made by this
research are that women tend to use speech for forming emotional and social bonds while men see speech primarily as a means of conveying information or maintaining social positions; and second, while men speak far
more than women in public situations, in private men are far less verbally
available.[54]

This second point is most relevant to the issue of the laconic style,
and it has received some powerful interpretations. According to Jack Sattel, in a celebrated 1976 article,

> Silence and inexpression are the ways men learn to consolidate power,
> to make effort appear as effortless, to guard against showing the real
> limits of one's potential and power by making it all seem easy. Even
> among males, one maintains control over a situation by revealing only
> strategic proportions of oneself.[55]

Similarly, in her book on the Western novel and film Jane Tompkins
argues (in a wonderful if misleading phrase) that silent men exercise a
"conversational *droit de seigneur*."[56] For her, "the Western hero's silence
symbolizes a massive suppression of the inner life" (p. 66).

> To be a man is not only to be monolithic, silent, mysterious, impene-
> trable as a desert butte—it is to *be* the desert butte. By becoming a
> solid object, not only is a man relieved of the burden of relatedness
> and responsiveness to others, he is relieved of consciousness itself,
> which is to say, primarily, consciousness of self. (p. 57)

Whether this is true of the Western hero, or of the contemporary
American male, is not a matter I am in a position to determine. But as for
the figures, both fictional and historical, whom I have discussed in this
essay, this account is as inaccurate as is the canard of the medieval *droit*

de seigneur.[57] For it is precisely an excess of consciousness—or an excess of meaning, which is much the same thing—that motivates the terse concision of these men. When Beowulf displaces his understanding of his cultural and personal situation into the story of Hrethel and then the bereft father, it is not because he feels too little but too much. Like the speaker in "The Wanderer," he knows that laments—"grief-songs"—are not merely useless but inadequate, insufficient to the full meaning of his situation. He understands, with a clarity that contemporary popular culture has lost, the difference between sentiment and sentimentality, and the crucial importance of preserving not a merely visible honor but an inner integrity, a wholeness of self that direct expression would betray. This wholeness is not given but achieved, and achieved through the realization of the inevitability of death and the insignificance of human effort. In the face of such knowledge, what words could be adequate? "I am just going outside and may be some time."

chapter seven

Writing Amorous Wrongs

Chaucer and the Order of Complaint

"Death is the mother of beauty." Wallace Stevens's dictum reminds us of the long-standing, perhaps permanent link between poetry and loss, writing and absence. We write of and out of what we lack, what we imagine to be possible (happiness, understanding), and what we hope, by our writing, to discover or recover: this is what Stevens meant when he described us as "natives of poverty, children of malheur" for whom "the gaiety of language is our seigneur."[1] And if Chaucer seems to us one of the least impoverished, least unhappy of poets, we should remember that he maintained a persistent, intense interest in the kind of writing he and his contemporaries called complaint.[2] This was a ubiquitous albeit amorphous medieval form. The voice of lament pervades Germanic and Celtic writing, is shaped by biblical and classical models and rhetorical prescription into the *planctus* of the learned tradition, and permeates both the affective piety and the sentimental amorousness of the later medieval period.

Given the *murnung* of the Anglo-Saxon scop[3] and the *englynion* of the Welsh bard, the *planh* of the Provençal poet (Cercamon on Guillaume IX of Aquitaine, Bertran de Born on Henry the young king), the satirist's "complaint of the times" (Alain de Lille's *De planctu naturae*, Rutebeuf's "Complainte de Guillaume," Gower's *Vox clamantis*), and the *planctus Mariae* of pious and the *complainte d'amour* of courtly poets—it sometimes seems as if the Middle Ages must have been awash with tears.

Despite its taxonomic skill, medieval scholarship has not yet produced a full-scale account of the complaint.[4] Perhaps investigators have been understandably discouraged simply by the varieties of the form and the complexities of its history. Yet there is a deeper problem as well—one clearly recognized and neatly solved in an analogous area by Donald Howard. In his study of the *contemptus mundi* theme, Howard recognized that an analysis of the topoi of a single generic set, however inclusive or complex, could not adequately describe either the pervasiveness with which the theme permeated medieval writing or the profundity of its effect.[5] Consequently, he followed his discussion of the genre itself with characteristically acute readings of three Middle English poems, thus revealing the way the theme shaped these works both directly and by reaction. In effect, Howard showed how in the later Middle Ages the *contemptus mundi* theme was not merely an element in these poems but constitutive of them, a context so enveloping as to be both invisible and unavoidable, both taken for granted and always at issue.

Something of the same is true of the complaint: as I have suggested, it is virtually coextensive with poetry, indeed with writing itself. If language is a form of action that mediates between the subject and the world, then complaint interrogates its relation to these two presences. Can language express the subject? Can it have an effect upon the world? The first question is asked by the emotionalism that complaint takes as its special province, the claim it makes upon the affect of both speaker and audience. Complaint negotiates between feeling and form, asking a question that has been at the center of Western poetics since their inception: is poetry primarily a spontaneous expression of feeling (as the rhetor Ion tells Socrates) or is it an art (Aristotle's *techne*)? Is it the inspired language of the soul (the poet as *vates*) or a product of civilization at its most exacting (the *poeta doctus*)? When in 1795 Schiller distinguished between naive and sentimental poetry, rather than initiating a new stage in literary thinking he was projecting an age-old debate upon a historical axis. Paradoxically, however, the ahistorical lyricism of the Middle Ages, precisely because of its highly stylized and convention-bound nature, raises this question in larger, more unsettling terms, as Paul Zumthor has shown. Is the speaking subject of the medieval lyric created by its own discourse—a grammatical function, Jakobson's diegetic shifter—or is s/he a historical being endowed with the selfhood humans have typically taken as their own?[6] If the complaint is above all an act of self-expression, is there a self from which it issues and to which it can be referred for interpretation, or is there only a suprapersonal discourse, Zumthor's "great game of poetry"?[7]

If the affectivity of complaint raises with special urgency questions about the emotive function of language, it asks similar questions about the referential and conative functions.[8] This is not simply a matter of representation, as if that were simple at all. But representation is a question for all literary language, as for language per se: there is no reason to see complaint as privileged in its skepticism. But what is specific to complaint is that the claim it lays upon the world is virtually always self-cancelling, and so it raises questions about writing as a pragmatic activity. Not only does the plaintive voice typically assume the uselessness of its declarations, but its uselessness is programmatic. The *complainte d'amour*, for instance, not only presupposes the perpetual intransigence of the lady—were she to respond to the lover's pleading she would not be worthy of it—but is invalidated by its very articulation: the more eloquent the lover, the less reliably sincere his plea. An implication present throughout amorous lament, this point is made explicit by Andreas Capellanus: the lover who woos with service rather than words is to be preferred, says the noblewoman, to "the man who publicises to me the secrets of his heart explicitly in words, placing all his hopes in eloquence and doubtless trusting more to the elegance of his speech and the deceit of his words [*verborum duplicate*] than to the integrity of my will."[9] Complaint is not merely ineffective, in other words, but an illegitimate attempt to change a heart that will yield only to action. The poet's relation to the world is thus one of exclusion, even alienation: rather than participating, he stands to the side, claiming the privilege of irony because he lacks the efficiency of power. And again we touch one of the central issues of Western thinking about literature: does writing have any effect upon the world, whether moral or practical, or is it simply ornament and compensation?

The ubiquity of complaint within the medieval literary system, whether as a specific genre or an element present in all writing, thus stems in part from its capacity to stage questions central to literary culture as a whole. It provides a site for theorizing, a diminutive arena in which a poetics can be concentrated. Indeed, its modest dimensions and unprepossessing claims are part of its appeal: here radical speculation can be granted free play. And since the issues generated by the reflexivity of complaint focus upon the ground of writing, the form can be used to raise even larger questions about the foundations of cultural and even metaphysical truths. It is in this direction, at any rate, that Chaucer moves in his complaints. Put simply, he asks whether amorous wrongs can be righted by being written—whether, that is, the self can be repaired or justice be done through poetry. In two different but related moments of lament—the *Canticus Troili* and *The Complaint of Mars*—Chaucer shows that not only can the question not be answered but that its very asking initiates a process of interrogation that has no natural stopping point.

I

After his vision of Criseyde in the temple, Troilus retreats to his room, the first of the many acts of withdrawal to be enacted in this poem of almost obsessive inwardness. His initial instinct is to continue this inward path—"Thus gan he make a mirour of his mynde" (1.365)—but he shortly turns from the pleasures of narcissism to the empirical demands of courtship. "Thus took he purpos loves craft to suwe" (379), and he begins to plot strategy, deciding "What for to speke, and what to holden inne, / And what *to arten hire* to love he soughte" (387–88). The famous Petrarchan sonnet he now rehearses derives from this wish "to arten" Criseyde, a verb derived from *ar(c)tere* and so meaning "to constrain, compel, or force" but whose phonetic form inevitably links it to the artful Ovidian "craft" (379) to which Troilus has just committed himself— a phonetic link that in fact led many of the scribes to rewrite the line so as to enforce the neologistic meaning "to manipulate."[10] In fact, the word is usefully ambiguous: Troilus will artfully coerce Criseyde, a program that links together passion and strategy.

The song he now sings is both part of this program and an expression of its central paradox. In changing the Petrarchan original—changes that commentators have usually, and mistakenly, described as errors—Chaucer renders the song not simply a display of the oxymoronic psychology of love but rather an interrogation of its ontological status.[11] For Petrarch, as we would expect, the object of scrutiny was his own emotion: "If it is not love, what then is it that I feel? But if it is love, by God, what kind of thing is it?"[12] But Troilus takes the emotion as a given and queries its source: "If no love is, O God, what fele I so? / And if love is, what thing and which is he?" (400–401). In moving the interjection from the second line to the first, and rendering it not an assertion ("by God") but an apostrophe ("O God"), Troilus makes it clear that his poem is in fact addressed to the very God of Love whose existence he is simultaneously questioning and affirming, the god from whom comes the "torment and adversite" (404) of which he complains. But then in the second stanza Troilus poses the alternative possibility: perhaps "at *myn owen lust* I brenne" (407). If this is the case, he asks, in another significant change from Petrarch, "How may [there be] of the [i.e., love] *in me* swich quantite, / But if that I consente that it be?"(412–13).[13] Hence when his third stanza then invokes the simile of the rudderless boat "posed to and fro . . . bitwixen wyndes two" (415–17), we can see that he is caught not simply between conflicting emotions but also between two different conceptions of love: love as a transcendent deity who imposes his power upon his subjects versus love as an inward and conflicted emotion. And as the dramatic context of the song shows, these two conceptions are symmetrically related to the double impulse of coercion and submission that motivated the song in the first place: proceeding from Troilus's own conflicted motives, the song extends them into a metaphysical question. Not surprisingly, Troilus cannot sustain this conflict, and the two succeeding stanzas immediately resolve his dilemma in favor of transcendence.

> And to the God of Love thus seyde he
> With pitous vois, "O lord, now youres is
> My spirit, which that oughte youres be."
>
> (421–23)

In sum, then, at the very moment he begins to enact his desire, Troilus has come to question it. Although initially defining the emotion that moves him as a transcendent force by which he is wholly possessed, his plaintive song has unexpectedly led him to acknowledge that it may be in fact a merely human feeling, and hence marked with the impure complexity that by definition characterizes the human; but the uncertainty thus elic-ited is then hastily submerged within a commitment to a divine source so unwavering as to raise even Criseyde, at least momentarily, into the realm of the divine: "But wheither goddesse or womman, iwis, / She be, I not, which that ye do me serve" (425–26).

The dynamic enacted here is a miniaturized instance of the erotic economy that obtains throughout *Troilus and Criseyde*. The love upon which Troilus habitually calls is, whether deified or invoked simply as a guiding power, conceived as a transcendent force that possesses and trans-figures those who are its devoted recipients. Deriving from the *fons et origo* of being itself, its unifying force promises to overcome the difference or "unlyklynesse" (1.16) that does not merely disfigure but constitutes the *regio dissimilitudinis* of history. Not only does it claim the power to make one of two—"ye two," says Pandarus, "ben al on" (4.592)—but it can reconcile the lover to both the largest movements of the universe and to himself, endowing him with an inner coherence that repairs his self-alienation and makes him whole. For the true lover is by definition a being possessed of a single *entente,* an *intentio naturalis* (as Boethius would call it [3, pr. 11]) wholly directed toward a unification whose enactment may be sexual but that nonetheless promises to confirm a sacramental cosmic harmony. But in fact, as Troilus's song shows *in parvo,* love serves not to overcome the lover's alienation but to intensify it. At odds with itself in its very motivation, Troilus's artful song develops into an unpremeditated acknowledgment of the complexity of a self whose initial claim upon Cri-seyde had been its now discredited singleness of purpose. And far from being the first step in a process of courtship, it turns back on the entangled lover and reconfirms the narcissistic self-enclosure it was originally meant to counter. Written "to arten hire to love he soughte" (388), it is a song Criseyde never hears: the linear movement of amorous communication is converted to the circularity of psychological self-reflection.

The almost inevitable reaction to the inability of Troilus's love to fulfill its ambitions is to measure it against the love defined by medieval theology and philosophy, whether the Christian love of "sothefast Crist" (5.1860) that the poem comes finally to commend, or the Boethian *amor conversus* that is everywhere allusively invoked. The strengths of this in-terpretive procedure are obvious, as is the force of the readings it produces. But it also elicits resistance, and for a number of reasons. One is that bringing these systematic intellectual structures to bear upon a multivalent textuality creates a feedback effect that destabilizes the interpretive structures themselves. Hence, for instance, efforts to apply the elaborate medieval distinctions among different kinds of love to *Troilus and Criseyde* have as one effect an awareness of just how rigid these taxonomies are—a rigidity that in turn witnesses to an impeaching insecurity. So too, the invocation of Boethian standards of judgment must come to acknowledge that even the Boethian experience of *amor* is itself irresolubly ambiguous, as Boethius himself tacitly acknowledges in the famous Orpheus meter at the end of Book 3 of the *Consolation of Philosophy*. Moreover, this interpretive strategy requires the interpreter to stand apart from and above the object of his scrutiny, and so both to disavow the sympathy that was the initial basis for understanding in the first place and, more seriously, to foreclose attention to the dynamics of the love that is itself the object of understanding. When understood as simply the negative obverse of a legitimate *amor*, in other words, Troilus's love loses its value as an object of interpretive interest. And yet it remains the subject of Chaucer's poem, and surely not simply so that it can call up its absent opposite.

These general comments have a particular relevance to the *Canticus Troili*, because Chaucer prefaces the song with a well-known stanza that shows how he is himself implicated within the divisive dynamic of Troilus's self-reflections, and implicated not as would-be lover but specifically as a writer:

> And of his song naught only the sentence,
> As writ myn auctour called Lollius,
> But pleinly, save oure tonges difference,
> I dar wel seyn, in al that Troilus
> Seyde in his song, loo! every word right thus
> As I shal seyn; and whoso list it here,
> Loo, next this vers he may it fynden here.
>
> (393–99)

Chaucer promises here to introduce into the course of his narratorial account a privileged moment of Troilian discourse. In a way evidently unlike the other instances of Troilus's speech recorded in the poem, the

Canticus Troili is authentic: we are to be given not just the "sentence" but "every word." Just as Troilus's song begins by asserting his closeness to the very origins of love—"every torment and adversite / . . . cometh of *hym*" (404–5), the God to whom the poem is addressed—so does the song itself derive directly from Troilus. Yet here too the initial claim reaches an unlooked-for conclusion: as Troilus discovers that the transcendent singularity he had posited as the source of love cannot be sustained, so too is the narrator's claim to unmediated access belied by his recourse to Petrarch. And in fact, as we have seen, the univocal Petrarchan lyric—an examination of love as simply a psychological phenomenon—becomes in Chaucer's rewriting an equivocal debate between love-as-deity and love-as-affect. Neither Troilus's love nor the poet's representation of Troilus's song about love bespeaks an authoritative origin: just as Lollius is revealed upon inquiry to be a mumbling together of sources, so is the *entente* to love (as this moment suggests and as the poem as a whole demonstrates) an unfathomable mixture of appetite and idealism, self-regard and altruistic self-sacrifice.

"To write is to have the passion of the origin."[14] This Derridean dictum is above all true of the logocentric Middle Ages, which tended to conceive of its cultural activity as an effort, however necessarily incomplete, to ground itself upon a divinely authored source. But it is just this theology of origins—whether conceived in amorous, literary, or historiographical terms—that *Troilus and Criseyde,* and so much of Chaucer's poetry, interrogates. In writing a Trojan poem Chaucer invoked the founding moment of Western secular history. But in saturating his narrative with allusions to a Theban prehistory he let this Trojan origin give way to reveal beneath it another foundational narrative, and one in which—as the form of the Theban legend argued—beginnings are always re-beginnings, action always repetition. As the very reduplicative form of *Troilus and Criseyde* itself argues, history is not the linear *translatio imperii* medieval secular historiography asserted but rather a recursive labyrinth, an echo chamber of tragic reenactment.[15]

The same economy controls as well the *translatio* of writing, revealing it to be subversively conditioned by an unavoidable "tonges difference." The governing assumption of medieval literary culture was that the same thing can be said in different words: the *res*—the signified that underwrites and legitimates all verbal expression—can be articulated in an infinite number of different *verba* and yet remain always the same. The task of the medieval writer is not to discover new matter—hence the withering away of *inventio* in late classical and medieval rhetorical theory—but to rewrite the original, the authoritative text bequeathed to the present by the past. This rewriting is accomplished in large part by recourse to the tropes—the *translationes*—catalogued by the rhetorical handbooks. But figuration, as the Middle Ages well knew, is never innocent: verbal *translatio* is the transfer of a word from its proper use to an improper one, a displacement that always runs the risk of vagrancy. The success of literary transfer, in other words, is always threatened by the truancy of the mediatory figures by which it is to be accomplished. Just as within the economy of the individual text figuration retards the unfolding of the narrative line, so in the larger economy of literary history does it invert the linearity that connects imitation to source into a periphrastic circumlocution. That this periphrasis is a source of anxiety is shown both by the injunctions to writers to restrain figuration within the limits of propriety and the preemptive hermeneutics with which medieval exegetes sought to protect readers from the seductions of the letter. The task of the medieval reader is to rewrite the *signa translata* of figurative language back into the *signa propria* of the literal truth, a task accomplished by recourse to an extratextual source of authority able to cut through the laterally extended veil of words to the truth within. Absent such an instrument, the reader will find himself trapped within the *regio dissimilitudinis* of the letter. Just as the purposive linearity of secular history cannot maintain itself, but gives way to a compulsive recursiveness that calls into question all merely historical beginnings and endings, so writing threatens to declare its ineluctably mediatory status—its condition as a process of *translatio* undertaken without access to an authoritative source and with no guarantee of successful conclusion. And it is just this sense of writing as ceaseless rewriting that characterizes the work of the man whom Deschamps rightly designated, in a poem based on the topos of *translatio studii*, a *grant translateur*.

In writing the song with which he will "arten" Criseyde to love, Troilus comes upon some disquieting facts about his own integrity—a term with ontological meanings that are as important as its more familiar ethical significance.[16] Promising to make one out of two, love has had the ironic effect of introducing ambiguity into what was formerly thought to be integral. And the poem as a whole comes to define a subjectivity that is less that of identity than a site where different selves are constituted and decomposed. Nowhere is this subjectivity made more fully present than in the act of complaint. And it is also in the complaint that we can best understand Chaucer's own inscription within the economy of amorous duplication.

II

A second example that can usefully illuminate this unsettling dynamic is one of Chaucer's most innovative and enigmatic poems, the *Complaint of Mars*.[17] The poem is presided over by Venus—"þe double goddesse of love," as John Shirley called her in a notorious rubric to the poem[18]— and is itself almost obsessively equivocal. It represents its protagonists as both planets and gods, and yet has their embarrassing celestial doings described by a bird as the subject of a Valentine's Day aubade. This complex siting apparently serves to establish an opposition between the nighttime misbehavior of the planetary gods and the orthodox natural mating of the birds. But in fact it comes to present these alternative modes of love-making less as opposites than equivalents. For its very status as the subject of amorous bird song endows the adultery of Mars and Venus with a certain legitimacy, as does their enactment of an astronomically detailed celestial itinerary. Adulterous they may be, but they are tracing a course prescribed for them by a divinely established "hevenysh revolucioun" (30), and their conjunction—a celestial event designated by the astrologers a *copulatio*—is as much in the nature of things as is the love service of the birds.[19] Similarly, Venus's astrological amelioration of Mars is simultaneously a shameful unmanning and the sign of a harmonious *discordia concors*: Venus is indeed, as the mythographers and astrologers say, *duplex*— both "the mother of all fornications" and the deity whom Boccaccio called *Venus magna* and whom Bernard Silvestris described as "the harmony of the world, that is, the even proportion of worldly things, which some call Astrea, and others call natural justice."[20] The "binding" (47–48) and "knitting" (50) by which Mars and Venus are joined is simultaneously an expression of the Boethian "byndynge" by which Nature "restreyneth alle thynges by a boond that may nat be unbownde" (3.ii.6–7) and the constraint with which "amyable Fortune byndeth with the beaute of false goods the hertes of folk that usen them" (3.8.19–21).[21]

Critics have virtually unanimously read Venus's effect on Mars in this poem in negative terms, and have denied or devalued the relevance of the notion of *discordia concors*, arguing that this is a classical topos that reappears only in the Renaissance. Chauncey Wood provides a forthright account:

> The fact of the matter is that Chaucer's attitude, as well as that of the audience, toward the story of Mars and Venus was rather well fixed in the direction of condemnation, and the "good" interpretation of Mars and Venus that became common in the Renaissance was only used outside of any reference to planetary conjunction or mythological adultery in the Middle Ages and so cannot fit the situation in the *Complaint of Mars*. . . . A close inspection of the evidence suggests that while the idea that Venus could temper the fury of Mars was well-known in the Middle Ages, the more positive idea that the union of the two produced Harmony seems to be discoverable only in the Renaissance.[22]

It is quite true that Ficino's illustration of the philosophic idea of universal harmony by means of the adultery of Mars and Venus finds its precedent not in medieval tradition but in Plutarch's *Moralia*. But the idea, in however ironically inflected a form, was always implicit in the myth, and Chaucer would have found it made explicit in Book 3 of the *Thebaid*. There Venus seeks to prevent Mars from inciting the Argives against the Thebans, a race descended from their daughter, Harmonia. In explaining that he is constrained by Jove and the Fates, Mars acknowledges Venus's tempering power, describing her as "my repose from battle, my sacred joy and all the peace my heart doth know: thou who alone of gods and men canst face my arms unpunished, and check even in mid-slaughter my neighing steeds, and tear this sword from my right-hand" (3.295–99).[23] In his commentary on these lines, Lactantius Placidus describes the effect of Venus on Mars in both astrological and cosmic terms. He first glosses *sacra voluptas* ("sacred joy") astrologically: "Si enim mixtus aliis sideribus Mars fuerit, uehementior truculentiorque fit, econtra si Iouis, bonus, si Veneris, supplex fiet." And he then glosses *unaque pax animo* ("and all the peace my heart doth know") by citing an important passage from Lucretius (otherwise unavailable to the Middle Ages) that describes Venus's pacific effect on Mars: "For thou alone canst delight mortals with quiet peace, since Mars mighty in battle rules the savage works of war, who often casts himself upon thy lap wholly vanquished by the everliving wound of love."[24] My point is not that in the *Complaint of Mars* Chaucer presents a vision of *discordia concors*, but rather that the conjunction of Mars and Venus, both as stars and as deities, was understood in the classical world in ambivalent terms; and that the beneficial effects of the goddess Venus upon Mars would have been known to Chaucer both implicitly through the tradition of *Venus duplex* and explicitly by means of this passage in the *Thebaid* and its commentary. In fact, the ambivalence of at least the astrological conjunction is neatly articulated in Chaucer's other two uses of it, once (positively) in the Hypermnestra story of the *Legend of Good Women* and then (negatively) in the Wife of Bath's Prologue. And the *Complaint of Mars* does *not* tell the story of the humiliating entrapment of Mars and Venus by Vulcan but allows it to remain a suppressed middle: we are given the initial discovery by Phoebus Apollo and the subsequent history of the Brooch of Thebes with which Vulcan avenged himself, but not the entrapment itself—a deliberate textual omission that ought to restrain the reader from simply importing the values of that part of the myth into the poem.

The ambivalence of the conjunction of these deities/stars is neatly expressed in the stanza that describes the consummation of the love:

> The grete joye that was bitwix hem two,
> When they be mette, ther may no tunge telle.
> Ther is no more, but unto bed thei go;
> And thus in joy and blyse I lete hem duelle.
> This worthi Mars, that is of knygthod welle,
> The flour of feyrnesse lappeth in his armes,
> And Venus kysseth Mars, the god of armes.
>
> (71–77)

The allusion to Corinthians is at once elevating and bathetic; the assertion of verbal insufficiency that is thrice repeated in the consummation scene in the *Troilus*—"I kan namore" (3.1193, 1273, 1314)—is here both invoked and transformed into a statement of sexual urgency; and the meeting of opposites promises both a moment of cosmic harmony and future discord. Indeed, even the largest of the oppositions by which the poem is structured is in fact insolubly equivocal. The mythographical narrative records the collapse of the "perpetuall" love that Mars and Venus have plighted "for evere" (47–48), while the birds are brought together to confirm that their mutual love will last "perpetuely" (20): the fickleness of Olympian adultery is set against the steadfastness of natural instinct, change against permanence. Yet from another perspective the very fact that the birds return each year to "renovel[en]" (19) their vows—and that they choose to sing this particular song—raises the prospect of reparation: if Mars and Venus are driven apart "by hevenysh revolucioun" (30) they will also be brought back together. Evidently, there can be no change without permanence, and inconstancy promises renewal. So too with the other major thematic opposition in the poem, freedom and constraint. The act of moral judgment that the poem everywhere calls for assumes moral freedom; and yet the agents—whether birds, gods, or planets—are constrained to their acts by dispositions that serve to constitute their very natures. The birds are engaged in a ritual that witnesses to the ineluctable processes of nature, and yet they have come together to *choose* their mates, an assertion that is enforced by having the word repeated in three successive lines (16–18). For Mars and Venus not to conjoin would require them to be something other than Mars and Venus; and yet the consequences of their conjunction are represented in terms that assume ethical judgment and presuppose freedom of choice. The point is, then, that the poem represents behavior as both externally compelled and self-chosen, as an effect of both necessity and free will. Once again, opposites become counterparts, and the exclusive binarism of either/or becomes the inclusive— and destabilizing—dualism of both/and.

The most telling instance of this pervasive doubleness is Mars's complaint itself. "His nature was not for to wepe" (94), but having been first divested of his "cruelte, and bost, and tyrannye" (37) by Venus, and then further chastened by her loss, he has now discovered the *alter ego* of a previously unknown plaintive self. It is this geminated, amartial self that now engages in the quintessentially self-duplicating act of complaint. The aporetic context thus established gives special, ironic point to the subject of the complaint, which is nothing less than the search for a cause:

> The ordre of compleynt requireth skylfully
> That yf a wight shal pleyne pitously,

Ther mot be *cause* wherfore that men pleyne;
Or men may deme he pleyneth folily
And *causeles*; alas, that am not I!
Wherfore the *ground and cause* of al my peyne,
So as my troubled wit may hit atteyne,
I wol reherse; not for to have redresse,
But to declare my *ground* of hevynesse.

(155–63)

This initial invocation of a forensic purpose promises to endow the complaint with a secure discursive definition: Mars appears as plaintiff, appealing for redress for the wrongs he has suffered at the hands of some malefactor. Yet the course of the complaint itself subverts this discursive stability, for Mars discovers that he can specify with confidence neither the nature of the wrong done him, nor the perpetrator, nor an audience to whom he can appeal.[25] What instead emerges from his ruminations is the far more disturbing awareness that the economy of desire contains at its center an apparently irremediable repetitiveness. As day follows night so does need follow fulfillment, an imperative of reenactment that is emblematized in the Brooch of Thebes, itself a sign of the fatal repetition of a Theban history that doubles back on itself in a frustrated return to an always absent origin.

Mars designates this economy a "double wo and passioun" (255) and recognizes his own inscription within it. But what eludes him is its source: "What meneth this? What is this mystihed?" (224). Mars carefully exempts Venus from blame. She is, to be sure, the "verrey sours and welle . . . Of love and pley" (174–78) and as a "double goddesse" might be thought responsible for the doubleness of love. But such a thought is for Mars unthinkable, and he instead represents Venus as herself helpless before malevolent forces and so in his own condition of thwarted lament: "My righte lady, my savacyoun, / Is in affray, and not to whom to pleyne" (213–14). But in shying away from Venus as *fons et origo* Mars in fact allows for a far more destabilizing thought. By a process of logical regress he now designates as the source of his "double wo" the First Mover himself, "the God that sit so hye" (218). And with this assertion Mars now finds himself forced to identify this First Mover with the misshapen Vulcan and to see both the "hevenysh revolucioun" that has brought him to this impasse and the processes of history as motivated by the jealous malevolence of a wronged husband.

Mars's speculations have thus arrived at a self-evident absurdity, and we are invited to regard them as simply the product of his "troubled wit." His love for Venus persuades him to exempt her from responsibility for the erotic dynamic over which she herself presides, and he instead impeaches the basis of his own existence, the "ground and cause" of his very being. Hence he is unable to find anyone to whom to direct his bill of complaint, and concludes by instead leading "hardy knyghtes of renoun" and "ladyes that ben true and stable" (272, 281) in a choral lament for the Venus whom he thinks is abandoned but who is even now being comforted by the Mercury who will father upon her the illicit Hermaphrodite. And just as Mars becomes a figure of pathetic self-delusion, so his benighted complaint arrives at a philosophical impasse that can be resolved only by a Christian truth to which he himself has no access. Indeed, as critics have argued, the ambiguity of the poem's language calls up the absent other of Christian doctrine. Perhaps the most compelling instance of this ambiguity is Mars's description of God as a malevolent fisherman who baits his hook with "som pleasaunce" (238) that grants the lover "al his desir, and therwith al myschaunce" (241):

> And thogh the lyne breke, he hath penaunce;
> For with the hok he wounded is so sore
> That he his wages hath for evermore.
>
> (242–44)

Neil Hultin has shown that the image of woman as bait on the hook of sin was common in medieval didactic literature, and Rodney Merrill has argued that this image invokes as well the medieval trope of *amor* as a hook (*hamus*), which would allude not just to the biblical image of Christ as a fisher of men but also to the iconographic representation of God as baiting his hook with Christ in order to catch Satan.[26] In effect, then, Mars's discovery of the doubleness that pervades experience as a whole is taken as requiring as its antidote the singular truth of Christian doctrine: the endless dissatisfaction of venerean desire reminds the reader of the fulfillment offered by Christian love. Christ is the answer to Mars's questions, the love of God the means by which the unquiet heart of wayfaring man can find peace.

This strategy of stabilizing an equivocal text by locating it within a univocal interpretive context is not only authentically medieval, but is clearly solicited by the religiously charged language of the poem. But the poem also casts an interrogative light upon the procedures by which the strategy is enacted. If Christian interpretation is the necessary supplement by which that which is missing from the *Complaint of Mars* can be pro-vided, supplementarity has its own recursive habit of revealing what Der-rida has called "the anterior default of a presence."[27] That such a revelation may be a function of more than simply contemporary critical fashion is suggested by the poem itself, which is after all about the ubiquity of the equivocal. It delineates a world in which the either/or of singularity is sub-verted by a dualistic both/and, in which oppositions are revealed to be counterparts; and this must make us hesitant to endow one element of a pair with the power wholly to sublate much less to efface the other. So too does it delineate a mind engaged in a process of mental regress in order to discover a "ground and cause" for its experience, just as does the reader of the poem. Mars is constrained in his speculations by his avoidance of the unthinkable thought that Venus is herself complicit in the double-ness that characterizes the rest of the world. But is not the reader also constrained by the unthinkable? Is there not an orthodoxy that we too cannot transgress, a limit beyond which we cannot go, an origin (whether historical, metaphysical, or theological) we are reluctant to undo? In a post-Enlightenment world this question may seem overly dramatic, but that can hardly have been the case for Chaucer's audience.

III

Historians of medieval French literature have shown that in the fourteenth century previously freestanding lyrics began to be grounded within narra-tives.[28] This process was accomplished both through the *dit* form popu-larized by Guillaume de Machaut and through the development of lyric collections such as the *Cent ballades* or (to take a non-French example) Petrarch's *Rime sparse*.[29] This is a process of historicization, a strategy by which the abstract voice of lyric, issuing from no one in particular and re-ceived by everyone in general, is situated within a specific historical con-text: a singular person speaks to a determinate audience. And such a prac-tice can naturally be understood as seeking to contain the regressive irony implicit within lyricism. Chaucer himself participates in this literary innovation: poems like *Anelida and Arcite* and *The Legend of Good Women*, as well as *Troilus and Criseyde* and the *Complaint of Mars*, locate plaintive lyricism within a narrative context.[30] But the examples we have examined suggest that lyric irony cannot be domesticated by narrative. On the contrary, the narrative context is itself ironized, becomes itself subject to the self-reflexive uncertainties of the plaintive voice. Once introduced, irony metathesizes, subverting all efforts at sequestration. As Paul de Man has suggested, "Lyric poetry . . . [is] an enigma which never stops asking for the unreachable answer to its own riddle," and an enigma whose endless quest reveals unanticipated weaknesses within the body of the host.[31]

Genre and Source in Troilus and Criseyde

The purpose of this essay is to answer two questions. The first is so familiar that to ask it is—at least according to received opinion—already to answer it: why, at the end of *Troilus and Criseyde*, does Chaucer define his poem as a "tragedye" (5.1786)? The second, despite its obviousness, seems never to have been asked at all, much less answered. C. S. Lewis told us many years ago "What Chaucer Really Did to *Il Filostrato*," but he— and evidently everyone else—declined to ask the prior question: why *Il Filostrato* at all? As we shall see, these questions and their answers are interconnected.

As everybody knows—or at least thinks they know—Chaucer derived the term *tragedy* from a sentence in Boethius's *Consolation of Philosophy* and its attendant gloss.[1]

> What other thynge bywaylen the cryinges of tragedyes but oonly the dedes of Fortune, that with an unwar strook overturneth the realmes of greet nobleye? (*Glose. Tragedye is to seyn a dite of a prosperite for a tyme, that endeth in wrecchidnesse.)*[2]

Accepting this definition as a guide to Chaucer's use of the term in the *Troilus*, many critics have tried to accommodate the poem's densely complex narrative to this simple (not to say simplistic) model.[3] The results are generic gyrations that were wittily summed up twenty-five years ago by Alice Kaminsky. A "survey of various attempts to define the genre of *Troilus* is very clarifying," said Kaminsky, somewhat sardonically. [It] "reveals that *Troilus* is a comic tragedy with romantic and epic elements." She goes on to cite Alan M. F. Gunn, who defines the poem as a "polylithic romance," then describes it as "historical, amorous, . . . chivalric, comic, elegiac, tragic, pathetic, philosophical, psychological . . . allegorical, problematic, ironic, quasi-realistic, [and] myth-oriented."[4] This taxonomic chaos derives, I shall argue, from not attending to the context of Boethius's definition, by ignoring or misinterpreting the Monk's tragedies in the *Canterbury Tales*, and then—misled by these mistakes—by assuming that Chaucer's use of the term in the *Troilus* should be interpreted by reference to Boethius at all.

In Book 5 of the *Consolation* Lady Philosophy posits a straightforward Platonic epistemology. Knowledge is obtained through four ascending modes: *sensus* (which Chaucer translates as "wit"), *imaginatio* ("ymaginacioun"), *ratio* ("resoun"), and finally *intelligentia* ("intelligence") (5, pr. 4, 151–66). Of these four, only the first three are available to human beings.[5] Since Philosophy's task is to raise the prisoner's mind from a dependence on imagination to the use of reason, her instruction in the *Consolation* is organized according to these two epistemological modes. In the first two books Philosophy is the prisoner's "noryce" (1, pr. 3, 6) and he is her "nory" (1, pr. 3, 13) or nursling. Here the prisoner is taught by means of the imagination, and most extensively by the *prosopopeia* by which Philosophy speaks as if she were Fortune, "usynge the woordes of Fortune" (2, pr. 2, 2). Before she begins, Philosophy makes it clear that her account of the workings of Fortune—to repeat, an account spoken not by Fortune but by Philosophy *as if* she were Fortune—is preliminary and philosophically facile. Philosophy says that she is now going to instruct her "nory" with "softe and delitable thynges," using "the suasyoun of swetnesse rethorien" (2, pr. 1, 37, 40–41). At the end of the self-description that Philosophy has "Fortune" provide, the prisoner says: "thise ben faire thynges and enoyted with hony swetnesse of Rethorik and Musike; and oonly whil thei ben herd thei ben delycious, but to wrecches it is a deppere felynge of harm" (2, pr. 3, 8–12). Lady Philosophy agrees with him:

"For thise ne ben yet none remedies of thy maladye, but they ben a maner norisschynges of thi sorwe, yit rebel ayen thi curacioun" (2, pr. 3, 19–20). The point for us is that these preliminary and philosophically inadequate teachings include tragedy. A form of the dangerous poetry purveyed by the Muses whom Philosophy expels at the outset (see 1, pr. 1, 44–77), tragedies do not instruct the reason but, through the imagination, move the emotions. That is why they are described as "cryinges" that can only "bywaylen" Fortune. Only later, when Philosophy is confident that "the norisschynges of my *resouns* descende now into the" can she "usen a litel strengere medicines" (2, pr. 5, 1–3), the primary one being the reasoned demonstration that bad fortune is actually good. In sum, then, for Boethius the speaking personification of Fortune and the genre of tragedy are suspect for three reasons. Appealing to the imagination rather than reason, they arouse emotions rather than impart knowledge; they present Fortune as a powerful figure, although in reality good and bad events occur because of divine providence; and they grant to this fictitious figure named Fortune control over human happiness, although true happiness depends not upon the goods of fortune (which are arbitrarily bestowed and withdrawn) but upon philosophic wisdom (which is permanent).

The Monk's Tale shows that Chaucer fully understood Boethius's condemnation of tragedy. As almost every critic has pointed out, the Monk's tragedies are philosophically incoherent.[6] More to the point for my argument, they appeal to the emotions through what the Monk evidently thinks are powerful images rather than to the reason through philosophical instruction. This is why he begins his tale by saying that he "wol *biwaille* in manere of tragedie / The harm of hem that stoode in heigh degree" (1991–92) and later paraphrases the passage in which Philosophy dismisses the very form he will now (relentlessly) deploy:

> Tragedies in noon oother maner thyng,
> Ne kan in syngyng *crye ne biwaille*,
> But for that Fortune alwey wole assaille
> With unwar strook the regnes that been proude.
>
> (2760–63)

The best example of tragedy's incapacity to move beyond the emotional is the story of Ugolino with which the modern instances (and in all likelihood the tale itself) closes.[7] Dante presented Ugolino in *Inferno* 33 as a demonstration of the power of language to misrepresent the most violent sins,[8] but the Monk surpasses that self-exculpation with an even more extravagantly misleading version of Ugolino's story, larded with scriptural allusions and drenched in pathos.[9] That the Monk's Tale is in fact directed against his own misreading of Boethius is enforced by having him cite, approvingly, Philosophy's repudiation of tragedy not once but three times (VII.1973–79, 1991–98, 2760–65)—a sign of his pride in a learning that is all too shallow.[10]

We must therefore dismiss the definition of tragedy that Philosophy gives in the *Consolation* as defining a form that Chaucer could have taken seriously. So what else could he have meant by calling the *Troilus* a tragedy? Oddly enough, a clue is provided by a comment the Monk adds to his rehearsals of the Boethian definition. Tragedies, he says, "ben versified communely / Of six feet, which men clepen exametron" (1973–79). Over a century ago, in one of the many insights from the early days of Chaucer studies that appears to have been neglected by contemporary critics, Skeat understood that the Monk's reference to hexameter verse was relevant to the *Troilus*:

> Chaucer is speaking of Latin, not of English verse; and refers to the common Latin hexameter used in heroic verse; he would especially be thinking of the *Thebaid* of Statius, the *Metamorphoseon Liber* of Ovid, the *Aeneid* of Virgil, and Lucan's *Pharsalia*. This we would easily have guessed, but Chaucer has himself told us what was in his thoughts. For near the conclusion of his *Troilus and Criseyde*, which he calls a *tragedie*, he says, "And kis the steppes, wheras thou seest pace / Virgile, Ovyde, Omer, Lucan, and Stace."[11]

Skeat is certainly right, and we can begin to see that the Monk has muddled together two definitions of tragedy. One is the Boethian; the other is what we may call, in shorthand, the Dantean. Not that Dante invented this definition, for in having Virgil call his *Aeneid* "alta mia tragedìa" (*Inf.* 20.113) he was referring to a long medieval tradition.[12] While the Middle Ages soon lost any sense of the classical theater, the connection between elevated characters and tragedy remained. For Isidore of Seville, tragedies are not dramas but poems (*carmina*) that treat "public matters and the history of kingdoms" (*tragici vero res publicas et regum historias [praedicant]*) or, in a later account, "the ancient deeds and

sorrowful crimes of wicked kings" (*antiqua gesta atque facinora scelerato-*
rum regum luctuosa).[13] In a literary culture that lacked any clear generic
category in which to locate what in antiquity was known as an *epos* or *car-*
men heroicum, the works that we now call epics were instead designated
as tragedies. This shift in nomenclature was complete by at least the
twelfth century. In an *accessus* to Ovid's *Amores*, the student is told that
"Tragedy is . . . poetry about the deeds of nobles and kings,"[14] and by the
early fourteenth century Albertino Mussato defined a tragedy as a poem
written in heroic meter—hexameters—and dealing with the "open wars
in the field waged by sublime kings and dukes." For Albertino, tragedians
include Ennius, Lucan, Virgil, and Statius.[15]

So the epic of Antiquity was in the Middle Ages called tragedy.
And for the Middle Ages tragedy dealt with history. Medieval readers and
writers understood the *Aeneid*, the *Thebaid*, and the *Pharsalia* as accounts
of things that really happened, as histories. After recounting the plot of
the *Aeneid*, Conrad of Hirsau says that "Virgil has taken both the subject-
matter and his intention from this history." Speaking of the *Thebaid*, he
says that "Statius . . . took the subject-matter of his work from the beginning or the end of the actual war."[16] Indeed, Servius—followed by
Isidore—complained that "Lucan did not deserve to be reckoned among
the poets, for he seems to have written a history, not a poem," and Arnulf
of Orléans said bluntly that Lucan's "intention is to deal with the *historia*"
of the civil war.[17] Bernard Silvestris included Virgil among the *historici*,
and Alexander Neckham told his students to read the "historians" (*ystori-*
ographi) Virgil, Statius, and Lucan.[18] And when Petrarch came to write his
own *carmen heroicum*, the *Africa*, he chose as his topic an unquestionably
historical event, the life of Scipio Africanus.[19] Indeed, even the Monk
seems to know that his miserable little narratives are in fact histories: as he
says in the first line of his definition: "Tragedie is to seyn, a certeyn *storie*"
(1973)—that is, a history.

Chaucer could have derived this understanding of tragedy from many
sources, but he almost certainly learned it from Dante. As we have seen,
in canto 20 of the *Inferno* Virgil refers to the *Aeneid* as *l'alta mia tragedìa*
(20.113). He calls his poem a *high* tragedy because it is written in an elevated style (in the *De vulgari eloquentiae* [2.6.5] Dante says that tragedy
is written in a *stilus superior*) and because it deals with important matters. As the commentary known as the *Anonimo Fiorentino* (c. 1400) says,

tragedy treats "the magnificent deeds and the crimes of powerful men, as did Virgil, Lucan and Statius."[20] But fully to understand Chaucer's debt to Dante we need to locate this definition of tragedy in its context in the *Commedia*. Shortly after Virgil identifies the *Aeneid* as a tragedy, he and Dante meet the Malebranche, a squadron of devils with vulgar names and the manners of Neapolitan street urchins. Taunting each other and Virgil, they are nonetheless unable to shake the ancient poet's severe, even haughty demeanor. But Dante is also unable to persuade Virgil that the devils do in fact represent a real threat. Hence the travelers soon discover that the Malebranche have tricked Virgil into thinking that there is a bridge over the sixth *bolgia*, whereas in fact it had been destroyed by the earthquake that occurred at the moment of Christ's death. The travelers are thus forced to escape the pursuing devils by an undignified slide down the side of the sixth *bolgia*. There they are met by the hypocrites, one of whom replies to Virgil's complaint that the devils lied to him with a laconic comment:

> Once in Bologna, I heard discussed
> the devil's many vices; one of them is
> That he tells lies and is the father of lies.
> $\qquad$ (*Inf.* 23.142–44)[21]

Virgil stalks off angrily, discomfited by his inability to recognize the diabolical, perhaps understandably since his interlocutor is quoting John 8.44. We now see that the episode as a whole is designed to highlight the limitations of Virgil's pre-Christian understanding: hence he is "amazed" (24.124) when he sees the crucified Caiaphas, unaware both of his identity and of the symbolic meaning of his crucifixion. In sum, the scurrilous events of cantos 21 through 23 are a stark (and ironic) contrast to the heroic action and *stilus superior* of Virgil's *alta tragedìa*.[22]

For our understanding of the *Troilus*, the most important point is that it is within these very cantos—just a few lines after Virgil's identification of the *Aeneid* as a *tragedìa*—that Dante designates the genre of the poem he is writing as *la mia comedìa* (*Inf.* 21.2). And it is in these cantos that Dante shows that his *Commedia* can include elements that a *tragedìa* cannot, specifically these cheerfully vulgar devils, with their adolescent squabbles and a magnificent fart. To be sure, the curve of the action from

"wo to wele" (as Egeus says in the Knight's Tale) is central to Dante's definition, but so too is the stylistic variation that characterizes comedy. As
Pietro Alighieri says in his commentary, comedy is written "in a style that
is, in the main, lowly . . . [yet also] in the high and elevated style."[23] The
mixed style of comedy, as Dante shows in these cantos, can accommodate
elements that the uniformly high style of tragedy cannot. But equally important as these two criteria—the shape of the action, the level of the
style—is subject matter. Tragedy deals with the world of public events, of
history: according to Donatus, "tragedy aspires to historical truth."[24] But
comedy describes not events but, as one medieval description of Terence
put it, "the habits of men, both young and old"—*mores hominum, iuve-
numque senumque*.[25] According to the schoolbook definitions, it concerns
itself with *privatae personae, privati homines, res privatorum, et humiliae personae*.[26] The subject matter of comedy is what we would call character: it
represents men and women not in terms of their social existence but as
individuals, as the unique and individualized personalities—or souls—
whom we meet throughout the *Commedia*.[27] Are these cantos in the *Inferno* the proximate source of Chaucer's understanding of tragedy? Two
lines after designating the *Troilus* a "tragedye," and just before telling it
to kiss the footprints of the great classical tragedians—"Virgile, Ovide,
Omer, Lucan and Stace" (an invocation itself taken from the end of the
Thebaid)—Chaucer prays God for the "myght to make in some comedye"
(5.1788). Just as Dante contrasts Virgil's *tragedìa* with his own *comedìa*,
then, so does Chaucer contrast the tragedy of *Troilus* with an unnamed
future work—a work that is surely the *Canterbury Tales*.[28]

Before turning to our second question—why *Il Filostrato?*—I cannot
leave the topic of genre without disposing of a ubiquitous but unexamined assumption that has persistently muddied the discussion. This is the
notion that the poem should be called a romance. In 1938 Karl Young
entitled an article "Chaucer's *Troilus and Criseyde* as Romance"; in 1957
Charles Muscatine saw elements of both romance and the psychological
novel in the poem; in 1992 Barry Windeatt applied to the poem, among
other generic terms, romance; in 2002 Roy Pearcy described the poem
under the rubric of tragedy and romance; and in 2004 *A Companion to Romance* includes, apparently inevitably, a discussion of *Troilus and Criseyde*.[29]
Indeed, there are few discussions of the poem in which the word "romance"
does not appear.[30] The problem with using the term *romance* to describe

the poem is not only that it ignores Chaucer's own generic identification of the poem as a tragedy but that *romance* was one of the few generic terms that had a distinctive meaning for medieval readers. Although the term covered a broad lexical field, and never (so far as I know) received any sustained theoretical attention, most readers and writers had a pretty clear idea what it meant. In England it originally signified French as opposed to Latin: in his *Story of England* (completed in 1338), Robert Mannyng of Brunne wrote that "Frankysche speche ys cald Romaunce," and he described one of his main sources, Pierre Langtoft's *Le regne d'Edouard Ier*, as written "in romance."[31] But the primary medieval meaning—romance as a narrative—developed in the twelfth century, when Chrétien de Troyes used the term *roman* to designate his work: "Cest romanz fist Crestiens," he says in the Prologue to *Cligés*.[32] Occasionally, to be sure, the term was applied to works that we would hardly consider romances. The English translation of Robert Grosseteste's *Chasteau d'amour*, a personification allegory about the battle between the vices and virtues, opens with a firm generic marker: "Here begynnes a romance of Englische of the beginning of the world." Other works that call themselves romances include the *Myrour of Lewed Men*, the *Trental of St. Gregory*, and *Meditations on the Life and Passion of Christ*.[33] But on the whole the term was restricted to the narratives that fit the primary definition now offered by the Middle English Dictionary: "A written narrative of the adventures of a knight, nobleman, king, or an important ecclesiastic, a chivalric romance." Two presuppositions are important here: the focus on an individual hero and the absence of any requirement that the adventures be amorous.[34] Indeed, the contemporary meaning of romance as a love affair, or as designating specifically the erotic rather than the fanciful or exotic, did not emerge at all—surprisingly—until the second half of the nineteenth century.[35] Yet this is certainly the dominant meaning of the word now: if you Google *romance* the first web site that pops up is "Lovingyou.com: Love, Romance and Relationship Resources" and all of the ads on the Google web page are of a similar nature, ranging from "Find Romance Online" to "In Home Sex Toy Parties." It is this modern definition of romances as designating the amorous and erotic that accounts for its erroneous application to *Troilus and Criseyde*.

Having answered the question of genre, we can now turn to question number two: why the *Filostrato*? C. S. Lewis said that in revising the

Filostrato Chaucer "approached his work as an 'Historial' poet contributing to the story of Troy."[36] This is certainly true, but to a degree that Lewis did not fully appreciate. Boccaccio had virtually no interest in the historical context of his narrative. Indeed, in a letter written contemporaneously he refers to the presumed Trojan source of the noble families of Italy with skeptical disdain.[37] Chaucer, on the other hand, for all his narrator's disclaimers about his lack of interest in history, is in fact extraordinarily diligent in both maintaining the consistency of his classical context and in reminding us of the historical significance of his narrative. The poem contains well over a hundred classical allusions, almost all of them additions to Boccaccio's poem and with the vast majority showing both an impressive range of classical learning and unusual precision. I shall give only one example. After their first night of love Boccaccio has the lovers lament the coming of day in the general terms typical of the medieval aubade: "But the unfriendly day drew near, as was clearly perceived by signs, which each of them cursed angrily, for it seemed to them that it came much sooner than it usually came, which for a certainty grieved each of them."[38] But Chaucer has Troilus lament in terms specific to his cultural moment:

> Quod Troilus: "Allas, now am I war
> That Pirous and tho swifte steedes thre,
> Which that drawen forth the sonnes char,
> Han gone som bipath in dispit of me;
> Thus maketh it so soone day to be;
> And for the sonne hym hasteth to rise,
> Ne shal I nevere don hym sacrifise."
>
> (3.1702–8)

Troilus not only invokes the name of one of the four horses that pull the chariot of the sun—almost every scribe stumbled over *Pirous*, the Englished version of Pyrois—but he also refers, here as throughout the poem, to the pagan rites, and especially his devotion to Apollo, that the Christian narrator will later reject with righteous indignation.[39]

Chaucer's poem is part of a widespread interest in the Trojan story in late medieval England. More or less contemporaneous with the *Troilus* are two Middle English poems, the alliterative *Destruction of Troy* and the so-called *Laud Troy Book*, plus the rather inept *Seege of Troye* and the vernacular chronicle *Brut*, which promoted London's Trojan origins and its unofficial name of Troynovaunt. Then in the early fifteenth century Lydgate produced his massive *Troy Book* at the behest of Henry V, a very brief prose *Sege of Troy* was composed at the same time, and about 1475 Caxton printed as his first book an English translation of Raoul Lefevre's French translation of Guido delle Colonne's *Historia destructionis Troiae*. But if Chaucer thought of his poem as a history like these other works — and calling it a tragedy, as well as his careful historical contextualization, certainly encourages us to think so — then why, given the vast amount of Trojan material available to him, did he choose as his source the *Filostrato*? Boccaccio's poem is in no way a history (or "tragedye") but a *cantare*, a genre that deals almost entirely with the amorous doings of the courtly world.[40]

An answer can be proposed by recalling that the received versions of Trojan history provide no clear explanation for either the cause of the war or its outcome. The problem is not the absence of explanations but their proliferation: Laomedon inadvertently refuses Jason and Hercules hospitality on their way to Colchis, and so they sack the city on the way home, abducting Laomedon's daughter Hesione; then after Priam, Laomedon's son, has rebuilt the city, the Trojans authorize Paris to abduct Helen in revenge; during the subsequent war the fate of Troy is sealed when Achilles treacherously kills Hector and Troilus; and then Aeneas and Antenor plot to betray the city, allowing the wooden horse within the walls. In even this briefest of summaries, the causes for the fall of the city mount up, until finally no single explanation is adequate — including one that Chaucer adds to Benoît-Guido, that Laomedon did not pay Apollo and Neptune the wages he had promised them when they originally raised the walls of the city (4.120–26). In sum, then, the versions of the Troy story available to Chaucer presented the insecure origins of secular history in a form that failed to explain their insecurity.[41]

How can this puzzle lurking at the very inception of the medieval version of Western history be solved? Chaucer's way is to try to explain the large by the small: if the collapse of a Trojan love affair could be understood, then perhaps so too could the collapse of Troy.[42] Chaucer uses the erotic to gloss the historical, a strategy that explains his choice of the *Filostrato*. For while Benoît (and after him Guido) included an account of Briseida's betrayal of Troilus, only Boccaccio described the *beginning* of the love affair as well as its unhappy ending. Although he ignored the historical in favor of the erotic, Boccaccio nonetheless did tell a story of origins—a foundation myth, as it were, albeit one that is entirely amorous and individual. For Chaucer, the erotic—which in this poem includes all those qualities we designate by the term *character*—offered at least a possibility for understanding. So we have answered our two questions. Chaucer called his poem a *tragedye* because he thought of it as dealing with history; he chose the *Filostrato* as his source because he sought to explain the meaning of an original catastrophe by exploring the origins of a catastrophic love affair. But these answers raise a third question: did he succeed in this attempt? Did the small disaster of a failed love affair explain the larger disaster of a destroyed city?

In one sense, the answer is quite straightforward. The word *trouthe* appears in the poem, in its various grammatical forms, over a hundred times, and almost always as an addition to the *Filostrato*. Occasionally it is used as a conventional, almost unthinking oath—Pandarus is especially fond of swearing "by my trouthe"—yet as the poem proceeds even these casual usages come to bear a weightier significance. "To trusten som wight is a preve / Of trouth" (1.690–91), Pandarus says early in the poem to Troilus, and then later tells Criseyde that she will be saved from Poliphete's machinations "bi thi feyth in trouthe" (2.1503).[43] In Book 3 he reminds her that she has her "trouthe y-plight" (3.782) to Troilus, and she later confirms her commitment to Troilus himself:

> And I emforth my connyng and my might
> Have, and ay shal, how sore that me smerte,
> Ben to yow trewe and hool with al myn herte;
> And dredeles that shal be founde at preve.
>
>   (3.999–1002)

"Have here my trouthe" (3.1111), she later says to Troilus, and he replies, "Beth to me trewe, or ellis were it routhe, / For I am thyn, by god and by my trouthe" (3.1511–12). After the Trojans have decided to exchange Criseyde for Antenor, when Pandarus suggests to Troilus that he seek out a new lady, he replies angrily, "syn I have trouthe hire hight, / I wol nat ben untrewe for no wight" (4.445–46). And as Criseyde prepares to leave Troy, after promising to return, Troilus begs her to have "vertue of youre trouthe" (4.1491). Criseyde promises in turn not to be "untrewe" (4.1617)—a promise that is all the more poignant when she tells Troilus, in a reversal of what Chaucer found in the *Filostrato*, that she fell in love with him because she saw in him "moral vertue grounded upon trouthe" (4.1672).[44]

But Criseyde *is* untrue, despite Troilus's epistolary plea "that she wol come ageyn and holde hire trouthe" (5.1585). The significance of this failure is made explicit in a line that Chaucer not only added to his source but has Troilus say twice: "Who shal now trowe on any othes mo?" (5.1263, 5.1681). That this lament can be applied both to the love affair and the fall of the city is clear—and there is no reason to doubt that Chaucer meant his audience to respond to this rather straightforward moral lesson. If Laomedon had paid Neptune and Apollo; if Jason and Hercules had been granted the hospitality they had a right to expect; if Jason had been true to Medea; if vengeance had not been taken on Troy by the treacherous abduction of Hesione; if the next act of revenge had not been the seduction of the unfaithful wife Helen; if Achilles had not tricked Hector into an ambush; if Paris had not used Achilles's love for Polyxena to render him helpless; if Aeneas and Antenor had not broken faith with their countrymen; if Ulysses had not betrayed Penelope with Circe, bearing the son Telegonus who would ultimately kill him; and so on and so on. All of these actions—including those of the self-destructive Thebans whose history preceded the Trojan War, and whom Chaucer never lets us forget through some of his most extensive additions to Boccaccio—can be understood as failures of *trouthe*.[45]

Moreover, as Richard Green has shown, in the fourteenth century *trouthe* came to include the meaning "reality," as in "the truth of things."[46] And in *Troilus and Criseyde* we are encouraged throughout to see the narrator as being *true* to the history he is recounting, however much he might wish to avoid its ultimate unhappiness. He invokes Clio, the muse of history, at the beginning of Book 2 (and in Book 3, Calliope, the muse of heroic poetry[47]); reminds us that if we don't understand someone's behavior that the story took place long ago, and that "eech contree hath hise lawes" (2.42); and assures us no less than six times that "myn auctour shal I folwen as I konne" (2.49; see also 3.90–91, 3.575–81, 3.1196, 3.1325; 3.1817). Then, in the final book, when Criseyde admits that "now is clene ago / My name of trouthe in love for evere mo" (5.1054–55), the narrator insists not once but three times that he is following "the storie," i.e., the historical record, "trewely" (5.1037–57). And he goes on to say that "trewly . . . non auctour" (5.1086–88) tells how much time passed between Criseyde's arrival in the Greek camp and her acceptance of Diomede as her lover.

> Ne me ne list this sely womman chyde
> Ferther than *the storye* wol devyse.
> Hire name, allas, is publisshed so wyde,
> That for hir gilt it oughte ynough suffyse;
> And if I mighte excuse hir any wyse,
> For she so sory was for hir *untrouthe,*
> Y-wis, I wolde excuse hir yet for routhe.
>
>   (5.1093–99)

In this single stanza Chaucer presents us with his rueful, rather awkward narrator, who will not "falsen" the history he is recounting, set against the charming heroine who does, alas, "falsen" Troilus. George Kane has rightly said that *trouthe* is "the principal formative concern of Chaucer's mature writing."[48] In the Franklin's Tale we are told that "Trouthe is the hyeste thyng that man may kepe"; the refrain of the "Balade de Bon Conseyl" is "And trouthe thee shal delivere, it is no drede." To deny the centrality of *trouthe* to *Troilus and Criseyde,* despite the old-fashioned quality of such an interpretation, would be willfully perverse. And this moral seriousness, along with its aspiration to historical understanding, is what most distinguishes Chaucer's poem from Boccaccio's, with what C. S. Lewis called—rather ungenerously but not inaccurately—its "cynical Latin gallantries."[49]

Yet this reading in an odd way not only does not account for Chaucer's choice of the *Filostrato* as the vehicle for his own version of the Troy story but actually makes the problem more difficult. If Chaucer wanted to explain the fall of Troy in terms of a failure of *trouthe,* why turn to a version that so assiduously avoids both historical context and moral import? Let us not forget that Chaucer wanted not merely to assign a judgment to the collapse of both a love affair and a city, but to understand the *meaning* of that judgment. If we can say that at the start of secular history lies a great and terrible failure of *trouthe,* what is the cause of *that?* Are we just to say that human beings are fallen creatures who often behave disgracefully? Or can we understand moral frailty in more precise terms? What exactly *is* the source of people's inability to behave as they know they should? And surely Chaucer chose to ask this question in a poem set in classical times precisely in order to avoid the foreclosure of the Christian answer. In his Epistle to the Romans Paul laments that "I do not that good which I will; but the evil which I hate, that I do," explaining this self-division by invoking original sin: "Now then it is no more I that do it, but sin that dwelleth in me."[50] But this solution to the problem of wrongdoing—inevitable to the medieval Christian audience—Chaucer was careful to make unavailable to the carefully specific classical world of *Troilus and Criseyde*.

In order to explain the love affair's disastrous ending, Chaucer explored in remarkable detail its beginning. His account of the initiation of the love affair in Books 1 through 3 is where he made the most extensive changes to Boccaccio's poem. In the first three books he expanded the *Filostrato* by over three thousand lines, in the last two by less than a thousand.[51] What he added to Boccaccio is a dauntingly complex beginning to the love affair. The effect of his extraordinarily delicate account is to show not only that desire is experienced by Criseyde as an external force that comes upon her, but that even when it has become a part of her—when it has become *her* desire—she is unable to represent it to herself as her own. Aroused first by Pandarus's words, her feelings are intensified by the sight of Troilus returning from battle to the point where she can understand what is happening to her only as a form of almost chemical change: "Who yaf me drynke?" She then retreats to a small private room, and then retreats yet further into her own mind where she debates the question of love in order, we assume, to make a deliberated decision. But the debate remains unresolved, so that what follows is a series of events (all of them of Chaucer's invention) that present desire as at once a part of and apart from the female subject who experiences it. First Criseyde overhears her lady-in-waiting Antigone sing a song that presents love as a benign mutuality. But the song alienates Criseyde's desire from itself by a double vicariousness: the song is not even Antigone's—much less Criseyde's—but that of an unnamed "goodlieste mayde / Of gret estat in al the town of Troye" (880–81). What then follows is a "lay / Of love" (921–22) sung by a nightingale in the cedar tree, a wordless song that by its allusion to Philomela images passion as a function only of the rapacious male. And finally Criseyde dreams that a bone-white eagle with his "longe clawes" (927) rends her heart from her breast and replaces it with his own, fulfilling the promise of mutuality offered in Antigone's song but also staging the violence implicit in the nightingale's lay of love. By this point, Criseyde has, as she will later, passively, say, "ben yold" (3.1210), but her accession to that yielding—as her use of the passive voice implies— remains unspoken and unacknowledged. She knows and doesn't know that she desires: she has felt it, heard it, dreamt it—but has she done it or had it done to her?

Chaucer's point in having love come upon Criseyde in this unreflective, subterranean way is to suggest, I think, that the moral issue, dependent as it is upon consciously willing and choosing, has become so deeply entangled with psychology as to be in some sense almost irrelevant. We cannot say Criseyde is a passive victim—she knows what is happening to her and allows it to happen—but neither can we say that she makes a deliberate decision. So too, Criseyde's betrayal is described so that actions again unfold with such imperceptible gradualism, and are so compounded of motives and circumstances, that the search for an explanation—"the cause whi"—is inevitably thwarted. At the conclusion of Diomede's first interview with Criseyde in her tent, "he roos and tok his leve." The passage continues:

> The brighte Venus folwede and ay taughte
> The wey ther brode Phebus down alighte;
> And Cynthea hire char-hors overraughte
> To whirle out of the Leoun, if she myghte;
> And Signifer his candels sheweth bright
> Whan that Criseyde unto hire bedde wente
> Inwith hire faders faire brighte tente,
>
> Retornyng in hire soule ay up and down
> The wordes of this sodeyn Diomede,
> His grete estat, and perel of the town,
> And that she was allone and hadde nede
> Of frendes help; and thus bygan to brede
> The cause whi, the sothe for to telle,
> That she took fully purpos for to dwelle.
>
> (5.1016–29)

The astronomical machinery represents not only the relentless passage of time—Criseyde had earlier promised Troilus she would return "Er Phebus suster, Lucina the sheene, / The Leoun passe out of this Ariete" (4.1591–92)—but also the workings of forces that operate in ways unavailable to self-reflection. As the moon leaves Leo so does Criseyde leave the lover who has just been described as "Yong, fressh, strong, and hardy as lyoun" (5.830). Venus is somehow in Diomede's train here, and she in turn dominates Phoebus Apollo: to say that love overcomes wisdom translates the astronomical symbolism, but it is hardly adequate as an account of Criseyde's behavior. The Zodiac bears signs, but their meaning is unclear to her, an ignorance that is both the condition of her very existence and a key constitutive of her actions. Lying in bed, Criseyde "returns" Diomede's words in her mind as the heavens turn, a scene that itself returns to the night some three years before when "lay she stille and thoughte" (2.915) of Troilus's words, of Pandarus's, and of Antigone's. Then she had heard the "lay / Of love" sung by the nightingale, had dreamed the dream of the eagle, and had awakened (we were prepared to believe) in love.

In staying with Diomede, Criseyde not only repeats her earlier behavior but reveals her life to be a continuous process that cannot be endowed with a precisely demarcated beginning and ending, in the sense of either a single motive or an intended goal. If it were true, as Pandarus had said, that "th'ende is every tales strengthe" (2.260), when we reach the conclusion we should be able retrospectively to evaluate the meaning of the events that have occurred: "But natheles men seyen that at the laste, / For any thing, men shal the soothe se" (5.1639–40). Criseyde's liaison with Diomede ought to tell us what her liaison with Troilus meant: the end of her career in the poem should make clear the meaning of its beginning. But in fact, far from clarifying the enigma of her character and motivation, much less of human actions in general, Criseyde's behavior serves to compound the difficulty: her end does not gloss but replicates her beginning.

The narrator himself finds this inconclusiveness painful—or so we might judge from his last-minute attempt to suppress it. In the midst of Diomede's second and successful assault on Criseyde, he suddenly introduces into the poem portraits of the three protagonists. The presence of these portraits is sanctioned by the historiographical tradition: Dares, Benoît, and Joseph of Exeter all include similar passages in their histories, and

Chaucer's version may owe some details specifically to Joseph. But the point about their late appearance in *this* version of the story is that they evade the very problem of interpretation on which Chaucer had hitherto insisted. By substituting for the detailed representation of subjectivity woodenly externalized *effictiones* ornamented with brief judgments— Diomede has the reputation of being "of tonge large" (804), Criseyde is "slydvnge of corage" (825), Troilus "trewe as stiel" (831)—the narrator suddenly implies that the relation of character to action has become self-evident. But nothing could be further from the truth: the narrative these portraits are meant to gloss mocks their oversimplifications.

We are left, then, where we began, with questions. What have we learned from a poem that uses the *Filostrato* as the basis for a *tragedye?* What is the relation of small individual choices—if choices they be—to the large events of history? Given that the poem ends, if indeed it ends at all, in what Talbot Donaldson has called "a kind of nervous breakdown in poetry,"[52] we are entitled, I think, to conclude with the poet that no conclusion is possible. The questions are pressing, then as now, but the answers remain unavailable.

chapter nine

"Rapt with Pleasaunce"

The Gaze from Virgil to Milton

I

In Book 1 of the *Aeneid* Aeneas and Achates enter Carthage shrouded in a protective mist and make their way to a temple sacred to Juno where they await the coming of Dido. As they wait, Aeneas sees a "wonderful thing" that for the first time gives him hope of safety and the promise of better things.[1] On the walls of the temple, representations of the battles of Troy are laid out *ex ordine*, evidence that news (*fama* [457]) of the war has traveled throughout the world. "Here," Aeneas cries to Achates, "things worthy of praise find due reward: here there are tears for human happenings (*lacrimae rerum* [462]) and mortal sufferings touch the heart. Be free of fear; this fame will bring you some deliverance" (*feret haec aliquam tibi fama salutem* [463]). Eight scenes are presented, organized in pairs: first Greeks being chased by Trojans matched with Trojans fleeing before Achilles;

then the nighttime slaughter of the sleeping Rhesus by Diomedes balanced with Achilles's ambush of the unarmed Troilus; next the Trojan women's useless supplication of an implacable Pallas Athene paired with Priam giving gold to Achilles for Hector's defiled body; and finally pictures of two later, doomed Trojan allies, Memnon and Penthesilea, the latter a vision of heroic independence and feminine grace, caught by the artist "in the act of buckling her golden girdle beneath her naked breast" (492).[2] Aeneas, we are told, "feeds his soul upon these empty pictures" (*pictura inani* [464]); as Dido approaches he stands wonderingly (*miranda* [494]), stupefied and fixed fast in a gaze (*stupet obtutuque haeret defixus in uno* [495]).

Aeneas is a hero who has entered upon his poem with unpropitious hesitancy. We see him first at the mercy of the storm and lamenting that he did not die at Troy, then offering his men an encouragement he does not believe himself. Even his mother Venus quickly tires of his self-pitying account of his misfortunes and responds to his notorious self-identification— *sum pius Aeneas* (378)—with cruelly feigned incomprehension: "Whoever you are, you are hardly, I think, hated by the gods" (387). But Aeneas thinks he has been abandoned, and burgeoning Carthage fills him with envy: "How fortunate are those whose walls already rise!" (437). Hence the consolation afforded by this pictured reenactment of the past: not only does it assure him that this is a country that honors the brave deeds of Troy but, more tellingly, it monumentalizes a heroism that may have been tragic but remains nonetheless preeminent, a *fama* that will never pass away.[3] Yet Aeneas forgets that if his welcome depends upon who he has been, it necessarily ignores what he will become, the founder of the empire that will obliterate the very Carthage he now envies. Similarly, while his Trojan past may help him to find a temporary home, it is one that comes to threaten the Roman future in which he will find his true fame. But these larger understandings are, for the moment, closed to him. Suspended in passivity, Aeneas gazes at both city (*miratur . . . miratur* [421–22]) and ecphrasis (*miratur* [456], *miranda* [494]) with a trance-like stupor that bespeaks his incomprehension.

Yet it is in this very ecphrasis, in the pictures that solicit his eye only to deaden his attention, that paradoxically resides a saving knowledge. The pictures interpret as well as represent the past, and in their interpretation provide a salutary premonition of the future.[4] They expound the motifs that will come to dominate Aeneas's experience: the implacable gods, the implacable hero needed to do their will, and the innocent victims who must be sacrificed to historical necessity. *Saevus Achilles* (458) dominates the scenes, mentioned even before the specific pictures are passed in review; fierce to both Priam and the Atrides, he is described as an enemy to friend and foe alike. The agent of Troy's destruction, he accounts for the deaths of all but five of the pictured Trojan victims. Moreover, that these details are not merely incidental to the gradual collapse of Trojan resistance is shown both by the animosity of Pallas and by the fact that the deaths of Rhesus and Troilus are part of the *fata Troiana*: it was prophesied that Troy would never fall as long as the horses of Rhesus fed on Trojan meadows nor if Troilus lived to his twentieth year. But Troy must fall, and the pictures conclude with the breathtaking beauty of *Penthesilea bellatrix* (493), a prefiguration not just of Camilla but of the regal leader, *forma pulcherrima Dido* (496), who is at this very moment sweeping toward the temple to assume her throne and exercise her lordly power. For *infelix Dido*, like the Troilus who is here poignantly described as *infelix puer* (475), is herself a victim as, ironically, is Aeneas himself: these pictures are in Juno's temple because they commemorate her triumph over her Trojan enemies.

The immediate lesson the ecphrasis offers Aeneas is that the promise of safety is false, that Carthage is a place not of security but danger. But in a larger sense the ecphrasis expresses the central problem of the Virgilian epic as a whole, the relation of the individual to historical destiny. It speaks most immediately to the dilemma of Aeneas's own heroism: can he at once renounce the savagery of Achilles and fulfill his mission, or must he not also be an enemy to friend and foe alike? This is a question, however, that Aeneas cannot ask himself. Rather than use this representation of the past to understand his future, Aeneas falls into a trance that avoids understanding altogether. To be sure, the pictures are themselves complicit in their own misuse, *visibilia* that by the force of their affective appeal preempt cognition. But if they are *picturae inanes* it is because Aeneas empties them of their historical force by ignoring their commentary upon his own situation. This is, doubtless, why he himself figures in the ecphrasis only marginally, in a single, vague line (488): when his own story is to be told it is rendered not in pictures but through a narrative. Awakened from the trance of his gaze by Dido, he is invited to tell the tale of his sufferings. What was previously offered as vision is now transformed into narration: Book 2 provides a critique of Greek heroism and a definitive statement of the divine necessity that required the fall of Troy, while Book 3 describes the homing instinct that has brought Aeneas to the false home of Carthage and will drive him on to Latium. His discourse, then, explicates the images on the temple walls by unfolding them into a narrative that makes available the meanings they encapsulate. And in making Aeneas the narrator of his own tale, Virgil asserts his hero's capacity for self-reflection and begins him upon the journey of self-knowledge that constitutes the first, Odyssean half of the poem.

The entranced gaze upon a significant image is a telling moment that appears and reappears throughout medieval and Renaissance literature. My purpose here is less to provide a history of the topos than to examine several salient instances and the patterns of allusion that link them together. My primary exhibits are Perceval's gaze upon the blood drops in the snow in the *Conte du Graal* by Chrétien de Troyes, Dante's fix on Beatrice in *Purgatorio* 32, and Satan's twice-repeated contemplation of Eve in *Paradise Lost*, but other scenes could be added: the Narcissus gaze of the *Roman de la Rose*, the vision of the Heavenly Jerusalem at the end of *Pearl*, or Calidore "rapt with pleasaunce" by the sight of the dance at the summit of Mount Acidale in Book 6 of the *Faerie Queene*.[5] Not all of these moments look back directly to Book 1 of the *Aeneid*, but Virgil does provide a crucial precedent both in his critical attitude toward the gaze and in the dialectical relationship within which he places it. The point is not only that full knowledge cannot be mediated by images, but that the gaze is one pole of a dialectic of which the other is some form of discursive exposition. The gaze implies a nostalgic evasion of understanding, a lowered state of consciousness that is figured by a trance-like stupor that must be broken, both to disarm its dangerous seductions and to unlock the riches its object contains. Indeed, even in intellectual contexts in which visionary experience is regarded less dubiously, such as Neoplatonic philosophy and the traditions of medieval mysticism cognate to it, the gaze is often seen as needing a discursive complement for its potential to be realized.

A representative and influential example from late antiquity is Boethius's *Consolation of Philosophy*. As soon as the prisoner's eyes have been wiped free of tears by Philosophy, he tells us, "I turned my eyes and fixed my gaze upon her" (*deduxi oculos intuitumque defixi* [1, pr. 3]),[6] an act of recognition that is later given its philosophical meaning by Lady Philosophy's withdrawal into self-contemplation as she prepares to unfold the mysteries of the *summum bonum* to her pupil. She stands for a moment "with her gaze fixed [*defixo . . . visu*] as if withdrawn to the exalted source [*augustam . . . sedem*] of her mind" (3, pr. 2). In the great Platonic prayer of 3, 9 this *augustam sedem* is then explicitly defined as the source from which all being flows and to which it returns, and as the point upon which seekers after truth must fix their gaze: "Grant, Father, that my mind may ascend to your exalted seat, grant that it may see the source of goodness, grant light that the clear gaze of the soul may be fixed on you" (*in te conspicuos animi defigere visus* [3, m. 9]).[7] The prisoner's initial gaze upon Philosophy, then, is authorized by Philosophy's own gaze within herself, and both stand as preliminary signs of that full possession of the truth that allows the wise man to be "securely fixed" (*stabiliter fixa* [4, pr. 6]) at the center of things. The gaze itself, however, must be abrogated in order to allow for a pedagogical discourse by which its value can be recovered at the highest level. It is at once a retarding pause and a prefiguration of the goal, both impediment and encouragement—a paradox which, as we shall see, continues to mark its later appearances.

II

The *Conte du Graal* records the hero's apparently smooth development from a Welsh naif to a fully accomplished Arthurian knight, complete with a lady to be loved (Blancheflor) and a land to be defended (Belrepaire). But as soon as this optimistic conclusion is projected it begins to be qualified, a characteristically revisionary pattern in Chrétien's romances. Here the agents of qualification are a series of damsels who gradually reveal to Perceval that in the very process of his success he has committed a number of grievous moral errors. One was his abandonment of his mother, but the most important was his silence at the Grail Castle: presented with the marvels of the castle—the bleeding lance and the Grail procession— he forbore asking the crucial questions that would have healed the Fisher King and restored his waste land. Having earlier been told by his chivalric mentor that a knight should not talk too much, Perceval had been silent here out of fear that "he should be thought a *villain*" (3210–11).[8] These marvels, he assumed, had nothing to do with him. Having understood his quest solely within the martial and erotic context of the Arthurian court, he naturally thought that his winning of Blancheflor and rescue of Belrepaire marked his accession to a fully chivalric identity.

But in fact Chrétien had rendered this success with an elaborate Christian imagery that had alerted us, if not Perceval, to the fact that he is not merely a chivalric hero but a figure of salvific value. Hence the damsels now upbraid him in order to force him to realize that he has misunderstood both himself and his quest, that his growth into chivalry has left him with a narrowed vision that is both culpable and naive, and that his quest is not almost over but barely begun. Perceval is now forced to realize that the very condition of human action, imaged here in his fatal departure from his mother in order to revive the chivalric values of his dead father, entails an impurity that cannot be self-purged. This is why he first becomes aware of his own name—Perchevax li Galois (3575)— at the very moment that his culpability is forced upon him, and his self-identification is immediately revised by the damsel who tells him that his name ought to be "Perchevax li chaitis, . . . Perchevax maleurous" (3581–82): the access to self-consciousness and a recognition of sinfulness are correlative, even synonymous, events. We now also understand that when Perceval misread a comment about knightly behavior (be sparing of speech) as if it were the rigid prescription of a code, he revealed a literalism of mind that is at one with his passivity before the Grail procession, a willingness to accept appearance (*semblance*) as itself sufficient reality.

It is at just this moment of dismay and self-doubt that Perceval enjoys the respite of an entranced gaze. The trance is a moment of withdrawal and recollection that both restores to him a nostalgic sense of his innocent past and yet offers an occasion for future understanding. The reader comes to understand its significance for Perceval by the way he and his Arthurian companions misread the event. The scene is as follows:

> [On a spring morning], according to custom, Perceval had risen early because he wished to seek and to meet adventure and chivalry; and he came to a meadow covered with frost and snow, where the king's company [the Arthurian court] was encamped. But before he reached

the tents a flock of wild geese, blinded by the snow, flew overhead. Perceval saw them and then heard their honking as a falcon came streaking after them. When one goose became separated from the rest the falcon struck and knocked it to the ground. But because it was too early in the morning the falcon chose not to seize upon its prey and instead flew away. The goose had been wounded and three drops of blood had fallen from its neck, spreading out on the whiteness of the snow and creating a natural color. By the time Perceval had ridden up the goose itself had flown away, for its wounds were not serious enough to keep it down. When he saw the hollow in the snow where the bird had been struggling, and the blood around it, he leaned on his lance to gaze at the sight. The mingling of the blood and the snow reminded him of his lady's fresh complexion and he fell into such a deep contemplation that he forgot himself, for her face showed red on white just like the three drops of blood on the white snow. His gazing so pleased him that he thought he was actually seeing the fresh color of his fair lady's face. And Perceval mused on the drops of blood until the whole morning passed by.[9]

In reading the blood drops as reminders of Blancheflor Perceval retreats into chivalric eroticism. This is also the interpretation offered by the Arthurian court. First the two chivalric anti-heroes, Sagramor and Kay, mockingly attack the pensive knight, but are easily defeated. Then the courtly Gawain offers a more generous interpretation: "This thoughtfulness is not base," he declares, "but rather it is courteous and sweet" (4458–59).[10] So Gawain rides out to Perceval and, after waiting for the sun to melt the snow, invites him to join the court where his *chevalerie* (4577) can be fully confirmed.

The second half of the romance persistently and at times harshly subjects this chivalry to ironic qualification, and with it both Perceval's reading of the blood drops and Gawain's meta-reading of Perceval. The primary target of the irony is Gawain, whose reenactment of Perceval's earlier adventures reveals chivalry to be a mixture of bullying and predatory eroticism.[11] Perceval, on the other hand, virtually disappears from the action, to reappear in a context that now calls into question that very possibility of narrative romance. Having set off to return to the Grail Castle, Perceval has fallen into a forgetfulness that blots out both his specific quest and all knowledge of the Christian dispensation from which it derives its meaning. He is simply a knight *en aventure* who is seeking *chevalerie* (6226), precisely his condition when he fell into the first forgetfulness of his trance. He is awakened this time, however, not by the courtly Gawain but by a group of penitents "who, for the salvation of their souls, went on foot doing penance for their sins" (6250–52). They inform Perceval that this is Good Friday, when no Christian should bear arms, and they direct him to a providentially nearby hermit. The hermit provides Perceval instruction both in the elements of his faith and in the mysteries of the Grail Castle. Now we learn that the penitential values that are here made explicit have in fact been present throughout the poem, controlling the action in ways that the uninstructed Perceval could never have recognized. The hermit is thus the last and authoritative instance of that retrospective revaluation which the damsels had previously initiated.

From this perspective, then, the trance of the blood drops is revealed to have been a futile avoidance of the accession into religious meaning that the hermit definitively accomplishes. Bemused by erotic nostalgia, Perceval turned back to the uncomplicated past of Blancheflor and Belrepaire. But the whole of the scene actually required not bemusement but interpretation, precisely the kind of reading that the hermit now offers for the Grail procession. The falcon striking the goose, the blood-drops disposed in the significant *figura* of three, the blazing sun that absorbs the enameled snow—it is not difficult to allegorize this scene into a recapitulation of Christian history itself: the fall of Adam, the bleeding of Christ, the resurrection and *repaire* to heaven.[12] Even should we not settle on this particular interpretation, readers will agree that *some* allegorization is required. In other words, the scene offers itself to Perceval as an occasion not for self-absorption but for instruction, as did the procession in the Grail Castle, an instruction that he now belatedly receives. Similarly, in the trance scene itself, the red-on-white that Perceval ought to be remembering is not Blancheflor's complexion but the red blood drops rolling down the white shaft of the lance at the Grail Castle.[13] The blood on the snow, in short, belongs to that structure of events which ironized chivalry and authorizes the hermit. In placing it in the structure that dreams of innocence Perceval misread it by refusing to read it at all, just as he refused to read the Grail procession itself.

Perceval's choice of absorption over instruction is thus not only wrong but sinful. This lesson has, however, been avoided throughout the narrative not only by the chivalric hero but by the romancer himself. For the hermit's explication, however correct, removes the narrative from the shadowy forest of romance and locates it in the clear cenobitic desert of allegory. The central mysteries that provided the romance with both thematic allure and narrative motivation have now been stripped bare; and once their significance has been revealed, and revealed to be part of an authorized and institutionalized ideology, the events themselves become little more than signs for a higher reality. The demystification the hermit offers demystifies romance itself. This is no doubt why Perceval disappears from the action for good, replaced by a Gawain whose ever more trivial adventures peter out in an embarrassing contretemps. What lies ahead for literary history are both fresh attempts at remystification and, inevitably, the complete subordination of narrative to ideology. The best known instance of this triumph of exegesis is the *Queste del Saint Graal* (c. 1220). Here the all-too-human Perceval is replaced by the impeccable Galahad, an elect endowed with what Albert Pauphilet elegantly called "le sublime egoisme de la vertu,"[14] and the narrative enigmas are deconstructed by a whole flock of holy men. In reading this relentless subordination of image to idea we realize that the discarded enchantments of romance were the enchantments of literature itself. The interpretive activity that Perceval withheld at the Grail Castle and before the blood drops dominates the *Queste*, so privileging the spiritual sense that the letter of the narrative becomes a mere veil that parts at will before the importunities of a discursive pedagogy and forcing chivalric *aventure* to serve simply as the occasion for monastic homilies that pass an apocalyptic judgment upon the Arthurian world. Here, then, the dialectic between the enigmatic gaze and its discursive explication, between the mystified moment and its cognitive fulfillment, breaks down. As so often happens throughout the Middle Ages, the literary impulse finds itself caught between polarized values, between a letter that celebrates the cultic values of secular society and a spirit that declares unavoidable theological imperatives. For Chrétien, then, the moment of gaze is a pause of reconciliation before an inevitable and irreparable rupture, a dissociation, moreover, that brings into question the very possibility of a Christian literature, even of a literature of instruction in general. Yet both Dante and Milton are ostentatiously, even aggressively, free from this anxiety. How, then, do they deploy the topos of the gaze, and what might this tell us about the protocols that govern their poetic activity?

III

The Grail procession and its entranced observer are the crucial precedents for a central moment in Dante's *Commedia*: the procession of sacred history in the Earthly Paradise.[15] Dante's Eden is located at the summit of Mount Purgatory and is guarded by a wall of fire that stands as the final purgatorial barrier. Dante is drawn through this fire by Virgil, who "kept talking of Beatrice as he went, saying: 'I seem to see her eyes already'" (*Purg.* 27.52–54).[16] These are the same eyes that, shining "brighter than the stars" (*Inf.* 2.55), came to Limbo to initiate the saving mission that now draws to a close. "Li occhi lucenti" (*Inf.* 2.116) stand, then, at both the beginning and the end of Virgil's mission, although not of Dante's; and in promising the lover that these eyes await him he is assuring Dante that the amorous Paradise he once lost is now to be regained.[17]

But Dante in fact receives something different. A sudden flash of lightning announces the arrival of a mysterious procession, in the midst of which is a car drawn by a Gryphon. And in the midst of the car is discovered Beatrice herself: at last the lover finds himself face to face with his beloved. Her attendants urge her to grant him the supreme gift: "'Turn, Beatrice, turn thy holy eyes on thy faithful one,' was their song, 'who for sight of thee has made so great a journey'" (*Purg.* 31.133–35). In gracious response Beatrice "disveils" herself (136) and stands fully "opened" (145) before the poet. This is the crucial moment of transcendence—but it is also, curiously, a moment of failure:

> So fixed and intent (*fissi e attenti*) were my eyes in satisfying their ten years' thirst that every other sense was quenched in me and they had, on the one side and the other, a wall of indifference, so did the holy smile draw them to itself with the old net, when my face was turned perforce to my left by those goddesses, for I heard from them a "Too fixed!" (*Troppo fiso!*) And the condition of the sight that is in eyes just smitten by the sun left me for a time without vision. (*Purg.* 32.1–12)

When Beatrice's attendants warn Dante that his gaze is *troppo fiso* they turn him away from Beatrice herself and toward the procession of which she is at once centerpiece and expositor. This procession consists of the Scriptures, the Church and Christ, and the Gryphon, which in its composite nature expresses the miracle of the Incarnation. As Charles Singleton has taught us, this procession is indeed a *processus,* an unfolding of the ultimate reality in time.[18] It is also an imaginary event—one constituted, that is, by images, as the Gryphon serves to remind us: for the Middle Ages the gryphon was a standard example of an object that has only an imaginary life. This does not mean that the procession is untrue, only that its function is exclusively pedagogical: it is there in order that Dante may see it. There are thus two aspects to the procession: first, it is a statement about God in history; second, it is designed for instruction. We can now understand why Dante's absorption in Beatrice is unacceptable, for it violates both of these values. It removes him from time, both because he is absorbed in this moment to the exclusion of all others and because his access to Beatrice is a nostalgic reaccess to the past: it is the "ten years' thirst" that he now satisfies, the "old net" that grips him. Second, in focusing his senses upon that one point he builds about him a wall of indifference that denies him the possibility of cognition, a denial that is graphically represented in the blindness that succeeds upon his dazzled gaze. Consequently, as soon as his sight returns he is subjected to an elaborate instruction. "Hold thine eyes now on the car," commands Beatrice, and Dante, "who at her command was wholly bowed down and devout, gave over [his] mind and eyes as she wished" (*Purg.* 32.104, 106–8).

The process which we witness here is crucial to our understanding of both the Earthly Paradise and of Dante's poetic method as a whole. As with the Earthly Paradise itself, the gaze upon Beatrice is both a nostalgic return to a vanished past and a prefiguration of the goal toward which the traveler is moving. It is a pause that at once retards the pilgrim with its transfixion and impels him forward toward full possession. When Dante gazes at Beatrice she herself stands with "her shining eyes . . . still fixed on the Gryphon, and even like the sun in a mirror the two-fold beast shone within them" (*Purg.* 31.119–22). If Beatrice is the means by which vision takes place, she is also a model of the visionary act itself: Dante sees the Gryphon both in and through her eyes. Her goal is to instruct Dante so that, as she later says, "you may see . . . as do I" (*Par.* 7.123) and that he may "fix [*ficcar*] [his] look on the eternal light" (*Par.* 33.83). In *Paradiso* 33 Dante describes his final gaze in language that unmistakably recalls this scene in the Earthly Paradise: "Thus my mind, all rapt, was gazing, fixed, still and intent [*fissa, immobile e attenta*] and ever enkindled with gazing"

(97–99), a gazing that is further authorized by the example of St. Bernard: "Bernard, who saw my eyes fixed and intent [*fissi e attenti*] on the fire that warmed him [that is, on the Virgin], turned his own on her with so great affection that he made mine more eager in their gazing" (*Par.* 31.139–42).

Beatrice, says Dante, is "she who emparadises my mind" (*Par.* 28.3), but what is the mechanism of this emparadising? It is a ten-times repeated enactment of this scene in the Earthly Paradise as Dante ascends in the *Paradiso*. The account of the ascent to the first sphere recalls that first gaze and provides the model for the rest of the ascents throughout this *cantica*. Beatrice looks at the sun—"never eagle so fastened on it [*li s'affisse*]" (*Par.* 1.48)—and "from her action," says Dante, "infused by the eyes into my imagination, mine was made, and beyond our wont I fixed [*fissi*] my eyes on the sun. . . . Beatrice stood with her eyes fixed [*fissa*] only on the eternal wheels, and on her I fixed [*fissi*] mine, withdrawn from above" (1.52–54; 64–66). The Earthly Paradise thus provides the materials from which Dante fashions the metaphor of his celestial ascent, but its prefigurative, even archetypal, function is more detailed than even this dependence suggests. For in the Earthly Paradise Dante's experience is our now-familiar dialectic between an ineffable moment of illumination and a labored exposition of doctrine, between gaze and instruction. And in the *Paradiso* this dialectic is repeated in every sphere. It forms, in fact, the basic structure of the *cantica* as a whole. But now this dialectic is crucially revised. No longer does the moment of absorption stand over against the cognitive action which it frames; on the contrary, it now becomes identified with cognition itself. Dante ascends through the spheres by seeing as Beatrice sees, which means that he knows what and as she knows: the mechanism of ascent is a metaphor for the access of knowledge.

The implications of this strategy for poetry, and for reading, are profound. In the Earthly Paradise Dante responded to Beatrice's teachings by complaining that they were over his head: "Why do your longed-for words fly so far above my sight that the more it strives the more it loses them?" (*Purg.* 33.82–84). Beatrice's answer was that the difficulty of her language was itself a pedagogical device. She speaks as she does, she says, "so that you may recognize what school you have followed and see if its teachings can follow my words" (85–87). The *Paradiso* is a continuation of this "high talk," a poetry not of image but instruction, in which what was previously literal becomes metaphoric and in which image is ornament rather than substance.[19] We now know that Dante composed the *Commedia* according to a scheme of the three modes of vision that was originally devised by Augustine to explain St. Paul's enigmatic claim that he had been carried up to the third heaven (2 Cor. 12.2–4).[20] According to Augustine, Paul is referring to three ways of knowing: *visio corporalis, visio imaginativa,* and the highest or "third" heaven, *visio intellectualis.* These three modes of vision provide the media for the three parts of Dante's journey. The *Inferno* is the realm of the corporeal, and is therefore dominated by the densest object in the universe, Satan. The *Purgatorio* is a world of images, ranging from the figured pavement of the first terrace through to the pageant in the Earthly Paradise. And the *Paradiso* is a world of intellectual vision, the *luce intellectual* (*Par.* 30.40) which everywhere illuminates the celestial spheres and its inhabitants. The blessed spirits are themselves filled with light (see, e.g., *Par.* 9.7–8), and Dante's ambition is to be so "illuminated" (*illustra* [*Par.* 4.125]) or "enlightened" (*chiarirti* [*Par.* 5.120]) that he can join their company. And how does the *etterna luca* (*Par.* 5.8) come to and finally penetrate the pilgrim? Through the *gran sentenza* (*Par.* 7.24), the "great doctrine," that Beatrice and the other pedagogues of Paradise offer him. Our reading of the *Paradiso,* then, provides us with an experience analogous to that of Dante himself, as he himself continually reminds us: "Stay now, reader, on thy bench, thinking over this of which thou hast a foretaste, and thou shalt have much delight before thou art weary; I have set before thee, now feed thyself" (*Par.* 10.22–25; see also 2.1–18; 5.109–14; et al.). As Dante is literally "informed" (*informar* [*Par.* 2.110]) by his journey through the spheres, so does our reading of his journey similarly inform us.

The process of information is described by Beatrice in a simile that by its striking reminiscence of Perceval's love trance recalls us to our theme:

> Now, as the substance of the snow, smitten by the warm rays, is left bare both of its former color and its cold, so I would inform you, similarly uncovered in your mind, with a light so living that it will sparkle in your sight. (*Par.* 2.106–11)[21]

As in the *Conte de Graal* the sun melted the snow and defaced the three drops of blood, so here the *luce intellectual* of instruction has burned away the "false imaginings" (*falso imaginar* [*Par.* 1, 89]) of Dante's terrestrial perception. But it has burned them away in order to recover them at a higher level. The process by which the prefigurative images of the Earthly Paradise are fulfilled in the celestial spheres is enacted throughout the *Paradiso*, and nowhere more brilliantly than in the sphere of the Sun (*Par.* 10–14). The account opens by invoking the erotic pastoralism with which Matelda first drew Dante to the Earthly Paradise: here the blessed spirits dance a *ballata* about Dante and Beatrice, forming a circle that one of them describes as a "garland which surrounds with looks of love the *bella donna*" (10.92–93). But just as Matelda and the regressive impulses she aroused in Dante were transcended by Beatrice, so here the *ballata* gradually expands into an abstract wheeling of three concentric circles, proleptic of the final Trinitarian vision. More cogently, the pastoral moment itself decomposes into a careful scholastic exposition, one that provides glosses on its own text and laborious scholastic *distinctiones* (*distinzione* [*Par.* 13.116]). Pastoral sexuality gives way, in other words, to a scholastic exposition that both prepares for and constitutes the transcendent vision. This threefold process is itself one, a Trinitarianism that reflects the divine ontology. During his stay in this sphere Dante is told that the created universe itself is "nothing but the splendor of the Idea which our Sire, in loving, begets" (*Par.* 13.53–54). After passing itself down through creation the divine light then reflects itself back to itself in the Platonic pattern of procession and return. This "spiration," as Dante calls it, controls as well the threefold movement of history, which is marked into stages by the appearance first of Adam, then of Christ the redeemer, and finally of Christ the judge, a movement also described in this canto. These stages of growth, whether personal or poetic, are then subsumed into an overarching unity, a unity that is here expressed by a bold act of Dantean identification: both the dancing master and the pedagogue of the sphere of the Sun are the same person, and he is none other than the quintessential wise man, Thomas Aquinas.

The pastoral of desire gives way to an indoctrination that allows for the higher pastoral of fulfillment; the amorous gaze is abrogated by an instruction that allows the contemplative gaze to be refixed upon its highest object. In the Earthly Paradise Beatrice is garlanded by three attendants who represent the theological virtues. In cantos 24 through 26 of the *Paradiso* these virtues reappear, but not as maidens: they are now the subject matter of three separate examinations conducted by Saints Peter,

James, and John, examinations that are presented in the authorized language and form of the medieval university. This transformation of maidens into university curricula eloquently declares the supercession of pastoral by instruction, of images by intellectual light. And so, when pastoral returns in its highest, redeemed form in the *giardino* of the Empyrean, with its gradually dilating rose, we can now recognize that a poetry of absence, of nostalgia and desire, has been fulfilled into a poetry of presence.

IV

Twice in *Paradise Lost* Satan falls into a rapturous trance, and on both occasions he enjoys, as we should expect, both a respite from his quest and a nostalgic reenactment of his original purity. In Book 4, with his sight of Adam and Eve "Imparadised in one another's arms" (506), Satan stands "still in gaze, as first he stood" (356). Here the pun on "still" and the ambiguity of "first" recall to us, and to him, the placid self-composure of his original rectitude. In Book 9 the description is more extended and explicit. Eve's

> heavenly form
> Angelic, but more soft, and feminine,
> Her graceful innocence, her every air
> Of gesture or least action overawed
> His malice, and with rapine sweet bereaved
> His fierceness of the fierce intent it brought:
> That space the evil one abstracted stood
> From his own evil, and for a time remained
> Stupidly good.
>
>   (9.457–65)[22]

In both instances Satan has arrived to destroy the very beauty that for a moment holds him prisoner, and we can recognize in his pause remnants of that "original brightness" which, we were told in Book 1, "his form had yet not lost" (1.591–92). The anguish of Satan's condition derives from just this inextinguishability of goodness, and from the inner warfare that now rages within him. Having lost the original oneness of the good, he now hopes to lose himself in the corresponding simplicity of evil: "Evil be thou my good" (4.110). This Satanic ambition is as unattainable as his others, and his downward metamorphosis into the serpent, in both the garden and later in Hell, is merely a short-lived "illusion" (10.571) rather than a final escape into pure evil. Thus Satan's amorous gaze both recalls with its uprightness what once he was and foreshadows with its stupor what he desires to become.

The place of this gaze in the economy of the Satanic condition shows us Milton's reliance upon the romance tradition, but it also witnesses to a crucial revision.[23] For the gaze is marked from the beginning precisely as Satanic, and it never sheds this dubiousness. It is true that both Adam and Eve are granted moments of trance, but in every instance these moments are either part of their earliest and least reliable lives or illicit attempts to return to that earliness.[24] This is most clearly the case with Eve. At the moment of her first awakening Eve gazes into a "watery gleam" (4.461) at her own image, and there, she tells us, "I had fixed / Mine eyes till now" (465–66) had she not been led away to Adam. But this leading outward is immediately resisted: "back I turned," preferring "that smooth watery image" (480) to the "less fair, / Less winning soft, less amiably mild" Adam (478–79). Appropriately, then, Satan exploits the attractions of the gaze in his seduction of Eve. In the dream of Book 5 he tells Eve he has come to her "with ravishment / Attracted by thy beauty still to gaze" (46–47); and in Book 9 he says he cannot help but "gaze / Insatiate" on her whom "all things living gaze on" (535–36, 539). Correspondingly, when Eve is led to the fatal tree, "Fixed on the fruit she gazed" (9.735), a dark reminiscence of Dante's garden gaze in the *Commedia*. The Dantean background to this line also reminds us that if Eve's gaze is a relapse back to her narcissistic origins it is also proleptic of the omniscient vision that is, she thinks, her goal. Hence Satan tells Eve that as soon as he ate of the tree "with capacious mind / [He] Considered all things visible in heaven, / Or earth, or middle" (603–4), and in the dream of Book 5 he ascends with her "up to the clouds" where she "underneath beheld / The earth outstretched immense, a prospect wide / And various" (87–89). The fruit, and Satan's commentary, thus allow Eve both to reenact her narcissistic enclosure and to project an omniscience that is, in its assertion of the centrality of the self, a sublated version of narcissism.

What Satan's account leaves out, as we now understand, is the process of cognition that falls between beginning and end. This process of cognition—of education—is offered in two forms in *Paradise Lost*: first in the conversation between Raphael and Adam in Books 5 through 8; then in Books 11 and 12 with Michael's theology of history.[25] The first pedagogy is an education for innocence, gradually providing Adam with the knowledge that he needs in order to know himself and his place in God's scheme of things. That this education fails is an effect of Adam's forgetfulness when he gazes upon Eve: as he has already confessed to Raphael, "All higher knowledge in her presence falls / Degraded" (8.551–52). The second pedagogy is an education for experience that provides for Adam, with its assertion of the meaningfulness of history, a necessary consolation: "Greatly instructed I shall hence depart," he says, "Greatly in peace of thought" (12.557–58).

Each of these teachings is enacted according to the familiar dialectic between vision and narration. Books 5 through 8 operate according to a pattern of instruction that is repeated in both the small movements of Adam's self-development and in the larger pedagogical structure of the books as a whole. In Book 8 Adam describes his awakening into life as having been accomplished in three stages. His first movement was a gaze towards heaven:

> Straight toward heaven my wondering eyes I turned,
> And gazed a while the ample sky, till raised
> By quick instinctive motion up I sprung,
> As thitherward endeavouring, and upright
> Stood on my feet.
>
> (8.257–61)

But rather than allowing his gaze to remain fixed upon the heaven that is his ultimate goal, Adam turned to the created world about him, "Hill, dale, and shady woods, and sunny plains" (262). The final stage of this process was then a turn towards the self—"My self I then perused" (267) and, more generally, an effort to understand this self in the largest perspective. This effort is then itself enacted in three similar stages: first, a direct vision of God ("Whom thou sought'st I am" [316]), then an inventory of Eden (8.349–54), finally a realization that his human nature renders him in need of companionship (8.354–436). This threefold pattern also structures the whole of this pedagogical project as it is disposed throughout the poem's central books. We begin with the War in Heaven, but

Raphael's attempt to "relate / To human sense the invisible exploits / Of warring spirits" (5.564–66) is a visionary endeavor that leaves Adam puzzled and in "deep muse" (7.52): these events are to him literally "unimaginable" (54). Adam then turns to "what nearer might concern him" (62) and has Raphael tell the story of creation, "How this world / Of heaven and earth conspicuous first began" (62–63). The final stage of the process is then reached with his own narration of his earliest memories, an act of self-reflection that recalls him not merely to himself but to himself in relation both to the created world of which he is the head and to the Creator to whom he owes obedience. He defines for himself, in other words, his place within the scheme of creation and the moral imperatives that this place imposes upon him. That these three stages are, on this largest scale, interrupted by the speculations on astronomy is a diversion designed to show us just how tempting visionary ambitions can be. For in trying to comprehend "spaces incomprehensible" (8.20), Adam is not merely entering upon "studious thoughts abstruse" (40) but aspiring to a prospect that rivals that of God Himself.[26] "Heaven is for thee too high," cautions Raphael, "Be lowly wise" (172–73), and Adam forgoes the imperfect knowledge that later searchers will achieve only "through optic glass" (1.288) in order to return to the narrative of his own experience.

Books 11 and 12 repeat this pattern of vision set aside in favor of narration. Michael's instruction of Adam in the providential order of history appropriately recalls Beatrice's instruction of Dante in the same subject: both teachings take place in Eden, both pedagogues rely upon the Augustinian scheme of the seven ages. But for Milton the visionary mode carries crucial dangers. "O visions ill foreseen!" (11.763), cries Adam, and only Michael's careful commentary averts his despair. The whole of Book 12 is in fact just such a commentary. As recent criticism has shown, the narratives of the last six ages in Book 12 match precisely, "in themes, episodes, and figures," the six visions in which the first age is bodied forth in Book 11.[27] These narratives now raise up the fallen Adam, providing for him the crucial knowledge that it is in and through fallen history itself that paradise shall be regained. Only through "the race of time" shall "time stand fixed" (12.554–55), and any attempt to preempt this process, to accomplish God's purpose in, as Satan says, "a moment" (4.51), is worse than futile. As Leopold Bloom reminded himself, after his long gaze at Gerty McDowell, "Longest way round is the shortest way home."[28]

V

If for Milton the immediacy of vision prefigures the goal, he nonetheless insists that fulfillment requires the long way round of history. Analogously, he shows us that the processes of understanding are also continually required: nobody can be stupidly good. This is a dynamic that is also at work in *Paradise Regained*: Satan's impatience, his unwillingness to tolerate temporality, is expressed in the immediacy of his visionary mode, Christ's wise passiveness in the patient unfolding of his instructive discourses. With Milton, then, the alternation between vision and narration that was for Dante a dialectic begins to move toward opposition, and an opposition that also begins to draw a familiar, romantic line between the *poésie pure* of the image and the cold abstractions of doctrine. Milton is the great transitional figure in English literary history, and the versions of him that criticism gives us bespeak his liminality. An older tradition locates him as the last poet of the philosophical epic, writing a poem that is not merely historically true but, more profoundly, itself a form of knowledge.[29] "All Virgil is full of wisdom," says Servius, an assumption that governed both Virgilian commentary and the writing of epic until well after Milton's day.[30] On the other hand, the Renaissance conception of the epic was capacious, and more recent literary historians have found warrant for seeing in Milton a visionary bard who preserved the heritage of romance for the English line that was to follow.[31] Although this study of a single topos does indeed argue for the primacy of the first view, such a complicated issue can hardly be resolved by these preliminary soundings. More to the point is the fact that the choice between these alternative modes of interpretation is itself central to Milton's way of writing. Why this should be so, why given the example of Dante a choice should even have been necessary, is a question that would move us into the tangles of theology.

chapter ten

Brother Fire and St. Francis's Drawers

Human Nature and the Natural World

One of the most familiar of the many stories of Francis and the natural world is the tale of the wolf of Gubbio. First briefly reported about 1290, it is now best known in the elaborate version that appears in the popular *Fioretti* or *Little Flowers of Saint Francis*. A ravenous wolf that is terrorizing the town is reprimanded by a fearless St. Francis, who says that if the wolf will stop eating the townspeople they will in turn provide it with less distressing food. The wolf not only agrees but at Francis's request "raised its front paw and meekly and gently put it in St. Francis' hand as a sign that it was giving its pledge." Francis then brings the now-reformed wolf into town, where he repeats the pledge scene in front of the people. "From that day," says the author,

> the wolf and the people kept the pact that St. Francis made. The wolf lived two years more, and it went from door to door for food [not

unlike a friar, one observes]. It hurt no one, and no one hurt it. The
people fed it courteously. . . . Then the wolf grew old and died. And
the people were sorry.[1]

Despite the debate among scholars, the historical veracity of this narrative is the least interesting thing about it.[2] The interesting question is
whether the story is simply a hagiographical topos or an expression of specifically Franciscan values. For the story attributes moral consciousness to
an animal; it displays the saint's ability to command obedience from even
the most savage of beasts; and above all, it describes the making of a formal pact with an animal, a gesture that implies, at the least, a sense of the
equality of animals and humans, the ability of animals not merely to obey
but to negotiate with man, and their worthiness to receive the touch of
the saint's hand. It stresses not just the harmony that Francis sought to establish between the human and animal worlds but, more important, something of the motives that drew him to the natural world.

The purpose of this essay is to define both what is unique in Francis's
relation to nature and, above all, *why* the natural world was so valuable to
him at a time when, for many of his contemporaries, it was a site of distaste and apprehension.[3] For the city-dweller the countryside was most
often understood as inhabited by a rapacious, violent nobility, a peasantry
sunk in rural idiocy, and dangerous animals; for the country-dweller the
natural environment was either a place of unremitting labor or a source of
wealth grindingly wrung from uncooperative, even defiant, workers whose
very humanity was often in question.[4] And beyond the area of cultivation lay the wilderness, where holy men and outlaws went to lose themselves *in deserto*, to be tested by dark temptations and threatened by wild
animals as fierce as the wolf of Gubbio. Yet while for Francis the natural
world at times fit into these conventional categories, his ultimate relation to it was, I shall argue, not merely different from his contemporaries
but unique.

This uniqueness derives, I believe, not from his hagiographical identity as an *alter Christus* nor as the sixth angel of the apocalypse but rather
from the complexities of his struggle with his own sainthood. Admittedly,
to try to understand Francis psychologically is to be vulnerable to the
many traps laid for us by the number and diversity of the texts that record his life. Nor can the "questione francescana" that has preoccupied

Franciscan scholarship for much of the last century simply be ignored. But the intricate and so far inconclusive debates about the chronology and status of the various Franciscan texts must not be allowed to foreclose investigation into what remains a deeply mysterious—and immensely influential—personality. For one thing, it is the very power of that personality that accounts for the extraordinary proliferation of texts: there is literally no other medieval person who generated the amount of writing that surrounds Francis and his order. And for another, the meaning of Francis's life that emerges from the *interpretation* of these texts is itself part of the evidence to be included in any final judgment (should one indeed be possible) about the status of each individual text and its relation to the others. Thematic meanings are as much evidence as the *dispositio* of the text, its presumed author, or the date of the manuscript in which it survives—however open to revision the nature of these meanings must inevitably be. In what follows, therefore, I have sought for Francis among the texts that one can say, with at least some confidence, record Francis's life with a special intimacy. Without denying myself access to other texts when it seemed legitimate, I have focused almost exclusively on Francis's own writings, the *Vita prima* of Thomas of Celano, the *Anonymous of Perugia*, the *Legend of the Three Companions*, and especially the *Assisi Compilation* (more commonly known as the *Legend of Perugia*). In choosing these texts I have relied primarily upon the discrimination and learning of the editorial team that has just produced a new English translation of the works—a group of scholars that is *au courant* with the issues of the Franciscan Question and that provides each text with a headnote explaining what is known of its provenance, granting the reader easy access to long and complex debates.[5]

These texts show Francis relating to nature in several distinctive ways. The first and most familiar is the idea that the Book of Nature everywhere expresses God in symbolic terms, an idea with scriptural sources. Not only does Jesus tell us to consider the ravens and the lilies (Luke 12.24–27), but in Romans 1.20 Paul famously says, "For the invisible things of him, from the creation of the world, are clearly seen, being understood by the things that are made."[6] This use of nature appears at the very origins of the eremitical life—Antony tells a visitor that "my book is the nature of created things. In it when I choose I can read the words of God"[7]—and is familiar throughout the Middle Ages, continually referred to by spiritual writers for whom the natural world is important not in and of itself but as a means of reading a divine message. As for Francis, we are told that "whenever he had to walk over rocks, he would walk with fear and reverence out of love for Him who is called 'The Rock.'"[8] In his *Vita prima*, Thomas of Celano tells us that

> among all the different kinds of creatures, [Francis] loved lambs with a special fondness and spontaneous affection, since in Sacred Scripture the humility of our Lord Jesus Christ is frequently and rightly compared to the lamb. He used to embrace more warmly and to observe more gladly anything in which he found an allegorical likeness to the Son of God.[9]

The very conventionality of this idea, and its implicit contradiction with other, more original attitudes toward nature that we find elsewhere in the texts, may well mean that this is an expression less of Francis's own views than of the conventions of hagiography. But it is nonetheless present throughout the texts, and we cannot dismiss the possibility that it was indeed an attitude that Francis entertained.

The second Franciscan relation to nature is one that would become much more prominent after Francis's death — thanks to Bonaventure's *Itinerarium* — but was also ascribed to Francis while he was alive. This is nature as an occasion for contemplation. In the *Vita prima* Thomas makes explicit the way in which Francis's contemplative practices were dependent on the natural world:

> Who could ever express the deep affection he bore for all things that belong to God? Or who would be able to tell of the sweet tenderness he enjoyed while contemplating in creatures the wisdom, power, and goodness of the Creator? From this reflection he often overflowed with amazing, unspeakable joy as he looked at the sun, gazed at the moon, or observed the stars in the sky. What simple piety! What pious simplicity! . . . He used to call all creatures by the name of "brother" and "sister" and in a wonderful way, unknown to others, he could discern "the secrets of the heart" of creatures (1 Cor. 14.25) like someone who has already passed "into the freedom of the glory of the children of God" (Romans 8.21).[10]

So too, the less official *Assisi Compilation* tells us that Francis commu-
nicated with God's creatures "with joy, . . . and for that reason he was
often caught up in the contemplation of God [*rapiebatur in contempla-
tione Dei*]."[11] And it adds, "We who were with him saw him always in such
joy, inwardly and outwardly, over all creatures, touching and looking at
them, so that it seemed his spirit was no longer on earth but in heaven."[12]
It is probably the case that Francis responded more immediately and
powerfully to the natural world than many others in the contemplative
tradition, but again the familiarity of this motif in earlier hagiography
makes it difficult to claim that he is, as is sometimes claimed, a "nature
mystic."[13]

The third relation toward nature that we find expressed throughout the texts is also conventional, although its ubiquity in the early texts
suggests that it expresses an authentically Franciscan attitude. This is the
notion that the saint, by his simplicity and holiness, has himself recovered the original paradisal relation of man to animal: as God says in Genesis, "let [man] have dominion over the fishes of the sea, and the fowls
of the air, and the beasts, and the whole earth, and every creeping creature that moveth upon the earth" (Genesis 1.26). Francis becomes, in effect, the new Adam. As John Fleming has shown, this is a theme especially
dear to the Spirituals drawn to a Joachamite interpretation of Francis.[14] But
it is also a common theme from the earliest years of Christian eremitism.
Athanasius tells us, in an allusion to Job 5.22, that Antony "made the wild
beasts become peaceful with him," and Jerome says that Paul of Thebes
explained to his companions that "if someone possesses purity, all things
will be subject to him, as they were to Adam when he was in Paradise before he disobeyed the divine command."[15] The theme of holy men taming
wild animals is in fact everywhere in early medieval hagiography:

> Penitent bears, humiliated wolves, and scared rabbits mutely obey a
> saint's imperious command. Sea-birds stop raiding a saint's newly sown
> fields and accept imprisonment as their punishment. Deer leap from
> the deep woods of Brittany to plow the saint's fields, but refuse to work
> on Sundays.[16]

In fact, several of these stories go further than simply asserting the recovery of human authority over the natural world and instead reveal the

holy man's paradisal harmony with nature. Bede tells us of St. Cuthbert praying throughout the night while standing in the frigid sea up to his neck. When he emerged at daybreak two otters "bounded out of the water, stretched themselves out before him, warmed his feet with their breath, and tried to dry him on their fur."[17] Then there is Gregory's story of Florentius. Abandoned by his fellow monk Euthicius and desperately lonely, Florentius prays for a companion and is joined by a kindly bear, who becomes both his shepherd, leading the sheep out to pasture and back at the designated times, and Florentius's beloved companion.[18] Francis also recovers a prelapsarian authority over animals, like the wolf of Gubbio, or—most famously—the swallows he commands to be quiet while he preaches.[19] Bonaventure makes the meaning of this ability clear in a passage in the *Legenda Minor*:

> It came to pass by a supernatural influx of power that the nature of brute animals was moved in some gracious manner toward him. Even inanimate things obeyed his command, as if this same holy man, so simple and upright, had already returned to the state of innocence.[20]

"Simple and upright": Bonaventure is here citing the Book of Job (1.8 and 2.3), where Job is called *vir simplex et rectus*, a phrase also used of one of Francis's disciples by Thomas of Celano in his *Vita prima*.[21] This analogy is drawn to Francis not because Job is an archetype of the faithful man who suffers (as he will figure in late medieval hagiography[22]) but because Eliphaz promises Job that "[you] will not fear the beasts of the earth. For you shall be in league with the stones of the field, and the beasts of the field shall be at peace with you" (Job 5.22–23).

But Francis goes much further. Cuthbert's and Florentius's harmony with the natural world is largely a decorative motif rather than one of their defining spiritual virtues. But for Francis it is central, as in his calling both creatures and natural objects "Brother" and "Sister." There is no real hagiographical precedent for this passionate desire to establish intimacy with the natural world. Although he does insist that creation was made for man—he ascribes to the flowers the cry, "God made me for you, o people!"—he also sees the natural world as something other than man, as having an existence of its own which man aspires to join but from which he is in his sinfulness always in danger of being excluded. The best evidence for this understanding of Francis's naturalism is the *Canticle of the Creatures*. In the *Assisi Compilation* he says that he will compose a song "for [God's] creatures [*de suis creaturis*], which we use every day, and without which we cannot live. Through them the human race greatly offends the Creator."[23] That the *Canticle* is not a celebration of God's creation but actually a celebration of God *by* his creation—and a creation that explicitly excludes humans—is clear from the poem. Given its ambiguity, and what I consider to be its habitual mistranslation, I include here the original Umbrian with a literal translation of the nine-verse *Canticle* as Francis initially composed it.[24]

1. Altissimu, onnipotente, bon signore,
   tue so le laude, la gloria e l'honore
   et onne benedictione.

2. Ad te solo, Altissimo, se konfano,
   et nullu homo ene dignu te mentovare.

3. Laudato si, mi signore, cun tucte le tue creature,
   spetialmente messor lo frate sole,
   lo qual'è iorno, et allumini noi per lui.

4. Et ellu è bellu e radiante cum grande splendore,
   de te, Altissimo, porta significatione.

5. Laudato si, mi signore, per sora luna e le stele,
   in celu l'ài formate clarite et pretiose et belle.

6. Laudato si, mi signore, per frate vento,
   et per aere et nubilo et sereno et onne tempo,
   per lo quale a le tue creature dai sustentamento.

7. Laudato si, mi signore, per sor aqua,
   la quale è multo utile et humile et pretiosa et casta.

8. Laudato si, mi signore, per frate focu,
   per lo quale enn'alumini la nocte,
   ed ello è bello et iocundo et robustoso et forte.

9. Laudato si, mi signore, per sora nostra matre terra,
   la quale ne sustenta et governa,
   et produce diversi fructi con coloriti flori et herba.

1. Most high, all-powerful good Lord,
   to you are the praise, the glory and the honor
   and all blessings.

2. To you alone, Most High, do they belong
   and no man is worthy to praise you.

3. Praised be you, my Lord, with all your creatures,
   especially my lord brother sun,
   by whom exists for us the day, and light, by him.

4. And he is beautiful and radiant, with great brightness:
   of you, Most High, he bears the likeness.

5. Praised be you, my Lord, by sister moon and the stars:
   in heaven you made them clear and precious and lovely.

6. Praised be you, my Lord, by brother wind,
   and by the air and clouds and clearness and all weather
   by which you sustain all your creatures.

7. Praised be you, my Lord, by sister water,
   which is very useful and humble and precious and pure.

8. Praised be you, my Lord, by brother fire,
   by whom the night is lit up:
   and he is beautiful and joyful and robust and strong.

9. Praised be you, my Lord, by our sister mother earth,
   who sustains and controls us,
   and produces various fruits with colored flowers and grass.

Notice that the *Canticle* says of God that "no man is worthy to praise you" (*nullu homo ene dignu te mentovare*).[25] The human voice is explicitly excluded, which means that the elliptical *per* that appears throughout verses 5 through 9 should be translated as neither "for" nor "through" but as "by": "Praised be you, my Lord, *by* sister moon and the stars," and so forth.[26] And immediately after the exclusion of the human, the *Canticle* goes on to say: "Praised be you, my Lord, *with* all your creatures" (*cum tucte le tue creature*). Nature is thus seen as simultaneously dependent upon the human to give it voice and yet as independent of and even superior to the human. The human exclusion from nature is neither complete nor irremediable, but Francis does insist that our primary response must be one of grateful praise for a natural world that ministers to us. In the same passage in the *Assisi Compilation* he says, after composing the *Canticle,* that "at dawn, when the sun rises, everyone should praise God, who created it, because through it the eyes are lighted by day. . . . Because of this, we must always praise the glorious Creator for these and for His other creatures which we use every day."[27]

Over fifty years ago Lynn White argued that

> the older view of the natural creation as symbol was completely an-
> thropocentric: everything existed solely for man's spiritual benefit and
> for nothing else. Against this human egotism the humility of St. Fran-
> cis rebelled. To him the things of nature were indeed symbols, but
> they were more than that: they were fellow creatures placed on earth
> for God's inscrutable purposes, praising him in their proper ways as
> we do in ours. . . . It may be said without exaggeration that St. Fran-
> cis first taught Europe that nature is interesting and important in and
> of itself. . . . He forced man to abdicate his monarchy over the cre-
> ation, and instituted a democracy of all of God's creatures.[28]

Whatever exaggeration these words may contain, White is right in stress-
ing that Francis often saw the natural world as set apart from, even set
over against, humanity. Indeed, for Francis nature represented a realm of
being that relates to God in a way that is unaffected, spontaneous, and
authentic—an ideal to which fallen man could only aspire.[29]

Having identified what is truly new in Francis's relation to nature,
we are now able to deal with our central question: *why* was nature so important to Francis in the first place? Whatever we may decide about the
precise content of his views, we must be struck—as his contemporaries
were and as posterity has always been—by his constant, loving attention
to nature, by Francis's desire virtually to lose himself within nature. There
are at least two possible answers to this question, one historical, the other
psychological.

First, the historical. Franciscanism developed within a context of religious turmoil, in which the laity was becoming increasingly active in
searching for a spiritual life more authentic than that which was available
within the Church's institutions. The Petrobrusians, the *Humiliati*, the Be-
guines, the Apostolic Brethren, the Waldensians, the Brothers and Sisters
of Penitence, the *Continentes*, the *peregrini*—all these groups and others
were active during Francis's lifetime. But the most powerful and threat-
eningly independent movement in northern Italy was Catharism. Francis
was acutely aware of the danger these groups posed to his fledgling movement, especially since many of them were committed to values very similar to the Friars Minor: humility, poverty, public displays of penance, and

severe asceticism. Indeed, Peter Waldo was apparently converted by the same scriptural text that, at least according to the *Anonymous of Perugia*, led Francis to change his life: "If thou wilt be perfect, go sell what thou hast and give to the poor and thou shalt have treasure in heaven and come follow me" (Matt. 19.21).[30] Francis was careful to make certain that neither his various rules nor anything else about the order could be construed as a challenge to Church authority. He was also remarkably shrewd in finding powerful patrons within the Church hierarchy.[31] But the most powerful and threatening movement in northern Italy were the Cathars, and they posed a special problem. The emphasis by the Cathar *perfecti* on humility, poverty, and purity of life, as well as their practice of traveling in pairs in their missionary work, made them all too similar to the Friars Minor.[32] Cathars were known in Assisi itself, there was a Cathar bishopric in the nearby Val del Spoleto, and there were several cases of Franciscan tertiaries and even the lector at a Franciscan convent who either converted to Catharism or defended it before the authorities.[33] And after Francis's death charges of Catharism continued to be brought against the Fraticelli.[34]

Given this context, the rationale of much of Francis's teaching becomes clear.[35] The Cathars were committed to reading the Scriptures in the vernacular and composed their own spiritual texts to the extent that reading itself was seen as a characteristic activity of the *perfecti*.[36] Francis, on the other hand, consistently denigrates reading, even to the point of claiming to be himself illiterate—*ignorans et idiota*—and to denying one of his followers access to a breviary.[37] Again, the Cathars would eat no meat but only fish because it was thought that fish was generated by water rather than coition. Francis, despite several ostentatious displays of penitence for eating chicken, meat, and lard, insisted that the friars eat meat by invoking the Gospel injunction, "And into what city soever you enter, and they receive you, eat such things as are set before you" (Luke 10.8). Indeed, in his *Vita secunda* Thomas of Celano includes an anecdote about how a Cathar attempted to embarrass Francis by telling his audience that the great ascetic had just eaten from a capon. But when the Cathar sought to display the remains of the capon as evidence, it had been transformed into a fish.[38] Similarly, the Cathars insisted that a corrupt priest could not perform the sacraments, but Francis not only insists throughout his ministry that priests must be granted the greatest respect, but on occasion specifically commands a brother to confess to a priest who is known for his irregular life.[39] For the dualist Cathars, with their rejection of the material world, Christ was only "apparently" a man created when pure spirit entered Mary's ear, and the suffering of the Passion was also only "apparent." But Francis's famous enactment of the Nativity at the crib at Greccio was a way of insisting on Christ's human birth, and he sought to imitate Christ's bodily suffering not only through asceticism but to the point of stigmatization. All of this helps us to understand that Francis's celebration of the natural world—a material world that was despised by the Cathars and ascribed to an evil deity—was not merely a personal idiosyncrasy but an effort to insist, in opposition to the *perfecti* who were in other ways so like him, that even the smallest and most trifling part of God's creation, even the worms he would carefully remove from the path so they would not be crushed,[40] was an expression not merely of God's power but of his goodness. In his loving care for the natural world Francis could not have expressed more directly his rejection of Cathar dualism.

But the real heart of Francis's relation to the natural world is not finally historical but psychological. It derives from the deepest level of his existence, the conflict between his humanity and the sanctity he knew to be his destiny. Unlike so many saints' lives, the copious material we have about Francis reveals a figure of great complexity. This is not by any means the explicit goal of these writings. Thomas of Celano's *Vita prima*, written as a dossier for his canonization, seeks to chart Francis's life on a trajectory from the innocence of childhood through the struggle and conflict of adolescence and then back to the innocence of sanctity. Throughout the *Vita prima* Thomas insists that the virtue Francis most fully possessed was "holy simplicity," that he was "simple by grace, not by nature," that "he was simple in everything": "What simple piety! What pious simplicity!"— the word is found not only on virtually every page of Thomas's book but throughout the corpus of writings about Francis.[41] There are few terms that are applied to Francis more abundantly in the early texts than *simplicitas* and its cognates.[42] Moreover, Francis himself consistently invokes *simplicitas* as the central virtue that distinguishes him and his order. "The Spirit of the Lord," he says, "strives for . . . pure simplicity and true peace of the spirit," and he insists that the Franciscan vocation consists above all else in "pure and holy simplicity, prayer, and our Lady Poverty."[43] In the *Tes-*

tament he says that he had the *Rule* "written down simply and in a few words" and exhorts his brothers that "as the Lord has given me to speak and write the Rule and these words simply and purely, may you understand them simply and without gloss."[44]

Yet as Chrysogonus Waddell has said, "In the context of Christian literature, few terms offer so many complexities as does *simplicitas*."[45] Of course it refers to the Franciscan manner of life, and in this the Franciscans owe a substantial debt to the Cistercians.[46] But it also refers to a spiritual condition, most often described as the childlikeness that Jesus insisted was a prerequisite for understanding his message: "Thou hast hidden these things from the wise and prudent, and hast revealed them to little ones" (Luke 10.21); "Yea, have you never read: Out of the mouth of infants and of sucklings thou hast perfected praise?" (Matt. 21.16, citing Psalm 8.2); and, most explicitly: "Jesus, calling them together, said: Suffer children to come to me, and forbid them not: for of such is the kingdom of God. Amen, I say to you: Whosoever shall not receive the kingdom of God as a child, shall not enter into it" (Luke 18.16–17; and see Mark 10.15). It is in quest of this ideal—of simplicity as both moral innocence and psychological clarity—that Francis says that "God has called me by the way of simplicity and showed me the way of simplicity. . . . And the Lord told me what He wanted: He wanted me to be a new fool in the world."[47] By this he means not only that the wisdom of God is folly to the world but, more important, that true simplicity consists in, as Thomas Merton put it in relation to St. Bernard, "a gradual simplification and unification of the spiritual faculties"—what we would call psychological integrity, a wholeness of the self, or even the emotional security that comes from commitment and a singleness of purpose.[48] But as Francis's own life demonstrates, few virtues are more difficult to attain. For what the texts show is a Francis who is not only actively engaged in the ongoing drama of constructing his own saintly identity but is acutely aware of the complexity—even the duplicity—involved in the process.[49]

Francis's career begins with the ostentatious discarding of an unwanted identity when he rejects his patrimony before Bishop Guido and the townspeople of Assisi:

> When he was in front of the bishop, he neither delayed nor hesitated, but immediately took off and threw down all his clothes and returned

them to his father. He did not even keep his trousers on, and he was completely stripped bare before everyone. The bishop, observing his frame of mind and admiring his fervor and determination, got up and, gathering him in his own arms, covered him with the mantle he was wearing. He clearly understood that this was prompted by God and he knew that the action of the man of God, which he had personally observed, contained a mystery.[50]

The most important aspect of this scene is what is missing: the words that the silent Francis might have been expected to offer as explanation for his act. As is so often the case, he presents himself as a stubborn fact whose significance must be elicited by others.[51] In the *Testament* Francis instructs his followers "not to place glosses upon the Rule or upon these words."

> But as the Lord has given me to speak and write the Rule and these words *simply and purely,* may you understand them *simply and without gloss* and observe them with holy activity until the end.[52]

And in the *Assisi Compilation,* when some of the brothers express concern about the severity of the Rule, Francis's radical literalism is ratified in the most authoritative way possible:

> The voice of Christ was then heard in the air, saying, "Francis, nothing of yours is in the *Rule:* whatever is there is all mine. And I want the *Rule* observed in this way: to the letter, to the letter, to the letter, and without a gloss, and without a gloss, and without a gloss.[53]

Ad litteram, ad litteram, ad litteram, et sine glossa, et sine glossa, et sine glossa: over and over we are reminded of Francis's insistence that only through the most literal imitation of the life of Christ is salvation possible. Francis refuses to soak vegetables the night before they are to be eaten because that would violate the injunction to take no thought for the morrow (Matt. 6.34); he abandons the cell in which he is living because a brother casually refers to it as "*your* cell," and Christ said "Foxes have holes and the fowls of the air have nests, but the Son of Man hath not where to lay his head" (Matt. 8.20).[54] As the *Assisi Compilation* says, "he observed the holy Gospel *to the letter* from the day he began to have brothers until the day of his death" (my italics).

Yet there is no such thing as pure literalism, just as absolute simplicity is unavailable to the complex creatures that are human beings. Bishop Guido, by covering Francis, is simultaneously honoring the mystery of his nakedness and yet appropriating it, providing as it were the gloss of his mantle to cover the letter of Francis's body. The act of covering is a recognition of uninterpretability: "the action of the man of God, which he had personally observed, contained a mystery." Unlike Francis's father, Pietro Bernardone, for whom the discarding of the clothes represents Francis's rejection of his patrimony, and specifically of Pietro's vocation as a cloth merchant, Bishop Guido knows that nakedness is not transparent but enigmatic, and that Francis cannot be fully understood within traditional categories.[55] Yet there is another side: in covering Francis he absorbs him into the Church, thus beginning the process of institutional incorporation that would soon generate the political tension at the heart of Franciscan history. Four years after Francis's death in 1226, his great protector Bishop Ugolino, now Pope Gregory IX, issued the bull *Quo elongati* in which he released the brothers from the severity of Francis's *Rule,* saying that "scarcely or never could all of [Francis's injunctions] be obeyed to the letter."[56]

Yet Francis's quest for the singularity of selfhood that would constitute perfect simplicity, like his quest for absolute literalism, is enacted—as here—with an ostentatious theatricality that would seem to cancel out the very values that are sought. The examples of Francis's theatricality are almost endless. Matthew Paris tells how Francis went to see Innocent III, but his disheveled appearance led the pope to treat him as if he were a swineherd: "Go and find your pigs," he said, "and preach to them as much as you like." Francis rushed off to a pigsty, smeared filth over himself, and returned to the pope. After prudently telling Francis to go and wash, Innocent then granted him an audience.[57] He not only saves a lamb from among a flock of goats but then takes it to the bishop of Osimo's palace in order to instruct him in Jesus's use of the division of the sheep and the goats as a parable for the Last Judgment (Matt. 25.32). Francis leads the sheep into the palace of the bishop, who—not unexpectedly—"was surprised both at the sheep the man of God was leading and at [his] affection for it." Nor is the episode complete until Francis, having delivered his message, cannily off-loads the now-extraneous sheep onto a nearby community of Poor Clares, who complete the transaction by later making a tunic for Francis of the sheep's wool—an ironically apt allusion to Francis's previous life as a cloth merchant.[58] And Francis insists that the other brothers engage in the same public displays of foolishness, and not just by begging. When the brothers meet a priest, they are to kiss not only his hands but, if he is on horseback, the hooves of his horse; an insulted brother must place his foot on the mouth of the one who has insulted him; a brother who has touched money must carry it in his mouth and place it on a pile of ass's dung.[59]

Examples of these staged displays of holy foolishness could be easily multiplied, all pointing to the central paradox of the drama of Francis's saintly identity—the fact that his "pious simplicity" is displayed and achieved only through strategies that witness to the very complexity he wishes to erase.[60] These ostentatious displays are a way of acknowledging, by their very extravagance, Francis's awareness of the gap between the simplicity he seeks and the complexity that characterizes the human. Indeed, a number of the anecdotes about Francis reveal that he is himself all too aware of this strategy, and of the paradox—simplicity always bespeaks complexity, authenticity always carries with it the aura of performance—that makes it necessary. At the palace of Bishop Ugolino he leaves during dinner to beg alms in the street, returning with the scraps of food he has collected and distributing them to the dinner guests. If we should think this to be simply the act of a man who is *idiota et simplex*, a new holy fool or *novellus pazzus*, we are disabused by his private comment to the bishop: "I must be a model and example of your poor" because there will be brothers "who, held back by shame and because of bad habit, are and will be scorned by humbling themselves, by demeaning themselves, by begging alms, and by doing this kind of servile work. Therefore I must teach by deed those who are or will be in religion, that they might be without excuse."[61] This sense of constantly having to play a role, of having to provide a model, pervades Francis's life. Hence he turns away praise for his saintliness by comparing himself to a picture:

> As in a painting of the Lord and the Blessed Virgin on wood, it is God and the Blessed Virgin who are honored, and God and the Blessed Virgin are held in memory. The wood and the paint attribute nothing to themselves because they are merely wood and paint. In the same way, a servant of God is a painting, that is, a creature of God, in whom God is honored because of His goodness. Like wood or paint, he must not attribute anything to himself, but give all honor and glory to God.

He should not attribute anything to himself while he is alive except shame and trouble, because, while he is alive, the flesh is always opposed to God's gifts.[62]

The servant of God is a painting, a metaphor that simultaneously reduces the servant to a mere signifier of something greater than himself and yet also suggests that there is something artificial about him, perhaps even something artful, something deceptive. He seems to be something other than what he is.

The dilemma of enacting rather than simply inhabiting a saintly identity is expressed with real poignancy in an episode found in a fourteenth-century text. Francis instructs Brother Leo to write down what Francis considers to be true joy. As is his way, he explains the abstract in terms of the concrete, in this case by confecting a story about himself. Suppose, he says,

> I return from Perugia and arrive here in the dead of night. It's winter time, muddy, and so cold that icicles have formed on the edges of my habit and keep striking my legs and blood flows from such wounds. Freezing, covered with mud and ice, I come to the gate and, after I've knocked and called for some time, a brother comes and asks: "Who are you?" "Brother Francis," I answer. "Go away!" he says. "This is not a decent hour to be wandering about! You may not come in!" When I insist, he replies: "Go away! You are simple and stupid! Don't come back to us again! There are many of us here like you—we don't need you!" I stand against the door and say: "For the love of God, take me in tonight!" And he replies, "I will not! Go to the Croziers' place and ask there!" I tell you this: If I had patience and did not become upset, true joy, as well as true virtue and the salvation of my soul, would consist in this.[63]

What a remarkable fiction Francis has constructed here! He simultaneously imagines his rejection by his own brothers and yet, in telling this story, presents himself as the indispensable leader who defines for them their own spiritual aspirations. He is at once unworthy and yet essential, at once desiring the *apatheia* of the holy man and yet expressing that desire in a tale that bespeaks throughout his profound and inevitably conflicted feelings not just for his brothers but for his position among them.

Perhaps the most telling anecdote concerns his relationship with the companion named Brother John, a *vir mire simplicitatis*, a man of wonderful or perhaps even peculiar simplicity. "Because blessed Francis greatly loved and was always pleased by pure and holy simplicity in himself and in others," we are told, "he immediately dressed [John] in the clothing of the religion and took him for his companion." The story continues:

> He was a man of such simplicity that he believed he was bound to do everything blessed Francis would do. So, whenever blessed Francis was in some church or in some other place to pray, he wanted to watch and observe him so that he could imitate all his gestures. If blessed Francis knelt, or joined his hands toward heaven, or spat, or coughed, he would do the same. With great joy, blessed Francis began to reprove him for these kinds of simplicity. But he answered: "Brother, I promised to do everything you do. Therefore I want to do everything you do." And blessed Francis marveled and rejoiced, seeing him in such purity and simplicity. For he began to be perfect in all virtues and good habits, so that blessed Francis and the other brothers greatly marveled at his perfection. A short time afterwards he died in that holy perfection. Therefore, with great inner and outer joy, blessed Francis used to tell the brothers about his manner of living and would call him not "Brother John," but "Saint John."[64]

"Not Brother John, but Saint John": this man whom we would say, with the careful reticence of our time, had an intellectual disability is the perfect instance of the literalistic sanctity toward which Francis constantly aspired but which necessarily eluded him. Unencumbered by self-consciousness, unafraid of the burden of perfection, Saint John transcends the psychological dilemma that afflicts his master. It is, indeed, a sign of Francis's own generosity of spirit that when confronted by this exemplar of all that he would wish to but cannot be, he responds "with much amusement" and celebrates "with great delight" the pious simplicity and simple piety he can himself never attain.

What has the psychological drama of Francis's sainthood to do with his love for nature? The episode that provides the title for this essay concerns not the famous cauterization of Francis's face by Brother Fire, but a more bizarre event.[65] Once when he was sitting close to a fire his pants or drawers—one text describes them as *pannos eius juxta crus,* "the rags next to his leg," another as *pannos eius de lino sive bracas,* "his linen rags or breeches"—caught fire. Francis prevents his companion from putting out the fire: "No, dearest brother, do not hurt Brother Fire." Only when another friar comes to the rescue are the flames extinguished.[66] This episode does not reveal Francis to be a nature mystic, or a heretical animist ascribing moral being to the natural elements, or a Coleridgean pantheist for whom a divine spirit rolls through all things, or even simply a lover of the natural world. Rather, it shows a Francis who subordinates himself to a force that is able to enact its very being with an unselfconscious immediacy. Brother Fire is untroubled by taking what he desires; Brother Fire requires no Gospel model for his behavior; and yet Brother Fire—simply by being what he is and doing what he does—is, like all of God's creation, good. Brother Fire, in short, is *idiota et simplex.* And the same can be said for all of the natural world: it embodies the beneficent simplicity for which the human Francis so powerfully yearns and yet which remains always beyond his reach.

━━━━━━━━━━━━━━━━━━━━━

Preface

1. Harold Pinter is quoted from Michael Billington, "The Evil that Men Do," in *The Guardian*, June 30, 2001.

2. I am referring here to the oft-quoted sentence that opens L. P. Hartley's novel *The Go-Between*: "The past is a foreign country; they do things differently there."

one. Historical Criticism and the Development of Chaucer Studies

1. Recent examples of these two different kinds of work are L. O. Aranye Fradenburg, *Sacrifice Your Love: Psychoanalysis, Historicism, Chaucer* (Minneapolis: University of Minnesota Press, 2002), and Alastair Minnis, *Fallible Authors: Chaucer's Pardoner and Wife of Bath* (Philadelphia: University of Pennsylvania Press, 2008).

2. In *Parler du moyen âge* (Paris: Editions de Minuit, 1980), Paul Zumthor playfully invokes psychoanalytic language to describe medieval studies. He speaks of "le médiévisme de papa" (p. 31) and suggests that the antiquarianism that has traditionally motivated so much medieval scholarship is itself expressive of Freudian instincts: "l'érudition devient le refuge des Oedipes ratés" (p. 29), who are denied a more direct return to the maternal origin. Zumthor's analysis in fact takes psychoanalysis no more seriously than does my own.

3. A bibliography of Robertson's writings through 1977 is available in his *Essays in Medieval Culture* (Princeton: Princeton University Press, 1980), pp. 283–84.

4. E. Talbot Donaldson, "Patristic Exegesis in the Criticism of Medieval Literature: The Opposition," in Dorothy Bethurum, ed., *Critical Approaches to Medieval Literature* (New York: Columbia University Press, 1960), pp. 1–26, reprinted in *Speaking of Chaucer* (New York: Norton, 1970), pp. 134–53, along with the analogous "Medieval Poetry and Medieval Sin," pp. 164–74; Francis Lee Utley, "Robertsonianism Redivivus," *Romance Philology* 19 (1965): 250–60, reprinted as "Chaucer and Patristic Exegesis" in A. C. Cawley, ed., *Chaucer's Mind and Art* (Edinburgh: Oliver and Boyd, 1969), pp. 69–85; Morton W. Bloomfield, "Symbolism in Medieval Literature," *Modern Philology* 56 (1958): 73–81, reprinted in *Essays and Explorations: Studies in Ideas, Language, and Literature* (Cambridge, Mass.: Harvard University Press, 1970), pp. 82–95; Donald R. Howard, "Medieval Poems and Medieval Society," *Medievalia et Humanistica*, n.s. 3 (1972): 99–115; Robert E. Kaske, "The Defense," in *Critical Approaches to Medieval Literature*, pp. 27–60, and "Chaucer and Medieval Allegory," *ELH* 30 (1963): 175–92.

5. Donaldson opens his attack on Exegetics with a disarming admission that in fact serves as a familiar empiricist enabling move: "I am not aware of any valid theoretical objection to the use of patristic exegesis in the criticism of medieval literature," he says, thereby protecting his own practice from theoretical examination and appealing to shared standards of value that remain powerfully unarticulated. A theoretical attack on Exegetics was in fact offered by Ronald S. Crane in "On Hypotheses in 'Historical Criticism': Apropos of Certain Contemporary Medievalists," in *The Idea of the Humanities* (Chicago: University of Chicago Press, 1967), 2.236–60. Crane's claim is that Robertsonian exegesis violates canons of interpretive correctness, a claim that contemporary criticism, with its stronger sense of the conventional nature of all interpretive activity, would be less likely to make.

6. Examples of the polemical nature of Exegetics include the critical writings of Judson B. Allen, *A Distinction of Stories* (Columbus: Ohio State University Press, 1981) (with Theresa Anne Moritz) and *The Ethical Poetic of the Later Middle Ages* (Toronto: University of Toronto Press, 1982), and John V. Fleming, *Reason and the Lover* (Princeton: Princeton University Press, 1984). While it is true that in *A Distinction of Stories* Allen and Moritz "state bluntly and categorically" that they are not "Robertsonian" (p. 34 n. 20), both this book and Allen's *Ethical Poetic* are premised on the assumptions of Robertson's brand of historicism and are directed against the Robertsonian targets of "modern critical expectations" (*Distinction*, p. x) and the "solipsism" and "mere aestheticism" that is said to characterize contemporary modes of critical understanding (*Ethical Poetic*, pp. xi and 38). Fleming, Robertson's successor at

Princeton, opens his book on the *Roman de la rose* with an anathema against what he calls "The Ithacan Heresy" promoted by such irreligious Cornellians as Winthrop Wetherbee and Thomas D. Hill. On the other side, critical anxiety about the historicist claims of Exegetics were ubiquitous. Two examples, chosen not because they are egregious but because they are at once typical and oblique, are comments by Donald R. Howard in *The Idea of the Canterbury Tales* (Berkeley: University of California Press, 1976), and Jill Mann in "Troilus' Swoon," *Chaucer Review* 14 (1980): 319–35. Throughout his book Howard skirmishes with Exegetics but evades direct engagement in favor of nervous dismissal: "It is all very dreary" (p. 51). Similarly, Mann concludes her discussion with an apparently superfluous dismissal of "self-conscious historicism" (p. 332) in favor of a more direct emotional response, a conclusion that makes sense only in terms of an unarticulated antagonism to the explicitly historicist claims of Exegetics. Again, throughout *Chaucer and the Imagery of Narrative* (Stanford: Stanford University Press, 1984), V. A. Kolve takes great pains to distinguish his interpretive use of visual materials from that of the Exegetes, with the perhaps predictable result that he was chided by reviewers for not being exegetical enough: see James I. Wimsatt in *South Atlantic Quarterly* 85 (1986): 98–101.

7. An apparently notorious instance of an essay that highlights these differences is my own "Chaucer's Pardoner on the Couch: Psyche and Clio in Medieval Literary Studies," *Speculum* 76 (2001): 638–80; reprinted in *Temporal Circumstances: Form and History in Chaucer's Poetry* (New York: Palgrave Macmillan, 2006), pp. 67–96.

8. There were of course exceptions to this general avoidance. A positive valence for the Miller's bagpipes has been demonstrated both by Robert Boenig, "The Miller's Bagpipe: A Note on the *Canterbury Tales* A 565–566," *English Language Notes* 21 (1983): 1–6, and by V. A. Kolve, *Chaucer and the Imagery of Narrative*, p. 75. As for the Wife of Bath's deafness and the Pardoner's eunuchry, in both cases the exegetical meaning of these details ought to be set in opposition to their narrative function. For example, the Wife's deafness is read by Exegetics as an iconographical detail that defines her as one of those who have ears and hear not (Psalm 113); hence her deafness comments on her "rampant 'femininity' or carnality" (Robertson, *A Preface to Chaucer* [Princeton: Princeton University Press, 1963], p. 321). But the narrative of the Prologue tells us that in the course of her violent struggles with Jankyn over his book of wicked wives "he smot me so that I was deef" (3.668), a narrative detail that defines the deafness as an effect not of female inadequacy but of male violence. It is also an evidently enabling handicap: unable to hear the overbearing discourse of male superiority in all its authority, the Wife reproduces instead a parody that inscribes and legitimizes female difference. In showing how male authority undoes itself, then, the literal narrative of the Wife's deafness both offers an explanation in terms other than the exegetical ones

prescribed by the dominant clerical culture and demystifies that very dominance by disclosing the violence upon which it is based. I expanded on this
reading in "'For the Wyves Love of Bathe': Feminine Rhetoric and Poetic Resolution in the *Roman de la Rose* and the *Canterbury Tales*," *Speculum* 58 (1983):
656–95; reprinted in a revised form in *Chaucer and the Subject of History* (Madison: University of Wisconsin Press, 1991), pp. 280–321.

9. A few instances are John P. Hermann and John J. Burke, eds., *Signs
and Symbols in Chaucer's Poetry* (University: University of Alabama Press,
1981); David Lyle Jeffrey, ed., *Chaucer and Scriptural Tradition* (Ottawa: University of Ottawa Press, 1984); Chauncey Wood, *The Elements of Chaucer's Troilus*
(Durham: Duke University Press, 1984); and Paul A. Olson, *The Canterbury
Tales and the Good Society* (Princeton: Princeton University Press, 1986). Even a
book as critically *au courant* as R. A. Shoaf's *Dante, Chaucer, and the Currency
of the Word* (Norman: Pilgrim Books, 1983) was directed (and, in my view, ham-
strung) by the norms of Exegetical interpretation.

10. John V. Fleming, "Chaucer and Erasmus on the Pilgrimage to Can-
terbury: An Iconographical Speculation," in Thomas J. Heffernan, ed., *The
Popular Literature of Medieval England*, Tennessee Studies in Literature 28
(Knoxville: University of Tennessee Press, 1985), p. 152.

11. The obvious exception was the work of Hans Robert Jauss; see his
Aesthetic Experience and Literary Hermeneutics, trans. Michael Shaw (Minneapolis: University of Minnesota Press, 1982), *Toward an Aesthetic of Reception*,
trans. Timothy Bahti (Minneapolis: University of Minnesota Press, 1982), and
the influential essay "The Alterity and Modernity of Medieval Literature," trans.
Timothy Bahti, *New Literary History* 10 (1979): 181–229, from *Alterität and
Modernität der mittelalterlichen Literatur* (Munich: Fink, 1977). Broadly speaking, Jauss attempts to reconcile the tradition of humanist hermeneutics deriving from Dilthey with the *wissenschaftliche* positivism of traditional literary
history; hence he insists on "intersubjective communication" as the defining
quality of literary understanding ("Art History and Pragmatic History," *Toward
an Aesthetic of Reception*, p. 52), yet designates as the object of a truly historical literary study (i.e., one that respects the work's "alterity") not the work itself but the work's "horizon of expectation," by which he means the expectations of the work's original readers. This "horizon" is to be discovered by three
means: "first, through familiar norms or the immanent poetics of the genre;
second, through the implicit relationships to familiar works of the literary-
historical surroundings; and third, through the opposition between fiction
and reality, between the poetic and the practical function of language, which
is always available to the reflective reader during the reading as a possibility of
comparison" ("Literary History as a Challenge to Literary Theory," *Toward an
Aesthetic of Reception*, p. 24). What this amounts to is traditional literary history
(items one and two mean comparing the work to others of its kind and to other

literary works) supplemented with a comparison of the work to "reality," a reality whose availability is never defined. Moreover, Jauss declines to confront the historicity of the observer. In "The Alterity and Modernity of Medieval Literature," the modern reader is described as being able to recognize both the culturally confirmatory aspects of the medieval text (its alterity) and its disruptive elements (its modernity) because both these aspects correspond to an analogous opposition within the modern situation—an analogy that remains unexamined. As Robert Holub says, in *Reception Theory* (London: Methuen, 1984), "In contradistinction to Gadamer's insistence on historicality, we are asked [by Jauss] to ignore or bracket our own historical situatedness. Despite his struggle to escape a positivist-historicist paradigm, then, Jauss, in adopting objectivity as a methodological principle, appears to fall back into the very errors he criticizes" (p. 60). In sum, Jauss's work seems to me to represent a sophisticated reconceptualization of the problems of historicism that promises a theoretical solution that it does not deliver.

12. I have outlined my own views on historicist methodology in a variety of essays, the fullest account being chapter 2 of *Negotiating the Past: The Historical Understanding of Medieval Literature* (Madison: University of Wisconsin Press, 1987), pp. 41–74.

13. On nineteenth-century medievalism in England, see the general study by Alice Chandler, *A Dream of Order: The Medieval Ideal in Nineteenth-Century English Literature* (Lincoln: University of Nebraska Press, 1970). The best account of the conservative strain of medievalism is by Mark Girouard, *The Return to Camelot: Chivalry and the English Gentleman* (New Haven: Yale University Press, 1981). Girouard stresses the crucial importance of Kenelm Henry Digby's *The Broad Stone of Honour* (1823) in forming the nineteenth-century ideology of chivalry by which the class and economic violence of the nineteenth century was successfully mystified.

14. Lord John Manners, *England's Trust and Other Poems* (London: J. G. F. and J. Rivington, 1841), p. 16.

15. From a letter of 1842, cited by Chandler, *Dream of Order*, p. 164.

16. The Oxford Movement—which Matthew Arnold characterized as one of the "last enchantments of the Middle Ages"—ought to be enrolled among the promoters of a conservative medievalism, and Manners's explicitly reactionary program can be tellingly matched with an equally obscurantist comment uttered by the future Cardinal Newman: "I do not shrink from uttering my firm conviction that it would be a gain to the country were it vastly more superstitious, more bigoted, more gloomy, more fierce in its religion than at present it shows itself to be." Cited by Basil Willey, *Nineteenth-Century Studies* (New York: Columbia University Press, 1949), p. 75; for the citation from Arnold, see p. 73.

17. John Ruskin, "The Nature of Gothic," *Works*, ed. E. T. Cook and Alexander Wedderburn (London: George Allen, 1904), 10.188. Given the com-

plexity of his personality and career, it would be wrong to ascribe to Ruskin any single attitude toward the Middle Ages. Despite his commitment to the Working Men's College in Red Lion Square in the 1860s, the vehicle for educational and social reform that Ruskin proposed in the 1870s was the Guild of St. George, an organization governed by the laws of *quattrocento* Florence — an image of medieval society radically at odds with that represented in "The Nature of Gothic" in 1852. Indeed, "The Nature of Gothic" is discontinuous with itself, juxtaposing a primitivist Gothicism with a careful iconographical exegesis of St. Mark's Cathedral in Venice. For Ruskin's exegetical interests, see George P. Landow, *The Aesthetic and Critical Theories of John Ruskin* (Princeton: Princeton University Press, 1971), pp. 319–457. The curriculum of Ruskin's St. George's schools was to consist in books by seven authors: Moses, David, Hesiod, Virgil, Dante, Chaucer, and St. John the Divine. Significantly, however, all of Chaucer's works (including the spurious) were to be read *except* the *Canterbury Tales*: see *Fors Clavigera* 61 in *Works* 28.500. For Ruskin the Companions of St. George are "a band of achieving knights — not churls needing deliverance." See Margaret E. Spence, "The Guild of St. George: Ruskin's Attempt to Translate His Ideas into Practice," *Bulletin of the John Rylands Library* 40 (1957): 156.

18. Morris's *A Dream of John Ball* is an attack on "the degradation of the sordid utilitarianism that cares not and knows not of beauty and history" in the name of "the Fellowship of Men" that motivated the Peasants' Revolt and that, Morris asserts, "shall endure." See *Collected Works*, ed. May Morris (London: Longmans, 1910–15), 16.215, 284. In *William Morris: Romantic to Revolutionary* (New York: Monthly Review Press, 1961), E. P. Thompson describes *A Dream of John Ball* as perhaps Morris's "greatest meditation upon the meaning of life, both in its individual and its historical context" (p. 836). For the appeal to the tradition of Saxon liberty, see Christopher Hill, "The Norman Yoke," in John Saville, ed., *Democracy and the Labour Movement* (London: Lawrence and Wishart, 1954), pp. 11–66, reprinted in *Puritanism and Revolution* (London: Seeker and Warburg, 1958), pp. 50–122. Morris's conception of the Germanic origins of English society is matched by the picture of Saxon life presented by the Anglo-Saxonist J. M. Kemble and the "Whig" historians J. R. Green and E. A. Freeman; see J. W. Burrow, *A Liberal Descent: Victorian Historians and the English Past* (Cambridge: Cambridge University Press, 1981), pp. 155–92. The politically ambiguous medievalism of Morris's Pre-Raphaelite colleagues is examined by John Dixon Hunt, *The Pre-Raphaelite Imagination* (Lincoln: University of Nebraska Press, 1968). As for Tennyson's *Idylls of the King*, Swinburne's suggestion that it be retitled the *Morte d'Albert* neatly crystallizes the poem's political valence (as if its dedication to the Queen were not sufficient indication).

19. For an account of this strain in nineteenth-century medievalism, see Lionel Gossman, "Literature and Education," *New Literary History* 13 (1982): 341–71, and, more generally, Raymond Williams, *Culture and Society*,

1780–1950 (Harmondsworth: Penguin Books, 1961), pp. 137–61, 187–91. While beyond the scope of this discussion, the link between a primitivist reading of medieval culture and a liberal commitment to the unification of society is of central importance to the development of medieval studies on the Continent. The intense politicization of the Middle Ages in France, for example, and its co-option by a conservative state apparatus, had the result of driving liberal medievalists like Michelet into a violent rejection of all things medieval. As a countermeasure, scholars who wished to remain loyal both to the Middle Ages and to their liberal principles insisted that what validated modern interest in the medieval past was not an admiration for its political or religious values but the immediacy with which both a common human nature and a shared national culture were represented in medieval art. A good example of this attitude is provided by Gaston Paris, son of the Paulin Paris who was holder of the first chair of medieval French at the Collège de France (1863), and himself holder of the first chair in the same subject at the École Pratique des Hautes Études (1872). Throughout his writings Paris insists that medieval literature can be all things to all readers because it offers a full representation of the French nation in its original form; see, e.g., his comments at two of the early meetings of the Société des Anciens Textes Français in the *Bulletin de la Société des Anciens Textes Français* 3 (1877): 53–58, and 5 (1879): 46–52, and the manifesto of *Romania*, founded in the dark days of 1871 and seen as an agency by which France could reunite itself to withstand the challenge of a monolithic Germany: *Romania* 1 (1872): 1–22. For the politicization of the Middle Ages in nineteenth-century France, see Janine Dakyns, *The Middle Ages in French Literature, 1851–1900* (Oxford: Oxford University Press, 1973), and Hans Ulrich Gumbrecht, "'Un souffle d'Allemagne ayant prise': Friedrich Diez, Gaston Paris, and the Genesis of National Philologies," *Romance Philology* 40 (1986): 1–37. This process went so far that Fustel de Coulanges could actually claim that the disasters of 1870–71 were the result of the divisions brought about by partisan misrepresentations of the Middle Ages. Hence, "La connaissance du moyen âge, mais la connaissance exacte et scientifique, sincère et sans parti-pris, est pour notre société un intérêt de premier ordre" (cited by Dakyns, p. 196). It was by recuperating a Middle Ages unified by a national spirit or character rather than by institutions that were by their very nature divisive that a unified France could be recovered.

20. Complaints about the government's neglect of historical records and monuments are a persistent feature of nineteenth-century English scholarly writing; brief overviews are offered by Thomas P. Peardon, *The Transition in English Historical Writing, 1760–1830* (New York: Columbia University Press, 1933), and by Dom David Knowles, *Great Historical Enterprises* (London: Nelson, 1964), whose parallel accounts of the Monumenta Germaniae Historica and the Rolls Series provide a dismaying insight into English amateurism and

disorganization. For the state control of medievalism in France, see, e.g., William R. Keylor, *Academy and Community: The Foundation of the French Historical Profession* (Cambridge, Mass.: Harvard University Press, 1975), and Paul Léon, *La vie des monuments français: destruction, restauration* (Paris: Picard, 1951). In England, the feebleness of the aristocratic Royal Society of Antiquaries should be set against the vigor of the voluntary publishing and scholarly societies (which should themselves be distinguished from antiquarian book clubs like the Roxburghe): see Joan Evans, *A History of the Society of Antiquaries* (Oxford: Oxford University Press, 1956), and Harrison Ross Steeves, *Learned Societies and English Literary Scholarship* (New York: Columbia University Press, 1913). On the independent scholar of nineteenth-century England, general surveys are offered by John Gross, *The Rise and Fall of the Man of Letters* (London: Macmillan, 1969), and Richard D. Altick, *The Scholar Adventurers* (New York: Macmillan, 1960).

21. On the politics of the leaders of the historicist movement, see Georg G. Iggers, *The German Conception of History* (Middletown: Wesleyan University Press, 1968), and Peter Hanns Reill, *The German Enlightenment and the Rise of Historicism* (Berkeley: University of California Press, 1975).

22. The brevity of this account simplifies complex issues that are given full treatment by Hayden White, *Metahistory: The Historical Imagination in Nineteenth-Century Europe* (Baltimore: The Johns Hopkins University Press, 1973).

23. Kemble's attack on the Anglo-Saxon establishment is detailed by Hans Aarsleff, *The Study of Language in England, 1780–1860* (Princeton: Princeton University Press, 1967); see also Raymond A. Wiley, "Anglo-Saxon Kemble: The Life and Works of John Mitchell Kemble, 1807–1857, Philologist, Historian, Archaeologist," in S. C. Hawkes, D. Brown, and J. Campbell, eds., *Anglo-Saxon Studies in Archaeology and History* 1, British Archaeological Reports, British Series 72 (Oxford: British Archaeological Society, 1979), pp. 165–273. The best account of the Swinburne-Furnivall dispute is provided by William S. Peterson, ed., *Browning's Trumpeter: The Correspondence of Robert Browning and Frederick J. Furnivall, 1872–1889* (Washington, D.C.: Decatur House Press, 1979); see also William Benzie, *Dr. F. J. Furnivall, Victorian Scholar Adventurer* (Norman: Pilgrim Books, 1983).

24. Benzie, *Dr. F. J. Furnivall*, p. 48; Peterson, *Browning's Trumpeter*, p. xxiv. For the liberal values that motivated the rise of English studies in general, see Chris Baldick, *The Social Mission of English Criticism, 1848–1932* (Oxford: Clarendon Press, 1983).

25. Eric Stanley, *The Search for Anglo-Saxon Paganism* (Cambridge: Brewer and Boydell, 1975), p. 8; for the eighteenth-century roots of this primitivism, see Reill's account in *German Enlightenment and the Rise of Historicism* of the career of the founder of German literary medieval studies, Johann Jacob Bodmer

(1698–1783), who was inspired by Thomas Blackwell's *Enquiry into the Life and Writings of Homer* (1735) to search for a German Homeric Age and who then succeeded in discovering/creating one.

26. Whig historiography was first christened by Herbert Butterfield, *The Whig Interpretation of History* (London: G. Bell, 1931); its monuments are perceptively analyzed by Burrow, *Liberal Descent.*

27. "Prospectus of the Engraving of Chaucer's Canterbury Pilgrims," *Poetry and Prose of William Blake,* ed. Geoffrey Keynes (London: Nonesuch Press, 1943), p. 637.

28. Of course there were nineteenth-century exceptions. Early in the century John Wilson, professor of moral philosophy at Glasgow, insisted that Chaucer's poetry was allegorical and motivated by a commitment to "the wonderful political institution of Chivalry," and in his *Encyclopaedia Britannica* article of 1876, William Minto, professor of logic and English at Aberdeen University, argued that "the 'Canterbury Tales' are really in their underlying design an exposition of chivalrous sentiment, thrown into relief by contrast with its opposite." The citations from Wilson (who wrote under the pseudonym "Christopher North") and Minto are taken from Derek Brewer, ed., *Chaucer: The Critical Heritage* (London: Routledge and Kegan Paul, 1978), 2.59, 187. For surveys of Chaucer criticism, see Brewer's introduction to this collection and his essays "Images of Chaucer, 1386–1900," in Brewer, ed., *Chaucer and Chaucerians* (University: University of Alabama Press, 1966), pp. 240–70, and "The Criticism of Chaucer in the Twentieth Century," in *Chaucer's Mind and Art,* pp. 3–28.

29. Examples are John S. P. Tatlock, "The Epilog of Chaucer's *Troilus,*" *Modern Philology* 18 (1920–21): 625–59, and "Boccaccio and the Plan of Chaucer's *Canterbury Tales,*" *Anglia* 37 (1913): 69–117 (Tatlock published over thirty-five separate items on Chaucer, including seven books); George Lyman Kittredge, "The Authorship of the English Romaunt of the Rose," *Harvard Studies and Notes in Philology and Literature* 1 (1892): 1–65, and "Chaucer's Lollius," *Harvard Studies in Classical Philology* 28 (1917): 47–133 (twenty-two items, three books); John Livingston Lowes, "Chaucer and the *Miroir de Mariage,*" *Modern Philology* 8 (1910–11): 165–86, 305–34, and "The Loveres Maladye of Hereos," *Modern Philology* 11 (1913–14): 491–546 (thirty items, one book). Judging from the extent to which the findings and arguments of these scholars (and of the remarkably erudite and intelligent W. W. Skeat) have been inadvertently repeated in later discussions, we should acknowledge their importance and regret their current neglect.

30. John M. Manly, *Some New Light on Chaucer* (New York: Holt, 1926). More recent examples of occasional criticism are D. W. Robertson, Jr., "The Historical Setting of Chaucer's *Book of the Duchess,*" in John Mahoney and John Esten Keller, eds., *Mediaeval Studies in Honor of Urban Tigner Holmes, Jr.* (Chapel Hill: University of North Carolina Press, 1965), pp. 169–95, reprinted

in *Essays in Medieval Culture*, pp. 235–56; Larry D. Benson, "The Occasion of *The Parliament of Fowls*," in Benson and Siegfried Wenzel, eds., *The Wisdom of Poetry: Essays in Early English Literature in Honor of Morton W. Bloomfield* (Kalamazoo: Medieval Institute Publications, 1982), pp. 123–44; and Larry D. Benson, "The 'Love-Tydynges' in Chaucer's *House of Fame*," in Julian N. Wasserman and Robert J. Blanch, eds., *Chaucer in the Eighties* (Syracuse: Syracuse University Press, 1986), pp. 3–22.

31. Gustav Gröber, *Grundriss der romanischen Philologie*, 2d ed. (Strassburg: Trübner, 1904–6), 1.194: "Die Erscheinung des menschlichen Geistes in der nur mittelbar verständlichen Sprache and seine Leistunge in der künstlerisch behandelten Rede der Vergangenheit also bilden den eigentlichen Gegenstand der Philologie." For Humboldt, see his "Über die Aufgabe des Geschichtsschreibers," translated as "On the Historian's Task," *History and Theory* 6 (1967): 57–71, esp. 70. The idealism of his project is well discussed by Hayden White, *Metahistory*, pp. 178–87.

32. The crisis of historicism is usually understood as the relativizing of value, but the insistence upon the self-sufficiency of each historical period— "that," in Ranke's famous words, "each period is immediate vis-à-vis God, and that its value depends not at all on what followed from it, but rather on its own existence, on its own self"—also sacrificed the historian's responsibility to connect the past with the present. For the citation from Ranke, and a lucid discussion of this issue, see Jauss, *Toward an Aesthetic of Reception*, pp. 7–8.

33. Despite being accomplished critics, as shown by their books on other authors and periods, neither Edith Rickert (1871–1938) nor Caroline Spurgeon (1869–1942) wrote books on Chaucer. The most important woman Chaucerian of the next generation, Margaret Schlauch (1898–1986), wrote widely on Middle English literature, including the ground-breaking Marxist book, *English Medieval Literature and Its Social Foundations* (Warsaw: Państwowe Wydawnictwo Naukowe, 1956).

34. John Livingstone Lowes, *Chaucer and the Development of His Genius* (Boston: Houghton Mifflin, 1934), p. 6.

35. C. S. Lewis, *The Discarded Image* (Cambridge: Cambridge University Press, 1964).

36. Robert K. Root, *The Poetry of Chaucer*, 2d ed. (Boston: Houghton Mifflin, 1922), p. 32.

37. Ronald S. Crane, *The Languages of Criticism and the Structures of Poetry* (Toronto: University of Toronto Press, 1953), pp. 123–24; see Jonathan Culler, *The Pursuit of Signs* (Ithaca: Cornell University Press, 1981), p. 5. On New Criticism, see Murray Krieger, *The New Apologists for Poetry* (Minneapolis: University of Minnesota Press, 1956), and Gerald Graff, *Poetic Statement and Critical Dogma* (Evanston: Northwestern University Press, 1970), among many others. A Marxist reading of New Criticism is offered by John Fekete,

The Critical Twilight: Explorations in the Ideology of Anglo-American Literary Theory from Eliot to McLuhan (London: Routledge and Kegan Paul, 1977); see also Frank A. Ninkovich, "The New Criticism and Cold War America," *Southern Quarterly* 20 (1981): 1–24.

38. E. Talbot Donaldson, *Chaucer's Poetry: An Anthology for the Modern Reader* (New York: Ronald Press, 1958). Important early New Critical readings were those by Charles Owen, "The Crucial Passages in Five of the *Canterbury Tales*: A Study in Irony and Symbol," *Journal of English and Germanic Philology* 52 (1953): 294–311, and "Chaucer's *Canterbury Tales*: Aesthetic Design in Stories of the First Day," *English Studies* 35 (1954): 49–56; Charles Muscatine, "Form, Texture, and Meaning in Chaucer's *Knight's Tale*," *PMLA* 65 (1950): 911–29; Arthur W. Hoffman, "Chaucer's Prologue to Pilgrimage: The Two Voices," *ELH* 21 (1954): 1–16; and the fine essays on Chaucerian irony published by Earle Birney in two groups, one in 1939–41 and the other in 1959–60. Birney's essays have been collected in *Essays on Chaucerian Irony*, ed. Beryl Rowland (Toronto: University of Toronto Press, 1985).

39. E. Talbot Donaldson, "Chaucer the Pilgrim," *PMLA* 69 (1954): 928–36, and "The Ending of Chaucer's *Troilus*," in *Early English and Norse Studies Presented to Hugh Smith* (London: Methuen, 1963), pp. 26–45, both reprinted in *Speaking of Chaucer*, pp. 1–12, 84–101.

40. Charles Muscatine, *Chaucer and the French Tradition* (Berkeley: University of California Press, 1957); further references will appear in the text.

41. Muscatine's precursor and partial model in thus situating characterization at the heart of stylistic history is Erich Auerbach: see the references to Auerbach in the index to *Chaucer and the French Tradition*, Muscatine's review of *Mimesis* in *Romance Philology* 9 (1956): 448–57, and his acknowledgment of indebtedness in *Poetry and the Age of Chaucer* (Notre Dame: University of Notre Dame Press, 1972), pp. 1–14. Auerbach's project in *Mimesis* was to understand the formation not of realism per se but rather of a sublime realism that imbues the *sermo humilis* of biblical style with the values of classical humanism. Such a synthesis makes possible what Auerbach called "realistic works of serious style and character" ([Princeton: Princeton University Press, 1953], p. 556), by which he meant above all else Dante's *Commedia*. For Auerbach, Dante's representation of Farinata and Cavalcante in *Inferno* 10 stood as the highest achievement of European literature, an achievement that "overwhelms everything else, a comprehension of human realities which spreads as widely and variously as it goes profoundly to the very roots of our emotions, an illumination of man's impulses and passions which leads us to share in them without restraint and indeed to admire their variety and their greatness" (pp. 201–2). For a full and trenchant discussion of Auerbach's work and of the key concept of synthesis, see Paul A. Bové, *Intellectuals in Power: A Genealogy of Critical Humanism* (New York: Columbia University Press, 1986).

42. Wilhelm Worringer, *Formprobleme der Gotik* (1912), trans. Herbert Read as *Form in Gothic* (London: Putnam, 1927); Max Dvořák, "Idealismus und Naturalismus in der gotischen Skulptur und Malerei," *Historische Zeitschrift* 119 (1919): 1–62, 185–246 (cited by Muscatine, *Chaucer and the French Tradition*, p. 258 n. 33). An analogous if less *geistesgeschichtliche* definition of "Gothic Chaucer" is offered by Derek Brewer in his *Geoffrey Chaucer*, Writers and Their Background (London: Bell, 1974), pp. 1–32, and by Robert M. Jordan, *Chaucer and the Shape of Creation* (Cambridge, Mass.: Harvard University Press, 1967). See also Brewer's *English Gothic Literature* (New York: Schocken Books, 1983).

43. For a discussion of Lamprecht and his *Kulturgeschichte*, see Karl J. Weintraub, *Visions of Culture: Voltaire, Guizot, Burckhardt, Lamprecht, Ortega y Gasset* (Chicago: University of Chicago Press, 1966).

44. Johan Huizinga, "The Task of Cultural History," *Men and Ideas*, trans. James S. Holmes and Hans van Marle (New York: Meridian Books, 1959), p. 76.

45. Karl Mannheim, "On the Interpretation of *Weltanschauung*" (1923), *Essays on the Sociology of Knowledge*, ed. and trans. Paul Kecskemeti (London: Routledge and Kegan Paul, 1952), p. 38.

46. Ibid., p. 58.

47. Ernst Gombrich, *In Search of Cultural History* (Oxford: Clarendon Press, 1969), p. 32. Gombrich represents *Geistesgeschichte*, in Popperian fashion, as a proto-Nazi Hegelianism, an oversimplification that Leo Spitzer took pains to refute in his famous debate with Arthur O. Lovejoy: see *Journal of the History of Ideas* 2 (1941): 257–78; 5 (1944): 191–203, 204–19.

48. On Dilthey and his successors, see David Couzens Hoy, *The Critical Circle* (Berkeley: University of California Press, 1978).

49. Edgar Wind, "Some Points of Contact between History and Natural Science," in Raymond Klibansky and H. J. Paton, eds., *Philosophy and History: Essays Presented to Ernst Cassirer* (Oxford: Clarendon Press, 1936), p. 257.

50. Leo Spitzer, *Linguistics and Literary History* (Princeton: Princeton University Press, 1948), p. 24.

51. A good account of the Gothic revival is Charles Dellheim, *The Face of the Past* (Cambridge: Cambridge University Press, 1982).

52. See Léon, *Vie des monuments français*. For a German counterpart, see the account of the completion of Cologne Cathedral given by W. D. Robson-Scott, *The Literary Background of the Gothic Revival in Germany* (Oxford: Clarendon Press, 1965), pp. 287–301.

53. James F. White, *The Cambridge Movement: The Ecclesiologists and the Gothic Revival* (Cambridge: Cambridge University Press, 1962), pp. 68–79.

54. Emile Mâle, *The Gothic Image: Religious Art in France in the Thirteenth Century*, trans. Dora Nussey (New York: E. P. Dutton, 1913), p. viii. Mâle's career and impact are discussed by Harry Bober in the editor's foreword to *Religious Art in France: The Twelfth Century*, trans. Marthiel Mathes (Princeton:

Princeton University Press, 1970); see also André Grabar, "Notice sur la vie et les travaux de M. Emile Mâle," *Académie des Inscriptions et Belles-Lettres, Comptes Rendus*, Séance du 16 Novembre 1962: 328–44.

55. Robertson, *Preface to Chaucer*, p. 6.

56. Robertson, *Essays in Medieval Culture*, p. 4. A more recent expression of the same view of medieval culture is expressed by Allen, *Ethical Poetic*: "late medieval Europe was a system—a universe with no parts left over, corresponding as a whole, but only as a whole and not part by part, with all other systems. In this late medieval system, texts were made whose textuality we still possess, and which we are pleased to call poems. Between our system and the late medieval one, this textuality persists—an ordered series of words in a particular language. Beyond this, of course, there is nothing—no certain correspondence. Our enterprise must begin by admitting this nothing, lest we impose our categories on the past" (p. 4). The problem here is that a totalizing view of period consciousness forecloses any possibility of transhistorical understanding.

57. The dominating influence of Augustine has been recently extended to the *Roman de la rose* by John Fleming, who in *Reason and the Lover* argues that the paradigmatic texts for the poem are Augustine's *Soliloquies*.

58. Saint Augustine, *On Christian Doctrine*, trans. D. W. Robertson, Jr. (Indianapolis: Bobbs-Merrill, 1958), p. 93.

59. Claude Lévi-Strauss, *The Savage Mind* (Chicago: University of Chicago Press, 1966), p. 247.

60. Michel Foucault, *The Order of Things* (New York: Vintage Books, 1973), p. xxiii.

61. Charles Peirce, "Issues of Pragmaticism," *The Monist* 15 (1905): 485; cited by Edgar Wind, "Some Points of Contact between History and Natural Science," p. 258.

62. Foucault, *Order of Things*, p. 326.

63. For a discussion of an instance—the Wife of Bath's deafness—see above, n. 8.

64. This positivizing of *Geistesgeschichte* in literary studies finds a parallel development in art history. In *Studies in Iconology* (New York: Oxford University Press, 1939), Erwin Panofsky defined iconology as a *geistesgeschichtliche* quest for "those underlying principles which reveal the basic attitude of a nation, a period, a class, a religious or philosophical persuasion" (p. 7) and contrasted it to a "narrower" iconography concerned only with "specific *themes* or *concepts* manifested in *images, stories* and *allegories*" (p. 6; and see the added comments in *Meaning in the Visual Arts* [Garden City, N.Y.: Doubleday, 1955], pp. 31–32). But Panofsky's *Early Netherlandish Painting* (Cambridge, Mass.: Harvard University Press, 1953) sets aside this quest for *Weltanschauung* (a goal at the heart of the entire cooperative project initiated by Aby Warburg, himself

a pupil of Karl Lamprecht) and restricts iconology simply to iconography—to, that is, the articulation of the intended meaning. This point is well made by Otto Pächt in his review of *Early Netherlandish Painting* in *Burlington Magazine* 98 (1956): 110–16, 267–77. The "premeditated programmes" that motivate Dutch painting are, according to Pächt, no longer "looked upon as historic data that required interpretation (alongside the stylistic evidence). . . . At least no direct suggestion is made that this interpretation has to be transcended in the search for the intrinsic, inner meaning." This narrowing of analytic focus represents "a clear manifestation of the newly won autonomy of iconographic research" and its triumph over the stylistic approach characteristic of *Geistesgeschichte*, which "rested on the belief that the stylistic data were more reliable guides to the inner meaning, to the true character of a work of art than the most perfect knowledge of its author's intentions could provide" (p. 276). For explicit attacks on *Geistesgeschichte* from the perspective of Anglo-American empiricism, see Ernst Gombrich, *In Search of Cultural History*, Ronald S. Crane, *Critical and Historical Principles of Literary History* (Chicago: University of Chicago Press, 1971), and Jeffrey L. Sammons, *Literary Sociology and Practical Criticism* (Bloomington: Indiana University Press, 1977).

65. "The Allegorist and the Aesthetician," in *Essays*, pp. 85–101.

66. The quoted phrase is from Howard, *The Idea of the Canterbury Tales*; see above, n. 6.

67. Gerhart Ladner, "The Future of Medieval Studies," in *Memory and Promise: From the Special Convocation upon the Fiftieth Anniversary of the Pontifical Institute of Mediaeval Studies, 20 October 1979* (Toronto: Pontifical Institute of Mediaeval Studies, 1980), pp. 20, 16.

68. For Robertson's proposals for "a new professionalism in graduate training," see *Essays*, pp. 83–84.

69. The most recent contribution to this sense of the limitations of the medieval studies paradigm is James Simpson, "Diachronic History and the Shortcomings of Medieval Studies," in David Matthews and Gordon McMullan, eds., *Reading the Medieval in Early Modern England* (Cambridge: Cambridge University Press, 2007), pp. 17–30.

two. The Disenchanted Classroom

1. T. W. Adorno, *Minima Moralia: Reflections from Damaged Life*, trans. E. F. N. Jephcott (London: New Left Books, 1974), p. 81.

2. One effort at a serious investigation is Charles R. Cooper, ed., *Researching Response to Literature and the Teaching of Literature: Points of Departure* (Norwood, N.J.: Ablex Publishing Co., 1985).

3. *The Pedagogy of the Oppressed*, trans. Myra Bergman Ramos (New York: Continuum, 1993 [1970]), p. 64 (emphases in the original).

4. Kostas Myrsiades and Linda S. Myrsiades, "Introduction," to Kostas Myrsiades and Linda S. Myrsiades, eds., *Margins in the Classroom: Teaching Literature* (Minneapolis: University of Minnesota Press, 1994), p. viii.

5. A book that provides illuminating insights into the actual conditions of one form of student life is Michael Moffatt, *Coming of Age in New Jersey: College and American Culture* (New Brunswick: Rutgers University Press, 1989). A young anthropologist, Moffatt lived as a student for a term at Rutgers University, studying student life as one might any foreign culture. His report disabuses one of naive assumptions about the importance of the classroom in the lives of many students. Critiques of Freire have been offered by, among others, Richard E. Miller, "The Arts of Complicity: Pragmatism and the Culture of Schooling," *College English* 61 (1998): 10–28; Elizabeth Ellsworth, "Why Doesn't This Feel Empowering? Working Through the Repressive Myths of Critical Pedagogy," *Harvard Educational Review* 59 (1989): 296–324; and Maureen M. Hourigan, *Literacy as Social Exchange: Intersections of Class, Gender, and Culture* (Albany: State University of New York Press, 1994).

6. I have taught Chaucer seminars for both graduate students and high school teachers, but since these groups have specialized needs and interests I shall confine my comments in this essay to undergraduate teaching.

7. An example of such an account is the much-discussed article by Jane Tompkins, "Pedagogy of the Distressed," *College English* 52 (1990): 653–60; for reactions, see *College English* 53 (1991): 599–604, 714–17; 54 (1992): 358–60, 474–80; Marshall Gregory, "Curriculum, Pedagogy, and Teacherly Ethos," *Pedagogy* 1 (2001): 69–90; and Robert P. Yagelski, "The Ambivalence of Reflection: Critical Pedagogies, Identity, and the Writing Teacher," *College Composition and Communication* 51 (1999): 32–50. Nowhere in Tompkins's article and the ensuing discussion are questions of class size, reasons for student enrollment, nor the actual subject matter of literature courses addressed.

8. "University English Teaching: Observations on Symbolism and Reflexivity," in *Demarcating the Disciplines: Philosophy, Literature, Art*, Glyph Textual Studies 1 (Minneapolis: University of Minnesota Press, 1986), p. 218.

9. In order to stress the fact that the course is about Chaucer and not about my approach to Chaucer, I make it clear to the students that there is no requirement that they attend lectures: the knowledge the course seeks to impart is not in the sole possession of the instructor but can be obtained quite independently. Hence while the course does require weekly quizzes or worksheets, students who choose not to attend can fulfill this part of the requirement by taking an optional final exam. In other words, I try (probably unsuccessfully, I admit) to provide a structural resistance to the notion that students are taking "my" Chaucer course, or that Chaucer's poetry can only be read and understood in the terms in which he is presented in class.

10. Even in a lecture course this requirement can be met in a variety of ways, including assigning short interpretive exercises and, perhaps most important, by providing examples of close readings in the lectures with a special emphasis on the complexity of Chaucerian language. I am aware that the responsibility to teach reading and writing conflicts with the encouragement of performance, which shows that teaching is always a compromise.

11. Max Weber, "Science as a Vocation," in *From Max Weber: Essays in Sociology*, trans. and ed. H. H. Gerth and C. Wright Mills (New York: Oxford University Press, 1946), pp. 129–56.

12. For a recent version of this charge, see Bruce Robbins, *Secular Vocations: Intellectuals, Professionalism, Culture* (London: Verso, 1993), pp. 122–25.

13. For the issue, and the citation from Rosenberg, see Peter Novick, *That Noble Dream: The "Objectivity Question" and the American Historical Profession* (Cambridge: Cambridge University Press, 1988), pp. 496, 501. The deadly effects of the particularism of identity politics on contemporary political life, and especially on the poor, are well analyzed by Michael Lind, *The Next American Nation: The New Nationalism and the Fourth American Revolution* (New York: Free Press, 1995), and Todd Gitlin, *The Twilight of Common Dreams: Why America Is Wracked by Culture Wars* (New York: Henry Holt, 1995).

14. For "heroic cynicism," see Fredric Jameson's appreciative account of Weber in "The Vanishing Mediator; or Max Weber as Storyteller," in *The Ideologies of Theory: Essays 1971–1986*, vol. 2: *The Syntax of History* (London: Routledge, 1988), pp. 3–34; the charge of a spiteful apologetics is made by Herbert Marcuse in *Negations: Essays in Critical Theory* (Boston: Beacon Press, 1966), pp. 201, 208.

15. "Science as a Vocation," p. 139. All subsequent references to this essay will be included in the text.

16. "'Objectivity' in Social Science and Social Policy," in Max Weber, *The Methodology of the Social Sciences*, trans. and ed. Edward A. Shils and Henry A. Finch (New York: Free Press, 1949), p. 57. The essay was published originally in 1904 in the *Archiv für Sozialwissenschaft und Sozialpolitik* as a statement of policy for the journal.

17. *The Protestant Ethic and the Spirit of Capitalism*, trans. Talcott Parsons (New York: Scribner's, 1958), p. 104; all citations in this paragraph are from this work and are included in the text. Unless otherwise indicated, all other page numbers in the text refer to "Science as a Vocation" (see n. 11 above).

18. A useful account of the relevance of Weber's analysis of capitalism to modernity and post-modernity is Robert J. Holton and Bryan S. Turner, *Max Weber on Economy and Society* (London: Routledge, 1989), pp. 68–102.

19. *Past and Present*, 3.11. For Weber's own "work asceticism," see Arthur Mitzman, *The Iron Cage: An Historical Interpretation of Max Weber* (New York: Knopf, 1970), pp. 48–49. In *The Cultural Contradictions of Capitalism* (London: Heinemann, 1976), Daniel Bell analyzed how the ideology of vocation had

been undermined by the hedonism required by consumer capitalism, developing what he called "the Dynosiac pack" as a threatening alternative to the well-regulated labor force. One effect of the economic squeezing of working people in the last thirty years, as of the assault upon the poor (which provides working people with both a political scapegoat and a cautionary example of what happens to the unproductive in the world of capitalist monopoly), has been to reinforce the idea that labor is necessary to a meaningful life.

20. "Politics as a Vocation," in *From Max Weber*, pp. 122, 121.

21. Wolfgang Schluchter, "Value-Neutrality and the Ethic of Responsibility," in Guenther Roth and Wolfgang Schluchter, *Max Weber's Vision of History: Ethics and Methods* (Berkeley: University of California Press, 1979), p. 87.

22. As Weber says, "In the lecture-room we stand opposite our audience, and it has to remain silent. I deem it irresponsible to exploit the circumstance that for the sake of their career the students have to attend a teacher's course while there is nobody present to oppose him with criticism" ("Science as a Vocation," p. 146).

23. Max Weber, "Value-judgments in Social Science," in *Weber: Selections in Translation*, ed. W. G. Runciman, trans. Eric Matthews (Cambridge: Cambridge University Press, 1978), p. 70. This essay is also translated as "The Meaning of 'Ethical-Neutrality' in Sociology and Economics," in Max Weber, *The Methodology of the Social Sciences*, trans. and ed. Edward A. Shils and Henry A. Finch (New York: Free Press, 1949), pp. 1–47.

24. For an excellent discussion, see Fritz Ringer, *The Decline of the German Mandarins: The German Academic Community, 1890–1933* (Hanover: University Press of New England, 1990 [1969]), pp. 86–89, 104–5; for Weber's anti-Mandarin views, see pp. 180, 188, 356–57.

25. Robert Nisbet, "Max Weber and the Roots of Academic Freedom," in Charles Frankel, ed., *Controversies and Decisions: The Social Sciences and Public Policy* (New York: Russell Sage Foundation, 1976), pp. 103–22. When in 1908 his student Robert Michels, an atheist and Social Democrat, was denied the right to teach, Weber "urged that the continual references to the autonomy of scholarship be dropped 'in the interests of taste and also of truth.' 'In Germany,' [he said,] 'the freedom of learning exists only within the limits of officially accepted political and religious views'" (Ringer, *Decline of the German Mandarins*, p. 143). Weber began his lecture on "Science as a Vocation" with a grim statement—not a prescription—that in contemporary Germany there was no place for a Jew in the academic world, a statement all the more powerful for its brutal abruptness.

26. The passage continues: "They presuppose that there is an interest in partaking, through this procedure, of the community of 'civilized men.' But they cannot prove 'scientifically' that this is the case" (p. 145). In terms of the critique of the educational system offered by Pierre Bourdieu and Jean-Claude Passeron, *Reproduction in Education, Society and Culture*, trans. Richard Nice

(Beverly Hills: Sage, 1977), Weber could be accused of naively asserting that education in the "cultural sciences" is nothing other than the acquisition by a bourgeois elite of the "cultural capital" it will employ to maintain its privileged status. According to Andrew Ross, "As humanists and social scientists, we have . . . begun to recognize that the often esoteric knowledge which we impart is a form of symbolic capital that is readily converted into social capital in the new technocratic power structures." Therefore, Ross asks, "what is our most available guarantee of challenging this *system* of cultural power?" (*No Respect: Intellectuals and Popular Culture* [New York: Routledge, 1989], p. 211). As we shall see, Weber has a more carefully thought out if less self-proclaimedly "revolutionary" rationale for cultural studies than this passage would imply; and at any rate, one could assent to Bourdieu and Passeron's critique, and Ross's, only if one accepted the idea that the primary if not the sole function of cultural knowledge is status competition.

27. The distinction between *meaning* and *significance* is central to the interpretive theory developed by E. D. Hirsch, Jr., *Validity in Interpretation* (New Haven: Yale University Press, 1967). Although incapable of being maintained with the absolutist precision Hirsch sometimes claimed, and certainly mistaken in its assumption that meaning (whether historical or not) can be equated with conscious intention, the distinction is nonetheless useful in providing a way to describe the different interests that motivate interpretation. For a good discussion, see David Couzens Hoy, *The Critical Circle: Literature, History, and Philosophical Hermeneutics* (Berkeley: University of California Press, 1982), pp. 11–40.

28. "Value-judgments in Social Science," p. 71.

29. Ibid., p. 73. In "Science as a Vocation," Weber says that "The primary task of a useful teacher is to teach his students to recognize 'inconvenient' facts—I mean facts that are inconvenient for their party opinions. . . . I believe the teacher accomplishes more than a mere intellectual task if he compels his audience to accustom itself to the existence of such facts" (p. 147). We see here Weber's resistance to the rightist politics of his student audience.

30. "Value-judgments in Social Science," pp. 76–77.

31. Talcott Parsons, "Value-freedom and Objectivity," in Otto Stammer, ed., *Max Weber and Sociology Today* (New York: Harper, 1971), pp. 38, 33.

32. "'Objectivity' in Social Science and Social Policy," pp. 55, 81; emphasis in the original.

33. "Value-judgments in Social Science," p. 69. A useful definition of bias in scholarly investigation is provided by Abraham Kaplan, *The Conduct of Inquiry: Methodology for Behavioral Science* (New York: Chandler Publishing, 1964): bias is when "a proposition is accepted or rejected, not on the basis of its origin, but on the basis of its outcome. It is believed or not according to whether our values would be better served if it were true than if it were false. . . . What constitutes bias is that the will to believe is motivated by interests external to the context of inquiry itself" (pp. 373–74).

34. "Value-judgments in Social Science," p. 70. Nor did Weber feel required to avoid boredom: Max Horkheimer provides a vivid account of his disillusionment when he went to hear Weber lecture on the Russian Revolution in 1919: "It was all so precise, so scientifically exact, so value-free that we all went sadly home. . . . As we left the lecture-theatre that day with such disappointment, we thought that Max Weber must be ultra-conservative. This conclusion was however over-hasty" (Stammer, ed., *Max Weber and Sociology Today*, pp. 51, 53).

35. As Weber understood: "One cannot demonstrate scientifically what the duty of an academic teacher is" ("Science as a Vocation," p. 146).

36. "The Return to Philology," a contribution to "Professing Literature: A Symposium of the Study of English," *The Times Literary Supplement* 4158, 10 December 1982, 1355–56; reprinted in *Resistance to Theory* (Minneapolis: University of Minnesota Press, 1986), p. 24.

37. *Resistance to Theory*, pp. 10–11.

38. The politics of historicism have drawn considerable interest, especially in relation to the now rather timeworn New Historicism. Perhaps the best commentary is by Catherine Gallagher, "Marxism and the New Historicism," in H. Aram Veeser, ed., *The New Historicism* (New York: Routledge, 1989), pp. 37–48. For a description of a historicist course that has an explicitly party-political orientation, see Richard Ohmann, "Teaching Historically," in Maria-Regina Knecht, ed., *Pedagogy Is Politics: Literary Theory and Critical Teaching* (Urbana: University of Illinois Press, 1992), pp. 173–89.

39. Clearly a teacher has the responsibility to explain to students what motivates the kind of approach pursued in the classroom: there can be no question of pretending that "the facts speak for themselves" or that one is simply pursuing a "natural" or "commonsensical" way of studying literature. I myself understand the political meaning of a historicist pedagogy as addressing two aspects of the disenchanted world: one is a culturally fostered amnesia about the past and about historical understanding generally; the other is a radical individualism that seeks to efface the socio-economic determinants that condition people's lives. Although I explain this to undergraduates, they seem on the whole uninterested in either my motives or in the details of current critical controversies. In my experience the undergraduate reaction to courses that attempt to "teach the [critical] conflicts," as Gerald Graff (among others) recommends, is one of impatience and/or bewilderment with the amount of energy that academics invest in issues that strike them as narrowly professional. Graff's program is described in *Professing Literature: An Institutional History* (Chicago: University of Chicago Press, 1987).

40. As Weber said, "The historical and cultural sciences . . . teach us how to understand and interpret political, artistic, literary, and social phenomena *in terms of their origins*" ("Science as a Vocation," p. 145, emphasis added).

41. Adorno, *Minima Moralia*, p. 18.

42. This is the rather shopworn charge that Louise O. Fradenburg levels against "historical exegesis" in "'Voice Memorial': Loss and Reparation in Chaucer's Poetry," *Exemplaria* 2 (1990): 169–202. She further claims that historicism is a form of mourning that bespeaks a psychological incapacity to face the fact of loss, a weak-minded escape from the rigors of modernity. As the present argument suggests, however, much historicism is perhaps better understood as deriving from a clear-eyed acceptance and affirmation of modernity.

43. H. Marshall Leicester, *The Disenchanted Self: Representing the Subject in the Canterbury Tales* (Berkeley: University of California Press, 1990), p. 28.

44. The essays in the appendix are listed alphabetically by author, not in the order in which they are read. For graduate students and high school teachers I add two books to the syllabus: M. M. Postan, *The Medieval Economy and Society: An Economic History of Britain in the Middle Ages* (Harmondsworth: Penguin Books, 1975), and Maurice Keen, *English Society in the Later Middle Ages 1348–1500* (Harmondsworth: Penguin Books, 1990). Unfortunately, the excellent Postan book must be ordered directly from England.

45. The poem's concern with language has been treated in a variety of ways by, for example, Philip Boardman, "Courtly Language and the Strategy of Consolation in the *Book of the Duchess*," *ELH* 44 (1977): 567–79; Lisa J. Kiser, *Truth and Textuality in Chaucer's Poetry* (Hanover: University Press of New England, 1991), 11–24; and Glenn Burger, "Reading Otherwise: Recovering the Subject in the *Book of the Duchess*," *Exemplaria* 5 (1993): 325–41. Narcissism is also a traditional topic of critical discussion: the most recent and theoretically charged treatment may be found in Gregory B. Stone, *The Death of the Troubadour: The Late Medieval Resistance to the Renaissance* (Philadelphia: University of Pennsylvania Press, 1994). The topic of the poem as self-consciously beginning a literary tradition is treated by, among others, Robert Edwards, "The *Book of the Duchess* and the Beginnings of Chaucer's Narrative," *NLH* 13 (1982): 189–204. The issue of the poem's consolatory function goes back at least to John Lawlor's article on "The Pattern of Consolation in *The Book of the Duchess*," *Speculum* 31 (1956): 626–48, but was given a Derridean and Lacanian refurbishing by Maud Ellmann, "Blanche," in Jeremy Hawthorn, ed., *Criticism and Critical Theory*, Stratford-upon-Avon Studies, 2d ser. (London: Arnold, 1984), pp. 98–110. For Ellmann, "*The Book of the Duchess* certainly invites a psychoanalytic reading. . . . A work of mourning, it anticipates the talking cure" (p. 101). Ellmann's essay also stresses the erasure of the woman implicit in courtly writing: "If Blanche stands for the whiteness of the page, the Black Knight represents the ink with which it is deflowered" (pp. 106–7): Blanche is the feminine other that must always be excluded so that the two men can converse. Ellmann is the inspiration for subsequent feminist and psychoanalytic discussions of the poem by Louise O. Fradenburg, "'Voice Memorial,'"

(n. 42), Elaine Tuttle Hansen, *Chaucer and the Fictions of Gender* (Berkeley: University of California Press, 1992), pp. 58–86, and Gayle Margherita, *The Romance of Origins: Language and Sexual Difference in Middle English Literature* (Philadelphia: University of Pennsylvania Press, 1994), pp. 100–128.

46. The date at which the poem was written remains uncertain: see the note to lines 1314–29 in *The Riverside Chaucer*, 3rd ed., gen. ed. Larry Benson (Boston: Houghton Mifflin, 1987), p. 976. Blanche died in September 1368; in January 1372 Gaunt assumed the title of king of Castile and León; in July 1372 Gaunt abandoned the title of earl of Richmond when the earldom was returned to John, duke of Brittany (Michael Jones, "The Seals of John IV, Duke of Brittany, 1364–1399," *Antiquaries Journal* 55 [1975]: 369 n. 1). The ending of the poem refers to the black knight as "this kyng" (1314) and directs him to a long castle with white walls "on a ryche hil" (1319). If we take these references as accurately denoting Gaunt's titles—and I don't know why we shouldn't— then the poem would seem to have been written between January and July 1372. As I shall argue, there are other reasons to prefer this late date to one immediately following Blanche's death.

47. See Margaret J. Ehrhart, "Machaut's *Dit de la fonteinne amoureuse*, the Choice of Paris, and the Duties of Rulers," *PQ* 59 (1980): 119–39.

48. Guillaume de Machaut, *La Fonteinne amoureuse* in *Œuvres*, ed. Ernest Hoepffner, SATF 57 (Paris: Champion, 1921), vol. 3, l. 2618.

49. Elizabeth Salter makes a similar point in less political terms in *Fourteenth-Century English Poetry: Contexts and Readings* (Oxford: Clarendon Press, 1983), pp. 122–23. By far the best discussion of the relative position of English and French at mid-century is by Rolf Berndt, "The Period of the Final Decline of French in Medieval England (Fourteenth and Early Fifteenth Centuries)," *Zeitschrift für Anglistik und Amerikanistik* 20 (1972): 341–69.

50. Martin M. Crow and Clair C. Olson, eds., *Chaucer Life-Records* (Oxford: Clarendon Press, 1966), p. 271.

51. The only sustained effort to answer this question is by D. W. Robertson, "The Historical Setting of Chaucer's *Book of the Duchess*," in John Mahoney and J. E. Keller, eds., *Mediaeval Studies in Honor of Urban Tigner Holmes, Jr.* (Chapel Hill: University of North Carolina Press, 1965), pp. 169–95. Unfortunately, Robertson's reading of the poem, and his understanding of John of Gaunt, is imbued with a piety supported by neither contemporary accounts of the duke nor the social environment of the court as reflected in its literary tastes. In *The Life of Geoffrey Chaucer* (Oxford: Blackwell, 1992), Derek Pearsall suggests with characteristic pungency that the tenor of the poem implies "a certain intimacy" between Gaunt and Chaucer—"A young pipsqueak of an esquire would not have presumed to write on such a subject in such a way had he not been assured of a sympathetic reception" (p. 84)—but he tactfully declines to speculate on any local effect the poem might have been intended to

have. Whether Chaucer was, or was perceived to be, a pipsqueak must remain a matter of pleasant conjecture, but he was no longer young, in medieval terms, in 1368 when Blanche died. If we accept the traditional date of 1340 for Chaucer's birth, he and Gaunt were exact contemporaries.

52. Sidney Armitage-Smith, *John of Gaunt* (New York: Barnes and Noble, 1964 [1904]), pp. 460–61. Anthony Goodman, *John of Gaunt: The Exercise of Princely Power in Fourteenth-Century Europe* (London: Longman, 1992), discusses Gaunt's contemporary reputation for "lechery" (p. 357). Is it only coincidence that Gaunt's daughter by Constance was named Catherine?

53. This passage finds its source in Machaut's *Remede de Fortune* (Barry A. Windeatt, *Chaucer's Dream Poetry: Sources and Analogues* [Cambridge: D. S. Brewer, 1982], pp. 58–59), but the line that elicits a note of bitterness — "Therfore hit ys with me laft" (791) — is added by Chaucer.

54. See above, n. 47.

55. For these characterizing terms, see Goodman, *John of Gaunt*, pp. 355, 357, and Simon Walker, "Lordship and Lawlessness in the Palatinate of Lancaster, 1370–1400," *Journal of British Studies* 28 (1989): 325–48.

56. In arguing for the value of specialization I am not endorsing the kind of professionalism celebrated by Stanley Fish in *Professional Correctness* (Oxford: Clarendon Press, 1995). While I agree with Fish's rejection of the idea that literary study ought or even can be "part of the war effort," his justification for criticism — "I do it because I like the way I feel when I'm doing it" (p. 110) — might be termed an ethic of self-satisfaction, in both senses of the term. The book's lack of interest in teaching is striking, and nowhere in Fish's account of the profession of literary critic and scholar, either here or elsewhere, is any serious consideration given to the idea that the profession should be thought of as providing a service, either to students or to society as a whole.

57. Noam Chomsky, *Language and Responsibility*, trans. John Viertel (New York: Pantheon Books, 1979), p. 3; further citations are included in the text.

three.   Court Poetry and the Invention of Literature

1. P. P. Howe, ed., *Complete Works of William Hazlitt* (London: Dent, 1930), 4.214–15.

2. Pioneers in providing political readings of Chaucer's works were Stephen Knight, with his article "Chaucer and the Sociology of Literature," *SAC* 2 (1980): 15–51 and book, *Geoffrey Chaucer* (Oxford: Blackwell, 1986); and David Aers, *Chaucer* (Atlantic Highlands, N.J.: Humanities Press International, 1986). In "Medieval Literature and Historical Enquiry," *Modern Language Review* 99 (2004): xxxi–xlii, Derek Pearsall laments this turn toward political meanings because it devalues "the wonderful resilience and transformative

power that distinguishes literature" (xlii) from other forms of writing. Unfortunately, Pearsall's representation of the kind of criticism he dislikes (represented by the work of Aers, myself, and James Simpson) is embarrassingly reductive.

3. Janine Dakyns, *The Middle Ages in French Literature, 1851–1900* (Oxford: Oxford University Press, 1973), p. 196. Gaston Paris founded *Romania* in 1871 and the Société des anciens textes français in 1873 explicitly in order to counter German domination of medieval studies.

4. These citations are from Paris's annual report to the Société des anciens textes français printed in its *Bulletin* 3 (1877): 57.

5. Paul A. Olson, *The* Canterbury Tales *and the Good Society* (Princeton: Princeton University Press, 1986), pp. 3, 15.

6. Paul Strohm, *Social Chaucer* (Cambridge, Mass.: Harvard University Press, 1989), pp. 55, 63, 75, 80, 82. The claim that the development of Middle English literature is to be explained by the rise of a "middle class" is pursued in detail by Janet Coleman, *Medieval Readers and Writers 1350–1400* (New York: Columbia University Press, 1981); see also, for a much more nuanced account, Anne Middleton, "Chaucer's 'New Men' and the Good of Literature in the *Canterbury Tales*," in Edward Said, ed., *Literature and Society*, Selected Papers from the English Institute, 1978 (Baltimore: The Johns Hopkins University Press, 1980), pp. 15–56.

7. *Medieval to Renaissance in English Poetry* (Cambridge: Cambridge University Press, 1985), p. 34. For the importance of Dante, see also Elizabeth Salter, *Fourteenth-Century English Poetry: Contexts and Readings* (Oxford: Clarendon Press, 1983), p. 123; and David Wallace, "Chaucer's Continental Inheritance: The Early Poems and *Troilus and Criseyde*," in Piero Boitani and Jill Mann, eds., *The Cambridge Chaucer Companion* (Cambridge: Cambridge University Press, 1986), pp. 21–22, 29–30.

8. Clanvowe's career, and religious commitments, are treated most fully by K. B. McFarlane, *Lancastrian Kings and Lollard Knights* (Oxford: Clarendon Press, 1972).

9. His only appearance in the *Life-Records* is when he, along with his friends and fellow chamber knights William Neville and William Beauchamp (also chamberlain of the king's household) and two prominent London merchants, witnessed Cecily Champaigne's writ releasing Chaucer from the charge of rape: Martin M. Crow and Clair C. Olson, eds., *Chaucer Life-Records* (Austin: University of Texas Press, 1966), p. 343. For the literary relation to Chaucer, see R. T. Lenaghan, "Chaucer's Circle of Gentlemen and Clerks," *Chaucer Review* 18 (1983–84): 155–60; Paul Strohm, "Chaucer's Audience," *Literature and History* 5 (1977): 26–41; Derek Pearsall, "The *Troilus* Frontispiece and Chaucer's Audience," *YES* 7 (1977): 68–74.

10. All citations are from V. J. Scattergood, ed., *The Works of Sir John Clanvowe* (Cambridge: D. S. Brewer, 1975); I have also benefitted from Erich

Vollmer, ed., *Das Mittelenglische Gedicht "The Boke of Cupide,"* Berliner Beiträge zur germanischen und romanischen Philologie 17, Germanische Abteilung 8 (Berlin: Ebering, 1898). Scattergood discusses the poem's authorship in the introduction to his edition and more fully in "The Authorship of *The Boke of Cupide,*" *Anglia* 82 (1964): 37–49.

11. For a history of the criticism, see Russell A. Peck, *Chaucer's* Romaunt of the Rose *and* Boece, Treatise on the Astrolabe, Equatorie of the Planets, *Lost Works, and Chaucerian Apocrypha: An Annotated Bibliography, 1900–1985* (Toronto: University of Toronto Press, 1988), pp. 309–12. The poem is discussed in Strohm's *Social Chaucer,* pp. 78–82. Subsequent to the original publication of this essay, the poem has received more sustained attention: see David Chamberlain, "Clanvowe's Cuckoo," in David Chamberlain, ed., *New Readings of Late Medieval Love Poems* (Lanham: University Press of America, 1993), pp. 41–65; Lynn Staley, "Gower, Richard II, Henry of Derby, and the Business of Making Culture," *Speculum* 75 (2000): 68–96; John M. Bowers, "Three Readings of The Knight's Tale: Sir John Clanvowe, Geoffrey Chaucer, and James I of Scotland," *Journal of Medieval and Early Modern Studies* 34 (2004): 279–307.

12. Gervase Mathew, *The Court of Richard II* (London: John Murray, 1968), p. 30. The distinction between poetry of the court and courtly poetry is drawn, in somewhat different terms, by Derek Pearsall, *Old English and Middle English Poetry* (London: Routledge and Kegan Paul, 1977), p. 212.

13. The first phrase is from R. N. Swanson, *Church and Society in Late Medieval England* (Oxford: Blackwell, 1989), p. 337; the others from Rossell Hope Robbins, "The Structure of Longer Middle English Court Poems," in Edward Vasta and Zacharias P. Thundy, eds., *Chaucerian Problems and Perspectives: Essays Presented to Paul E. Beichner* (Notre Dame: University of Notre Dame Press, 1979), p. 245. See also Robbins's "The Middle English Court Love Lyric," in W. T. H. Jackson, ed., *The Interpretation of Medieval Lyric* (New York: Columbia University Press, 1980), pp. 205–32.

14. According to J. M. W. Bean, *From Lord to Patron: Lordship in Late Medieval England* (Philadelphia: University of Pennsylvania Press, 1989), "When indentures in the vernacular appear in the fifteenth century, the language is generally 'beleft and witholden.' In the late thirteenth and fourteenth centuries indentures of retinue were almost always in French, the words used being *demore et retenu* or similar language" (p. 33 n. 1; for examples, see pp. 111, 113–14). This is also a Chaucerian usage: Melibee comments on the "chesynge and . . . withholdynge of my conseillours" (1233), and in the General Prologue we are told that the Parson has not "been withholde" (511) by a guild as its chaplain; for a perhaps even closer usage, in the F-Prologue to the *Legend of Good Women,* when speaking of the companies of the flower and the leaf Chaucer says that "I nam withholden yit with never nother" (192); see also The Tale of Melibee (2202).

15. Chris Given-Wilson, *The Royal Household and the King's Affinity: Service, Politics and Finance in England 1360–1413* (New Haven: Yale University Press, 1986), p. 243.

16. For the relevant portions of Theseus's speech, see the Knight's Tale 1785–90, 1799–1805. All citations from Chaucer's poetry are from Larry D. Benson, gen. ed., *The Riverside Chaucer* (Boston: Houghton Mifflin, 1987).

17. As Strohm points out, "The irony is double in that it places two contradictory propositions before us: love *is* great, but great in its capacity to make fools of its servants" (*Social Chaucer*, p. 79).

18. See Margaret Schlauch, "Chaucer's Doctrine of Kings and Tyrants," *Speculum* 20 (1945): 155, and J. D. Burnley, *Chaucer's Language and the Philosopher's Tradition* (Cambridge: D. S. Brewer, 1979), pp. 11–43.

19. Given-Wilson, *Royal Household*, p. 162.

20. For his dismissal, see Chris Given-Wilson, "The King and Gentry in Fourteenth-Century England," *TRHS*, 5th ser. 37 (1987): 91 n. 18.

21. According to McFarlane, "The contemporary spirit in religion was puritan, biblical, evangelical, anarchic, anti-sacerdotal, hostile to the established order in the Church. Hence there was widespread sympathy with at least the moral content of the Lollard teaching. And it is doubtful how far the knights accepted or even grasped the theological implications of their views. Theirs was a moral revolt by the laity against the visible Church, a rejection of sacerdotalism in favour of the personal, immediate contact between believer and his Creator" (*Lancastrian Kings*, p. 225).

22. Anthony J. Tuck, "Carthusian Monks and Lollard Knights: Religious Attitudes at the Court of Richard II," in Paul Strohm and Thomas J. Heffernan, eds., *Studies in the Age of Chaucer, Proceedings 1, 1984: Reconstructing Chaucer* (Knoxville: New Chaucer Society, 1985), pp. 149–61.

23. See especially John Stevens, *Music and Poetry in the Early Tudor Court* (London: Methuen, 1961); Robbins, "Middle English Court Love Lyric," pp. 205–32; and Glending Olson, "Toward a Poetics of the Late Medieval Court Lyric," in Lois Ebin, ed., *Vernacular Poetics in the Middle Ages* (Kalamazoo: Medieval Institute Publications, 1984), pp. 227–48.

24. For the first two phrases, see "La Belle Dame Sans Merci," in Walter W. Skeat, ed., *Chaucerian and Other Pieces*, Supplement to the *Complete Works of Geoffrey Chaucer*, vol. 7 (Oxford: Oxford University Press, 1897), lines 328–29 (p. 309); for "parler mignot," see Christine de Pizan, *Cent ballades d'amant et de dame*, ed. Jacqueline Cerquiglini (Paris: Union Générale d'Editions, 1982), poem 8, line 11 (p. 39).

25. See C. Stephen Jaeger, *The Origins of Courtliness: Civilizing Trends and the Formation of Courtly Ideals 939–1210* (Philadelphia: University of Pennsylvania Press, 1985), pp. 162–68; on the meaning of *facetus*, see Alison Goddard Elliott's introduction to her translation of "The *Facetus*: or, The Art

of Courtly Living," *Allegorica* 2 (1977): 27–57. Jaeger's book provides a power-ful critique of the too-common assumption that the courtly personality is a phenomenon of the Renaissance.

26. This definition is given by Donatus in his commentary on Terence's *Eunuchus*, cited by Laura Kendrick, *The Game of Love: Troubadour Wordplay* (Berkeley: University of California Press, 1988), p. 53.

27. Stevens, *Music and Poetry*, p. 163; part 1 of the Knight's Tale itself provides the occasion for a *demande d'amour*, as do the Franklin's Tale and the debate among the noble suitors in the *Parliament of Fowls*. Apparently *demandes* were not always as high-minded as these instances: for a collection of *demandes* that turn on racy *doubles entendres* and so require fast-paced verbal ban-ter rather than lofty eloquence, see Eustache Deschamps, *Oeuvres complètes*, ed. Gaston Raynaud, SATF, t. 8 (Paris: Firmin-Didot, 1893), pp. 112–25. For examples of linguistically playful poems in English, see Rossell Hope Robbins, ed., *Secular Lyrics of the XIVth and XVth Centuries*, 2d ed. (Oxford: Clarendon Press, 1955), poems number 172, 173, and 177.

28. Thomas Usk, *Testament of Love*, in Skeat, ed., *Chaucerian and Other Pieces*, p. 12.

29. William W. Kibler, "Poet and Patron: Froissart's *Prison amoureuse*," *L'Esprit Créateur* 18 (1972): 38.

30. *Le livre messire Ode*, in Arthur Piaget, *Oton de Grandson, sa vie et ses poésies*, Mémoires et documents publiés par la Société d'Histoire de la Suisse Ro-mande, 3ième série, tome 1 (Lausanne: Librairie Payot, 1941), line 1478 (p. 439).

31. George Puttenham, *The Arte of English Poesie* (London: Richard Field, 1589 [printed in facsimile: London: Scolar Press, 1968]), p. 155.

32. See especially Richard Firth Green, *Poets and Princepleasers: Literature and the English Court in the Late Middle Ages* (Toronto: University of Toronto Press, 1980), pp. 101–34.

33. Many years ago, in *Chaucer's Official Career* (Menasha, Wisc.: George Banta, 1912), James R. Hulbert showed that Chaucer's career as a king's esquire was exactly analogous, in functions as in rewards, to those of his cohort who were not poets; for the official documents that record the poet's career, none of which mentions his literary activity, see the *Chaucer Life-Records*.

34. Mathew, *Court of Richard II*, p. 30; Green, *Poets and Princepleasers*, p. 107; Glending Olson, "Deschamps' *Art de dictier* and Chaucer's Literary En-vironment," *Speculum* 48 (1973): 714–23.

35. A list of English aristocratic poets of the late fourteenth and fifteenth centuries (compiled largely from Green's discussion) includes John Montagu, earl of Salisbury; Edward Plantagenet, second duke of York; Richard Beau-champ, earl of Warwick; William de la Pole, duke of Suffolk; John Tiptoft, earl of Worcester; Anthony Woodville, Earl Rivers; Sir Richard Roos; and of course Sir John Clanvowe. Non-English noble *littérateurs* include Marshall Boucicault

and his friends, like the Duc de Berri, who composed the *Livre de cents ballades*; James I of Scotland; René of Anjou and his son, Jean, duc de Calabre; Wenceslas de Brabant; Charles d'Orléans; and Jean II, duc de Bourbon. As K. B. McFarlane has said, "In what other century has the peerage been so active in literature?" (*The Nobility of Later Medieval England* [Oxford: Clarendon Press, 1973], p. 242).

36. See Kibler, "Poet and Patron," 32–46, and Peter F. Dembowski, *Jean Froissart and His Méliador: Context, Craft, and Sense* (Lexington: French Forum, 1983).

37. According to Robbins, "The Middle English Court Love Lyric," there survive perhaps three hundred love lyrics and thirty "love aunters," by which he means poems such as Lydgate's *Temple of Glass, The Flour and the Leaf,* and *The Court of Love* (p. 207).

38. The influence of the *dits amoureux* on Chaucer has been most vigorously argued by Rossell Hope Robbins, "Geoffroi Chaucier, Poète Français, Father of English Poetry," *Chaucer Review* 13 (1978–79): 106; see also Robbins's "Chaucer and the Lyric Tradition," *Poetica* 15/16 (1983): 107–27, and "The Vintner's Son: French Wine in English Bottles," in William W. Kibler, ed., *Eleanor of Aquitaine: Patron and Politician* (Austin: University of Texas Press, 1976), pp. 147–72; and by James I. Wimsatt, *Chaucer and the French Love Poets* (Chapel Hill: University of North Carolina Press, 1968). For the lyric presence in the *Troilus,* see Wimsatt, "The French Lyric Element in *Troilus and Criseyde,*" *Yearbook of English Studies* 15 (1985): 18–32. For an argument that Chaucer's poetry develops out of these lyric moments, see W. A. Davenport, *Chaucer: Complaint and Narrative,* Chaucer Studies 14 (Cambridge: D. S. Brewer, 1988).

39. Daniel Poirion, *Le poète et le prince: L'évolution du lyrisme courtois de Guillaume de Machaut à Charles d'Orleans* (Paris: Presses Universitaires de France, 1965), p. 77.

40. The poem is the fifteenth-century *Lay of Sorrow,* in Kenneth G. Wilson, "*The Lay of Sorrow* and *The Lufaris Complaynt*: An Edition," *Speculum* 29 (1954): 708–27. In MS Bodley Tanner 346, the *Boke of Cupide* is followed by four rhyme royal stanzas dedicating it to an unnamed lady; the same four stanzas also appear in MS Fairfax 16, here appended to the *Book of the Duchess*; see Vollmer, ed., *Das mittelenglische Gedicht,* pp. 46–47.

41. For "jeu des formes," see Robert Guiette, "D'une poésie formelle en France en Moyen Age," *Romanica Gandensia* 8 (1960): 17; for the *hortus conclusus* and "culte égocentrique," see Paul Zumthor, *Essai de poétique médiévale* (Paris: Seuil, 1972), pp. 243, 267. See also Roger Dragonetti, *La technique poétique des trouvères dans la chanson courtoise* (Bruges: De Tempel, 1960). According to Poirion, courtly verse represents "une évasion, une fuite devant les responsabilités sociales"; "ces gens attendaient sans doute de la poésie un apaisement, une sérénité que leur destin leur refusait" (*Le poète et le prince,* pp. 23, 25).

As he says, "Cultiver la beauté, ce sera désormais renoncer à l'action morale" (p. 95). In speaking of twelfth-century troubadour poetry, Erich Köhler points out that it is a way for aspirants to "dissimuler leur impuissance à maîtriser dans la vie les réalités qui répondent à ces notions" ("Observations historiques et sociologiques sur la poésie des troubadours," *Cahiers de civilisation médiévale* 7 [1964]: 34). Much the same point is made about the Italian sonnet sequences of the *quattrocento* by Lauro Martines, *Power and Imagination: City-States in Renaissance Italy* (New York: Knopf, 1979), p. 325.

42. Brian Stock, *Listening for the Text: On the Uses of the Past* (Baltimore: The Johns Hopkins University Press, 1990), p. 23. See also Stock's *The Implications of Literacy* (Princeton: Princeton University Press, 1983).

43. For "rhetorical man," see Richard Lanham, *The Motives of Eloquence* (New Haven: Yale University Press, 1976), p. 4. Historians of English Renaissance literature have assumed, largely under the influence of Burckhardt, that both a sophisticated court culture and the self-fashioning it entailed are specifically Renaissance phenomena, and that together they constitute an essential element of modernity. As the evidence presented in this paper suggests, neither of these assumptions is true. For well-informed accounts of medieval court culture, see Jaeger, *The Origins of Courtliness* (n. 25 above), and Joachim Bumke, *Medieval Court Culture* (Berkeley: University of California Press, 1991).

44. For the account offered in the next two paragraphs, see Anthony Tuck, *Richard II and the English Nobility* (New York: St. Martin's, 1974), and Given-Wilson, *Royal Household*. I have also been much aided by Patricia Eberle's splendid article, "The Politics of Courtly Style at the Court of Richard II," in Glyn S. Burgess and Robert A. Taylor, eds., *The Spirit of the Court: Selected Proceedings of the Fourth Congress of the International Courtly Literature Society* (Cambridge: D. S. Brewer, 1985), pp. 168–78.

45. Cited by Given-Wilson, *Royal Household*, pp. 146–47.

46. These low-born men included Richard Stury, a chamber knight who was later to be associated with Chaucer, Richard Lyons and John Peche, London merchants, Adam Burt, a London skinner, and Hugh Fastolf and William Ellis, members of the Great Yarmouth merchant oligarchy (Given-Wilson, *Royal Household*, pp. 148–51).

47. The cited phrase is from D. A. L. Morgan, "The House of Policy: The Political Role of the late Plantagenet Household," in David Starkey, ed., *The English Court: From the Wars of the Roses to the Civil War* (London: Longmans, 1987), p. 37. Morgan argues, wrongly, I believe, that the long-term shift from retinue to court did not occur until the 1430s and 40s, at which time "the style of the household as a war-band" was supplanted by that of the court. It may be true that the mid-fifteenth century was the time at which this shift became permanent, but it certainly was in effect during the latter years of Edward III's reign and throughout Richard II's; and it may be that we should understand the policy

of Henry IV and especially Henry V as a conservative return to an earlier mode of household organization. The *camera regis* is described by R. F. Green as "an inner sanctum . . . in which the king and his most intimate companions spent the majority of their time and where the most important business of the familia was conducted," "a kind of household within the household" (*Poets and Princepleasers,* pp. 35, 37). For the relative absence of the nobility at court, see Chris Given-Wilson, *The English Nobility in the Late Middle Ages* (London: Routledge and Kegan Paul, 1987), pp. 175–78.

48. For this interpretation of Richard's court, see Tuck, *Richard II,* and Richard H. Jones, *The Royal Policy of Richard II: Absolutism in the Later Middle Ages* (Oxford: Blackwell, 1968).

49. The citation, from the *Rotuli Parliamentorum,* is derived from Tuck, *Richard II,* p. 55.

50. Tuck, *Richard II,* p. 84.

51. For the citation, see Mathew, *Court,* p. 17; for the much-discussed Wilton Diptych, see for example J. J. N. Palmer, *England, France and Christendom, 1377–99* (London: Routledge and Kegan Paul, 1972), pp. 242–44. I have discussed Richard's absolutism in more detail, with further references, in *Temporal Circumstances: Form and History in Chaucer's Poetry* (New York: Palgrave Macmillan, 2006), pp. 55–58.

52. In 1386 he tourneyed at Smithfield wearing red armor and a red gown embroidered with golden suns; at the tournament of October 1390, itself preceded by an elaborate procession, his team wore the device of the white hart; and in 1392 he ratified the readmission of London to royal favor with a procession that amazed observers. For the Smithfield tournaments, see Juliet R. V. Barker, *The Tournament in England, 1100–1400* (Woodbridge: Boydell, 1986), pp. 100, 185; Sheila Lindenbaum, "The Smithfield Tournament of 1390," *Journal of Medieval and Renaissance Studies* 20 (1990): 1–20; Richard of Maidstone's account of the 1392 procession is translated by Edith Rickert, *Chaucer's World* (New York: Columbia University Press, 1948), pp. 35–39.

53. See Mathew, *Court,* passim, and Green, *Poets and Princepleasers,* pp. 17–52. For this as a European phenomenon, see Bernard Guenée, *States and Rulers in Later Medieval Europe,* trans. Juliet Vale (Oxford: Blackwell, 1985), pp. 66–80. Richard's ambitions for his court have often been seen as emulating the Valois court: see Mathew, *Court,* p. 21, and Ralph A. Griffiths, "The Crown and the Royal Family in Later Medieval England," in Ralph A. Griffiths and James Sherborne, eds., *Kings and Nobles in the Later Middle Ages* (New York: St. Martin's Press, 1986), who describes Richard as having "a mind that was fascinated with heraldry and kingly dignity, and besotted with things French" (p. 19). For Richard's expenditures on ostentatious luxuries, see George B. Stow, "Chronicles versus Records: The Character of Richard II," in J. S. Hamilton and Patricia J. Bradley, eds., *Documenting the Past: Essays in Me-*

dieval History Presented to George Peddy Cuttino (Woodbridge: Boydell, 1989), pp. 155–76.

54. Eberle, "Politics of Courtly Style," pp. 174–75.

55. Ibid., p. 178.

56. See Kate Mertes, *The English Noble Household, 1300–1600* (Oxford: Blackwell, 1987); and Green, *Poets and Princepleasers*, p. 19.

57. John Silvester Davies, ed., *An English Chronicle*, Camden Series 64 (London: Nichols, 1856), p. 12; this entry is dated 1398.

58. For Richard's anger, with many citations, see Stow, "Chronicles versus Records."

59. For the centrality of chivalry (i.e., violence) to aristocratic identity, see Given-Wilson, *Nobility*, p. 2; Nigel Saul, *Scenes from Provincial Life: Knightly Families in Sussex 1280–1400* (Oxford: Clarendon Press, 1986), p. 163; Maurice Keen, *Chivalry* (New Haven: Yale University Press, 1985).

60. On the fashionableness of the Ricardian court, see Mathew, *Court*, p. 1; and on the idea of fashion generally, Sima Godfrey, "Haute Couture and Haute Culture," in Denis Hollier, ed., *A New History of French Literature* (Cambridge, Mass.: Harvard University Press, 1989), pp. 761–69.

61. Norbert Elias, *The Civilizing Process*, vol. 1: *The History of Manners*, and vol. 2: *Power and Civility*, trans. Edward Jephcott (New York: Pantheon Books, 1982 [1939]); unfortunately, Elias assumes this to be a post-medieval phenomenon. For Henry IV's return to a more militaristic household, see Given-Wilson, *Household*, p. 196.

62. H. T. Riley, ed., *Historia anglicana*, 2 vols., Rolls Series (London: Longmans, 1863–64), 2.156; cited and translated by Eberle, "Politics," p. 69. For the political interests that controlled Walsingham's changing accounts of Richard, see George B. Stow, "Richard II in Thomas Walsingham's Chronicles," *Speculum* 59 (1984): 68–102.

63. Thomas Favent, *Historia sive Narracio de Modo et Forma Mirabilis Parliamenti apud Westmonasterium*, ed. May McKisack, *Camden Miscellany*, vol. 14, 3rd ser. 37 (1926): p. 3; Favent is citing one of the charges laid by the Appellants in 1388.

64. John Gower, *Vox clamantis*, in Eric Stockton, trans., *The Major Latin Works of John Gower* (Seattle: University of Washington Press, 1962), pp. 232–33.

65. Josef Kail, ed., *Twenty-Six Political and Other Poems*, EETS OS 124 (London: Kegan Paul, Trench, Trübner, 1904), pp. 14–22.

66. Carleton Brown, ed., *Religious Lyrics of the Fourteenth Century*, 2d ed., rev. G. V. Smithers (Oxford: Clarendon Press, 1957), number 103, pp. 93–94. The fear that courtly conversation is motivated by malevolent self-interest is also implied in Alceste's warning to the God of Love in the F-Prologue to the *Legend of Good Women*: "in youre court ys many a losengeour, / And many a

queynte totelere accusour, / That tabouren in youre eres many a sown, / Ryght after hire ymagynacioun, / To have youre daliance, and for envie" (352–56).

67. F. J. Furnivall, ed., Early English Meals and Manners, EETS OS 32 (London: Kegan Paul, Trench, Trübner, 1868), pp. 244–46. This poem is also printed in Carleton Brown, ed., Religious Lyrics of the XVth Century (Oxford: Clarendon Press, 1939), pp. 280–82. See also, from a fifteenth-century Boke of Curtayse also printed by Furnivall, the warning that "In swete wordis þe nedder was closet, / Disseyuaunt euer and mysloset" (p. 183). In the twelfth-century Facetus the courtier is advised to "consider it a sin always to tell the truth" (Elliott, ed., Facetus, p. 33), and reminded that "in the world there is no such thing as a really faithful friend, for every man is shrewd at deception" (p. 51).

68. E. K. Chambers and F. Sidgwick, eds., Early English Lyrics: Amorous, Divine, Moral & Trivial (London: Sidgwick & Jackson, 1921), p. 192.

69. H. Rosamund Parsons, "Anglo-Norman Books of Courtesy and Nurture," PMLA 44 (1929): 409.

70. See, for example, Albertanus of Brescia, Tractatus de arte loquendi et tacendi, in Thor Sundby, ed., Brunetto Latinos Levnet og Skrifter (Copenhagen: Lunds, 1869), appendix, pp. lxxxiv–cxix; and The Babees Book, in Furnivall, ed., Early English Meals, p. 252.

71. See V. J. Scattergood, "The Manciple's Manner of Speaking," Essays in Criticism 24 (1974): 124–46, and n. 83, below.

72. George Kane and E. Talbot Donaldson, eds., Piers Plowman: The B-Version (London: Athlone Press, 1975), p. 233 (Prologue, 111).

73. Mabel Day and Robert Steele, eds., Mum and the Soothsegger, EETS OS 199 (London: Oxford University Press, 1936), Fragment M, 265, pp. 49–50.

74. See Andrew Wawn, "Truth-telling and the Tradition of Mum and the Sothsegger," Yearbook of English Studies 13 (1983): 270–87.

75. For an instance of the topical argument, see John H. Fisher, "Wyclif, Langland, Gower, and the Pearl Poet on the Subject of the Aristocracy," in MacEdward Leach, ed., Studies in Medieval Literature in Honor of Professor Albert Croll Baugh (Philadelphia: University of Pennsylvania Press, 1961), p. 151.

76. In Cleanness, when the poet has God say that he himself established courtship, he uses language that invokes the kind of dalliance in which Gawain and the lady engage: "þe play of paramorez I portrayed myseluen" (ed. J. J. Anderson [Manchester: Manchester University Press, 1977], line 700).

77. See Michael J. Bennett, Community, Class and Careerism: Cheshire and Lancashire Society in the Age of Sir Gawain and the Green Knight (Cambridge: Cambridge University Press, 1983), pp. 163–68, 208, 233–34. Bennett even suggests (p. 246) that the poem was written by one of Richard's household clerks, a suggestion that, given both its social meaning and the lack of royal interest in alliterative poetry, seems unlikely.

78. On "cointise," see H. Rosamund Parsons, "Anglo-Norman Books of Courtesy and Nurture," PMLA 44 (1929): 410.

79. Compare the F-Prologue to the *Legend of Good Women*, where Alceste commands the poet to write the legends by saying, "And thogh the lyk nat a lovere bee, / Speke wel of love" (490–91).

80. In the F-Prologue, the green and white of the landscape is embodied in Alceste, "Crowned with white and clothed al in grene" (242; cf. 214, 223, 227, 303, 341). At the end of the *Boke of Cupid,* the nightingale tells the narrator that his lovesickness will be ameliorated if he will "Euery day this May . . . / Goo loke vpon the fresshe flour daysye" (242–43), the same love service as the narrator performs in the F-Prologue.

81. For Clanvowe St. Valentine's Day comes in March (80); for the courtly cult of Valentine's Day initiated in the *Parliament of Fowls* and the various possibilities for the date and patron saint, see Jack B. Oruch, "St. Valentine, Chaucer, and Spring in February," *Speculum* 56 (1981): 534–65, and Henry Ansgar Kelly, *Chaucer and the Cult of Saint Valentine,* Davis Medieval Texts and Studies 5 (Leiden: Brill, 1986).

82. There is a further analogy between the *Boke of Cupid* and the Prologue to the *Legend of Good Women* that may cast light on the logic of Chaucer's revisions. As he begins to dream, Clanvowe's narrator tells us "a wonder thinge" (106), that "Me thoght I wist al that the briddes ment, / And what they seyde, and what was her entent, / And of her speche I had good knovynge" (108–10); in the G-Prologue to the *Legend of Good Women,* the narrator comments that "to herken [the birdsong] I dide al myn entente, / For-why I mette I wiste what they mente" (G, 139–40). On this allusion, see Vollmer, *Das mittelenglische Gedicht,* p. 50, and for a contrary opinion, J. L. Lowes, "The Prologue to the *Legend of Good Women* Considered in Its Chronological Relations," *PMLA* 20 (1905): 754–56 n. 2. The G-Prologue is revised so as to incorporate the discipline that the F-Prologue seeks to impose: in other words, it is a poem that has responded to the authoritarian demands the God of Love makes in the F-Prologue. The lines at issue are an expression of the élitist attitude both poems stage, as we can see from another Chaucerian allusion to them: in the Squire's Tale, Canacee's ring is described as "a wonder thyng" (248) because of which she "wiste what [the birds] mente / Right by hir song, and knewe al hire entente" (399–400).

83. Mathew, *Court of Richard II,* p. 68.

84. In the fifteenth century a courtier poet included Pandarus's warnings about the dangers of unbridled speech (3.302–22) in a poem on the dangers of truth-telling and the burdens of service at court: see Frederick J. Furnivall, ed., *Odd Texts of Chaucer's Minor Poems,* Chaucer Society, 1st ser. no. 23, 60 (London: Trübner, 1868–80), pp. xi–xii.

85. For the *Romaunt,* see *The Riverside Chaucer,* p. 696; Derek Pearsall, ed., *Piers Plowman: An Edition of the C-Text* (Berkeley: University of California Press, 1978), p. 243; Alice Miskimin, ed., *Susannah: An Alliterative Poem of the Fourteenth Century* (New Haven: Yale University Press, 1969), p. 111.

86. Thomas E. Vesce, trans., *The Knight of the Parrot (Le Chevalier du Papegau)*, Garland Library of Medieval Literature 55B (New York: Garland Press, 1986).

87. Day and Steele, eds., Fragment M, pp. 152–55; the editors gloss the passage, "Once some of the commons discussed their grievances with some one of higher rank, and consequently suffered fines and imprisonments. Now they dare not speak, except privately among themselves" (p. 108).

88. The use of the term "popinjay" to signal these characteristics seems to have become common only in the sixteenth century, but here it seems to make an early, as yet unrecorded appearance. Clanvowe's usage does not appear in the *MED* entry; the first date at which the *OED* records the meaning "vain courtier" for "popinjay" is 1528.

89. The first citation is from Jaeger, *Origins of Courtliness,* p. 40, who shows that what Castiglione was describing was a widely recognized value as early as the eleventh century; the second is from Frank Whigham, *Ambition and Privilege: The Social Tropes of Elizabethan Courtesy Theory* (Berkeley: University of California Press, 1984), p. 33.

90. "Breaking" seems to refer to a mannered form of singing; complaining about its presence in church, a contemporary Wycliffite referred to the "smale brekynge þat stiriþ veyn men to daunsynge more þan to mornynge" (see Kenneth Sisam, ed., *Fourteenth-Century Verse and Prose* [Oxford: Clarendon Press, 1921], p. 123). In the Miller's Tale the spurious courtier Absolon sings "brokkyng as a nyghtyngale" (3377), which seems to refer to the same thing (see J. A. W. Bennett, *Chaucer at Oxford and Cambridge* [Toronto: University of Toronto Press, 1974], pp. 44–45).

91. It may well be that Clanvowe is here commenting on the use of French not just as a literary but as a spoken language in the royal court. That it was spoken is suggested by the court poetry of Froissart (1361–69), Jean de le Mote (c. 1360s), and Oton de Grandson (c. 1369–87, 1392–96): if their poems served as the occasion for amorous dalliance, then French must have been not only read but widely spoken in the court. Similarly, Gower addressed the *Cinquante balades* to Henry IV "por desporter vo noble Court roial," although they were probably written earlier for a non-court audience (see John H. Fisher, *John Gower: Moral Philosopher and Friend of Chaucer* [New York: New York University Press, 1964], pp. 72–75). Of course Chaucer's English court poetry shows that English was not only spoken at court but used for dalliance. Some scholars are certain that the language of the court in the 1350s and 60s was French: see James I. Wimsatt, *Chaucer and the Poems of 'CH' in University of Pennsylvania MS French 15* (Cambridge: D. S. Brewer, 1982) and Rossell Hope Robbins, "Geoffroi Chaucier, poète français." But this is less certain in the later years of Richard's reign, and if the royal court did speak French as a daily vernacular (as well as reading it, or using it for games), it was almost certainly the only social

circle in England that did. For a well-informed survey of this often discussed matter, see Rolf Berndt, "The Period of the Final Decline of French in Medieval England (Fourteenth and Early Fifteenth Centuries)," *Zeitschrift für Anglistik und Amerikanistik* 20 (1972): 341–69. The ambiguity of the situation is well illustrated by the fact that Richard II had two tutors, one English (Simon Burley) and one French (Guichard d'Angle). Linguistic nationalism, while widespread throughout the country in the later fourteenth century, became royal policy only with Henry V: see V. H. Galbraith, "Nationality and Language in Medieval England," *RHS*, 4th ser. 23 (1941): 113–28.

92. On Marcolf, see Francis Lee Utley, "Dialogues, Debates, and Catechisms," in Albert E. Hartung, gen. ed., *A Manual of the Writings in Middle English, 1050–1500*, vol. 3 (New Haven: Connecticut Academy of Arts and Sciences, 1972), pp. 737–38 (VII, 68e).

93. "The sense is 'For he who gets a little bliss of love may very soon find that his heir has come of age, unless he is always devoted to it.' This is a mild joke, signifying that he will soon find himself insecure, like one whose heir or successor has come of age, and whose inheritance is threatened" (Skeat, ed., *Chaucerian and Other Pieces*, p. 528; cited [slightly inaccurately] by Scattergood, p. 84).

94. Scattergood, ed., *Works*, pp. 69–70.

95. Here is the original in its entirety, as printed in Nicholas Harris Nicolas, ed., *The Controversy between Sir Richard Scrope and Sir Robert Grosvenor*, 2 vols. (London: Samuel Bentley, 1832), 1.184–85:

Mon[sieur] John Clanvowe del age de xxxv. ans armeez p[ar] xx ans & plus p[ro]duct p[ar] la p[ar]tie de mon[sieur] Richard Lescrop[e] jurez & examinez demandez si lez armez dazure ove une bende dor app[ar]teignent / & deyvent app[ar]teigner du droit & de heritage au dit mon[sieur] Richard. dist q[ue] oil qar il ne oiast unq[ue]s dire la contrairie. demandez p[ar] q[uoi] il sciet. dis q[ue] si un ho[m]me luy demande touz les int[er]rogatoirs du mond il luy respondera a un foitz p[a]r tout & dist c[er]teignement q[ue] p[ar] touz lez foitz ou il ad este armez en lez guerrez du Roy il ne vist unq[ue]s ho[m]me porter lez ditz armez ne lez armer ne user ne lez continuer mes ceux de no[u]n de Lescrop[e] ne ne ad oye p[ar]ler devant ceste debate riens dez Grovenors ne de lour auncestrie.

96. Anne Hudson, *The Premature Reformation: Wycliffite Texts and Lollard History* (Oxford: Clarendon Press, 1988), pp. 7, 387; McFarlane, *Lancastrian Kings*, p. 204.

97. Ibid., p. 205.

98. Kail, ed., *Twenty-Six Political and Other Poems*, p. 14 (see above, n. 74).

99. Derek Pearsall, *John Lydgate* (London: Routledge and Kegan Paul, 1970), pp. 92–93.

100. Cited from *PL* 207:45 by Jaeger, *Origins of Courtliness*, p. 59.

101. For "les rapports entre la terminologie féodale et la poésie courtoise," with bibliography, see Köhler, "Observations historiques," p. 34 n. 21.

102. The citation is from a poem ascribed to William de la Pole, duke of Suffolk, in Henry Noble MacCracken, "An English Friend of Charles of Orleans," *PMLA* 26 (1911): 166.

103. Cited by E. Jane Burns, "The Man Behind the Lady in Troubadour Lyric," *Romance Notes* 25 (1985): 261.

104. Robbins, ed., *Secular Lyrics*, number 129, lines 37–40.

105. Ibid., number 106, lines 3–4, 107–8.

106. See Piaget, *Oton de Grandson*; Diane R. Marks, "Poems from Prison: James I of Scotland and Charles d'Orleans," *Fifteenth-Century Studies* 15 (1989): 245–58; and MacCracken, "An English Friend."

107. Köhler, "Observations historiques"; and Herbert F. Moller, "The Social Cause of the Courtly Love Complex," *Comparative Studies of Society and History* 1 (1958): 137–59, and "The Meaning of Courtly Love," *Journal of American Folklore* 73 (1960): 39–52. Mertes, *Noble Household*, emphasizes how small were the number of women present in the noble households of late medieval England (pp. 6, 43, 57–59), although within the *camera regis* where this poetry was most likely read the ratio of men to women would probably have been more equal. The marriage of Chaucer to one of Queen Philippa's ladies-in-waiting, Philippa de Roet, suggests that court love poetry must sometimes have had an exclusively romantic meaning.

108. Robbins, ed., *Secular Lyrics*, number 127, lines 40–42.

109. Ibid., number 134, lines 50–53.

110. Ibid., number 162.

111. Ibid., number 169.

112. For "voix simplette," see Cerquiglini, ed., *Cent ballades*, poem 79, line 12 (p. 110); for "mignot," see above, n. 24.

113. Axel Erdmann, ed., *Lydgate's Siege of Thebes*, EETS ES 108 (London: Kegan Paul, Trench, Trübner, 1911), lines 253–54, 257.

114. Thus I would disagree with Louise Fradenburg's claim, in "The Manciple's Servant Tongue: Politics and Poetry in *The Canterbury Tales*," *ELH* 52 (1985), that the courtier "becomes a signifier in the totalized discourse of the sovereign. The servant ceases to be an individual and becomes a symbol in the service of his master's meaning" (89). This is, of course, what the sovereign desires, but the evidence of court writing, and of court politics, shows that this Foucauldian control was not possible.

115. Paul de Man, "The Rhetoric of Temporality," in *Blindness and Insight: Essays in the Rhetoric of Contemporary Criticism*, 2d ed. (Minneapolis: University of Minnesota Press, 1983), p. 207.

116. Another major site for the production of literary discourse was the "local society" of rural gentry from which emerged the Middle English romance

and to which *Piers Plowman* spoke with particular force: see P. R. Coss, "Aspects of Cultural Diffusion in Medieval England: The Early Romances, Local Society and Robin Hood," *Past and Present* 108 (1985): 35–79, and especially Anne Middleton, "The Audience and Public of 'Piers Plowman,'" in David Lawton, ed., *Middle English Alliterative Poetry and Its Literary Background* (Cambridge: D. S. Brewer, 1982), pp. 101–23, 147–54. But both the romances and Langland's poem play only a fitful role in post-medieval literary history.

four.   "What Is Me?"

1. M. C. Seymour, ed., *Selections from Hoccleve* (Oxford: Clarendon Press, 1981), p. 22, lines 393–94.

2. Any discussion of the issue of self-representation in Hoccleve's writing must acknowledge the ground-breaking analysis provided by J. A. Burrow in his lecture "Autobiographical Poetry in the Middle Ages: The Case of Thomas Hoccleve," *Proceedings of the British Academy* 68 (1982): 389–412. Burrow rightly points out that discussions of autobiography cannot be usefully organized by a distinction between the literarily conventional and the historically real, an argument made earlier if somewhat irresolutely (as Burrow notes) by Penelope B. R. Doob, *Nebuchadnezzar's Children: Conventions of Madness in Middle English Literature* (New Haven: Yale University Press, 1974), pp. 208–31.

3. Eva M. Thornley, "The Middle English Penitential Lyric and Hoccleve's Autobiographical Poetry," *Neuphilologische Mitteilungen* 68 (1967): 295–321; Charles R. Blyth, "Thomas Hoccleve's Other Master," *Mediaevalia* 16 (1993): 349–59; J. A. Burrow, "The Poet as Petitioner," *SAC* 3 (1981): 61–75 (see especially p. 66, n. 9); and Burrow, *Thomas Hoccleve*, Authors of the Middle Ages 4 (Aldershot: Variorum, 1994), p. 20.

4. Doob, *Nebuchadnezzar's Children*, pp. 208–31; Christina von Nolcken, "'O, why ne had y lerned for to die?': *Lerne for to Dye* and the Author's Death in Thomas Hoccleve's *Series*," *Essays in Medieval Studies: Proceedings of the Illinois Medieval Association* 10 (1993): 27–51.

5. "Balade to Edward, Duke of York" (*Selections*, p. 55). Burrow cites these lines in the course of arguing that "most of [Hoccleve's] works are occasional pieces, and of himself he certainly never speaks without occasion" (402)—a certainty this essay means to challenge. Other discussions that read the autobiographical material strategically, although often with a different rationale from that which Burrow offers, include David Greetham, "Self-Referential Artifacts: Hoccleve's Persona as a Literary Device," *MP* 86 (1989): 242–51; Antony J. Hasler, "Hoccleve's Unregimented Body," *Paragraph* 13 (1990): 164–83; David Lawton, "Dullness and the Fifteenth Century," *ELH* 54 (1987): 761–99; Derek Pearsall, "Hoccleve's *Regement of Princes*: The Poetics of Self-Representation,"

Speculum 69 (1994): 386–410; Larry Scanlon, "The King's Two Voices: Narrative and Power in Hoccleve's *Regement of Princes*," in Lee Patterson, ed., *Literary Practice and Social Change in Britain, 1380–1530* (Berkeley: University of California Press, 1990), pp. 216–47; James Simpson, "Madness and Texts: Hoccleve's *Series*," in Julia Boffey and Janet Cowen, eds., *Chaucer and Fifteenth-Century Poetry* (London: King's College, 1991), pp. 15–29; and Anna Torti, *The Glass of Form: Mirroring Structures from Chaucer to Skelton* (Cambridge: D. S. Brewer, 1991), pp. 87–106.

6. James Simpson, "Nobody's Man: Thomas Hoccleve's *Regement of Princes*," in Julia Boffey and Pamela King, eds., *London and Europe in the Later Middle Ages* (London: Queen Mary and Westfield College, 1995), p. 158.

7. *England's Empty Throne: Usurpation and the Language of Legitimacy 1399–1422* (New Haven: Yale University Press, 1998), p. 143. It may also be that contemporary readers availed themselves of the consoling bromides of orthodox moralization in an effort to accommodate Hoccleve's peculiarity— as did (I shall shortly argue) Hoccleve himself. An interpretation of one contemporary reception is proposed by David Lorenzo Boyd, "Reading Through the *Regement of Princes*: Hoccleve's *Series* and Lydgate's *The Dance of Death* in Yale Beinecke MS. 493," *Fifteenth-Century Studies* 20 (1993): 15–34; for an alternative account of this manuscript and, especially, of the meaning of its inclusion of Lydgate's *Dance of Death* (which is included in all manuscripts of the *Series* except the holograph of Durham Cosin V.iii.9), see the appendix to this chapter.

8. As Burrow says, "The autobiographical interpretation will be in danger of seeming merely anachronistic unless it can be supported by some historically plausible account of the poet's reasons for writing about himself" ("Autobiographical Poetry," p. 400). The hypothesis that Hoccleve would write about himself for the singular reason that he found himself unavoidable would thus be anachronistic and therefore wrong. Yet it is exactly this anachronism, I shall argue, that makes Hoccleve's selfhood a distressing puzzle to him—and therefore the unavoidable topic of his poetry.

9. On the self-reflexivity of the poetry as a whole, see especially the discussions by Greetham and Torti (see above, n. 5), and Manfred Markus, "Truth, Fiction and Metafiction in Fifteenth-Century English Literature, Particularly in Lydgate and Hoccleve," *Fifteenth-Century Studies* 8 (1983): 117–39.

10. Readings of the autobiographical passages that see them as oscillating between strategy and autobiography for its own sake—readings closer to the one I shall develop in this essay—are offered by Simpson, "Nobody's Man," pp. 149–80; and by Stephan Kohl, "More than Virtues and Vices: Self-Analysis in Hoccleve's 'Autobiographies,'" *Fifteenth-Century Studies* 14 (1988): 115–27.

11. This parallel has already been noted by Burrow, "Autobiographical Poetry," p. 402.

12. Citations of the *Regiment* are to the edition by Charles R. Blyth (Kalamazoo: Medieval Institute Publications, 1999).

13. For a summary of the Middle English material, see Francis Lee Utley, "Dialogues, Debates, and Catechisms," in Albert E. Hartung, gen. ed., *A Manual of the Writings in Middle English 1050–1500*, vol. 3 (New Haven: Connecticut Academy of Arts and Sciences, 1972), pp. 669–745, 828–902. See also Thomas L. Reed, Jr., *Middle English Debate Poetry and the Aesthetics of Irresolution* (Columbia: University of Missouri Press, 1990).

14. Burrow also mentions the old man in relation to the almsman, but only to dismiss him as a possible source ("Autobiographical Poetry," p. 402).

15. Stephen Medcalf, "Inner and Outer," in Stephen Medcalf, ed., *The Later Middle Ages* (London: Methuen, 1981), pp. 108–71, well describes Hoccleve's use of "an allegory so lightly stressed and all-pervading that we notice only its most obvious uses" (p. 133). As he says, "Hoccleve describes immediate and articulate consciousness allegorically" (p. 136). This quality of Hoccleve's writing was first brought to my attention by Charles Blyth in a paper delivered at the MLA Convention in 1980.

16. There are six mss of this work, none with a title; Durham University Library MS Cosin V.iii.9 was written by Hoccleve himself, but the first ten folios were lost and have been replaced by a copy of a later manuscript made by John Stowe—which means that it is at least possible that Hoccleve did entitle the work. For the title *Series*, see Eleanor P. Hammond, *English Verse between Chaucer and Surrey* (Durham: Duke University Press, 1927), pp. xix–xx.

17. For the *Complaint* and *Dialogue,* I have used J. A. Burrow, ed., *Thomas Hoccleve's Complaint and Dialogue,* EETS OS 313 (Oxford: Oxford University Press, 1999), and for the remainder of the work, Mary Ruth Pryor, *Thomas Hoccleve's Series: An Edition of MS Durham Cosin V iii 9,* Ph.D. dissertation, University of California, Los Angeles, 1968, to which I have added punctuation.

18. According to Doob, *Nebuchadnezzar's Children,* the "central theme [of the *Series* is] the usefulness of physical disorder for recalling men to spiritual sanity" (p. 220), a sanity that can only be achieved through confession. "The whole *Series* is thus united by the theme of the value of suffering and disease which preoccupied Hoccleve throughout his poetic career" (p. 225). Christina von Nolcken, "'O, why ne had y lerned for to die?'" argues that the spiritual as well as literal center of the *Series* is *Lerne to Dye,* and reads the Friend's interruptions as a distraction of Hoccleve from his proper spiritual duty. J. A. Burrow, "Hoccleve's *Series:* Experience and Books," in Robert F. Yeager, ed., *Fifteenth-Century Studies* (Hamden: Archon Books, 1984), pp. 259–73, promotes the notion of rehabilitation: the text "begins in solitary alienation, and it ends with the reassumption (albeit hesitant) of a social role proper to a man of fifty-three" (p. 268). A different version of the same argument is offered by

James Simpson, "Madness and Texts." A recent essay that stresses instead Hoccleve's self-disaffection—but deals with only the *Complaint* and *Dialogue* and thus avoids the problem of unity—is Matthew Boyd Goldie, "Psychosomatic Illness and Identity in London, 1416–1421: Hoccleve's *Complaint* and *Dialogue with a Friend*," *Exemplaria* 11 (1999): 23–52.

19. A. G. Rigg, "Hoccleve's *Complaint* and Isidore of Seville," *Speculum* 45 (1970): 564–74; J. A. Burrow, "Hoccleve's *Complaint* and Isidore of Seville Again," *Speculum* 73 (1998): 424–28.

20. Cf. *LGWP* G 452–63, in *The Riverside Chaucer*, gen. ed. Larry Benson (Boston: Houghton Mifflin, 1987), p. 601.

21. K. H. Vickers, *Humphrey Duke of Gloucester* (London: Constable, 1907), pp. 91–96, 125–29. Jacqueline had been previously married to John, the dauphin of France, who died in 1417. A. I. Doyle and M. B. Parkes, "The Production of Copies of the *Canterbury Tales* and the *Confessio Amantis* in the Early Fifteenth Century," in M. B. Parkes and A. G. Watson, eds., *Medieval Scribes, Manuscripts and Libraries* (London: Scolar Press, 1979), date the lines about Humphrey to September–December 1419 (p. 182 n. 39); Burrow, "Autobiographical Poetry," argues that the *Dialogue* was composed between December 30, 1419, and February 2, 1421 (p. 395 n.1), a position he explains in full in "Thomas Hoccleve: Some Redatings," *RES* 46 (1995): 366–72. Either dating is consistent with an allusion to the marriage negotiations.

22. Christopher Allmand, *Henry V* (Berkeley: University of California Press, 1992), pp. 167–68.

23. See Vickers, *Humphrey*, pp. 128–29.

24. For the evidence that supports this argument, see my *Chaucer and the Subject of History* (Madison: University of Wisconsin Press, 1991), pp. 231–43, 280–83.

25. For the source of the tale in the *Gesta*, and Hoccleve's changes, see Pryor's introduction, pp. 95–108, 112, and Jerome Mitchell, *Thomas Hoccleve: A Study in Early Fifteenth-Century English Poetic* (Urbana: University of Illinois Press, 1968), pp. 43–47, 86–95.

26. K. B. McFarlane, *The Nobility of Later Medieval England* (Oxford: Clarendon Press, 1973), p. 67.

27. *The Civilization of the Renaissance in Italy*, trans. S. G. C. Middlemore (London: Phaidon Books, 1965 [1860]), p. 81.

28. Thelma S. Fenster and Mary Carpenter Erler, eds. and trans., *Poems of Cupid, God of Love* (Leiden: E. J. Brill, 1990). For a primarily stylistic discussion of Hoccleve's changes to Christine's poem, see Roger Ellis, "Chaucer, Christine de Pizan, and Hoccleve: The Letter of Cupid," in Catherine Batt, ed., *Essays on Thomas Hoccleve*, Centre for Medieval and Renaissance Studies, Queen Mary and Westfield College, University of London (Turnhout: Brepols, 1996), pp. 19–54.

29. On this conceit, see Richard Firth Green, "The *Familia Regis* and the *Familia Cupidinis*," in V. J. Scattergood and J. W. Sherborne, eds., *English Court Culture in the Later Middle Ages* (London: Duckworth, 1983), pp. 87–108.

30. "C'est sa mere, c'est sa seur, c'est s'amie" (729); "C'est son droit per qui a lui est semblable, / La riens qui plus lui peut estre agreable" (731–32).

31. For this context, see J. C. Laidlaw, "Christine de Pizan, the Earl of Salisbury and Henry IV," *French Studies* 36 (1982): 129–43, and Nadia Margolis, "The Poetess as Historian," *JHI* 47 (1986): 361–75.

32. Richard Firth Green, "Troilus and the Game of Love," *Chaucer Review* 13 (1979): 201–220 (205). The vexed modern debate on the gender politics of the poem witnesses to Hoccleve's success, as critics play out the various arguments the poem allows: see Diane Bornstein, "Anti-Feminism in Thomas Hoccleve's Translation of Christine de Pizan's *Epistre au dieu d'amours*," *ELN* 19 (1981): 7–14; John V. Fleming, "Hoccleve's 'Letter of Cupid' and the 'Quarrel' over the *Roman de la Rose*," *Medium Aevum* 40 (1971): 21–40; Glenda K. McLeod, "A Case of Faux Semblans: *L'Epistre au dieu d'amours* and *The Letter of Cupid*," in Glenda K. McLeod, *The Reception of Christine de Pizan from the Fifteenth through the Nineteenth Centuries: Visitors to the City* (Lewiston: Edwin Mellen Press, 1991), pp. 11–24; Anna Torti, "Hoccleve's Attitude towards Women: 'I shoop me do my peyne and diligence / To wynne hir loue by obedience,'" in Juliette Dor, ed., *A Wyf Ther Was: Essays in Honour of Paule Mertens-Fonck* (Liège: University of Liège, 1992), pp. 264–74; Karen A. Winstead, "'I am al othir than yee weene': Hoccleve, Women, and the *Series*," *Philological Quarterly* 72 (1993): 143–55.

33. See above, chapter 3.

34. This point has often been made, most recently and in what I consider an exaggerated form by Paul Strohm, *England's Empty Throne*. For a different account of Henry IV, supported by considerable evidence, see A. L. Brown, "The Reign of Henry IV: The Establishment of the Lancastrian Regime," in S. B. Chrimes, C. D. Ross, and R. A. Griffiths, eds., *Fifteenth-Century England 1399–1509* (Manchester: Manchester University Press, 1972), pp. 1–28. Brown speaks of Henry's "genuine magnanimity" (p. 6) toward his defeated enemies in the early years, sees his notorious liberality as "a combination of necessity, insecurity, generosity and extravagance" (p. 20), and concludes that "he came to the throne an honourable, chivalrous man with old-fashioned ideas and ideals . . . but that these were not enough for the problems that he met" (p. 24). Perhaps the most balanced assessment remains that of K. B. McFarlane, who describes Henry IV as "a would-be autocrat hampered by financial weakness" (*Lancastrian Kings and Lollard Knights* [Oxford: Clarendon Press, 1972], p. 99), but not the paranoid megalomaniac described by Strohm.

35. Peter McNiven, *Heresy and Politics in the Reign of Henry IV: The Burning of John Badby* (Woodbridge: Boydell Press, 1987), p. 93.

36. Edward Maunde Thompson, ed. and trans., *Chronicon Adae de Usk*, 2d ed. (London: Henry Frowde, 1904), p. 222; the original is printed at pp. 58–59. For another case of punishing a man who spoke disparagingly of the king, also in 1401, see p. 229.

37. Mabel Day and Robert Steele, eds., *Mum and the Soothsegger*, EETS OS 199 (London: Oxford University Press, 1936), Fragment M, 265, pp. 49–50. For discussions of censorship and self-censorship in the early fifteenth century, see Andrew Wawn, "Truth-telling and the Tradition of *Mum and the Sothsegger*," *Yearbook of English Studies* 13 (1983): 270–87, and especially James Simpson, "The Constraints of Satire in *Piers Plowman* and *Mum and the Sothsegger*," in Helen Phillipps, ed., *Langland, the Mystics and the Medieval English Tradition* (Cambridge: D. S. Brewer, 1990), pp. 11–30.

38. McNiven, *Heresy and Politics*, p. 116. For a further account of the dampening effect of the Constitutions, see Nicholas Watson, "Censorship and Cultural Change in Late-Medieval England: Vernacular Theology, the Oxford Translation Debate, and Arundel's Constitutions of 1409," *Speculum* 70 (1995): 821–64. Nonetheless, it is important to remember that throughout Henry's reign there remained a persistent and vocal anticlericalism—often in concert with political resistance to royal authority—that stood against the regime's efforts to impose its will: see, for just one example, the bill introduced into the Parliament of 1410 that would have had the effect of annulling the force of *De haretico comburendo* (see Anne Hudson, *The Premature Reformation: Wycliffite Texts and Lollard History* [Oxford: Clarendon Press, 1988], p. 115).

39. For the politics of the reign of Henry IV, I have relied primarily upon E. F. Jacob, *The Fifteenth Century 1399–1485* (Oxford: Clarendon Press, 1961); John L. Kirby, *Henry IV of England* (London: Constable, 1970); McNiven, *Heresy and Politics*; and the sometimes unreliable but still indispensable James Hamilton Wylie, *History of England under Henry the Fourth*, 4 vols. (London: Longmans, Green, 1884–98).

40. For Henry's efforts in the Parliament of 1404 to alleviate his financial distress by "resuming" crown estates—in effect, reclaiming or "reassuming" them from those to whom they had previously been granted and then regranting them at a higher value—and the rejection of this ploy by Parliament, see B. P. Woolfe, "Acts of Resumption in the Lancastrian Parliaments 1399–1456," *EHR* (1958): 583–613.

41. McNiven, *Heresy and Politics*, p. 167; see also Woolfe, "Acts of Resumption," p. 590 n. 1.

42. See for this episode McNiven's articles, "The Betrayal of Archbishop Scrope," *BJRL* 54 (1971): 173–213, and "The Problem of Henry IV's Health, 1405–13," *EHR* 100 (1985): 747–72.

43. There are forty-four surviving manuscripts, a total surpassed only by the *Pricke of Conscience*, the *Canterbury Tales*, *Piers Plowman*, and the *Confes-*

sio Amantis: see M. C. Seymour, "The Manuscripts of Hoccleve's *Regiment of Princes*," *Edinburgh Bibliographical Society Transactions* 4, pt. 7 (1974): 253–97, and A. S. G. Edwards, "Hoccleve's *Regement of Princes*: A Further Manuscript," *Edinburgh Bibliographical Society Transactions* 5, pt. 1 (1978): 32. In the stemma proposed by Marcia Smith Marzec, twenty-nine further manuscripts are hypothesized: "The Latin Marginalia of the *Regiment of Princes* as an Aid to Stemmatic Analysis," *TEXT* 3 (1987): 269–84. It is sometimes argued, as by Pearsall, "Hoccleve's *Regement of Princes*," that the *terminus ad quem* has to be November 1411, when the king regained power from the prince; or, as Blyth argues in the introduction to his edition, that since Hoccleve's annuity was paid on time in 1411 it would have been unnecessary for him to complain about slow payment after that date. But Judith Ferster, *Fictions of Advice: The Literature and Politics of Counsel in Late Medieval England* (Philadelphia: University of Pennsylvania Press, 1996), has shown the weakness of Pearsall's arguments, while Hoccleve is always distraught about the unreliability of his income. Ferster thus concludes, rightly I believe, that there is "no reason to discard 1412 as a possible date for the completion of the poem" (p. 139).

44. For a shrewd analysis of the way in which the prince, during the period from January 1410 to November 1411 when he in effect controlled the government, could be seen as offering an opening for a less tightly controlled, less relentlessly defensive style of government, see McNiven, *Heresy and Politics*, pp. 136–57, 185–198. McNiven himself sees this possibility as beginning to close in March 1410 with the burning of the Lollard John Badby, engineered by Henry IV and Arundel as an object lesson to those who, like the members of the Commons who had once again just presented a petition to disendow the Church, would challenge the traditional order. According to McNiven, after the prince's failure to save Badby and frustrate his father's and Arundel's display of institutional intolerance, he "became the embodiment of traditional certainties" (p. 222). The centralizing and personalizing of rule during his own reign has been treated by a number of historians: see especially the essays collected in G. L. Harriss, ed., *Henry V: The Practice of Kingship* (Oxford: Oxford University Press, 1985), and Allmand, *Henry V*. Strohm, *England's Empty Throne*, presents a far darker picture of Henry V, but K. B. McFarlane's estimate of how Henry managed the unwieldy institution of the medieval English monarchy, however unfashionable it may be in the current, post-Foucauldian climate, should not be dismissed lightly: "Take him all round and he was, I think, the greatest man that ever ruled England" (*Lancastrian Kings and Lollard Knights*, p. 133).

45. Most treatments of the poem read it as supportive of Lancastrian orthodoxy: see, for example, Lawton, "Dullness and the Fifteenth Century"; Pearsall, "Hoccleve's *Regement of Princes*"; Paul Strohm, "Hoccleve, Lydgate and the Lancastrian Court," in David Wallace, ed., *The Cambridge History of Medieval English Literature* (Cambridge: Cambridge University Press, 1999),

pp. 640–61 (largely reprinted in *England's Empty Throne*). A reading of the poem as supportive of Henry which nonetheless grants to Hoccleve a sophisticated awareness of the relation of writing to power, and hence of the capacity of writing to resist power, is provided by Scanlon, "The King's Two Voices." Hasler's "Hoccleve's Unregimented Body" (see above, n. 5) reads the poem as more unreservedly anti-Henrician than these other critics, while Ferster, *Fictions of Advice*, pp. 137–59, offers a reading parallel to my own in its emphasis on the royal finances, although differing in other respects.

46. In September 1411 King Henry made plans to lead an expedition into northern France, probably to fight with the Armagnacs against the Burgundians—a plan that was canceled because of his ill health: see Wylie, *History of England under Henry the Fourth*, 4.37–40. Then in November 1411, the prince's troops supported the Burgundians and defeated the Armagnacs at St. Cloud: for this expedition, "unauthorized by the king but led by Thomas, earl of Arundel, the Prince's close asssociate and member of the royal council," see Allmand, *Henry V*, pp. 49–50.

47. It is often assumed that this is a forecast of the marriage of Henry with Catherine, the daughter of Charles VI, which took place in 1421 after Henry had conquered much of France; but it is far more likely that Hoccleve is referring to the contemporary negotiations for a marriage between Henry and Anne, the fifth daughter of John, duke of Burgundy (see Allmand, *Henry V*, pp. 48–49).

48. Thomas Hoccleve, *The Regement of Princes*, in *Works*, vol. 3, ed. Frederick J. Furnivall, EETS ES 72 (London: Kegan Paul, Trench, Trübner, 1897), p. 2 and n. 4. Scanlon, "The King's Two Voices," pp. 233–34, Pearsall, "Hoccleve's *Regement of Princes*," p. 391, and Ferster, *Fictions of Advice*, pp. 140–41, all accept Furnivall's interpretation. Another, even sharper instance of the dangers of kingship is found in lines 4068–74, in which a king is told that a dead lion becomes bird's meat. Hoccleve almost gloatingly concludes, "The answere of the kyng nat have I herd; / My book nat tellith how he was answerd" (4073–74).

49. As we have seen, Pearsall dates the poem prior to the prince's dismissal because it would have been tactless of Hoccleve to have written it later (see above, n. 44). But it is precisely tactlessness that characterizes Hoccleve's writing, both here and elsewhere.

50. See the persuasive and detailed account by McNiven, *Heresy and Politics*, pp. 200–202.

51. Hoccleve was quite well-informed about Badby's views: see McNiven, *Heresy and Politics*, pp. 199–200. That he was probably drawing not on the official documents of the case but on hearsay is suggested by the fact that he turns what is in the document a proper name, "John Rakyer of Bristol," into an occupation.

52. This is Harley 4866, the manuscript printed by Furnivall, who notes the cancellations. For the provenance of the manuscript, Seymour suggests

that it was made for either Edward, duke of York, or John, duke of Bedford ("Manuscripts of Hoccleve's *Regiment of Princes*," p. 269).

53. For a reading of the poem complementary to that offered here, but that stresses the gender politics of the poem rather than its emphasis upon the question of social identity per se, see Ruth Nissé, "'Oure Fadres Olde and Modres': Gender, Heresy, and Hoccleve's Literary Politics," *SAC* 21 (1999): 275–99.

54. All references are to the edition in Seymour, *Selections*, pp. 61–74.

55. Seymour notes this initial and the change of thematic direction: previously Hoccleve had written "more in sorrow than in anger. Now, in more vigorous mood, he refutes and condemns the Lollard beliefs. This second part may have been added later" (ibid., p. 131). Moreoever, while the rubric says that the poem was written when Henry was at Southampton preparing to go to Normandy, lines 499–500 imply that Henry and his men are already there—evidence that the second part of the poem was added later while the rubric was left unrevised.

56. *Rotuli parliamentorum*, 6 vols. (London, 1767–77), 3.623–24.

57. Hasler, "Hoccleve's Unregimented Body," usefully notes the presence of this theme in terms of the relation of Hoccleve to Chaucer. He observes that Hoccleve's name enters the poem only with that of the paternal Chaucer:

"What schal I calle thee? what is thy name?"
"Hoccleve, fadir myn, men clepen me."
"Hoccleve, sone?" "Ywis, fadir, that same."
"Sone, I have herd or this men speke of thee;
Thow were aqweyntid with Chaucer, pardee."
(1863–67)

For Hasler, this "moment implies that self-knowledge . . . emerges in the void of castration; Hoccleve's participation in the symbolic is now evident, his name fore-spoken by the Other" (175). Unfortunately, by reading the Chaucer-Hoccleve relation Oedipally one not only hides from view other father-son relations both in and outside the poem, especially that between Henry IV and the Prince of Wales, but reduces to a formula all the many ways in which men—including fathers and sons—compete with each other. For the fullest treatment of this theme, one that in part anticipates my own discussion, see Ethan Knapp, "Eulogies and Usurpations: Hoccleve and Chaucer Revisited," *SAC* 21 (1999): 247–73.

58. Pearsall, "Hoccleve's *Regement of Princes*," p. 386.

59. Hoccleve wrote a poem commemorating this event: Frederick J. Furnivall, ed., *Hoccleve's Works*, vol. 1, *The Minor Poems*, EETS ES 61 (London: Kegan Paul, Trench, Trübner, 1892), pp. 47–49.

60. A particularly striking instance of this concern for the truth-teller occurs in the discussion of largesse. Hoccleve is careful first to assert his own loyalty—"In al my book yee shul nat see ne fynde / That I youre deedes lakke

or hem despreise" (4397–98)—but then delivers a blistering attack on royal prodigality that is pointedly relevant to the notoriously precarious Lancastrian finances. Then after this attack he contrasts himself with "Favel": the "sweete venym of his tonge" (4443) ruins his lord while "the treewe man" (4446) is snubbed. But, says Hoccleve, with a certain self-satisfaction, it is better to suffer for the truth and win heavenly reward "Than richely enhaunced be for glose" (4461). Pearsall, "Hoccleve's *Regement of Princes*," takes these passages as a strategy by which Hoccleve legitimizes himself and in turn the entirely positive portrait of the prince that Pearsall sees in the *Regiment*.

61. Derek Pearsall has characterized Lydgate's political pronouncements as "the platitudes of his age," as "far too commonplace to have any particular topical import," and as betraying the absence of "any sort of coherent political philosophy" (*John Lydgate* [London: Routledge and Kegan Paul, 1970], pp. 15, 139, and 249). My own view, however, is that *The Siege of Thebes* (1421) is actually an acute analysis of the limitations of Lancastrian rule: see below, chapter 5. See also James Simpson, "'Dysemol Daies and Fatal Houres': Lydgate's *Destruction of Thebes* and Chaucer's *Knight's Tale*," in Helen Cooper and Sally Mapstone, eds., *The Long Fifteenth Century: Essays for Douglas Gray* (Oxford: Clarendon Press, 1997), pp. 15–33.

62. Elna-Jean Young Bentley, *The Formulary of Thomas Hoccleve*, Ph.D. dissertation, Emory University, 1965. The *Formulary* was the last of Hoccleve's works, composed after 1422, and after he had put together the manuscript(s) that were meant to represent his collected works: see John Bowers, "Hoccleve's Huntington Holographs: The First 'Collected Poems' in English," *Fifteenth-Century Studies* 15 (1989): 27–51. Valuable discussions of the formulary are provided by Ethan Knapp in "Bureaucratic Identity and Literary Practice in Lancastrian England," *Medieval Perspectives* 9 (1994): 64–72, and "Bureaucratic Identity and the Construction of the Self in Hoccleve's *Formulary* and *La Male Regle*," *Speculum* 74 (1999): 357–76.

63. According to R. H. Hall, "The Concept of Bureaucracy: An Empirical Assessment," *American Journal of Sociology* 69 (1963–64): "In a highly bureaucratized situation (along all dimensions) the highly competent person might not be able to exercise the full range of his competence due to specific procedural limitations, limited sphere of activity, limited authority due to hierarchical demands, etc." (p. 39).

64. Jacques Le Goff, *Time, Work, and Culture in the Middle Ages*, trans. Arthur Goldhammer (Chicago: University of Chicago Press, 1980), pp. 48–49.

65. R. A. Brown, "King Edward's Clocks," *Antiquaries Journal* 39 (1959): 284.

66. McNiven, *Heresy and Politics*, p. 224.

67. For an acute discussion of this paradox, see Georg Simmel, *On Individuality and Social Forms: Selected Writings*, ed. Donald N. Levine (Chicago: University of Chicago Press, 1971), pp. 277–80.

68. A good example is the passage where Hoccleve explains to the alms-man that his annuity cannot be paid through the Hanaper, the department of chancery that received fees for the sealing of documents (1881–83). The rea-son is because Henry IV had reinstituted in 1411 a policy of not paying annu-ities out of the Hanaper's income as a way of controlling the outflow of cash, and throughout his reign only two annuities were ever paid out of the Hanaper, neither to Hoccleve (Allmand, *Henry V*, pp. 386–87, 389).

69. This is not to say that the image does not also bear conventional meanings: Alan T. Gaylord, "Portrait of a Poet," in Martin Stevens and Daniel Woodward, eds., *The Ellesmere Chaucer: Essays in Interpretation* (San Marino: Huntington Library, 1995), pp. 121–41, argues persuasively that the portraits of Chaucer in the *Regement* manuscript Harley 4866 and in the Ellesmere manu-script, which are certainly related, both represent the poet as a venerable ad-visor to young men. The important point for my purposes is Hoccleve's insis-tence that the bodily image of Chaucer be made present so that the reader cannot reduce him to merely an abstract epitome of virtue.

70. This topic has recently been discussed, in very different terms, by Goldie, "Psychosomatic Illness and Identity in London, 1416–1421" (see above, n. 18).

71. Derek Keene, "Medieval London and Its Region," *London Journal* 14 (1989): 99–111. On Hockliffe, see *VCH Bedfordshire* 3 (1912): 383–86.

72. For the low estimate, see J. C. Russell, *British Medieval Population* (Al-buquerque: University of New Mexico Press, 1948), pp. 285–87, and Caroline Barron, "The Later Middle Ages, 1270–1520," in Mary D. Lobel, ed., *The City of London: From Prehistoric Times to c. 1520* (Oxford: Oxford University Press, 1989), p. 56; the high estimate is given by Derek Keene, "A New Study of Lon-don before the Great Fire," *Urban History Yearbook* (1984): 11–21.

73. See, for example, Henry Thomas Riley, ed. and trans., *Memorials of London and London Life in the XIIIth, XIVth, and XVth Centuries* (London: Longmans, Green, 1868), pp. 268, 480, 482, 502, 526, 535, 545, 585, and 636.

74. For this tournament, see Sheila Lindenbaum, "The Smithfield Tour-nament of 1390," *Journal of Medieval and Renaissance Studies* 20 (1990): 1–20. In *The Life of Geoffrey Chaucer* (Oxford: Blackwell, 1992), Derek Pearsall com-ments on the difference in scale between Theseus's amphitheater (a mile in circumference and built of stone) and the wooden scaffolds at Smithfield sur-rounding a jousting area just one-tenth of a mile in circumference (p. 212).

75. Eric W. Stockton, trans., *The Latin Works of John Gower* (Seattle: Uni-versity of Washington Press, 1962), p. 319.

76. Rossell Hope Robbins, ed., *Historical Poems of the XIVth and XVth Centuries* (New York: Columbia University Press, 1959), pp. 130–34.

77. David Wallace, "Chaucer and the Absent City," in Barbara Hanawalt, ed., *Chaucer's England: Literature in Historical Context* (Minneapolis: University of Minnesota Press, 1992), p. 82.

78. See Seymour, *Selections*, pp. 25–28, 110–12.

79. William Langland, *Piers Plowman: The B Version*, ed. George Kane and E. Talbot Donaldson (London: Athlone Press, 1975), Passus XIII, lines 282–85 (p. 501).

80. See Medcalf, "Inner and Outer," pp. 108–71.

81. Burrow, "Autobiographical Poetry," p. 404.

Appendix to Chapter 4

1. Barbara A. Shailor, *Catalogue of Medieval and Renaissance Manuscripts in the Beinecke Rare Book and Manuscript Library, Yale University*, vol. 2: MSS 251–500 (Binghamton: Medieval and Renaissance Texts and Studies, 1987), pp. 475–78.

2. Eleanor Prescott Hammond, ed., *English Verse between Chaucer and Surrey* (Durham: Duke University Press, 1927), p. 128.

3. John Lydgate, *The Dance of Death*, ed. Florence Warren and Beatrice White, EETS OS 181 (London: Oxford University Press, 1931). *Danse of Machabre* is Lydgate's title; see p. 6, line 46. For the meaning of "Machabre," see Robert Eisler, "Danse Macabre," *Traditio* 6 (1948): 187–225.

4. Jerome Mitchell, *Thomas Hoccleve: A Study in Early Fifteenth-Century Poetic* (Urbana: University of Illinois Press, 1968), p. 20.

5. Derek Pearsall, *John Lydgate* (London: Routledge and Kegan Paul, 1970), p. 243.

6. This question has been previously discussed by David Lorenzo Boyd, "Reading through the *Regement of Princes*: Hoccleve's *Series* and Lydgate's *The Dance of Death* in Yale Beinecke MS. 493," *Fifteenth-Century Studies* 20 (1993): 15–34. Boyd argues, plausibly enough, that since all three of these texts are copied by the same scribe and in the same format, they should be read as a large compilation on the same theme. The theme is governance (Hoccleve's *Regiment*), so that the manuscript offers a traditional account of the way in which people should behave in order to avoid the terrors of death (Lydgate's *Dance*) and the dire effects of madness (Hoccleve's *Series*).

7. M. C. Seymour, "The Manuscripts of Hoccleve's *Regiment of Princes*," *Edinburgh Bibliographical Society Transactions* 4, pt. 7 (1974): 253–97; A. S. G. Edwards, "Hoccleve's *Regiment of Princes*: A Further Manuscript," *Edinburgh Bibliographical Society Transactions* 5, pt. 1 (1978): 32; J. A. Burrow, *Thomas Hoccleve*, Authors of the Middle Ages 4 (Aldershot: Variorum, 1994), pp. 50–51.

8. Fol. 65a, next to stanza 43.

9. See John H. Fisher, *The Importance of Chaucer* (Carbondale: Southern Illinois University Press, 1992), and Fisher, "A Language Policy for Lancastrian England," *PMLA* 107 (1992): 1168–80.

10. The mss in which the picture survives are Harley 4866 (which actually has two portraits), Royal 17. D.vi, and Rosenbach MS 1083/30. Those in which it was cut out are Arundel 38 and Harley 4826; those in which the manuscripts are mutilated at the end, where the Chaucer portrait would have appeared, are Dugdale 45, Gg.vi.17, Queen's College Camb. 12, and HM 135.

11. This manuscript has been edited twice: Mary Ruth Pryor, ed., *Thomas Hoccleve's Series: An Edition of MS Durham Cosin V iii 9*, University of California, Los Angeles, Ph.D. dissertation, 1968, and Frederick Furnivall and I. Gollancz, eds., *Hoccleve's Works: The Minor Poems*, rev. ed. Jerome Mitchell and A. I. Doyle, EETS ES 61 and 73 (Oxford: Oxford University Press, 1970).

12. C. W. Dutschke, ed., *Guide to Medieval and Renaissance Manuscripts in the Huntington Library*, vol. 1 (San Marino: Huntington Library, 1989), p. 250. This manuscript has not been printed, but has been discussed in an important article by John Bowers, "Hoccleve's Two Copies of *Lerne to Dye*: Implications for Textual Critics," *Papers of the Bibliographical Society of America* 83 (1989): 437–72. I am grateful to Prof. Bowers for sharing his collations of the manuscripts with me. See also John Bowers, "Hoccleve's Huntington Holographs: The First 'Collected Poems' in English," *Fifteenth-Century Studies* 15 (1989): 27–51. In addition, a single stanza of *Lerne to Dye* survives as an interpolation in Chaucer's *Tale of Melibee* in Trinity College, Cambridge MS B.2.18: see Kate Harris, "Unnoticed Extracts from Chaucer and Hoccleve: Huntington MS HM 144, Trinity College, Oxford MS D 29 and *The Canterbury Tales*," *Studies in the Age of Chaucer* 20 (1998): 199. I am indebted for this reference, and for other kindnesses, to Prof. A. S. G. Edwards.

13. Seymour, "The Manuscripts of Hoccleve's *Regiment of Princes*," places S, B, and L together in a group (p. 263); he did not know of Y. In "Hoccleve's *Regiment*, p. 32, Edwards reported Y and linked it with S, B, and L, a grouping that Dr. Charles Blyth, editor of the *Regiment* (Kalamazoo: Medieval Institute Publications, 1999), has confirmed for me.

14. In "A New Chaucer Manuscript," *PMLA* 83 (1968), written with George B. Pace, A. I. Doyle dates S to "the second decade of the century" (p. 24), although since the poem was not completed until 1421 at the earliest he must mean the third. Doyle also says that the variants of the *Danse of Machabre* "support the descent S-B-L" (p. 24 n. 25). A date in the third decade of the fifteenth century for S has been independently confirmed for me by Dr. Ralph Hanna of Oxford University, to whom I am much indebted for this and other information.

15. This point has been made by Edwards, "Hoccleve's *Regiment*," p. 32. The most striking variant that links BLY is in *Lerne to Dye* 117–18. D reads: "Thy comyng vn to me was vncerteyn / Thow haast vp on me stolen and me bownde." In BLY eyeskip has led to the omission of the second half of 117 and the first half of 118, so that 117 reads, in all three manuscripts, "Thy comynge

vn to me stole and me bounde." Incidentally, in H line 117 reads: "Thyn *hour* was vn to me ful vncerteyn," an apparently authorial revision. This and similar variants suggest that the source for S's *Lerne to Dye* was, as we should expect, the complete D rather than the fragmentary H.

16. The critical discussion of the *Complaint* has largely sought to accommodate Hoccleve's poem to the conventions of medieval literature: see, for example, J. A. Burrow, "Autobiographical Poetry in the Middle Ages: The Case of Thomas Hoccleve," *Proceedings of the British Academy* 68 (1982): 389–412; however, in "Hoccleve and Chaucer," in Ruth Morse and Barry Windeatt, eds., *Chaucer Traditions: Studies in Honour of Derek Brewer* (Cambridge: Cambridge University Press, 1990), pp. 54–61, Burrow does say that "the *Series* represents something new in English poetry—nothing less than a long poem in which the poet himself plays the leading role" (p. 57). But even if this modest claim is true, it is obviously not the case for medieval poetry generally, as witness Dante's *Commedia* or Machaut's *Voir Dit*. The originality of the *Complaint* resides not simply in the foregrounding of the speaker as the subject of the poem, nor even in its unusually specific detail about the circumstances of Hoccleve's life, but rather in the exploration of the speaker's psychology as a condition that resists being located in the categories provided by conventional moral truths. Of the many discussions of this topic, the two that are closest to the position put forth here are Stephan Kohl, "More than Virtues and Vices: Self-Analysis in Hoccleve's 'Autobiographies,'" *Fifteenth-Century Studies* 14 (1988): 115–27, and James Simpson, "Madness and Texts: Hoccleve's *Series*," in Julia Boffey and Janet Cowen, eds., *Chaucer and Fifteenth-Century Poetry* (London: King's College, 1991), pp. 15–29.

17. K. B. McFarlane, *The Nobility of Later Medieval England* (Oxford: Clarendon Press, 1973), p. 67.

18. For the painting, see Abbé Valentin Dufour, *Recherches sur la Dance Macabre peinte en 1425 au Cimitière des Innocents* (Paris: Bibliophile Français, 1873).

19. Derek Pearsall, *John Lydgate (1371–1449): A Bio-bibliography*, English Literary Studies Monograph Series 71 (Victoria: University of Victoria, 1997), pp. 26–27.

20. The only extended critical discussion the poem has received is by Derek Pearsall, "Signs of Life in Lydgate's *Danse Macabre*," in James Hogg, ed., *Zeit, Tod und Ewigkeit in der Renaissance Literatur*, b. 3 (Salzburg: Institut für Anglistik und Amerikanistik, 1987), pp. 58–71. Pearsall is good on debunking the fevered reading of the poem as part of a cult of death, but ignores its satiric and social dimensions.

21. Joel Rosenthal, *The Purchase of Paradise: Gift Giving and the Aristocracy, 1307–1485* (London: Routledge and Kegan Paul, 1972).

22. M. C. Seymour, "Some Lydgate Manuscripts: *Lives of SS. Edmund and Fremund* and *Danse Macabre*," *Edinburgh Bibliographical Society Transactions* 5,

pt. 4 (1983–85): 10–24; John Stow, *A Survey of London,* reprinted from the text of 1603, with introduction and notes by Charles Lethbridge Kingsford, 2 vols. (Oxford: Clarendon Press, 1908).

23. In "Lydgate Manuscripts: Some Directions for Further Research," in Derek Pearsall, ed., *Manuscripts and Readers in Fifteenth-Century England: The Literary Implications of Manuscript Study* (Cambridge: D. S. Brewer, 1983), A. S. G. Edwards states that "a full picture of the readership and audience of Lydgate's writings would add to our understanding of late medieval taste and patronage. It would also quite probably establish Lydgate as possessing a much broader appeal than any other medieval English writer—including Chaucer" (p. 22).

24. Of the forty-three mss, seven are missing leaves at the end. I am indebted to Dr. Blyth for this information about the identification of Hoccleve as author in the mss of the *Regiment.* The two surviving patronal copies of the *Regiment* are Arundel 38 (prepared for Thomas Mowbray, first duke of Norfolk: see Kate Harris, "The Patron of British Library MS Arundel 38," *Notes and Queries* 229 [31] [1984]: 462–63) and Harley 4866 (prepared for either Edward, duke of York, or John, duke of Bedford); the third manuscript, closely associated with these, is BL Additional 18632 (see Seymour, "Manuscripts," pp. 274–75).

25. This drawing is described by Seymour, "Manuscripts," p. 278; see also A. S. G. Edwards, "The Chaucer Portrait in the Harley and Rosenbach Manuscripts," *Manuscript Studies* 4 (1993): 268–71.

26. H. N. MacCracken, "King Henry's Triumphal Entry into London, Lydgate's Poem, and Carpenter's Letter," *Archiv für das Studium der neueren Sprache* 126 (1911): 75–102.

27. Carol M. Meale, "*The Libelle of Englyshe Polycye* and Mercantile Literary Culture in Late-Medieval London," in Julia Boffey and Pamela King, eds., *London and Europe in the Later Middle Ages* (London: Queen Mary and Westfield College, 1995), pp. 181–227.

28. Whittington himself had founded the Grey Friars' Library in 1421, and he contributed four hundred pounds toward its cost: see Raymond Smith, "The Library at Guildhall in the 15th and 16th Centuries: Part I," *The Guildhall Miscellany* 1 (1952): 6.

29. See ibid.; Raymond Smith, "The Library at Guildhall in the 15th and 16th Centuries: Part II," *The Guildhall Miscellany* 6 (1956): 2–6; and Caroline M. Barron, *The Medieval Guildhall of London* (London: Corporation of London, 1974), pp. 33–35.

30. Carpenter's will is translated in Thomas Brewer, *Memoir of the Life and Times of John Carpenter* (London: Arthur Taylor, 1856), pp. 143–44.

31. Carpenter's bequest has been discussed in the context of similar charitable acts by Wendy Scase, "Reginald Pecock, John Carpenter and John Colop's 'Common-Profit' Books: Aspects of Book Ownership and Circulation in Fifteenth-Century London," *Medium Aevum* 61 (1992): 261–74.

32. Citations are from M. C. Seymour, ed., *Selections from Hoccleve* (Oxford: Clarendon Press, 1981).

33. The document recording this remarkable event may be found in R. W. Chambers and Marjorie Daunt, eds., *A Book of London English 1384–1425* (Oxford: Clarendon Press, 1931), pp. 140–42.

34. It should be pointed out that in the Hoccleve holograph, HM 111, the name Carpenter is in darker ink over an erasure: see C. W. Dutschke, *Guide to the Medieval and Renaissance Manuscripts in the Huntington Library*, vol. 1 (San Marino: Huntington Library, 1989), p. 146. This would suggest that the poem was written for someone else and then, after Carpenter had mediated the contretemps between the Brewers and Whittington, revised for him. This scenario does not affect the central point about the relationship between Hoccleve and Carpenter, however.

35. I am indebted to Ralph Hanna for bringing this detail to my attention before I had the opportunity to consult the manuscript myself. Interestingly, another manuscript of the *Series* that seems to derive directly from Selden, Coventry MS 325/1, is also a library copy, having originally belonged to the Coventry Grammar School. Its modern binding (according to the catalogue the book was rebound in 1968 and 1976 by the Coventry City Record Office) retains the clasp and a chain of twelve links. For the history and description of this MS, see A. I. Doyle, "New Chaucer Manuscript," 22–26.

36. This suggests another question: is it possible that the Friend with whom Hoccleve converses in the *Dialogue* is not a mere literary convention but the very John Carpenter whose protection Hoccleve was later to seek?

five. Making Identities in Fifteenth-Century England

1. Brian Stock, *Listening for the Text: On the Uses of the Past* (Baltimore: The Johns Hopkins University Press, 1990), p. 78.

2. *La Poésie du moyen âge* (Paris: Hachette, 1877), p. 220.

3. Isidore derived his definition (*Etymologiae* 1, 41) from classical authors such as Cicero and Cato: see Bernard Guenée, *Histoire et culture historique dans l'Occident médiévale* (Paris: Aubier, 1980), p. 18. Jacques Derrida, *Of Grammatology*, trans. G. C. Spivak (Baltimore: The Johns Hopkins University Press, 1976 [1967]), p. 158.

4. Dominick LaCapra, "Rhetoric and History," in *History and Criticism* (Ithaca: Cornell University Press, 1985), p. 17.

5. An example of such disregard, striking because of the very high level of the work, is Chris Given-Wilson's *The Royal Household and the King's Affinity: Service, Politics and Finance in England 1360–1413* (New Haven: Yale University Press, 1986), which discusses the Ricardian court while making no reference

to Richard Firth Green's important *Poets and Princepleasers: Literature and the Court in the Late Middle Ages* (Toronto: University of Toronto Press, 1980). Indeed, Given-Wilson refers only once to the court's most prominent literary figure, Geoffrey Chaucer, and then his name is misprinted (p. 61). Of course there are exceptions: David Aers's *Community, Gender, and Individual Identity: English Writing 1360–1430* (London: Routledge, 1988) has been put to good use by P. R. Coss in his important essay "Bastard Feudalism Revised," *Past and Present* 125 (1989): 27–64. A somewhat different example of the use of literary materials by a historian is G. L. Harriss's "Introduction: The Exemplar of Kingship," in G. L. Harriss, ed., *Henry V: The Practice of Kingship* (Oxford: Oxford University Press, 1985), 1–29, where Hoccleve's *Regiment of Princes* is used to provide the monarchical ideal that Henry sought to fulfill. But here the literary text is read as a straightforward expression of contemporary values—a reading that most literary critics would see as insufficiently alert to Hoccleve's inability to avoid embarrassing topics.

6. For example, Stephen Knight, *Geoffrey Chaucer* (Oxford: Blackwell, 1985); Paul Olson, *The Canterbury Tales and the Good Society* (Princeton: Princeton University Press, 1986); Susan Crane, *Insular Romance* (Berkeley: University of California Press, 1987); David Aers, *Community, Gender, and Individual Identity* (see above, n. 5); Paul Strohm, *Social Chaucer* (Cambridge, Mass.: Harvard University Press, 1989); Peggy Knapp, *Chaucer and the Social Contest* (London: Routledge, 1988); Peter Brown and Andrew Butcher, *The Age of Saturn: Literature and History in the Canterbury Tales* (Oxford: Basil Blackwell, 1991).

7. A good example—chosen not because it is egregious but because of the excellence of its literary analyses—is H. Marshall Leicester, *The Disenchanted Self: Representing the Subject in the Canterbury Tales* (Berkeley: University of California Press, 1990). Leicester's well-taken point is that most self-designated historicist criticism reduces both Chaucer and, more important, his tale-tellers, to agents of a supervening cultural practice they enact but are unable to conceptualize. But while he shows that the poet and his fictive surrogates have an ironic or "disenchanted" relation to their culture, he locates this disenchantment within the Weberian dynamic of modernization in only the briefest of ways (pp. 27–28). As he says, quite appropriately, "I regard the kind of work I do here as a preliminary contribution to a more properly historical account of the late Middle Ages" (p. 28).

8. Terry Eagleton, *Literary Theory* (Minneapolis: University of Minnesota Press, 1983), p. 150.

9. According to Frank Lentricchia, *After the New Criticism* (Chicago: University of Chicago Press, 1980), "On the matter of history, the deconstructionist position . . . appears equivalent to the position of the literary knownothing, newly reinforced with a theory of discourse that reassures him that history-writing is bunk" (p. 182).

10. Jacques Derrida, "Limited Inc., abc . . ." in *Glyph* 2 (1977): 236. As Derrida goes on to say, "All metaphysicians, from Plato to Rousseau, Descartes to Husserl, have proceeded in this way, conceiving good to be before evil, the positive before the negative, the pure before the impure, the simple before the complex, the essential before the accidental, the imitated before the imitation, etc. And this is not just *one* metaphysical gesture among others, it is *the* metaphysical exigency, that which has been the most constant, most profound, and most potent" (ibid.).

11. Derrida, "Differance," in *Speech and Phenomena* (Evanston: Northwestern University Press, 1973), p. 147.

12. See Christopher Norris, *What's Wrong with Postmodernism: Critical Theory and the Ends of Philosophy* (Baltimore: The Johns Hopkins University Press, 1990).

13. Jonathan Culler, *On Deconstruction: Theory and Criticism after Structuralism* (Ithaca: Cornell University Press, 1982), p. 157.

14. As K. B. McFarlane said, "In his capable hands at least the medieval kingship betrayed no sign that age had brought fragility" ("Henry V, Bishop Beaufort and the Red Hat, 1417–21" [1945], reprinted in *England in the Fifteenth Century* [London: Hambledon, 1981], p. 79).

15. Charles Lethbridge Kingsford, *Henry V: The Typical Mediaeval Hero* (New York: Putnam's, 1901). Of course there have been negative accounts, including the fundamental work by J. H. Wylie and (for volume 3) William T. Waugh, *The Reign of Henry V*, 3 vols. (Cambridge: Cambridge University Press, 1914–29) and, more recently, Desmond Seward, *Henry V: The Scourge of God* (New York: Viking, 1988), but these are very much minority opinions.

16. Derek Pearsall, *John Lydgate* (London: Routledge and Kegan Paul, 1970); see also Pearsall's essay, "Chaucer and Lydgate," in Ruth Morse and Barry Windeatt, eds., *Chaucer Traditions: Studies in Honour of Derek Brewer* (Cambridge: Cambridge University Press, 1990), 39–53. The earlier attempts to present Lydgate as proto-humanist were by Walter F. Schirmer, *John Lydgate: A Study of the Culture of the XVth Century*, trans. Ann E. Keep (London: Methuen, 1961 [1952]), and Alain Renoir, *John Lydgate: Poet of the Transition* (London: Routledge and Kegan Paul, 1967).

17. I take the term "traditionalistic" from Stock, *Listening for the Text*, p. 165.

18. I have discussed the monarchical value of the Trojan myth in relation to Henry II in *Negotiating the Past: The Historical Understanding of Medieval Literature* (Madison: University of Wisconsin Press, 1987), pp. 201–4, and its relevance to Richard II in *Chaucer and the Subject of History* (Madison: University of Wisconsin Press, 1991), pp. 161–62. That Henry understood this value is also suggested by his possession of a deluxe copy of Chaucer's *Troilus and Criseyde*, a manuscript adorned with his coat of arms as Prince of Wales

(the Campsall MS). Henry commissioned the *Troy Book* from Lydgate in the spring of 1412, after his reconciliation with his father and his apparent acceptance of the fact that he would accede to the throne only by the natural process of inheritance: see McFarlane, *Lancastrian Kings and Lollard Knights* (Oxford: Clarendon Press, 1972), p. 110.

19. Elmham produced a *Liber Metricus de Henrico Quinto* in 1418 and Walsingham wrote a defense of Henry's conquest of Normandy, the *Ypodigma Neustriae* in 1419.

20. Pearsall, *John Lydgate*, p. 169. Johnstone Parr, "Astronomical Dating for Some of Lydgate's Poems," *PMLA* 67 (1952): 251–58, has dated the chronographia with which the *Siege* opens to April 27, 1421.

21. Robert W. Ayers, "Medieval History, Moral Purpose and the Structure of Lydgate's *Siege of Thebes*," *PMLA* 73 (1958): 463–74.

22. All citations from the *Siege of Thebes* are from the edition by Alex Erdmann and (for volume 2) Eilert Ekwall, 2 vols., EETS ES 108, 125 (London: Oxford University Press, 1911–30). I have omitted scribal slashes and editorial diacritical marks and have on occasion altered the punctuation. Immediately after Henry's death, and while the governing circle was trying to sort out the responsibilties of his brothers the dukes of Bedford and Gloucester in the governance of England and France, Lydgate wrote a prose treatise warning against disunity that took both its title—the *Serpent of Division*—and its inspiration from this passage in the *Siege*. His historical instance was in this case not the Theban legend but the Roman civil wars. See H. N. MacCracken, ed., *The Serpent of Division* (London: Oxford University Press, 1911). In the *Fall of Princes*, written between 1437 and 1450 for Duke Humphrey of Gloucester, the lesson of Thebes is that "kyngdamys deuyded may no while endure": Henry Bergen, ed., *Lydgate's Fall of Princes*, 4 vols. (Washington: Carnegie Institution, 1923–27), 1.105 (Book 1, line 3822).

23. Lois Ebin, *Illuminator, Makar, Vates: Visions of Poetry in the Fifteenth Century* (Lincoln: University of Nebraska Press, 1988), pp. 19–48, and the earlier studies cited there.

24. This account of Amphion is Lydgate's addition to his source: see *Siege*, 2:100–101.

25. The role of Amphion in the *Siege* and the privileging of the "word" over the "sword" is discussed by Ebin, *John Lydgate* (Boston: Twayne, 1985), pp. 53–55.

26. In "Chaucer, Lydgate, and the 'Myrie Tale,'" *Chaucer Review* 13 (1978–79): 316–36, Ebin provides a more benign assessment of Lydgate's revisions of Chaucerian values in the *Siege*. A different but not incompatible account to that presented here is provided by A. C. Spearing, "Lydgate's Canterbury Tales: *The Siege of Thebes* and Fifteenth-Century Chaucerianism," in Robert F. Yeager, ed., *Fifteenth-Century Studies* (Hamden, Conn.: Archon, 1984),

pp. 333–64; see also Spearing's *Medieval to Renaissance in English Poetry* (Cambridge: Cambridge University Press, 1985), pp. 66–88.

27. John Bowers, "The *Tale of Beryn* and the *Siege of Thebes*: Alternative Ideas of the *Canterbury Tales*," *SAC* 7 (1985): 45.

28. In the *Troy Book*—Lydgate's version of the *historia* that Chaucer had so romantically retold in *Troilus and Criseyde*—he is even more insistent upon his *trouthefulnesse* as a historian: see the discussion in C. David Benson, *The History of Troy in Middle English Literature* (Woodbridge: Brewer, 1980), pp. 97–129.

29. It should also be noted that in the Prologue, Lydgate corrects what he would have seen as the Chaucerian misrepresentation of monasticism in the *Canterbury Tales*: Lydgate's Host suggests that Lydgate's name might be "Dan Piers" (82), the name of Chaucer's corrupt Monk, but is firmly corrected: "My name was Lydgate, / Monk of Bery" (92–93). The Host quickly responds: "Daun Iohn, . . . wel broke ʒe ʒoure name!" (96).

30. For law and order, see Edward Powell, *Kingship, Law and Society: Criminal Justice in the Reign of Henry V* (Oxford: Oxford University Press, 1989), and E. F. Jacob, *The Fifteenth Century 1399–1485* (Oxford: Clarendon Press, 1961): "In Henry V's first parliament (15 May 1413), . . . the commons spoke emphatically about the weakness of the last reign, of disobedience to the laws, and the lack of public order" (p. 133). For Henry IV's household, see Given-Wilson, *Royal Household*, pp. 140–41.

31. J. Kail, ed., *Twenty-Six Political and Other Poems*, EETS OS 124 (London: Kegan Paul, Trench, Trübner, 1904), pp. 50, 54 (lines 5 and 129–30). The poem is also printed by Rossell Hope Robbins, ed., *Historical Poems of the XIVth and XVth Centuries* (New York: Columbia University Press, 1959), no. 15.

32. Kail, *Political Poems*, p. 58 (lines 105–6); for Beaufort's speech, see Kail's introduction, pp. xix–xx, and V. J. Scattergood, *Politics and Poetry in the Fifteenth Century* (London: Blandford, 1971), pp. 49–50. According to the speech, the purpose of the Leicester Parliament was to root out Lollardy, enforce maritime truces, and restore public order at home; see Edward Powell, "The Restoration of Law and Order," in G. L. Harriss, ed., *Henry V: The Practice of Kingship* (Oxford: Oxford University Press, 1985), p. 63.

33. Cited from MS Bodley 649 by R. M. Haines, "Church, Society and Politics in the Early Fifteenth Century, as Viewed from an English Pulpit," in Derek Baker, ed., *Church, Society and Politics*, Studies in Church History 12 (Oxford: Blackwell, 1975), p. 156 n. 94.

34. Thomas Hoccleve, "On Richard II's Burial at Westminster," in *Minor Poems*, ed. F. J. Furnivall, EETS ES 61 (London: Kegan Paul, Trench, Trübner, 1892), lines 1–2.

35. John Capgrave, *The Chronicle of England*, ed. F. C. Hingeston (London: Longman, Brown, Green, Longmans, and Roberts, 1858), p. 309.

36. Friedrich W. D. Brie, ed., *The Brut, or, The Chronicles of England*, pt. II, EETS OS 136 (London: Kegan Paul, Trench, Trübner, 1908), p. 376.

37. "Address to Sir John Oldcastle," in Furnivall, *Minor Poems*, lines 37–38.

38. Hoccleve, "Balade au Tres Noble Roy Henry Le Quint," in Furnivall, *Minor Poems*, lines 60, 64.

39. Brie, *Brut*, pp. 373–74.

40. Frank Taylor, ed., "The Chronicle of John Strecche for the Reign of Henry V (1414–1422)," *BJRL* 16 (1932): 149; Robbins, ed., *Historical Poems*, no. 95, lines 86–90; see also no. 64, lines 57–64.

41. "A Defence of Holy Church," in H. N. MacCracken, ed., *The Minor Poems of John Lydgate: Part 1*, EETS ES 107 (London: Oxford University Press, 1911), p. 34 (lines 96–97).

42. F. Taylor and J. S. Roskell, eds., *Gesta Henrici Quinti* (Oxford: Clarendon Press, 1975), p. 17. The provenance of the *Gesta* is discussed by the editors in their introduction and in "The Authorship and Purpose of the *Gesta Henrici Quinti*," *BJRL* 53 (1970–71): 428–64; *BJRL* 54 (1971–72): 223–40.

43. Cited from Rymer's *Foedera* by C. T. Allmand, *Lancastrian Normandy 1415–1450: The History of a Medieval Occupation* (Oxford: Clarendon Press, 1983), p. 123 n. 5. Henry's policy of repopulating the duchy with English men and women could also be justified in these terms: see Robert Massey, "The Land Settlement in Lancastrian Normandy," in A. J. Pollard, ed., *Property and Politics: Essays in Later Medieval English History* (Gloucester: Alan Sutton, 1984), p. 78.

44. This Henrician theme is discussed by virtually all modern historians; see, for example, Jacob, *The Fifteenth Century*, p. 123. In his "Introduction: The Exemplar of Kingship," G. L. Harriss points out that "Henry V presented himself not as the conqueror but as the heir and saviour of France, the very terms in which his father had claimed the crown of England" (1).

45. E. F. Jacob, *Henry V and the Invasion of France* (London: Hodder and Stoughton, 1947), p. 76.

46. Taylor and Roskell, *Gesta*, pp. 2/3, 58/59, 94/95.

47. C. L. Kingsford, ed., "Extracts from the First Version of Hardyng's Chronicle," *EHR* 27 (1912): 744; John Lydgate, *Troy Book*, ed. Henry Bergen, part III, p. 870. Schirmer argues that the central theme of the *Troy Book* is that "strife and discord are poison, the root of all trouble and disorder in every land. It is a motto for the times, as well as a timeless one, when Lydgate says, in connexion with the quarrel between the Greek commanders: 'Lo what meschef lyth in variaunce / Amonge lordis, whan þei nat accorde'" (*John Lydgate*, p. 49).

48. Similar to this argument is the oft-repeated claim that Henry was interested only in peace but that he could attain that goal only by war. On October 25, 1416, the anniversary of Agincourt, Bishop Beaufort preached to

Parliament on the theme, "Bella faciamus, ut pacem habeamus, quia finis belli, pax" (Allmand, *Lancastrian Normandy*, p. 7). See also Henry's letter to the citizens of London of August 5, 1419: "And forasmoch as our aduerse partie wol noo pees nor accord haue wiþ vs, but finally haue refused al meenes of pees, We be compelled ayein to werre thorough þair default, as he wot þat al knoweþ" (R. W. Chambers and Marjorie Daunt, eds., *A Book of London English* [Oxford: Clarendon Press, 1931], p. 78).

49. Laments that were translated into English later in the century when England began to suffer its own civil war: see Diane Bornstein, ed., *The Middle English Translation of Christine de Pisan's 'Livre de corps de policie'* (Heidelberg: Winter, 1977), and Margaret S. Blayney, ed., *Fifteenth-Century English Translations of Alain Chartier's Le Traité de l'Esperance and Le Quadrilogue Invectif*, 2 vols., EETS OS 270, 281 (London: Oxford University Press, 1974–80).

50. The French and Latin versions of the treaty are printed in Thomas Rymer, ed., *Foedera, Conventiones et Litterae*, 2d ed., 20 vols. (London, 1727–35), 9.895–904; the English version is in 9.916–20.

51. Henry himself used this familial language of inclusion and exclusion: in a letter of July 12, 1421 to the citizens of London, he contrasted "oure fader of Fraunce," and "oure . . . trusty, louyng, and faithful brother," the Duke of Burgundy, to "the saide pretense Daulphin" (Chambers and Daunt, *Book of London English*, p. 84). According to an English chronicler, the murder of Philip of Burgundy was committed by the dauphin "ffalsly and vntrely and ayenst alle maner Lawe off Armes" (Charles L. Kingsford, ed., *Chronicles of London* [Oxford: Oxford University Press, 1905], p. 73).

52. For an illuminating commentary on this often-remarked process, see Rodney Hilton, "Were the English English?" in Raphael Samuel, ed., *Patriotism: The Making and Unmaking of the British National Identity*, vol. 1: *History and Politics* (London: Routledge, 1989), pp. 39–43.

53. That both English and French nationalisms were state sponsored rather than spontaneously generated by the conditions of the war has been argued by Bernard Guenée, "État et nation en France au moyen âge," *Revue historique* 237 (1967): 17–30 (much of which is translated in his *States and Rulers in Later Medieval Europe* [Oxford: Blackwell, 1985], pp. 49–65), and especially by P. S. Lewis, "War Propaganda and Historiography in Fifteenth-Century France and England," *TRHS*, 5th ser. 15 (1965): 1–21; reprinted in *Essays in Later Medieval French History* (London: Hambledon Press, 1985), pp. 193–213. Lewis shows that the authors of the nationalist propaganda generated in France during the fifteenth century were in the service of the state and were speaking for very specific political and class interests. As he says, "No amount of patriotic special pleading can obscure the fact that the majority of Frenchmen were, as far as action went, at least apathetic about the identity of their ultimate ruler and even about his nationality" (7). For a specific instance of the state enforc-

ing national identity upon resistant individuals, see André Bossuat, "L'Idée de nation et la jurisprudence du Parlement de Paris au XVe siècle," *Revue historique* 204 (1950): 54–61.

54. *Gesta*, pp. 16/17; *Versus rhythmici de Henrico Quinto*, in Charles A. Cole, ed., *Memorials of Henry Fifth, King of England* (London: Longman, Brown, Green, Longmans, and Roberts, 1858), lines 851, 1019 (pp. 137, 146).

55. W. R. Jones, "The English Church and Royal Propaganda during the Hundred Years War," *Journal of British Studies* 19 (1979): 28, citing the *Foedera* and the *Register of John de Grandisson*.

56. Capgrave, *Chronicle*, pp. 314–15; *Brut*, p. 395; for another example, see B. J. H. Rowe, "A Contemporary Account of the Hundred Years' War from 1415 to 1429," *EHR* 41 (1926): 504–13.

57. Robbins, *Historical Poems*, nos. 15 and 27.

58. "A Ballade, in Despyte of the Flemynges," in *The Minor Poems of John Lydgate: Part 2, The Secular Poems*, ed. H. N. MacCracken and Merriam Sherwood, EETS OS 192 (London: Oxford University Press, 1934), pp. 600–601.

59. Here is an advertisement, from *The Telegraph* (London) of February 21, 2008, for a televised broadcast of a rugby match between England and France: "Will the English stick it to 'em and ruffle hair to victory, or will French guile be too much? Tune in and find out."

60. John H. Fisher, "Chancery and the Emergence of Standard Written English in the Fifteenth Century," *Speculum* 52 (1977): 870–99 (the citation is from 877); Malcolm Richardson, "Henry V, the English Chancery, and Chancery English," *Speculum* 55 (1980): 726–50; still useful is V. H. Galbraith, "Nationality and Language in Medieval England," *TRHS*, 4th ser. 23 (1941): 113–28.

61. Chambers and Daunt, *Book of London English*, p. 139; the Latin original is printed on p. 16.

62. That French *was* a truly foreign language to the English in the late fourteenth and early fifteenth century is clear from the fact that French had by then become an entirely official language, the only exception being the possibility of its occasional use for social intercourse in the court of Richard II. An expert account that corrects previous misconceptions is Rolf Berndt, "The Period of the Final Decline of French in Medieval England (Fourteenth and Early Fifteenth Centuries)," *Zeitschrift für Anglistik und Amerikanistik* 20 (1972): 341–69. Contemporary chroniclers have recorded many incidents that make it clear that by the end of the fourteenth century inhabitants of the two realms rarely understood each other, and that they considered language use to be a definitive mark of national identity. Froissart tells the story of a skirmish in 1380 between a French squire and two English men-at-arms, who urged him to surrender. Not understanding them, the Frenchman continued to fight until a Burgundian ally of the English arrived on the scene and repeated the offer

to surrender in French, which was immediately accepted. Although the English complained to their commander that the Burgundian had robbed them of their prisoner, he was allowed to keep the booty he had won with his linguistic abilities. Jean Froissart, *Chroniques*, ed. Gaston Raynaud, t. 9 (Paris: Renouard, 1894), pp. 258–59. In the *Brevis historia* Walsingham records a less pleasant incident, the killing in 1404 of French raiders by peasant women near Dartmouth because they could not understand them when they tried to surrender. Cited by L. Douët-d'Arcq, ed., *La Chronique de Monstrelet*, vol. 1 (Paris: Renouard, 1857), p. 81 n. 1. For language as a marker of identity, the Bourgeois de Paris says that in January 1433 a marauding band of French soldiers attacked a convoy of merchants and then killed all those "who wore an English emblem or spoke English" (Janet Shirley, trans., *A Parisian Journal, 1405–1449 [Journal d'un Bourgeois de Paris]* [Oxford: Clarendon Press, 1968], p. 288).

63. Cited by Kingsford, *Henry V*, p. 281 (see above, n. 15).

64. Froissart, *Oeuvres*, ed. Kervyn de Lettenhove, t. 15 (Brussels: Devaux, 1871), pp. 114–15; Sir John Bourchier, Lord Berners, trans., *The Chronicle of Froissart*, vol. 6 (London: David Nutt, 1903), pp. 113–14.

65. The documents in this case are printed in *Foedera*, 9.655–56.

66. The five Latin biographies are the *Gesta Henrici Quinti* (1416–17); Thomas Elmham, *Liber Metricus de Henrico Quinto* (to 1418: written shortly after the *Gesta*); Titus Livius Frulovisi, *Vita Henrici Quinti* (1437–38), commissioned by Humphrey of Gloucester; John Capgrave, *Liber de illustribus Henricis* (1444); and the Pseudo-Elmham, *Vita et Gesta Henrici Quinti* (1446–1551). As for the English lives, the section on Henry V found in the Common Version of the *Brut* was excerpted as a separate biography in BL MS Cotton Claudius A.viii and entitled "The chronicle of King Henrie ye fifte." While this is the only surviving life written in English there were probably others. The text edited by Charles Kingsford as *The First English Life of King Henry V* (Oxford: Clarendon Press, 1911) was based in part on Titus Livius but also upon a lost book by someone in the service of James Butler, the fourth earl of Ormond (d. 1452). Kingsford also thought that the abridgment of the Pseudo-Elmham life in Harley 530 was based on a fifteenth-century work written in English. There is also the English biography thought by Benedicta Rowe to have been written by Peter Basset: B. J. H. Rowe, "A Contemporary Account of the Hundred Years' War from 1415 to 1429," *EHR* 41 (1926): 504–13. For bibliography on most of these texts, see Edward Donald Kennedy, "XII: Chronicles and Other Historical Writing," in *A Manual of the Writings in Middle English 1050–1500*, gen. ed. Albert Hartung (New Haven: The Connecticut Academy of Arts and Sciences, 1989), item 10, 2629–37, 2818–33, and 2826–27.

67. See Antonia Gransden, *Historical Writing in England*, vol. 2: *c. 1307 to the Early Sixteenth Century* (London: Routledge and Kegan Paul, 1982): "No other medieval king of England was honoured with such an abundance of lit-

erature" (p. 196). See also Jacob, *Henry V*, pp. 185–86. Kingsford's judgment in his *Henry V*—that Henry was "the most English of our Plantagenet kings, heart and soul in sympathy with his subjects, marked out by nature to be the leader of a united nation" (p. 93)—is a theme taken up by almost all later biographers; see, for example, G. L. Harriss's 1985 account of Henry as responsible for the "liberation of the national spirit" ("Introduction," p. 28).

68. Henry's memory exerted a powerful nostalgic influence on the later fifteenth century, a period bereft of royal leadership. When in the 1440s an anonymous author was arguing for a shift in English maritime policy he harked back to Henry V: "To speke of hym I stony in my witte," he says, an astonishment evidently shared by many: George Warner, ed., *The Libelle of Englyshe Polycye* (Oxford: Clarendon Press, 1926), line 1047. This nostalgia is also visible in Malory's account of Arthur's continental campaign against the Emperor Lucius, which in significant respects recalls Henry's Agincourt campaign: see Eugene Vinaver, ed., *The Works of Sir Thomas Malory*, 2d ed., 3 vols. (Oxford: Clarendon Press, 1967), 3.1368, 1396–98. Henry's "personal magnetism" is one of the persistent themes of modern historians, affecting even the hard-to-impress K. B. McFarlane: "Take him all round and he was, I think, the greatest man that ever ruled England" (*Lancastrian Kings*, p. 133).

69. Jacob, *Fifteenth Century*, p. 123.

70. For the disorder of the French, with citations from contemporaries, see Wylie, *Reign of Henry the Fifth*, 2.199–200. A fascinating account of the battle by a leading military historian is John Keegan, *The Face of Battle: A Study of Agincourt, Waterloo and the Somme* (Harmondsworth: Penguin, 1978), pp. 78–116.

71. *Gesta*, pp. 110–13.

72. For the Lancastrian changes in the coronation ceremony, and especially the introduction of the holy oil of Canterbury, see J. R. Lander, *The Limitations of English Monarchy in the Later Middle Ages* (Toronto: University of Toronto Press, 1989), pp. 42–45, and C. T. Wood, "Queens, Queans and Kingship: An Inquiry into Theories of Royal Legitimacy in Late Medieval England and France," in W. C. Jordan, B. McNab, and T. F. Ruiz, eds., *Order and Innovation in the Middle Ages* (Princeton: Princeton University Press, 1976), pp. 387–400. The development of *lèse majesté* is discussed by Christopher Allmand, *The Hundred Years War: England and France at War c. 1300–c. 1450* (Cambridge: Cambridge University Press, 1988), pp. 148–50.

73. For this interpretation of the canopy, see Dorothy Styles and C. T. Allmand, "The Coronations of Henry VI," *History Today* 32 (May 1982): 32.

74. James Gairdner, ed., *Historical Collections of a Citizen of London in the Fifteenth Century*, Camden Society, 2d ser. 107 (London: Camden Society, 1876), pp. 29–30.

75. *Brut*, p. 410.

76. For Frulovisi, see McFarlane, *Lancastrian Kings*, p. 123; Capgrave, *Chronicle*, p. 303.

77. Jacob, *Henry V*, provides a judicious account (pp. 72–73). John Strecche, who is one of the primary sources for the story, contrasts the *verba fellis eructantes* of the French messengers with Henry's *verbis brevibus, discretis et honestis circumstantibus* (Taylor, "Chronicle of John Strecche," p. 150).

78. *Brut*, p. 378.

79. Distrust of loquaciousness and a belief that silence befits the strong is an English characteristic as early as the Anglo-Saxons. As the speaker of the *Wanderer* says, "I know for a fact / In an earl it is always a noble habit / To seal fast the soul's chest." These lines are translated and discussed by James W. Earl, "*Beowulf* and the Origins of Civilization," in Allen J. Frantzen, ed., *Speaking Two Languages: Traditional Disciplines and Contemporary Theory in Medieval Studies* (Albany: State University of New York Press, 1991), p. 76. See also below, chapter 7.

80. For this process, see G. L. Harriss, "The King and His Magnates," in Harriss, *Henry V*, pp. 31–51.

81. Powell, "Restoration of Law and Order," p. 64.

82. Ibid., p. 71.

83. That Henry possessed a disinterested sense of justice was recognized even by the French, although the war he waged in France was probably not in any significant respect less brutal than those of his predecessors. Accounts of Henry's campaigns that give due weight to the French experience are provided by Seward, *Henry V*, and especially by Wylie and Waugh, *The Reign of Henry V*. For Henry's military discipline, see Richard A. Newhall, *Muster and Review: A Problem of English Military Administration 1420–1440* (Cambridge, Mass.: Harvard University Press, 1940).

84. Jacob, *Henry V*, pp. 162–63.

85. McFarlane, *Lancastrian Kings*, p. 117.

86. Jeremy Catto, "Religious Change under Henry V," in Harriss, ed., *Henry V*, p. 111.

87. Capgrave, *Chronicle*, p. 309.

88. Jacob, *Henry V*, p. 135; and see Mervyn James, *English Politics and the Concept of Honour, 1485–1642*, *Past and Present*, Supplement no. 3 (Cambridge: Cambridge University Press, 1978).

89. Jeremy Catto, "The King's Servants," in Harriss, *Henry V*, pp. 31–51.

90. Kingsford, ed., *Chronicles of London*, p. 69.

91. As McFarlane says, with undisguised enthusiasm, "The age of the Crusade was over and that of world empires not begun. But it is possible to believe that Henry V might have bridged the gap that divides Napoleon from Godfrey de Bouillon, and have succeeded where Richard I and St. Louis had failed" (*Lancastrian Kings*, p. 125).

92. *Foedera*, 9.883. For the difficulty of recruitment, see the letter from the bishop of Norwich, Sir Thomas Erpingham, and John Wodehouse, Esq., to the Chancellor on March 22, 1419, explaining that despite all their efforts among the local gentry they "can nat gete on þat wol wiþ his gode will go" (N. H. Nicolas, ed., *Proceedings and Ordinances of the Privy Council of England* [London: HMSO, 1834], 2.246). See also Kingsford, *Henry V*, p. 341; Lander, *Limitations*, pp. 15–17; C. T. Allmand, *Henry V*, Historical Association Pamphlet 68 (London: The Historical Association, 1968), p. 21. A concern was also expressed in the counties that the war was draining them of the men required to fill county offices: Simon Payling, *Political Society in Lancashire England: The Greater Gentry in Nottinghamshire* (Oxford: Clarendon Press, 1991), p. 139.

93. J. L. Kirby, "Henry V and the City of London," *History Today* 26 (1976): 231.

94. A. K. McHardy, "Liturgy and Propaganda in the Diocese of Lincoln during the Hundred Years War," *Studies in Church History* 18 (1982): 224. McHardy goes on to say, "Such unwillingness to contribute, even without cost, to the war effort, is particularly noteworthy on the morrow of Agincourt when, we are led to believe, enthusiasm for Henry and his war was very strong among his people."

95. Jacob, *Henry V*, p. 162.

96. *Foedera*, 9.919.

97. That the Commons had reason to be anxious is suggested by a contemporaneous letter written by Henry that "we ben advised for to have oon Chauncellor, bothe for our matiers that we have adoo in this land [France], and also for England" (cited by J. W. McKenna, "Henry VI of England and the Dual Monarchy: Aspects of Royal Political Propaganda, 1422–1432," *JWCI* 28 [1965]: 153 n. 26).

98. A survey of this material is provided by McKenna, "Henry VI of England and the Dual Monarchy" (see n. 97).

99. "The Kings of England," in MacCracken and Sherwood, *Minor Poems: Part 2*, p. 716. For an important discussion of the textual history of this poem, and of its officially sponsored dissemination, see Linne R. Mooney, "Lydgate's 'Kings of England' and Another Verse Chronicle of the Kings," *Viator* 20 (1989): 255–89.

100. The picture survives in BL MS Royal 15. E.vi, a book of poems and romances presented to Margaret of Anjou on her marriage to Henry VI by John Talbot, earl of Shrewsbury. It is reproduced here by permission of the British Library.

101. Ernst H. Kantorowicz, *The King's Two Bodies: A Study in Mediaeval Political Theology* (Princeton: Princeton University Press, 1957), p. 57.

102. MacCracken and Sherwood, *Minor Poems, Part 2*, pp. 613–22; line numbers are included in the text.

103. In a "Roundel for the Coronation of Henry VI," (MacCracken and Sherwood, ibid., p. 622), Henry VI is advised to be like his father, "Stable in vertue, withoute variaunce" (11); in a "Ballade to King Henry VI Upon His Coronation" (pp. 624–30), Edward and Louis, Arthur and Charlemagne are brought together in the figure of Henry VI, a unification that is analogized to the "soþefast vnytee / Of three persones in þe Trynyte" (28–29): Henry makes it possible for the royal lines to be "Grounded in feyth, with-outen varyaunce" (31–32). In "King Henry VI's Triumphal Entry in London, 21 Feb., 1432" (pp. 630–48), the citizens wear white "To showe the trouthe that they dyd[e] mene / Toward the Kyng" (40–41), the king's French and English subjects are now at peace, "theyre hertes made both oon" (98), and Henry's genealogical descent is represented by the natural metaphor of the tree (398–404). See also in MacCracken, *Minor Poems: Part 1, Religious Poems*, a "Prayer to St. Edmund" (pp. 124–27) and "A Prayer for Henry VI, Queen, and People, 1429" (pp. 212–16).

104. The relevant documents are available in William Abel Pantin, ed., *Documents Illustrating the Activities of the General and Provincial Chapters of the Black Monks, 1215–1540*, vol. 2, Camden 3rd ser. 47 (London: Camden Society, 1933), pp. 98–134.

105. Roy M. Haines, "'Our Master Mariner, Our Sovereign Lord': A Contemporary View of Henry V," *Mediaeval Studies* 38 (1976): 85–96. Subsequent references are included in the text; the translations from the Latin are mine. I have accepted Haines's proposals on authorship and occasion. This sermon is also discussed and in part translated by G. R. Owst, *Literature and Pulpit in Medieval England* (Oxford: Basil Blackwell, 1961), pp. 70–75. For another sermon by Pauntley, see Patrick J. Horner, F.S.C., "John Pauntley's Sermon at the Funeral of Walter Frocester, Abbot of Gloucester," *American Benedictine Review* 28 (1977): 147–66.

106. For examples of bad behavior by Polynices, see Lydgate's description of the "pompous Surquedye" (1076) that motivated both brothers at the outset of their dispute, and then the "hegh pride" (1323) that led Polynices to battle Tydeus in the porch of Adrastus's palace. As for the Argives, their refusal to negotiate with the Thebans, their killing of a tame tiger—the event that sparks the war—and their refusal to listen to the warnings of Amphiorax (3811–12) indicate their culpability.

107. Useful guides to the Theban materials available to the Middle Ages are Leopold Constant, *La Légende d'Oedipe étudiée dans l'antiquité, au moyen âge et dans les temps modernes* (Paris: Maisonneuve, 1881), and Lowell Edmunds, *Oedipus in the Middle Ages* (Baltimore: The Johns Hopkins University Press, 1985).

108. I have offered a full reading of the poem in these terms, and a discussion of the medieval understanding of Thebes, in *Chaucer and the Subject of*

History (Madison: University of Wisconsin Press, 1991), pp. 47–164. See also above, chapter 4.

six.   The Heroic Laconic Style

1. *The Iliad*, trans. Robert Fagles (Harmondsworth: Penguin Books, 1991), p. 523. Achilles is speaking here to Lykaon, a Trojan youth who is pleading for his life.

2. Ann Savours, *Scott's Last Voyage* (London: Sidgwick and Jackson, 1974), pp. 155–56. Ironically, Capt. Oates's nickname was "Titus," perhaps in acknowledgment of just how very different he was from the tireless self-promoter of the seventeenth-century Popish Plot. A famous painting of Oates going to his death hangs in the Cavalry Club in London; it is entitled "A Very Gallant Gentleman."

3. See L. M. Hollander, "Litotes in Old Norse," *PMLA* 53 (1938): 1–33. The classic discussion for Germanic literature generally is Alfred Hübner, *Die "mhd. Ironie" oder die Litotes im Altdeutschen* (Leipzig: Mayer und Müller, 1930).

4. Denton Fox and Hermann Pálsson, trans., *Grettir's Saga* (Toronto: University of Toronto Press, 1974), p. 37.

5. Ibid., p. 95. Charles Boardman, when an undergraduate at Yale, pointed out to me that toward the end of Werner Herzog's film *Aguirre, Wrath of God* a Spanish soldier on a river raft is run through with a javelin thrown by an Indian hidden in the foliage; as he looks down at the growing bloodstain he remarks, "These long-arrows are so fashionable" and hastily expires. Herzog had evidently read Icelandic sagas.

6. The definition of litotes is cited from E. E. Kellett, *The Northern Saga* (London: L. and Virginia Woolf, 1929), p. 66, by Frederick Bracher, "Understatement in Old English Poetry," *PMLA* 52 (1937): 915–34 (933); on understatement in heroic poetry generally, see A. T. Hatto, "Towards an Anatomy of Heroic/Epic Poetry," in J. B. Hainsworth, ed., *Traditions of Heroic and Epic Poetry*, 2 vols. (London: Modern Humanities Research Association, 1989): "In the tenser heroic societies, words have the status of deeds. . . . Laconism and understatement flourish" (2.224).

7. All translations, which are my own unless otherwise noted, are from the edition by Frederick Klaeber, 3rd ed. (Boston: Heath, 1950). I have also consulted George Jack, ed., *Beowulf: A Student Edition* (Oxford: Clarendon Press, 1994), and the translations by Howell D. Chickering, Jr., *Beowulf: A Dual-Language Edition* (New York: Anchor Books, 1977), and E. Talbot Donaldson (New York: W. W. Norton, 1966). I am indebted throughout my discussion of *Beowulf* to the tutelage of Fred Robinson, although he is responsible for none of my conclusions.

8. Bracher, 921. See also R. Baird Schuman and H. Charles Hutchings II, "The *un*-Prefix: A Means of Germanic Irony in *Beowulf*," MP 57 (1960): 217–22, and A. Leslie Harris, "Litotes and Superlative in *Beowulf*," *English Studies* 69 (1988): 1–11.

9. Fred C. Robinson, *Beowulf and the Appositive Style* (Knoxville: University of Tennessee Press, 1985), pp. 4, 13, 18.

10. Ibid., pp. 11, 13–14.

11. J. R. R. Tolkien, "*Beowulf*: The Monsters and the Critics," *PBA* 22 (1936): 245–95; cited from Donald K. Fry, *The Beowulf Poet: A Collection of Critical Essays* (Englewood Cliffs: Prentice-Hall, 1968), p. 21.

12. Edward B. Irving, Jr., *A Reading of Beowulf* (New Haven: Yale University Press, 1968), p. 111. See also Stanley B. Greenfield, "Geatish History: Poetic Art and Epic Quality in *Beowulf*," *Neophilologus* 47 (1963): 211–17, reprinted in R. D. Fulk, *Interpretations of Beowulf: A Critical Anthology* (Bloomington: Indiana University Press, 1991): "In *Beowulf*, it would appear, history subsumes the hero as an individual" (p. 126).

13. Harry Berger, Jr. and H. Marshall Leicester, "Social Structure as Doom: The Limits of Heroism in *Beowulf*," in Robert B. Burlin and Edward B. Irving, Jr., eds., *Old English Studies in Honour of John C. Pope* (Toronto: University of Toronto Press, 1974), p. 53.

14. Ian Duncan, "Epitaphs for Æglæcan: Narrative Strife in *Beowulf*," in Harold Bloom, ed., *Beowulf: Modern Critical Interpretations* (New York: Chelsea House, 1987), pp. 111–30. "Grendel himself [is] a figure for that *ecghete/wælnið* [84–85] which is self-destructively built into the dynastic codes of exchange and inheritance. . . . Grendel is a scapegoat who externalizes the treachery and murder-bale of the community, and Beowulf cleanses (*fælsian*) Heorot in an act of exorcism. In other words, the relationship between the two narrative modes proposes itself as a dialectic, in which the monster fight represents the symbolic resolution of the historical contradictions of the social world. But (and this is where the poem is so powerful) such resolution remains only symbolic, and thus limited, as we are made aware early on: Grendel, the descendant of Cain, may be destroyed, but the real heritage of Cain, and indeed the heritage of the Fall and of the Creation which rhetorically 'awakens' him for the narrative, is the secret *ecghete* [sword-hate, hostility], historical necessity in the hearts of men, which remains inscribed within the order of things at Heorot" (pp. 113, 118).

15. I accept Klaeber's emendation of the ms *sendep* to *snedep*, but see Jack's note to the line for another view. On the theme of battle and feasting, see Chickering's commentary on this passage, p. 302, and James L. Rosier, "The Uses of Association: Hands and Feasts in *Beowulf*," *PMLA* 78 (1963): 8–14.

16. On the notorious crux of lines 168–69, see the notes by Klaeber and Jack with helpful bibliographies. Whatever interpretation is chosen, one must agree with Klaeber that "the passage appears singularly awkward"—a clumsiness that is perhaps a sign of the poet's ambivalent desire to leave Grendel

shrouded in mystery while nonetheless remaining loyal to the clarity of his own Christian worldview. A similar syntactical clumsiness appears in the passage describing Thrith (1931b–54), perhaps because it describes a situation in which men are put to death at the command of a woman.

17. I follow Jack and others in rejecting Klaeber's emendation of the ms reading "woroldrædenne" (1142b); see Jack's note to the line. On the bitter irony of Hildeburh's return to "her people," see Gillian R. Overing, "The Women of *Beowulf*: A Context for Interpretation," in Peter S. Baker, ed., *Beowulf: Basic Readings* (New York: Garland, 1995), pp. 235–36.

18. The "envelope" or "ring pattern" described here is a well-recognized principle of narrative structure in *Beowulf* and heroic poetry generally: see Adelaine Courtney Bartlett, *The Larger Rhetorical Patterns in Anglo-Saxon Poetry* (New York: Columbia University Press, 1935); H. Ward Tonsfeldt, "Ring Structure in *Beowulf*," *Neophilologus* 61 (1977): 443–52; and John D. Niles, "Ring Composition and the Structure of *Beowulf*," *PMLA* 94 (1979): 924–35.

19. We also remember that Beowulf later tells us that Hrothgar himself told wondrous tales of past heroics: "wrapped in age, the old warrior spoke of youth, strength in battle; the heart within surged when he, old in winters, recalled many things" (2111b–14).

20. See Laurence N. de Looze, "Frame Narratives and Fictionalization: Beowulf as Narrator," *Texas Studies in Language and Literature* 26 (1984): 145–56; reprinted in Fulk, *Interpretations of Beowulf*, pp. 242–50.

21. Linda Georgianna, "King Hrethel's Sorrow and the Limits of Heroic Action in *Beowulf*," *Speculum* 62 (1987): 842. Georgianna insists, however, that Beowulf himself does not "see the story in this way" (p. 842), and that the effect of the speech "is to force the audience to distance itself from the hero and the action of the narrative present" (p. 834). But why should we deny the speaker access to the meaning of what he says?

22. Translated by E. T. Donaldson from the edition by John C. Pope, *Seven Old English Poems* (1966) in the *Norton Anthology of English Literature*, 6th ed. (New York: W. W. Norton, 1993), 1.69.

23. D. S. Brewer, "Introduction" to *The Morte Darthur: Parts Seven and Eight* (Evanston: Northwestern University Press, 1970), pp. 12, 17.

24. James Eli Adams, *Dandies and Desert Saints: Styles of Victorian Masculinity* (Ithaca: Cornell University Press, 1995), pp. 89–90.

25. Ibid., p. 91.

26. Joseph Bizup, "Walter Pater and the Ruskinian Gentleman," *English Literature in Transition* 38 (1995): 54, 58. I am indebted to Prof. Bizup for sharing with me his thoughts, and bibliographical knowledge, on this topic.

27. All citations from the novel are from this edition, published in London by Dent.

28. Roger Lancelyn Green, *A.E.W. Mason* (London: Max Parrish, 1952), p. 91.

29. Ibid.

30. The use of a white feather as a sign of cowardice apparently derives from cockfighting, where having a white feather is a proof that the bird is not pure bred; see the *OED*, s.v.

31. Personal communication.

32. There are of course no end of examples of the crude jingoism and emotional vulgarity that the war generated, but one is especially relevant to our topic. In his introduction to *The Muse in Arms* (1917), an anthology of celebratory war poems, E. B. Osborn wrote: "The Germans and even our Allies cannot understand why this stout old nation persists in thinking of war as sport: they do not know that sportsmanship is our new homely name, derived from a racial predilection for comparing great things with small, for the *chevaleries* of the Middle Ages." The passage is cited by Mark Girouard, *The Return to Camelot: Chivalry and the English Gentleman* (New Haven: Yale University Press, 1981), p. 285.

33. *Drum* was based on a novel of the same name by Mason published in 1937; Korda also made *Fire Over England,* based on Mason's 1936 novel about the Spanish Armada.

34. See Jeffrey Richards, "Boy's Own Empire: Feature Films and Imperialism in the 1930s," in John M. MacKenzie, ed., *Imperialism and Popular Culture* (Manchester: Manchester University Press, 1986), pp. 140–64 (145).

35. Friedrich von Schiller, "On Simple and Sentimental Poetry" (1795), in Walter Jackson Bate, *Criticism: The Major Texts* (New York: Harcourt Brace Jovanovich, 1970), pp. 410–11. Ker's Hegelianism—admittedly somewhat uneasy—is defined in "On the Philosophy of Art," published in 1883 when he was 28: *Collected Essays,* ed. Charles Whibley (London: Macmillan, 1925), 2.234–71 (hereafter cited in the text as *CE*).

36. See *Hegel on Tragedy,* ed. Anne Paolucci and Henry Paolucci (Garden City, N.Y.: Anchor Books, 1962), p. 288.

37. *Past and Present,* ed. A. M. D. Hughes (1858), pp. 240, 48; cited by Hugh A. MacDougall, *Racial Myth in English History: Trojans, Teutons, and Anglo-Saxons* (Hanover, N.H.: University Press of New England, 1982), p. 95.

38. *On Modern Literature: Lectures and Addresses,* ed. Terence Spencer and James Sutherland (Oxford: Clarendon Press, 1955), pp. 261, 184, and 8n.

39. J. W. Burrow, *A Liberal Descent: Victorian Historians and the English Past* (Cambridge: Cambridge University Press, 1981), p. 102.

40. *Epic and Romance* (New York: Dover Books, 1957 [1897]), pp. 324, 349. Further references will be included in the text. Ker gives the argument for 1100 as the division between medieval and modern in fuller form in *The Dark Ages* (London: Thomas Nelson, 1955 [1904]), pp. 1–23.

41. Ker disliked *Beowulf* because of its episodic and banal plot of monster killing, and especially the vulgarity of the dragon-killing episode (the points against which Tolkien argued in his famous essay). Less well known, however,

because it is not cited by Tolkien (who draws from Ker's *The Dark Ages*, rather than *Epic and Romance*), is his objection to what he called "a turn for edification, [so that it] cannot stand as anything like a pure example of the older kind of heroic poetry" (pp. 87–88). He was thinking, evidently, of the passage that has come to be known as Hrothgar's sermon. For Ker, Germanic poetry develops "from a more archaic and repressed to a more developed and more prolix kind of narrative" (p. 90), and *Beowulf* represents the second of these kinds. "The plot of *Beowulf* is not more serious than that of a thousand easy-going romances of chivalry, and of fairy tales beyond all number" (p. 167). For Ker the true drama of character that *Beowulf* contained lay in the feuds that were, in his view, pushed to the edge of the poem by the monsters — hence Tolkien's argument resuscitating the monsters as poetically effective.

42. W. P. Ker, "On the History of the Ballads," read December 15, 1900, and reprinted in *Form and Style in Poetry: Lectures and Notes*, ed. R. W. Chambers (London: Macmillan, 1929), p. 28.

43. See, for example, Peter Hallberg, *The Icelandic Saga*, trans. Paul Schach (Lincoln: University of Nebraska Press, 1962).

44. Eugene Vinaver, *The Rise of Romance* (New York: Oxford University Press, 1971).

45. See Patricia A. Parker, *Inescapable Romance: Studies in the Poetics of a Mode* (Princeton: Princeton University Press, 1979).

46. For Plarr's comment, see R. K. R. Thornton, *The Decadent Dilemma* (London: Edward Arnold, 1983), p. 15.

47. Cited by Masao Miyoshi, *The Divided Self: A Perspective on the Literature of the Victorians* (New York: New York University Press, 1969), p. 318.

48. Miyoshi, *Divided Self*, pp. 327, 331.

49. Linda Dowling, *Language and Decadence in the Victorian Fin de Siècle* (Princeton: Princeton University Press, 1986), p. 144.

50. Cited by Thornton, *Decadent Dilemma*, p. 19.

51. For Pater's mode of composition, see Dowling, *Language and Decadence*, p. 120. Ker's lecturing style is described by Charles Whibley in his introduction to the *Collected Essays* and by R. W. Chambers in his preface to W. P. Ker, *Form and Style in Poetry*.

52. Ker's fullest discussion of the ballad can be found in "On the History of the Ballads" (see n. 42 above).

53. The literature on the topic is vast, but an excellent collection of recent essays is Victoria L. Bergvall, Janet M. Bing, and Alice F. Freed, eds., *Rethinking Language and Gender Research: Theory and Practice* (London: Longman, 1996).

54. These claims have been popularized by Deborah Tannen, *You Just Don't Understand: Women and Men in Conversation* (New York: William Morrow, 1990). Tannen's book is unusual among those in the genre in that it tries hard to be non-judgmental. A careful and empirically based critique of these

arguments is made by Alice F. Freed, "Language and Gender Research in an Experimental Setting," in Bergvall, Bing, and Freed, eds., *Rethinking Language and Gender Research*, pp. 54–76. Freed's conclusion is that the differences asserted by earlier research are in fact determined less by gender than by other variables. For a judicious and well-informed (if now somewhat dated) survey of these contentious issues, see Philip M. Smith, *Language, the Sexes and Society* (Oxford: Blackwell, 1985), pp. 135–68.

55. Jack W. Sattel, "The Inexpressive Male: Tragedy or Sexual Politics," *Social Problems* 23 (1976): 469–77; revised and reprinted as "Men, Inexpressiveness, and Power," in Barrie Thorne, Cheris Kramarae, and Nancy Henley, eds., *Language, Gender and Society* (Rowley, Mass.: Newbury House Publishing, 1983), pp. 118–24 (quotation at p. 122).

56. Jane Tompkins, *West of Everything* (New York: Oxford University Press, 1992), p. 63. Further citations will be included in the text.

57. For the eighteenth-century invention of this presumed medieval practice, see Alain Boureau, *The Lord's First Night* (Chicago: University of Chicago Press, 1998).

seven. Writing Amorous Wrongs

1. The first citation is from "Sunday Morning," the second from "Esthetique du Mal": *The Collected Poems of Wallace Stevens* (New York: Knopf, 1968), pp. 68, 322.

2. The importance of the form to Chaucer's poetry has been stressed by W. A. Davenport, *Chaucer: Complaint and Narrative* (Cambridge: D. S. Brewer, 1988).

3. According to C. L. Wrenn, "It might almost be said that in Old English the lyric mood is always the elegiac" (*A Study of Old English Literature* [London: Harrap, 1967], p. 140).

4. There are a number of partial accounts: see especially John Peter, *Complaint and Satire in Early English Literature* (Oxford: Clarendon Press, 1956) (primarily on complaints of the times); Monika Wodsak, *Die Complainte: Zur Geschichte einer französischen Populärgattung* (Heidelberg: C. Winter, 1985) (primarily on postmedieval complaints of the times); Götz Schmitz, *Die Frauenklage: Studien zur elegischen Verserzählung in der englischen Literatur des Spätmittelalters und der Renaissance* (Tübingen: Niemeyer, 1984); and Prajapati Prasad, "The Order of Complaint: A Study in Medieval Tradition," Ph.D. diss., University of Wisconsin, 1965. See also below, n. 26.

5. Howard, *The Three Temptations: Medieval Man in Search of the World* (Princeton: Princeton University Press, 1966).

6. Paul Zumthor, "De la circularité du chant," *Poétique* 2 (1970): 129–40; Roman Jakobson, *Selected Writings* (Paris: Mouton, 1971), 2.130–32.

7. Paul Zumthor, "A Reading of a *Ballade* by Jean Meschinot," in W. T. H. Jackson, ed., *The Interpretation of Medieval Lyric Poetry* (New York: Columbia University Press, 1980), p. 162. As Zumthor says: "The 'first person' has passed by this way. He fades away, departs along a road known only to himself, to the beyond. He is calm: he has played his part for a little while, on the stage where traditional discourses make their speeches, and also far behind the scenes, hidden in the opacity of the work which was in course of being created" (ibid.).

8. For the terms "emotive," "conative," and "referential," see Roman Jakobson, "Linguistics and Poetics," in Thomas A. Sebeok, ed., *Style in Language* (Cambridge, Mass.: MIT Press, 1960), pp. 350–77.

9. P. G. Walsh, ed. and trans., *Andreas Capellanus on Love* (London: Duckworth, 1982), p. 191. Even if we read the *complainte d'amour* politically, as a literary exercise designed to promote not the lover but the courtier, self-cancellation remains at its center. On the one hand the best courtier is the most eloquent (for medieval court culture, *facetus* is often synonymous with *curialis*); yet on the other, verbal facility can be both dangerous in itself and the sign of an untrustworthy personality (hence the courtly praise of taciturnity). See above, chapter 3.

10. See the variants given in Geoffrey Chaucer, *Troilus and Criseyde*, ed. B. A. Windeatt (London: Longmans, 1984), p. 111. All citations are from *The Riverside Chaucer*, 3rd ed., gen. ed. Larry D. Benson (Boston: Houghton Mifflin, 1987). I have upon occasion altered the punctuation of the printed text.

11. The two major discussions of the song are by Ernest H. Wilkins, "Cantus Troili," *ELH* 16 (1949): 167–73, and Patricia Thomson, "The 'Canticus Troili': Chaucer and Petrarch," *Comparative Literature* 11 (1959): 313–28.

12. "S'amor non è, che dunque è quel ch' io slento? / ma s' egli è amor, per Dio, che cosa et quale?" Robert M. Durling, ed. and trans., *Petrarch's Lyric Poems* (Cambridge, Mass.: Harvard University Press, 1976), pp. 270–71. I have changed Durling's translation of *per Dio* from "before God" to "by God."

13. Petrarch instead asked his emotions how they could "have such power over me if I do not consent to it." It seems clear that Chaucer changed Petrarch's assertion of the dominion of love to his own description of its inward presence because Petrarch's phrasing inadvertently invoked the very divinity of love that Troilus initially asserted but that he is now, in this second stanza, calling into question.

14. Jacques Derrida, "Ellipsis," in *Writing and Difference,* trans. Alan Bass (Chicago: University of Chicago Press, 1978), p. 295.

15. I have provided a detailed reading of the Theban myth and its impact on *Troilus and Criseyde* in *Chaucer and the Subject of History* (Madison: University of Wisconsin Press, 1991), pp. 75–78, 84–164.

16. See Richard Firth Green, *A Crisis of Truth: Literature and Law in Ricardian England* (Philadelphia: University of Pennsylvania Press, 1999).

17. An appreciation of just how original Chaucer's poem is can be gained by comparing it with the texts discussed by Benedetto Soldati, *La Poesia astrologica nel quattrocento: ricerche e studi* (Florence: Sansoni, 1906). Despite its thoroughness, Chaucerian scholarship has been unable to discover either sources or analogues for the poem, a fact that should encourage us to be innovative in our own interpretive efforts.

18. Shirley's comments have been reprinted by Eleanor Hammond, *Chaucer: A Bibliographical Manual* (New York: Macmillan, 1908), p. 384.

19. On conjunction and *copulatio*, see Chauncey Wood, *Chaucer and the Country of the Stars* (Princeton: Princeton University Press, 1970), p. 147.

20. For Boccaccio, see *Genealogia deorum Gentilium*, 3, 22–23, ed. Vincenzo Romano (Bari: Laterza, 1951), 1.142–52; for Bernardus, see *Commentum super sex libros Eneidos Virgilii*, as cited and translated by Earl G. Schreiber, "Venus in the Medieval Mythographic Tradition," *JEGP* 74 (1975): 522–23. For further on *Venus duplex*, see George D. Economou, "The Two Venuses and Courtly Love," in Joan M. Ferrante and G. D. Economou, eds., *In Pursuit of Perfection: Courtly Love in Medieval Literature* (Port Washington, N.Y.: Kennikat Press, 1975), pp. 17–50; and Richard Hamilton Green, "Alan of Lille's *De Planctu Naturae*," *Speculum* 31 (1956): 667–68 (on Eriugena's commentary on Martianus Capella).

21. For further descriptions of the benevolent binding and knitting accomplished by divine *amor*, see 2.v.50–51; 2.viii.13–14; 3.ix.18; 5.iii.16–17; and 5.1.92–99. I have cited the *Consolation* according to the system used by commentators on the Latin text, using Roman numerals for the meters and Arabic for the prose. The ambiguous value of the Boethian concept has been well explored by Stephen Barney, "Troilus Bound," *Speculum* 47 (1972): 445–58.

22. *Chaucer and the Country of the Stars*, pp. 107–11. For other negative readings of the conjunction of Mars and Venus, see Neil C. Hultin, "Anti-Courtly Elements in Chaucer's *Complaint of Mars*," *Annuale Medievale* 9 (1968): 58–75; and Melvin Storm, "The Mythological Tradition of Chaucer's *Complaint of Mars*," *PQ* 57 (1978): 323–35.

23. Trans. J. H. Mozley (Cambridge, Mass.: Harvard University Press, 1928), 1.473.

24. nam tu, sola potes tranquilla pace iuuare
    mortales, quoniam belli fera moenia Manors
    armipotens regit, in gremium qui saepe tuum se
    reicit aeterno deuinctus [recte: devictus] uulnere amoris.

    (1.31–34)

Ed. Richard Jahnke (Leipzig: Teubner, 1898), pp. 157–58; trans. W. H. D. Rouse (New York: Putnam's, 1931), p. 5.

25. In his important discussion, "Chaucer's *Broche of Thebes*: The Unity of 'The Complaint of Mars' and 'The Complaint of Venus,'" *Literary Monographs* 5 (1973): 3–60, 187–95, Rodney Merrill also notices the forensic nature of the complaint, but then argues, unconvincingly to my mind, that it is structured as a classically defined judicial oration.

26. Hultin, "Anti-Courtly Elements in Chaucer's *Complaint of Mars*," pp. 70–72; Merrill, "Chaucer's *Broche of Thebes*," pp. 38–39. According to Merrill, "This unfulfilled desire, this aching thirst for 'reste,' is the 'line' of love by which God may 'catch' his fish. Man's desire for the fleeting things of the world leads to suffering; but this 'myschaunce' may be the very best fortune possible, if it causes him to seek more lasting goods. This is a Christian commonplace: in Mars' complaint we are made to see the psychological realities upon which it is based" (p. 39). He provides the most complete reading of the poem—and of the *Complaint of Venus*, which he designates a companion piece—in these terms. As he says, "Ignorant of the redeeming Christ, Mars can only look forward to an eternity of desire and frustration. . . . But human lovers who are not bound to an endless repetition of their allotted spans may take from him a serious warning with regard to the lower passion which he laments" (p. 41).

27. Derrida, *Of Grammatology*, trans. Gayatri Spivak (Baltimore: The Johns Hopkins University Press, 1976), p. 145. Derrida later provides a brief account of the law of supplementarity that bears a striking relevance to the *Complaint of Mars*:

> Through the sequence of supplements a necessity is announced: that of an infinite chain, ineluctably multiplying the supplementary mediations that produce the sense of the very thing they defer: the mirage of the thing itself, of immediate presence, of originary perception. Immediacy is derived. That all begins through the intermediary is what is indeed "inconceivable [to reason]." (p. 157)

28. See Jacqueline Cerquiglini, "Le nouveau lyrisme (XIVe–XVe siècles)" in Daniel Poirion, ed., *Précis de littérature française du Moyen Age* (Paris: Presses universitaires de France, 1983), pp. 275–92; Michel Zink, *La subjectivité littéraire autour du siècle de saint Louis* (Paris: Presses universitaires de France, 1985), pp. 47–74.

29. A connection between Petrarch's *Rime* and contemporary French practice is suggested by Sylvia Huot, *From Song to Book: The Poetics of Writing in Old French Lyric and Lyrical Narrative Poetry* (Ithaca: Cornell University Press, 1987), pp. 331–32.

30. In "Chaucer's *Complaint*, A Genre Descended from the *Heroides*," *Comparative Literature* 19 (1967): 1–27, Nancy Dean claims that Chaucer's narrativization of complaint reveals the primacy of classical models; see also Edgar F. Shannon, *Chaucer and the Roman Poets* (Cambridge, Mass.: Harvard

University Press, 1929), pp. 15–47. On the other hand, James Wimsatt locates Chaucer's usage in relation to the contemporary French *dit amoureux:* "Guillaume de Machaut and Chaucer's Love Lyrics," *Medium Aevum* 47 (1978): 66–87, and "*Anelida and Arcite:* A Narrative of Complaint and Comfort," *Chaucer Review* 5 (1970–71): 1–8. These genetic explanations are of course not exclusive.

31. Paul de Man, "Lyric and Modernity," in *Blindness and Insight: Essays in the Rhetoric of Contemporary Criticism,* 2nd ed. (Minneapolis: University of Minnesota Press, 1983), p. 186.

eight. Genre and Source in *Troilus and Criseyde*

1. Henry Ansgar Kelly, *Ideas and Forms of Tragedy from Aristotle to the Middle Ages* (Cambridge: Cambridge University Press, 1993), shows the wide range of meanings that were attached to the word *tragedy* in the Middle Ages. Nonetheless, he is confident that "Chaucer's primary source for his understanding of tragedy was Fortune's rhetorical question in Boethius's *Consolation of Philosophy*" (Henry Ansgar Kelly, *Chaucerian Tragedy* [Cambridge: D. S. Brewer, 1997], p. 50).

2. *Boece,* Book 2, prosa 2, lines 67–72; all citations from Chaucer, except those from *Troilus and Criseyde,* are from Larry D. Benson, gen. ed., *The Riverside Chaucer* (Boston: Houghton Mifflin, 1987). Citations from *Troilus and Criseyde* are from *Troilus & Criseyde: A New Edition of "The Book of Troilus"* by B. A. Windeatt (London: Longman, 1984). The gloss derives from the *Commentary* on the *Consolation* by Nicholas Trevet: "Tragedia est carmen de magnis iniquitatibus a prosperitate incipiens et in adversitate terminans." Chaucer omits the phrase *de magnis iniquitatibus,* thus returning the definition of tragedy to a more authentic Boethian meaning, in which the tragic fall is an effect solely of the workings of Fortune, which afflicts all who live under her sway, regardless of their moral condition. Alastair Minnis, "Chaucer's Commentator: Nicholas Trevet and Boece," in Minnis, ed., *Chaucer's Boece and the Medieval Tradition of Boethius* (Cambridge: D. S. Brewer, 1993), pp. 83–166, believes that Chaucer did this purposefully. On the other hand, Kelly argues that Chaucer used a manuscript of the *Consolatio* that had only an incomplete set of glosses taken from Trevet's *Commentary,* an example being CUL MS Ii.3.21 (the "Coucher" manuscript), in which the gloss reads simply "Tragedia dicitur carmen de prosperitate incipiens et in adversitate terminans" (*Chaucerian Tragedy* p. 52).

3. The most egregious example of Procrustean torture is D. W. Robertson's influential "Chaucerian Tragedy," *ELH* 19 (1952): 1–37, but there are literally dozens of interpretations that take as given that the Boethian definition of tragedy is central to the meaning of the poem. A brief listing of some

of them can be found in Karla Taylor, *Chaucer Reads "The Divine Comedy"* (Stanford: Stanford University Press, 1989), p. 214 n. 6. To that list one can add Derek Brewer, "Comedy and Tragedy in *Troilus*," in Piero Boitani, ed., *The European Tragedy of Troilus* (Oxford: Clarendon Press, 1989), pp. 95–109; Henry Ansgar Kelly, *Chaucerian Tragedy*; and Christine Herold, *Chaucer's Tragic Muse: The Paganization of Christian Tragedy* (Lewiston, N.Y.: Edwin Mellen Press, 2003).

4. Alice R. Kaminsky, *Chaucer's Troilus and Criseyde and the Critics* (Athens: Ohio University Press, 1980), p. 83.

5. Since the knowledge gained by *intelligentia* is immediate and non-discursive—intelligence "byholdeth alle thingis . . . by a strook of thought formely withoute discours or collacioun" (5.4.192–93)—it cannot be remembered by the prisoner but only be made available to him by Lady Philosophy herself. Hence Book 5 is an explanation by Philosophy of how human free will can coexist with divine foreknowledge. God is able to foresee that which will happen in an eternal presentness that does not prescribe its happening. How can this be done? The answer is that God's mode of knowing is so different from ours that we cannot understand how it could be done.

6. An early analysis along these lines is R. E. Kaske, "The Knight's Interruption of the Monk's Tale," *ELH* 24 (1957): 249–68.

7. I agree with Ralph Hanna that Hengwrt's location of these instances at the end of the tale is more likely to represent Chaucer's intention than the order in Ellesmere, where they are located mid-tale: Ralph Hanna, *Pursuing History: Middle English Manuscripts and Their Texts* (Stanford: Stanford University Press, 1996), p. 151.

8. Of the many commentaries on Ugolino in the *Inferno*, those especially relevant to Chaucer's rewriting are Marianne Shapiro, "Addendum: Christological Language in *Inferno* XXXIII," *Dante Studies* 94 (1976): 141–43; Ronald B. Herzman, "Cannibalism and Communion in *Inferno* XXXIII," *Dante Studies* 98 (1980): 53–78; Robert Hollander, "Inferno XXXIII, 37–74: Ugolino's Importunity," *Speculum* 59 (1984): 549–55; John Freccero, *Dante: The Poetics of Conversion* (Cambridge, Mass.: Harvard University Press, 1986), pp. 152–66; Rachel Jacoff, "The Hermeneutics of Hunger," in Robert F. Yeager and Charlotte C. Morse, eds., *Speaking Images: Essays in Honor of V.A. Kolve* (Asheville, N.C.: Pegasus Press, 2001), pp. 95–110; and Giuseppe Mazzotta, "*Inferno*: The Language of Fraud in Lower Hell," in Cormac Ó Cuilleanáin and Jennifer Petrie, eds., *Patterns in Dante: Nine Literary Essays* (Portland: Four Courts Press, 2005).

9. For Chaucer's revisions, see Piero Boitani, "The 'Monk's Tale': Dante and Boccaccio," *Medium Aevum* 45 (1976): 50–69; O. Rokutanda, "L'episodio dantesco del conte Ugolino in Chaucer," *Studi Italici* 35 (1986): 1–14; Richard Neuse, *Chaucer's Dante: Allegory and Epic Theater in* The Canterbury Tales

(Berkeley: University of California Press, 1991), pp. 140–200; Helen Cooper, "The Four Last Things in Dante and Chaucer: Ugolino in the House of Rumour," *New Medieval Literatures* 3 (1999): 39–66.

10. For different versions of this critique of the Monk's Tale, see Derek Pearsall, *The Canterbury Tales* (London: George Allen and Unwin, 1985), pp. 279–85; Jahan Ramazani, "Chaucer's Monk: The Poetics of Abbreviation, Aggression, and Tragedy," *Chaucer Review* 27 (1993): 260–76; and Piero Boitani, *The Tragic and the Sublime in Medieval Literature* (Cambridge: Cambridge University Press, 1989), pp. 20–55.

11. Walter W. Skeat, ed., *The Complete Works of Geoffrey Chaucer,* vol. 5 (Oxford: Clarendon Press, 1900), pp. 226–27. Skeat's observation is discussed by Kelly, *Chaucerian Tragedy,* who claims that Chaucer thought of Latin epics as tragic because some have unhappy episodes (*Chaucerian Tragedy,* pp. 61–62).

12. The connection goes back to Aristotle's *Poetics.* While alert to the differences of form and mode between drama and narrative, Aristotle notes a similarity of content: "Epic poetry agrees with tragedy in so far as it is an imitation in verse of characters of a higher type." S. H. Butcher, trans., *Aristotle's Theory of Poetry and Fine Art,* 4th ed. (New York: Dover, 1955), section 5.

13. *Etymologiae* 8.7.6 (*PL* 82.308) and 18.45.1 (*PL* 82.658). Isidore does add, in a gesture toward the drama, that tragedies were sung "while the people looked on" (*spectante populo concinebant*).

14. A. J. Minnis and A. B. Scott, eds., *Medieval Literary Theory and Criticism c. 1100–c. 1375: The Commentary Tradition,* rev. ed. (Oxford: Clarendon Press, 1991), p. 23.

15. Kelly, *Ideas and Forms of Tragedy,* p. 138. For other examples of medieval writers who define tragedy as describing historical events, see pp. 131 (Nicholas Trevet), 151 (Jacopo Alighieri), 153 (Pietro Alighieri), 155 (Benvenuto da Imola), 161 (an anonymous French translation of the *Consolation,* made in the early fourteenth century, which illustrates Boethius's comment about tragedies by reference to the *chansons de geste*) and 162 (Renaut de Louhans, who also gives as examples of tragedies *chansons de geste*).

16. Minnis and Scott, eds., *Medieval Literary Theory,* pp. 63, 61.

17. For Servius and Isidore, see Kelly, *Ideas and Forms of Tragedy,* pp. 83 and 115; for Arnulf, see Minnis and Scott, eds., *Medieval Literary Theory,* p. 155. For a full account of Servius's understanding of *historia,* see David B. Dietz, "*Historia* in the Commentary of Servius," *Transactions of the American Philosophical Association* 125 (1995): 61–97.

18. For Bernard Silvestris, see Maura K. Lafferty, *Walter of Châtillon's Alexandreis: Epic and the Problem of Historical Understanding* (Turnhout: Brepols, 1998), p. 45; for Alexander Neckham, see David Anderson, *Before the Knight's Tale: Imitation of Classical Epic in Boccaccio's Teseida* (Philadelphia: University of Pennsylvania Press, 1988), p. 148.

19. See *Seniles* 18.1 in James Harvey Robinson and Henry Winchester Rolfe, ed. and trans., *Petrarch, the First Modern Scholar and Man of Letters: A Selection from His Letters,* 2d ed. (New York: Knickerbocker Press, 1898), p. 70.

20. Almost all the early commentaries and many later ones can be accessed on the internet at the Dartmouth Dante Project. This specific citation appears in the Proemio to this commentary. The URL is http://dante.dartmouth .edu/search_view.php?doc=140051010000&cmd=gotoresult&arg1=0.

21. *Inferno,* trans. Allen Mandelbaum (New York: Bantam Books, 1982).

22. A good reading of the cantos in these terms is provided by C. J. Ryan, "*Inferno* XXI: Virgil and Dante, A Study in Contrasts," *Italica* 59 (1982): 16–31.

23. Minnis and Scott, eds., *Medieval Literary Theory,* p. 481.

24. Cited by Wilhelm Cloetta, *Beiträge zur Litteraturgeschichte des Mittelalters und der Renaissance,* 1: *Komödie und Tragödie im Mittelalter* (Halle: Niemeyer, 1890), p. 28.

25. Cited ibid., p. 34.

26. These definitions come, respectively, from Donatus, Isidore, and Lactantius Placidus; all are cited from Cloetta, pp. 28, 19, and 21.

27. An account of Dante's fascination with the individual is nowhere more persuasively or eloquently expressed than in Erich Auerbach, *Dante: Poet of the Secular World,* trans. Ralph Manheim (Chicago: University of Chicago Press, 1961 [1929]).

28. For the ways in which the *Canterbury Tales* fit medieval definitions of comedy, see Patterson, *Chaucer and the Subject of History* (Madison: University of Wisconsin Press, 1991), pp. 242–43. After completing this essay I discovered that the definition of Chaucer's *tragedye* as history, and the connection to Dante, is also discussed by Vincent Gillespie, "From the Twelfth Century to c. 1450," in Alastair Minnis and Ian Johnson, eds., *The Cambridge History of Literary Criticism,* vol. 2: *The Middle Ages* (Cambridge: Cambridge University Press, 2005), pp. 206–23.

29. Karl Young, "Chaucer's *Troilus and Criseyde* as Romance," *PMLA* 53 (1938): 38–63; Charles Muscatine, *Chaucer and the French Tradition* (Berkeley: University of California Press, 1957), p. 132; Barry Windeatt, *Troilus and Criseyde,* Oxford Guides to Chaucer (Oxford: Clarendon Press, 1992), pp. 138–79; Roy J. Pearcy, "'And Nysus doughter song with fressh entente': Tragedy and Romance in Troilus and Criseyde," *SAC* 24 (2002): 269–97; Corinne Saunders, "Chaucer's Romances," in Saunders, ed., *A Companion to Romance: From Classical to Contemporary* (Malden, Mass.: Blackwell, 2004), pp. 85–103.

30. This includes, alas, my own account in *Chaucer and the Subject of History,* pp. 104–14.

31. See the Middle English Dictionary, s.v. *romance,* 3.

32. See Rita Copeland, "Between Romans and Romantics," *Texas Studies in Literature and Language* 33 (1991): 215–24.

33. Paul Strohm, "*Storie, Spelle, Geste, Romaunce, Tragedie:* Generic Distinctions in the Middle English Troy Narratives," *Speculum* 46 (1971): 348–59.

34. Strohm shows that medieval discussions of romances witness to the assumption that they "deal with the deeds of a notable hero" (ibid., p. 355). As Jennifer Fellowes points out, "The modern connotations of the term 'romantic' might lead us to expect that love between the sexes is the primary focus of these narratives, but this is not normally the case. . . . This is not to say that love and marriage do not play an important part in most romances, but usually they subserve other themes such as the hero's growth to maturity . . . or are seen in relation to knightly prowess, honour . . . and loyalty" ("Introduction" in *Of Love and Chivalry: An Anthology of Middle English Romance*, ed. Fellowes [London: J. M. Dent, 1993], p. vi).

35. The first use of romance as signifying either an erotic event or—as an adjective—an erotic emotion that I have found occurs in George Meredith's *Diana of the Crossways* (1885), where Diana rather unkindly compares Thomas Redworth, the good man who has always loved her, to Lord Dannisburgh, the wicked but oh-so-exciting man who has nearly ruined her:

> Her hope of some last romance in life was going; for in him [Redworth] shone not a glimpse. He appeared to Diana as a fatal power, attracting her without sympathy, benevolently overcoming: one of those good men, strong men, who subdue and do not kindle. The enthralment revolted a nature capable of accepting subjection only by burning. . . . She could not now say she had never been loved; and a flood of tenderness rose in her bosom, swelling from springs that she had previously reproved with a desperate severity: the unhappy, unsatisfied yearning to be more than loved, to love.

In the OED, the first mention of *romance* as erotic is from George Bernard Shaw's 1912 play *Overruled*, in a hilarious scene where a young married man is trying to seduce a young married woman. He explains:

> To my English mind, passion is not real passion without guilt. I am a red-blooded man, Mrs. Lunn: I can't help it. The tragedy of my life is that I married, when quite young, a woman whom I couldn't help being very fond of. I longed for a guilty passion—for the real thing—the wicked thing; and yet I couldn't care twopence for any other woman when my wife was about. Year after year went by: I felt my youth slipping away without ever having had a romance in my life; for marriage is all very well; but it isn't romance.

My survey of nineteenth-century novels would have been impossible without the remarkable website http://victorian.lang.nagoya-u.ac.jp/concordance.html, where one can search concordances for a huge number of English language literary works, including some medieval ones.

36. C. S. Lewis, "What Chaucer Really Did to *Il Filostrato*," *Essays and Studies* 17 (1932): 56–75; reprinted in Richard J. Schoeck and Jerome Taylor, eds., *Troilus and Criseyde and the Minor Poems* (Notre Dame: University of Notre Dame Press, 1961), p. 19.

37. David Wallace, *Chaucer and the Early Works of Boccaccio* (Cambridge: D. S. Brewer, 1985), p. 176 n. 59. Commenting on the work of Maria Gozzi, "Sulle fonti del *Filostrato*: Le narrazione di argomento troiano," *Studi sul Boccaccio* 5 (1968): 123–209, Wallace says: "She finds that no single text may be identified as Boccaccio's source; this accords with her earlier observation that 'in design, in tone and even in size the *Filostrato* is a work that is very different from medieval narratives ("storie") of Troy.' . . . It appears, then, that Boccaccio read widely in Trojan matters, appropriating details not to create a consistent, historical account but to serve his own, highly individual purpose. . . . The Trojan material simply seems to have served Boccaccio as a pretext for the exploration of his own literary interests; he was not touched by the reverential respect with which Chaucer and other mature medieval poets approached the matter of Troy" (p. 74).

38. *Il Filostrato*, ed. Vincenzo Pernicone, trans. Robert P. apRoberts and Anna Bruni Seldis (New York: Garland Publishing, 1986), p. 168.

39. In his edition (see n. 2 above) Windeatt points out that this description is found in *Metamorphoses* 2.153–54; for scribal stumbles, see the list of variants Windeatt provides.

40. An excellent account of the *cantare* and Boccaccio's transformation of this popular form into a culturally more ambitious poem is provided by Wallace, *Chaucer and the Early Writings of Boccaccio*, pp. 76–95. Wallace usefully compares the Italian *cantare* to the English metrical romance as a mediator of courtly values to a nonaristocratic audience.

41. There were for the Middle Ages two versions of the Troy story. One was Virgil's account, which provided Geoffrey of Monmouth the inspiration for his brilliant fabrication, the *History of the Kings of Britain*, with King Arthur more or less playing the role of Aeneas. The other was Benoît de Saint-Maure's *Roman de Troie*, given its authoritative form in Guido delle Colonne's Latin prose translation. At first sight, the two narratives seem incompatible: Geoffrey's Virgilian view of history is presumably about the rise of an imperial future upon the ruins of the past, while the Benoît-Guido account is a tale of disaster. But in fact both narratives share a common interest in the instability of the very foundations of history that they are meant to establish. In Geoffrey's work this instability is symbolized by Vortigern's tower, which collapses after each rebuilding because two dragons are fighting in a pool beneath it—a succinct expression of the internecine warfare that was

occurring in Geoffrey's contemporary world and that continued to bedevil England throughout the Middle Ages. In the Benoît-Guido version—which was the source of the English Troy poems of the fourteenth and fifteenth centuries—the problem of origins is expressed through the multiplicity of causes that are invoked to explain the war. I have discussed Geoffrey's conception of the self-defeating nature of British history in *Negotiating the Past: The Historical Understanding of Medieval Literature* (Madison: University of Wisconsin Press, 1987), pp. 200–202. For a more detailed discussion of the Trojan material, see Francis Ingledew, "The Book of Troy and the Genealogical Construction of History: The Case of Geoffrey of Monmouth's *Historia regum Britanniae*," *Speculum* 69 (1994): 665–704, and James Simpson, "The Other Book of Troy: Guido delle Colonne's *Historia destructionis Troiae* in Fourteenth and Fifteenth-Century England," *Speculum* 73 (1998): 397–423.

42. A precedent for Chaucer's strategy here is Benoît's *Roman de Troie*, in which four love affairs are interspersed between scenes of violence: between Jason and Medea, Paris and Helen, Achilles and Polyxena, and Troilus and Briseida. These interludes offer themselves as explanatory glosses on the larger historical action, although in fact they explain little.

43. As Windeatt points out in his note to this line, "Pandarus's words echo Christ's in Luke 8.48 and 18.42." The anachronism of this allusion makes the echo all the more relevant to Chaucer's audience.

44. In the *Filostrato* it is Troiolo who describes Criseida's virtues; see Windeatt's note to these lines.

45. I have stressed the degree to which Chaucer saturates his poem with allusions to the story of Thebes, and the meaning of such allusions, in *Chaucer and the Subject of History*, pp. 129–36 and passim.

46. Richard Firth Green, *A Crisis of Truth: Literature and Law in Ricardian England* (Philadelphia: University of Pennsylvania Press, 1999), pp. 24–31.

47. Calliope is invoked, for instance, by Virgil (*Aeneid* 9.525) and by Statius (*Thebaid* 4.35 and 8.374), and in one of Statius's *Sylvae* (almost certainly not known by Chaucer) he has Calliope predict a career that will reach its apotheosis in an epic (2.7).

48. George Kane, *The Liberating Truth: The Concept of Integrity in Chaucer's Writings: The John Coffin Memorial Lecture* (London: Athlone Press, 1980), p. 12; see Green, *A Crisis of Truth*, p. 4.

49. Lewis, "What Chaucer Really Did to *Il Filostrato*," 75.

50. Romans 7.15–17.

51. And in Book 5 Chaucer actually leaves out a substantial amount of Boccaccio's poem, especially Troiolo's laments for the absent Criseida, whereas in the earlier books he excludes very little of the *Filostrato*, preferring to rewrite what he finds inappropriate to his purposes.

52. E. Talbot Donaldson, *Speaking of Chaucer* (London: Athlone Press, 1970), p. 91.

nine.   "Rapt with Pleasaunce"

1. My text of the *Aeneid* is that edited by R. D. Williams, 2 vols. (London: Macmillan, 1972–73); the translations are my own, but I have not hesitated to appropriate the wording provided by Allen Mandelbaum (New York: Bantam Books, 1971), C. Day Lewis (Garden City: N.Y. Doubleday, 1953), or W. F. Jackson Knight (Harmondsworth: Penguin, 1956), as well as that suggested by Williams in his notes.

2. This is Williams's translation.

3. On the ecphrasis as expressing the immortality conferred by art, see Adam Parry, "The Two Voices of Vergil's *Aeneid*," *Arion* 2 (1963): 66–80, and for a critique, W. R. Johnson, *Darkness Visible: A Study of Vergil's Aeneid* (Berkeley: University of California Press, 1976), pp. 99–105.

4. On the pictures themselves, see R. D. Williams, "The Pictures on Dido's Temple," *Classical Quarterly*, n.s. 10 (1960): 145–51, and J. Romeuf, "Les Peintures du temple de Carthage (*Enéide* 1.466–493)," *Annales Latini Montium Avernorum* 2 (1975): 15–27.

5. *Faerie Queene*, 6.9.17. Helpful guidance to the topic of ecphrasis is provided by Frederick Goldin, *The Mirror of Narcissus in the Courtly Love Lyric* (Ithaca: Cornell University Press, 1967), and Robert Morrissey, "Vers un topos littéraire: La préhistoire de la rêverie," *MP* 77 (1979–80): 261–90. Murray Krieger, *Ekphrasis: The Illusion of the Natural Sign* (Baltimore: The Johns Hopkins University Press, 1992), and Gottfried Boehm and Helmut Pfotenhauer, eds., *Beschreibungskunst, Kunstbeschreibung: Ekphrasis von der Antike bis zur Gegenwart* (Munich: W. Fink, 1995), appeared after this essay was written.

6. Ed. L. Bieler, Corpus Christianorum Series Latina 94 (Turnhout: Brepols, 1957). Translations are my own, with help from V. E. Watts (Harmondsworth: Penguin, 1969) and Richard Green (Indianapolis: Bobbs-Merrill, 1962).

7. On the Neoplatonic sources of this meter, see Joachim Gruber, *Kommentar zu Boethius De Consolatione Philosophiae* (Berlin: Walter de Gruyter, 1978), ad loc.

8. Ed. William Roach, Textes Littéraires Français 71 (Geneva: Droz, 1959); translations are my own.

9. Lines 4164–4212. This famous scene, well known even in the Middle Ages (see, e.g., *Durmart le Gallois*, lines 3655 ff.), has received a multitude of modern commentaries, of which the most notable are: Daniel Poirion, "Du Sang sur la neige: Nature et fonction de l'image dans le *Conte du Graal*," in R. J. Cormier, ed., *Voices of Conscience* (Philadelphia: University of Pennsylvania Press, 1977), pp. 143–65; Trude Ehlert and Gerhard Meissburger, "Perceval et Parzival: Valeur et fonction de l'épisode dit 'des trois gouttes de sang sur la neige,'" *Cahiers de civilisation médiévale* 71–72 (1975): 197–227; Joël Grisward, "Com ces

trois goutes de sanc furent qui sor le blanc noif parurent: Note sur un motif lit-téraire," in *Etudes de Langue et littérature du moyen âge offertes à Felix Lecoy* (Paris: H. Campion, 1973), pp. 157–64; Grace Armstrong, "The Scene of the Blood Drops on the Snow: A Crucial Narrative Moment in the *Conte du Graal*," *Kentucky Romance Quarterly* 19 (1972): 127–47; Susan Potters, "Blood Imagery in Chrétien's *Perceval*," *PQ* 66 (1977): 301–9. A closely analogous scene occurs in *Guillaume d'Angleterre*, uncertainly ascribed to Chrétien, where the protagonist proceeds "an veillant . . . a songier" (ed. W. Foerster [Halle: Niemeyer, 1899], 1.2600) and enjoys a vision that links past to future; see Morrissey, "Vers un topos littéraire," 266–68.

   10. On Perceval's trance as characteristic of the troubadours' *amor de lonh*, see Peter Haidu, *Aesthetic Distance in Chretien de Troyes* (Geneva: Droz, 1968), pp. 188–92; Herbert Kolb, "Die Blutstropfen-Episode bei Chretien und Wolfram," *Beitrage zur Geschichte der deutschen Sprache and Literatur* 79 (1957): 363–79, and Erich Köhler's response, "Die drei Blutstropfen im Schnee," *Germanisch-Romanische Monatschrift* 40 (1959): 421–25. The topos of the amorous trance is discussed by Alberto del Monte, "'En Durmen Sobre Chevau,'" *Filologia Romanza* 2 (1955): 140–47; D. R. Sutherland, "The Love Meditation in Courtly Literature," in *Studies in Medieval French Literature Presented to Alfred Ewert* (Oxford: Clarendon Press, 1961), pp. 165–93; and Elspeth Kennedy, "Royal Broodings and Lovers' Trances in the First Part of the Prose *Lancelot*," in *Mélanges de Philologie et de littératures romanes offerts à Jeanne Wathelet-Willem* (Liège: Marche Romane, 1978), pp. 301–14.

   11. The details of this repetition have been well described by Haidu, *Aesthetic Distance*, pp. 203–50.

   12. In the early-thirteenth-century *Perlesvaus*, Gauvain is distracted from the Grail procession by the beauty of one of the three damsels in attendance and fails to notice the three drops of blood that have fallen onto the white cloth of the altar. In their notes to this passage, the editors of the *Perlesvaus*, William A. Nitze and T. Atkinson Jenkins, suggest that "the three drops of blood are probably a symbol of the Trinity" and cite a passage from Gregory of Tours, *Libri Miraculorum* (PL 71:718) that describes the appearance of three blood drops during the celebration of the mass (*Le Haut Livre du Graal Perlesvaus* [Chicago: University of Chicago Press, 1932–37], 2.273).

   13. A point stressed by Armstrong, "Scene of the Blood Drops," 139–40, and by Pierre Gallais, *Perceval et l'Initiation* (Paris: Sirac, 1972), p. 166.

   14. *Études sur La Queste del Saint Graal* (Paris: H. Champion, 1921), p. 45.

   15. For an earlier suggestion of the link between this scene and the Grail romances, see Gallais, *Perceval et l'Initiation*, p. 119 n. 10, who refers to the scene of Gauvain at the Grail Castle in the *Perlesvaus* (see n. 12). References to other of Chrétien's romances, and to Arthurian parallels in general, are made by André Pézard, "Le Chevalier de la charrette et la dame du char," in *Studi in onore*

di Vittore Lugli e Diego Valeri (Venice: Neri Pozza, 1961), 2.733–63; Pio Rajna, "Dante e i Romanzi della Tavola Rotonda," *Nuova Antologia*, ser. 6, 206 (1920): 223–47; and Paget Toynbee in his *Dante Studies and Researches* (London: Methuen, 1902), pp. 1–37.

16. In my translations from Dante I have relied upon the version by John D. Sinclair (New York: Oxford University Press, 1961), corrected with reference to that by Charles S. Singleton (Princeton: Princeton University Press, 1970–75).

17. There are important parallels between Dante's entrance into the Earthly Paradise and the lover's entrance into the garden of Deduit in the *Roman de la Rose*: both gardens are preceded by an account of those who are excluded, both initiates must wash before entering, and of course both are paradises that contain the beloved. As the *Roman de la Rose* says, "Il n'est nus graindres parevis / D'avoir amie a son devis" (ed. F. Lecoy [Paris: H. Champion, 1965], 1, lines 1299–1300).

18. Charles S. Singleton, *Dante's Commedia: Elements of Structure* (Cambridge, Mass.: Harvard University Press, 1954), pp. 45–53.

19. For discussions especially relevant to my argument here, see Robin Kirkpatrick, *Dante's "Paradiso" and the Limitations of Modern Criticism* (Cambridge: Cambridge University Press, 1978), which usefully reviews the Italian debate; Charles S. Singleton, "The Irreducible Vision," in *Illuminated Manuscripts of the Divine Comedy*, by Peter Brieger, Millard Meiss, and Charles S. Singleton (Princeton: Princeton University Press, 1969), 1.1–29; and Marguerite Mills Chiarenza, "The Imageless Vision and Dante's *Paradiso*," *Dante Studies* 90 (1972): 77–91.

20. Francis X. Newman, "St. Augustine's Three Visions and the Structure of the *Commedia*," *MLN* 82 (1967): 56–78.

21. See also the use of this same image in *Paradiso* 33, where Dante describes how he is no longer able fully to recompose the final, ineffable vision: "Thus the snow loses its imprint in the sun" (64) or literally "unseals itself" (*si disigilla*).

22. All citations are from Alastair Fowler's edition of *Paradise Lost* (London: Longmans, 1971).

23. On Milton and romance, see Barbara Lewalski, "Milton: Revaluations of Romance," in *Four Essays on Romance*, ed. Herschel Baker (Cambridge, Mass.: Harvard University Press, 1971), pp. 57–70, and Patricia A. Parker, *Inescapable Romance: Studies in the Poetics of a Mode* (Princeton: Princeton University Press, 1979), pp. 114–58.

24. See, for example, the scene in Book 8 where Adam, "Abstract as in a trance" (462), dreams of Eve's creation, a trance that prefigures his fatal submission to her in Book 10. For the gaze as Satanic, see 3.671; 4.356; 9.524, 535, 578, 611; et al.

25. On education in *Paradise Lost*, see especially Barbara Lewalski, "Innocence and Experience in Milton's Eden," in Thomas Kranidas, ed., *New Essays on Paradise Lost* (Berkeley: University of California Press, 1969), pp. 86–117.

26. See Patrick Brantlinger, "To See New Worlds: Curiosity in *Paradise Lost*," *MLQ* 33 (1972): 355–69: "On a hill, on a wall, from a cloud, in flight, the characters of *Paradise Lost*, with or without telescopes and with or without eyesight, all gaze outward in search of 'new worlds' and 'the Book of knowledg fair' (3.47). And if they discover imperfections in that book—sunspots, craters in the moon, 'irregularities' and 'disproportions,' it is because of imperfections within, clouding and fogging their perceptions" (367).

27. Raymond B. Waddington, "The Death of Adam: Vision and Voice in Books XI and XII of *Paradise Lost*," *MP* 70 (1972–73): 9–21.

28. James Joyce, *Ulysses*, ed. Hans Walter Gabler (New York: Random House, 1986), p. 309.

29. An example of this tradition is Michael Murrin, *The Allegorical Epic* (Chicago: University of Chicago Press, 1980).

30. Quoted by Thomas Maresca, *Epic to Novel* (Columbus: Ohio State University Press, 1974), p. 29.

31. See Geoffrey Hartman, "False Themes and Gentle Minds," *PQ* 47 (1968): 55–68, reprinted in *Beyond Formalism* (New Haven: Yale University Press, 1970), pp. 283–97. In *Visionary Poetics* (San Marino, Calif.: Huntington Library, 1979), Joseph A. Wittreich has linked Milton to the Romantics through a tradition of apocalyptic poetry deriving in the first instance from the Book of Revelation.

ten.   Brother Fire and St. Francis's Drawers

1. The translation is by Raphael Brown, first published in *The Little Flowers of St. Francis* (Garden City, N.Y.: Hanover House, 1958), and reprinted in Marion A. Habig, ed., *English Omnibus of the Sources for the Life of St. Francis* (Chicago: Franciscan Herald Press, 1983), pp. 1348–51. The literary genealogy of the story is outlined by Habig in *Omnibus*, pp. 1502–4. An online edition of the Italian original is available at http://www.intratext.com/X/ITA0002.htm (the story appears in chapter 21); the Latin version can be found in the *Actus B. Francisci et sociorum eius* in Enrico Menestò and Stefano Brufani, eds., *Fontes Franciscani* (Assisi: Edizioni Porziuncola, 1995), pp. 2134–37.

2. The distinguished Franciscan scholar John Moorman, states flatly, "What could be more convincing than . . . the story of the Wolf of Gubbio?" (*Saint Francis of Assisi* [London: SCM Press, 1950], p. 76). On the other hand, Roger Sorrell points out that the story's "specific authenticity is shaky," but adds, rightly, that "much of its ideals are congruent with what we know of Francis"

(*St. Francis of Assisi and Nature: Tradition and Innovation in Western Christian Attitudes toward the Environment* [New York: Oxford University Press, 1988], pp. 169–70).

3. Vito Fumagalli, *Landscapes of Fear: Perceptions of Nature and the City in the Middle Ages,* trans. Shayne Mitchell (Cambridge: Polity Press, 1994); Gherardo Ortalli, *Lupi genti culture: uomo e ambiente nel Medioevo* (Torino: Einaudi, 1997).

4. Paul Freedman, *Images of the Medieval Peasant* (Stanford: Stanford University Press, 1999).

5. This team consists of Regis J. Armstrong, O.F.M. Cap., J. A. Wayne Hellmann, O.F.M. Conv., and William J. Short, O.F.M.; the three volumes of Franciscan texts they have produced, which they designate as *Early Documents,* are *Francis of Assisi: The Saint* (New York: New City Press, 1998), *Francis of Assisi: The Founder* (New York: New City Press, 2000), and *Francis of Assisi: The Prophet* (New York: New City Press, 2001). All citations are from these translations unless otherwise noted; they are cited by section and paragraph number, followed in parentheses by the volume and page number of the translation. For the editors' account of the Franciscan Question and their means of determining chronology, see 1.11–31; they also provide full introductions to each of the texts. Further—and supportive—guidance is also available in the Menestò and Brufani edition of the *Fontes Franciscani.*

6. All citations from the Bible are from the Douay-Rheims translation.

7. Cited by Sorrell, *St. Francis of Assisi,* p. 16.

8. *Assisi Compilation* 88 (2.192).

9. *Vita prima,* 28.77 (1.248). In the original the last sentence reads: "Sic et omnia illa, praecipue in quibus Filii Dei posset aliqua similitudo allegorica reperiri, amplexabatur carius et vident libentius" (*Fontes Franciscani,* p. 352).

10. *Vita prima* 24.80–81 (1.250–51).

11. *Assisi Compilation* 86 (2.191).

12. *Assisi Compilation* 88 (2.192).

13. As by Edward A. Armstrong, *Saint Francis: Nature Mystic: The Derivation and Significance of the Nature Stories in the Franciscan Legend* (Berkeley: University of California Press, 1973). Because of Bonaventure's *Itinerarium mentis ad Deum,* this element of Francis's response to nature has come to be seen as more prominent than is warranted.

14. John V. Fleming, *An Introduction to the Franciscan Literature of the Middle Ages* (Chicago: Franciscan Herald Press, 1977), p. 70.

15. Both passages are cited by William J. Short, O.F.M., *Saints in the World of Nature: The Animal Story as Spiritual Parable in Medieval Hagiography, 900–1200* (Rome: Pontificia Universitas Gregoriana, 1983), pp. 33, 76. For a thoughtful and original exploration of this theme, see George H. Williams, *Wilderness and Paradise in Christian Thought* (New York: Harper, 1962).

16. Short, *Saints in the World of Nature*, p. 40.

17. "The Life of St. Cuthbert" in D. H. Farmer, ed., *The Age of Bede*, trans. J. F. Webb (Harmondsworth: Penguin Books, 1988), p. 56. Bede also reports that when Cuthbert scolded ravens for eating the seed from his newly sown field, they not only stopped but apologized.

18. Gregory the Great, *Dialogues*, ed. Adalbert de Vogüé and trans. Paul Antin, 3 vols. (Paris: Editions du Cerf, 1979), 2.316–19.

19. Celano, *Vita prima*, 21.59 (1.235). For earlier examples of saints who quiet noisy birds, see Armstrong, *Saint Francis: Nature Mystic*, pp. 71–77.

20. *The Minor Legend of Saint Francis*, 3.6 (2.697). In his *Commentary on the Book of Sentences*, Bonaventure expands on this theme: "If you ask what is the virtue which makes a person love creatures, because they come from God and exist for him, I reply that it is compassion and a sort of natural affection. For example, we see that even now a person can be very fond of a dog because it obeys him faithfully. In the same way, man in his original state had a natural inclination to love animals and even irrational creatures. Therefore, the greater the progress a man makes and the nearer he approaches to the state of innocence the more docile these creatures become towards him, and the greater the affection he feels for them. We see this in the case of St. Francis; he overflowed with tender compassion even for animals, because to some extent he had returned to the state of innocence. This was made clear by the way irrational creatures obeyed him" (3 Sent., d. 28, q. 1, concl., *Opera Omnia* 3.622b, trans. Fr. Benen Fahy, in Habig, ed., *Omnibus of the Sources*, p. 879).

21. *Vita prima*, 10.25 (1.204; *Fontes*, p. 299).

22. Richard Kieckhefer, *Unquiet Souls: Fourteenth-Century Saints and Their Religious Milieu* (Chicago: University of Chicago Press, 1984), pp. 76–77.

23. *Assisi Compilation* 83 (2.186; *Fontes*, p. 1597). Oddly, the editors of *The Early Documents* translate the *de suis creaturis* as "for his creatures" in their translation of the *Assisi Compilation*, but in the headnote to the *Canticle* they translate the phrase as "about the Lord's creatures" (1.113). I believe the translation of the phrase in the *Assisi Compilation* to be more accurate.

24. For an account of the stages of composition, see the headnote in *The Early Documents* 1.113.

25. *The Canticle of the Creatures*, line 4 (1.113; *Fontes*, p. 39).

26. As the translators of the *Canticle* say, "It would seem that in these first nine verses Francis envisioned this as a song of God's creatures in which human beings, because of sin, had no part, a theme about which he hints in other writings" (1.113, note d). For the translation of *per*, for which they prefer "through" to "by", see 1.114, note a.

27. *Assisi Compilation* 83 (2.186). The five verses added later to the Canticle make explicit the role of humanity in praising God:

10. Praised be you, my Lord, by those who grant pardon
    for love of you, and those who endure sickness and trial.
11. Blessed are those who live in peace,
    by you, Most High, they will be crowned.
12. Praised be you, my Lord, by sister death,
    whom no living man can escape.
    Woe to those who die in mortal sin!
13. Happy those whom she finds doing your will,
    to whom the second death can do no harm.
14. Praise and bless my Lord and thanks
    and serve him with great humility.

28. Lynn White, Jr., "Natural Science and Naturalistic Art in the Middle Ages," *AHR* 52 (1947): 421–35 (432). For similar claims, see Clarence J. Glacken, *Traces on the Rhodian Shore: Nature and Culture in Western Thought from Ancient Times to the End of the Eighteenth Century* (Berkeley: University of California Press, 1967), p. 216, and Armstrong, *Saint Francis: Nature Mystic*, p. 157.

29. There is no sense in Francis that nature is in any sense a wholly autonomous realm capable of being understood in any way other than spiritually. In *Before Science: The Invention of the Friars' Natural Philosophy* (Aldershot: Scolar Press, 1996), Roger French and Andrew Cunningham argue that Franciscan scientific thought—unlike that of the Dominicans—resisted the Aristotelianism that was necessary for a true sense of the autonomy of nature, without which science is impossible.

30. *Anonymous of Perugia*, 2 (2.38). In Thomas of Celano's *Vita prima* it is Francis's first disciple, Bernard, who "fulfilled th[is] counsel of the holy gospel" (*Vita prima* 10.24 [1.203]), perhaps in order to distinguish Francis from Peter Waldo, perhaps in order to play down the role of poverty as the foundation of the order. It was also this verse that converted St. Antony, so that both Francis and Peter were following an authoritative precedent (see Athanasius, *Select Works and Letters,* in Philip Schaff and Henry Wace, eds., *Nicene and Post-Nicene Fathers,* series 2 [Peabody, Mass.: Hendrickson, 1994], p. 196; Evagrius's Latin translation of Athanasius is now available in English in Caroline White, trans., *Early Christian Lives* [London: Penguin Books, 1998]).

31. Francis's anxiety about heresy is well illustrated by the following passage from the *Testament* (1.126–27):

And let all the brothers be bound to obey their guardians and to recite the Office according to the Rule. And if some might have been found who are not reciting the Office according to the Rule and want to change it in some way, or who are not Catholics, let all the brothers, wherever they may have found one of them, be bound through obedience to bring him before the custodian of that place nearest to where they found him. And let the custodian be strictly bound through obedience to keep him securely day and night as a man in chains, so that he cannot be taken from his hands until he can personally deliver him into the hands of his minister. And let the minister be bound through obedience to send him with such brothers who would guard him as a prisoner until they deliver him to the Lord of Ostia [Ugolino, bishop of Ostia, later Pope Gregory IX], who is the Lord, the Protector and the Corrector of this fraternity.

32. For a brief account of the Cathars in Italy, see Malcolm Lambert, *The Cathars* (Oxford: Blackwell, 1998), pp. 171–214.

33. Carol Lansing, *Power and Purity: Cathar Heresy in Medieval Italy* (New York: Oxford University Press, 1998), pp. 133, 144; Lambert, *The Cathars*, pp. 171, 228–29, 291–96.

34. Bernadette Paton, *Preaching Friars and the Civic Ethos: Siena, 1380–1480* (London: Queen Mary and Westfield College, 1992), pp. 282–83, n. 48. Paton describes heresy trials in the later thirteenth century.

35. The fullest account of Francis's relation to Catharism is Kajetan Esser, "Franziskus von Assisi und die Katharer seiner Zeit," *Archivum Franciscanum Historicum* 51 (1958): 225–64.

36. Peter Biller, "The Cathars of Languedoc and Written Materials," in Peter Biller and Anne Hudson, eds., *Heresy and Literacy, 1000–1530* (Cambridge: Cambridge University Press, 1994), pp. 61–82 (80).

37. "A Letter to the Entire Order," 39 (1.119; *Fontes*, p. 103). Francis claims that it is because he is "ignorant and stupid" that he has not said the Office in the way or as often as his Rule prescribes, and in the *Testament*, 29 he says that because he is *simplex et infirmus* he wants to have a cleric with him to say the Office (1.126; *Fontes*, p. 230). In *The Legend of the Three Companions*, 7.21, as elsewhere, Francis is described as *idiota et simplex* (2.81; *Fontes*, p. 1394). For the episode concerning the breviary, see the *Assisi Compilation*, 104 (2.209), and of course Francis consistently warns the brothers against the dangers of learning.

38. *Vita secunda* 2.48.78–79 (2.298–99).

39. A similar anecdote about Francis is told by Stephen of Bourbon: see Lambert, *The Cathars*, p. 174.

40. *Vita prima* 80 (1.250): "Even for worms he had a warm love, since he had read this text about the Savior: 'I am a worm and not a man'" (Psalm 22:7).

41. "Fragments Found in a Manuscript in Worcester Cathedral," 51–52 (1.90); *Testament*, 15, 39 (1.125, 127); *Vita prima*, 1.16.44, 1.18.50, 1.27.75, 1.21.58, 1.29.82, 1.29.80 (1.221, 227, 247, 234, 253, 250).

42. See Pierre Beguin and CETEDOC, *Thesaurus fontium Franciscanorum*, Universitas Catholica Lovaniensis Lovanii Novi (Turnhout: Brepols, 1997), 45 microfiches, *sub verbum*.

43. *Anonymous of Perugia* 1.9 (2.37); *The Legend of the Three Companions* 7.21 (2.81); *Assisi Compilation* 103 (2.207).

44. *Testament* 14 and 39 (1.125 and 127).

45. Chrysogonus Waddell, "Simplicity and Ordinariness: The Climate of Early Christian Hagiography," in John R. Sommerfeldt, ed., *Simplicity and Ordinariness*, Studies in Medieval Cistercian History 4 (Kalamazoo: Cistercian Publications, 1980), p. 8.

46. As William of St. Thierry says in his *Golden Epistle*, "Holy simplicity is an unchanging will in the pursuit of a changeless good. Such was Job, 'a simple, direct and God-fearing man.' Simplicity, in fact, is properly the will fundamentally turned towards God, asking of the Lord only one thing, seeking it with fervor, with no ambition to multiply itself by becoming dispersed in this world. Simplicity is also, in the conduct of life, the true humility which has the virtue of attaching more importance to the evidence of the conscience than to reputation." Cited by Jean Leclercq, *The Love of Learning and the Desire for God: A Study of Monastic Culture*, trans. Catherine Misrahi (New York: Mentor Books, 1962), p. 205.

47. *Assisi Compilation* 18 (2.132–33).

48. Paraphrased by Waddell, "Simplicity and Ordinariness," p. 13, from Thomas Merton's essay "St. Bernard on Interior Simplicity," in Jean-Baptiste Chautard, *The Spirit of Simplicity: Characteristic of the Cistercian Order* (Trappist, Ky.: Gethsemani Abbey, 1948). For a historical account of the holy fool and its connection to simplicity, see John Saward, *Perfect Fools: Folly for Christ's Sake in Catholic and Orthodox Spirituality* (New York: Oxford University Press, 1980), especially pp. 54–55, 58–103.

49. The *Legenda maior*, the official life written by Bonaventure, elides even momentary signs of struggle in order to present the saint as always already having achieved the impassibility of sanctity.

50. *Vita prima* 6 (1.193–94).

51. Thomas dutifully provides the pious gloss that Francis deliberately eschews: "Look! Now he wrestles naked with the naked. After putting aside all that is of the world, he is mindful only of divine justice. Now he is eager to despise his own life, by setting aside all concern for it" (*Vita prima* 6 [1.194]).

52. *Testament* 38–39 (1.127).

53. *Assisi Compilation* 17 (2.132). For the historical context of this insistence on the literal, and especially its relation to Cistercianism, see Duncan Nimmo, *Reform and Division in the Franciscan Order: From Saint Francis to the Foundation of the Capuchins* (Rome: Capuchin Historical Institute, 1987), pp. 104–8.

54. *Assisi Compilation* 52 and 57 (2.152 and 159).

55. For an interpretation of the economic and familial meanings of this scene, see Richard C. Trexler, *Naked Before the Father: The Renunciation of Francis of Assisi* (New York: Peter Lang, 1989).

56. Cited by Rosalind B. Brooke, *The Coming of the Friars* (London: George Allen and Unwin, 1975), p. 36.

57. The story is retold by Armstrong, *Saint Francis: Nature Mystic,* pp. 115–16.

58. *Vita prima* 1.28 (1.249).

59. *Anonymous of Perugia,* 6, 8–9 (2.46, 48, 52).

60. As Aviad M. Kleinberg says of Francis's "ritual performances," while "the saint is supposed to react directly to situations, instead he is always thinking in terms of how others would react to his performance and regulating it by their assumed reaction. . . . Francis consciously and conscientiously performed for the sake of others" (*Prophets in Their Own Country: Living Saints and the Making of Sainthood in the Later Middle Ages* [Chicago: University of Chicago Press, 1992], pp. 140–41).

61. *Assisi Compilation* 97 (2.200–201).

62. *Assisi Compilation* 10 (2.124–25).

63. "True and Perfect Joy," 1.166–67. The source and authenticity of the document are discussed by the editors in their headnote.

64. *Assisi Compilation* 61 (2.164).

65. The theme of fire in Francis's life has been examined, in very different terms than those presented here, by Elpidius Pax, O.F.M., "'Bruder Feuer': Religionsgeschichtliche und volkskundliche Hintergründe," *Franziskanische Studien* 33 (1951): 238–49.

66. *Assisi Compilation* 86 (2.191; *Fontes,* p. 1607). The story is also told in the *Speculum Perfectionis,* where the phrase is *pannos eius de lino sive bracas* (*Fontes,* p. 2040).

index

LEE PATTERSON

is Frederick W. Hilles Professor of English

at Yale University.

He is the author of *Chaucer and the Subject of History*.